Human Rights and Human Liberties

Human Rights and Human Liberties

A Radical Reconsideration of the American Political Tradition

Tibor R. Machan

Nelson Hall Chicago

Library of Congress Cataloging in Publication Data

Machan, Tibor R
   Human rights and human liberties: a radical reconsideration of the American political tradition.

   Includes bibliographical references and index.
   1. Civil rights.   I. Title.
JC571.M22   323.4   74-26864
ISBN 0-88229-159-9

140580

Rome burns. There are those who fiddle—forming the dead weight of a culture indifferent to or ignorant of the rising flames. And there are those who are spreading the fire, whether or not they know that is what they are doing. But there is one spectacle even more disgusting—an alleged fireman who, speaking from the roof of the firehouse, proclaims that there is no such thing as fire.

Steve Wright

Wisdom and goodness to the vile seem vile.
Shakespeare (King Lear)

One's right to life, liberty, and property . . . and other fundamental rights may not be submitted to a vote; they depend on the outcome of no elections.
U.S. Supreme Court
319 U.S. 624, 638.

Contents

Preface

I became interested in human rights quite naturally in connection with my choice to become an American citizen. Since, as a boy in Hungary, I had been aware of numerous political events and took part in some, I later wanted to make sense of these for myself. Although it would be difficult to put a simple label on the type of community Hungary was back around 1950, I know that I wanted to leave it for *political* reasons and that I wanted to do so very much. I recall my being thrown out of class by a teacher of "constitutional government" for posing what to me seemed a natural question in relation to Marx's edict: "From each according to his ability, to each according to his need." I asked about two equally able persons who start with five dollars but one uses it to obtain wine, the other wood; the first ends up drunk, the second with a table he can trade for things he would like to have; would they have to share what "their" efforts produced? Can the builder justify keeping his earnings, or need he do so, and can the drinker justify sharing the other's earnings, and need he do so? This was the substance of my question—I can recall it vividly—and I was expelled from school, to be readmitted weeks later and assigned to a trade school with a nonacademic program.

I suppose questions such as that memorable one nagged at me on and off throughout the ensuing years, and I later decided that to answer them would require undertaking what turned out to be a philosophical and moral inquiry. The question I asked then sounds a bit different today but comes to the same thing: "Are there human rights each person has, and can we identify them?"

This book is my initial attempt to offer a systematic answer to the question. It is not as technical a work as I plan to write in the future, but it develops in straightforward terms the answer I have arrived at thus far. I have provided first of all an overview of the development of human rights theory as it came to maturity as a solution to some of the problems human beings face in life—in this case, in their effort to organize their communities in accordance with principles of justice and morality. I have then proceeded to develop what I take to be a sound argument for human rights, although many tangents obviously could not be developed in full. (I have attempted, however, to indicate the directions the argument would take at those points which could not be pursued further in this work.) I have also tried to provide some clues to the function of our knowledge of human rights in times when the community in which we live generally ignores them, and the legal system not only pays them minimal heed but is geared toward their systematic violation. Lastly, I have made efforts to answer some critical challenges, some reasonable and others not so reasonable, but popular, at least.

Henry David Thoreau wrote that "To be a philosopher is not merely to have subtle thoughts, nor even to found a school, but to so love wisdom as to live according to its dictates, a life of simplicity, independence, magnanimity, and trust. It is to solve some of the problems of life, not only theoretically, but practically." This book was written in the spirit of Thoreau's idea, one not widely shared by contemporary philosophers.

While I have aimed for a jargon-free text, I want to ask the reader to approach this work with the anticipation of some difficult passages that require patience, and also with the realization that I have not tried to write a neutral book on some political concept, one in which judgments as to what is right and wrong with human affairs are absent. In connection with the first hope let me quote a choice passage from the Preface to Albert Einstein and Leopold Infeld's book, *The Evolution of Physics,* a book designed for the "educated layman":

> Whilst writing the book we had long discussions as to the characteristics of our idealized reader and worried a good deal about him. We had him making up for a complete lack of any concrete knowledge of physics and mathematics by quite a great number of virtues. We found him interested in physical and philosophical ideas and we were forced to admire the patience with which he struggled through the less interesting and more difficult passages. He realized that in order to understand any page he must have read the preceding ones carefully. He knew that a scientific book, even though popular, must not be read in the same way as a novel.

It bears some mention that I have not tried to write an apology for the American political system, especially as it is generally perceived and administered these days, even though I do believe that it was conceived more closely in line with a theory of human rights than any other known to man. But I know that being closer than others has proved to be not close enough. Thus it is not helpful to make use of the American political experience as a sort of historical laboratory in which to test many aspects of a theory of human rights, though if tests there must be, we would find a place for them in America's history more than in that of other nations. Moreover, while the defense of rights which was offered in connection with the inception of America's political tradition drew on the best conclusions on the topic at that point in human history, that defense is neither without difficulties nor sufficient even in its best form (of its time) for our purposes. So a considerably different theory of human rights will emerge in these pages; it will draw on, but also seriously revise and improve the defense of natural rights generally associated with Locke, Paine, and many others who took part in the fervent intellectual life at the birth of the American nation.

Nevertheless, the idea of natural rights has been the most powerful and valuable contribution made to the political life of mankind. It has provided the best intellectual support for the liberation of millions of human beings from the caprice and malice of others, including those who have carried out their assault on the innocent "for reasons of state." It still has the most sustained answer to offer in the face of the only contending (but significantly more comprehensive) political doctrine afoot these days—albeit on its last leg—namely Marxism (in all of its patched-up versions).

On the other hand, contemporary philosophy has in the main deprived not just human rights theory, but ethics and politics in general of any grounding, what with the dominance of ultimately subjectivist ideas in these areas—and, of late, even in the areas of the "hard" sciences, interestingly enough! So while most people, when they resist oppression and abuse by others, including states, still refer to the basic rights of every individual, and while most states pay some homage to these rights in their basic legal documents, the intellectual climate has definitely turned against human rights. The most massive treatise on political philosophy to emerge in decades, John Rawls' book on justice, spends hardly a paragraph on the idea.

Human rights seem to me, therefore, worthy and in need of serious consideration. I have tried to do this with the aid of what I regard as some of the best philosophical ideas developed in recent as well as ancient times. In this respect I have not been original about the bits and pieces of the present theory, nor about its general thrust. I hope, however, to have developed an integrated position that will make good sense to those with that purpose in mind, i.e., the aim to make good sense of at least certain aspects of their lives, and to develop some realistic yet morally sound solutions to the problems they face.

For now I want simply to express my deep gratitude to several individuals and institutions for the help and guidance I have received. Professors Larry Houlgate, Merril Ring, and Joseph Ransdell have assisted me in connection with sections of the work devoted mainly to the justification of moral and political judgments. My friends R. A. Childs, Jr., Ned Dwelle, George Resch, J. Roger Lee, Eric Mack, Doug Den Uyl, and Doug Rasmussen have been patient with me as I tried out most features of my view during the many hours we spent discussing issues related to this project. Their suggestions and clarifications have found a place within various stages of it. I have benefited a good deal, I believe, from reading the works of many authors, as the text will make quite evident. My utilization of what I have learned from them must not be taken as proof of their agreement with my position nor, in fact, approval of my purpose. I do want to mention my friend and constant as well as severe critic, Jon Wheatley, who, while failing to persuade me to give up my views, did convince me that staying close to plain language is useful in thinking and writing about philosophy. In the final analysis, however, I received the most valuable help from my wife, Marty Zupan, who not only edited the manuscript (several times over and with the utmost thoroughness) but never let slip by a point that did not make good sense to her and seemed anything less than true and justified. And this gratitude is hardly sufficient to express my feelings about the pleasure and joy of having worked with her for months on to the completion of the book. Fortunately, that is not necessary to include in this acknowledgment, of course.

Two generous sources of financial help in this project were the Frederick C. Koch Foundation of Wichita, Kansas (whose administrator George Pearson has given me his personal encouragement as well), and the SUNY Summer Faculty Research Program. I thank both—especially since in the case of the latter the real "donors" could do little to make certain that their monies were well spent. I refer to the taxpayers of New York State, of course.

Not to break with all traditions, I want to assume full responsibility for what has finally emerged.

CHAPTER 1

The details of this new world, were not as yet clearly depicted; but faith ran high that a better world than any that had ever been known could be built where authority was distrusted and held in constant scrutiny; where the status of men flowed from their achievements and from their personal qualities, not from distinctions ascribed to them at birth; and where the use of power over the lives of men was jealously guarded and severely restricted. It was only where there was this defiance, this refusal to truckle, this distrust of all authority, political or social, that institutions would express human aspirations, not crush them.

Bernard Bailyn

Human History and Human Natural Rights

The Concern about What Is Right—and Why

THE most thorough account of the history of the idea of natural rights was written some decades ago by the eminent scholar and philosopher, the late Leo Strauss. In his *Natural Right and History*[1] he traced the idea from its origins in Greek thought to its present, rather muddled, conception in political philosophy and the humanities in general. In the following I will be relying on Strauss' teaching, although it will be obvious that I am not in full agreement with his views—e.g., those concerning the natural rights theory of John Locke.

Before I begin with the discussion of the idea of natural rights (the term in Strauss is purposefully "natural right" for reasons that will become clear shortly) I want to make a brief remark about Strauss and his conception of philosophy. There is what can be called a "Straussean School" of classical political philosophy—i.e., political philosophy in the Greek tradition. Strauss and his followers see a serious division between ancient and contemporary political thought. Some of them, as did Strauss himself, view this division as the major crisis of the modern age. Basically their idea is that in classical political philosophy human nature was conceived in terms of ethical or moral ideas and ideals. In the modern age, beginning with Machiavelli and continuing in contemporary positivist social science and political theory, human nature has been viewed more and more along reductivist, so called "scientific" lines. One of my aims in this work will be to argue further a point I made in my book which dealt with B. F. Skinner's views, namely that a genuinely scientific approach to the study of man in no way obviates moral and political considerations as conceived by the ancients.

So let me now turn to a brief sketch of the development of the idea of natural rights. Strauss is concerned with natural right, rather than the concept that emerged later, namely natural *rights*. But the two ideas are obviously related, as Strauss is the first to acknowledge. I too will begin by focusing on the development of natural right. In doing so it will help to start by explaining why it is important to understand this development, why a consideration of the validity of an idea can benefit greatly from a consideration of its origins.

Ideas emerge when people need and/or want to solve some problem, when they want an answer to a question for which no satisfactory answer exists as yet. The growth of ideas in human history can be compared to the growth of ideas in the repertoire of a child's thinking, only the pace is much slower and the detours, unfortunately, much longer. When children encounter new things in the world they may seek to understand and explain them. To do so they may ask to be taught (i.e., show interest when someone offers help in making things clear to them), or they may embark upon the effort to reach an understanding on their own. There is no guarantee for this, but unless children are abused, discouraged, or the like, they will generally set out to learn. Such learning will involve a perusal of what they already know, what they are familiar with, so that the new item can be compared to others, included among what is already understood, or provided with a place of its own among the things known. I am not now concerned with how all this starts in the case of a child—or for mankind as a whole.

But what happens in the case of a child is basically a highly accelerated version of what mankind has experienced. This generalization is not so much a historical discovery as a reconstruction on the basis of present understanding. By examining what ideas have emerged throughout recorded history, *and* by using philosophically defensible standards of success and failure in assessing their development, we can come to learn about what has, should have, and/or must have happened. By understanding a good deal about the context of some age, about what human beings must do to deal with their situation in that context, we can learn to distinguish between better and worse ways of being human, which includes learning to cope with the world. Here understanding is the first step.

In each age known to us there has been much dispute about whether certain ideas are meaningful or valid, whether using them can lead to clarity of thought and communication, whether reality and man's place in it could be correctly conceived of by the use of those ideas, given the available context. Some ideas like "phlogiston," "witch," "demon," or the like may have had limited functions and yet they were retained by some who were unwilling or unable to attend to developments that rendered them obsolete. Other ideas served a valid purpose, yet with the growth of knowledge required modification or revision. Yet others had a rough start but later came to prominence, depending on how well they served their purpose as well as how carefully people considered them.

To see if the idea of human/natural right ever had a place in the arsenal of mankind's meaningful ideas we can ask about its rendition, meaning, and function in the earliest of writings known to us. It turns out not, surprisingly, that among ancient thinkers, based on both narratives and theoretical writings, the idea of "right" (as well as "wrong") occupied an important place. People found out early enough the need for evaluating judgment, conduct, people, institutions, and so on. So there has always been a serious concern with what has come to be known as the issue of right and wrong. The actions of individuals, the practices of groups, the institutions of communities, the policies of governing bodies—all these have come under critical scrutiny at one time or another, however successfully or clumsily.

Now the question that arose quite naturally in connection with this concern is how human beings could (and thus should) discover what is right. There really is not that great a difference between the peoples of classical times and our own, and just as today many ask about the ways we might come to understand the rights and wrongs of personal and political affairs, so in ancient times this question arose quite naturally. Often the most sensible approach seemed to be that the right way to do things must be learned by consulting how things were done earlier. What had been done when these questions were first faced? This tended, of course, to lead to considerable reliance on the authority of elders. Old people had more experiences to draw on, they could recall more of what had happened in life. They could instruct about right and wrong because they had learned the ways of people. This traditionalism is still advocated by some and indeed it once made the best sense. But when it was noted that authorities differed, customs varied, conventions conflicted with one another, then something additional had to be done. Some answered, and still do, that these differences simply indicate the impossibility of finding the right way to do things. Without an alternative, that made some sense.

Thus many have accepted and settled for the utter impossibility of finding reliable guidance in the search for right answers to the questions and problems people face. Today, this is the turn taken by most people—in and out of intellectual circles. As a fact of our times we cannot fail to notice the widespread opinion that there are no right answers, that "all is relative," that truth, like (some say) beauty, is in the eyes of the beholder. This is especially so concerning matters of conduct, say many people. The *right* political system? Nonsense. The *right* moral code? Nonsense. The *right* way to conduct oneself as parent, doctor, presidential adviser, teacher, and the rest? Nonsense and more nonsense—"nonsense upon stilts,"[2] to quote the famous critic of natural rights, Jeremy Bentham.

The Idea of Natural Right

These responses reveal their own oddity at once. For *they* purport to be answers that are right, but if no right answers are possible these cannot be right either! Thus the search has gone on. And one answer that seemed to lie in much the same direction as traditionalism—namely "get back to first things"—emerged as promising. This answer was "nature." Nature antedated even the oldest of authorities, the oldest of conventions, the oldest of customs. Nature was first—whatever it was, however it was discovered, in whatever way it made its appearance. And it did not seem to be alterable and volatile as human opinions did. So if we could understand it, "grasp" it, perceive it correctly, then it held out promise of providing guidance for deciding what is right.

In short, the idea of natural right was born. To put it another way, to the question "What is right?" answers had been provided, and to some problems solutions had been offered. With the idea of natural right, only those answers and solutions were to receive acceptance that could be *shown* to be right by means of an investigation or study of nature. Not authority, convention, or custom, but nature was offered as the final arbiter in matters of dispute.

Saying this much does not, however, get one very far; what the concept of nature means is not always clear. Nor do people use it to mean the same thing. One philosopher has compiled more than sixty-five different meanings that the term "nature" has had within philosophical and related discussions. For example, we often talk about nature and have in mind everything there is in the universe; we also use the term in such expressions as "That is an unnatural way to act" or "The natural way to swim requires that this and that be done"; then there is the sense when we say, "The nature of government is to administer laws in some geographical area"; we also make use of the idea of nature when we think or speak of some individual's nature, as in "He is naturally enthusiastic." And we could go on to mention such technical uses as "natural numbers," "nature versus nurture," and "the beauty of nature as against the beauty of man's creations." It would be odd to maintain that of all these applications of the concept, only one is correct, the others mistaken. We can understand clearly enough what is meant in almost all the cases above, especially if we were to provide the appropriate context for each statement.

For our purposes, however, only two of the above are important. They are, where nature means "everything that exists" and "the nature of X." Natural right theory—the idea that some judgment is justified when we can support it by turning to nature—took these meanings as central for its purposes. Nature as such or the nature of something was thought to be common and open to us all. It does not depend on our wishes, beliefs, desires, will or whatever; it simply exists whether we like it or not. As such it could promise a *foundation* for our reasoning about anything.

None of this should give the impression that in natural right theory there were not considerable differences in how nature was understood, about the details of the meaning of the concept. From the beginning there developed conflicting theories about what nature is. This was to be expected. Typically in human affairs when an idea catches on many like to jump on the bandwagon. Different views incorporate the idea so as to gain plausibility. Just as in the modern age, once science gained its high reputation everyone from physicists, chemists, and biologists, to gurus, magicians, and the most blatant quacks, began calling themselves "scientists," so in earlier times everyone took to appealing to nature. Thus what seemed at first to provide an impartial ground upon which sound reasoning could rest and from which initial disagreements could be settled, turned out to provide no guarantee for agreement. (This in turn gave additional support to the views of those who believed that searching for a reliable basis of judgment in matters of concern to mankind must be considered futile, even dangerous.)

Later in this book I shall consider a problem with relying on nature for a *guarantee* of the truth of our beliefs, for support of our theories in or out of the special sciences. (Those who imagine that in the physical sciences all is in perfect harmony and no disagreements occur need only consult the scholarly periodicals in such professions as physics, chemistry, biology, astronomy, and the like. Perhaps because the concerns of these fields do not bear directly on our beliefs about ourselves, there is less fervency in the disputes. But they exist, even if relatively quietly, throughout these fields of study.) For the time being we need to take a brief look at the earliest notions of nature, what the two major Greek philosophers believed nature was, so that we can proceed with an understanding of the tradition that produced current ideas about rights.

Classical Ideas about Nature and Natural Right

The most influential as well as the first philosopher who offered us a well thought out idea of nature was Socrates. Before him there had been discussion related to the subject, and his own ideas were in part a response to these pre-Socratic views of nature.

For our purposes it will not be necessary to differentiate between the views of Socrates and Plato, although at a more specialized level of inquiry this could not be tolerated. Plato's writings are our most reliable source for Socrates' beliefs. But it is well established that in his later dialogues (Plato wrote by presenting Socrates engaged in dialogues with his students and adversaries) Plato used Socrates primarily as a mouthpiece for his own, often significantly different, views. Yet the two earliest recorded systematic thinkers in Western thought were close enough in bent of mind to justify omission of reference to differences between them in a brief overview.

Fundamental to Plato's system was his belief that there are two distinct and separate realms of reality, the visible realm and the intelligible realm. The manner in which these two are supposedly separated is not obvious, since when we speak of separation we usually have in mind two or more items of the same kind—separate tables, a separated couple and so on. But Plato's two realms of reality were very different from each other—roughly indicated by the difference that most of us believe exists between thoughts and things. But while we ordinarily take thoughts, whatever they are, to emanate from persons, Plato is more appropriately taken to have believed that the realm of the intelligible actually existed somewhere apart from where we spend our daily lives—this visible world of ours.

As in most other matters, there are different interpretations of Plato's thought. But virtually all commentators accept that he believed in two separate realms of existence. The main idea in Plato's theory is that the realm of the intelligible contains (or is made up of) ideas or forms, which are perfect but nonmaterial versions of everything that may ever be found in our visible world whether it does or could (but does not now) exist. For Plato every kind of thing is represented by an idea in the realm of the intelligible. And these ideas are supposed to be permanent, fixed, unchanging, and perfect.

Now why would Plato believe all this? Basically he would have answered that only by viewing matters along these lines could we make sense of things that may seem quite obvious to us anyway but, upon reflection, puzzle us. Things in the visible world change rapidly, so we need to make sense of the fact that we sometimes do have a clear understanding of what they are *essentially*. Take chairs, for example, or trees. They decay, grow, collapse, burn up, and undergo many different kinds of changes. Yet at least some people understand remarkably well *what* they are. Carpenters, for example, know what a chair is, what it must be, although any given chair changes, even drastically. And botanists understand trees despite the fact that any particular tree goes through stages of growth and change and may even disappear from sight during a forest fire.

In the face of this Plato argued that it must be true that there are permanent *ideas* of such things somewhere, and this would account for the knowledge we do have. We can thus study them in peace, independent of the constant change and destruction. And while we need to come across the imperfect versions (actual chairs, trees, people, actions, events, governments or virtues) *in the realm of the visible* so as to understand the perfect items, the imperfect versions have a lower level of importance for us since they last for only a brief period of time compared to their versions in the realm of the intelligible. To know *man* one must study *many* human beings at first; but we need to go much further than to simply experience them (visually, by sense perception) here on earth. We must gain an understanding of the idea or form of man to be able to claim with justice that we understand man (or any other kind of thing).

For Plato then nature, as we are concerned with it here, is constituted by the realm of the intelligible, the permanent collection of the perfect forms of things, an understanding of which can enable one to tell or know what is right. By grasping the *nature* of trees or some subclass of trees we can support our judgments about this or that tree with confidence. By understanding human nature, the ideal form of every individual person, we can justify our judgments about people, their lives, institutions, policies, and so forth. This is the point at which considerations of right enter into Plato's ideas. The realm of the intelligible—of the perfect ideas of anything that might ever be encountered here in our visible world—provides those of mankind who can ascend to it with the correct guidelines to judgment and action. While it is unlikely that we could ever implement the judgment based on some understanding of these ideas, we must always refer to them so as to make the best effort toward such implementation. (Thus while the ideal political community of Plato's *Republic* could exist only in the realm of the intelligible, not the visible, in their judgments and actions human beings were always to aspire to be guided by an understanding of such an ideal society. In this sense Plato was the first and greatest utopian/idealist in the history of Western thought.)

It is not important for now to examine what Plato thought about the role this picture of reality should play in our effort to conduct practical affairs—other than to note that those who have gotten a glimpse of it must be guided by it. Plato was an elitist, one who has often been interpreted to have advocated the absolute rule of the intellectuals and philosophers. But it seems more accurate to take him to have advocated that both personal and political life should be carried out with as much reliance on rational knowledge as it is possible for those concerned to generate. This view takes the idea of the philosopher king advanced by Plato in connection with the ideal political community symbolically, not literally. Thus it is what the philosopher king symbolizes—namely, wisdom and sound judgment, human excellence in political affairs—that we are all to implement to the best of *our* ability.

What is crucial for us here is that along Platonic lines the idea of nature emerged as an idealized version of what we encounter with our senses: the senses cannot be relied on to give us knowledge both because we can err in employing them and because what we perceive can change all to rapidly. But by turning our attention to the ideal versions of visible things, i.e., to the most accurate, truest statement about such things, we can relate our judgments and policies to fixed things, points of reference that must command the respect of any rational[3] investigator. (Of course not all investigators are rational; nothing follows about the reliability of understanding that is gained by having grasped the intelligible things from the fact that many people babble about matters they do *not* understand.)

This form of naturalism is perhaps not as easily assimilated to our general understanding of the concept of nature (e.g., in "Nature is everything and all there is'') as would be required in order to render it familiar to us all. But traces of it are to be found even today. When we speak of "the natural way" of doing things or of "the nature of something," we come close to using "natural" in this Platonist sense. We generally mean the appropriate, proper, or even ideal way of doing things as opposed to doing them without regard to standards of good and bad, of better and worse. The natural grip on a golf club is really the best, is it not? So we still retain elements of the Platonic meaning, even if it is no longer tied to the total theory.

There is an aspect of Plato's naturalism that cuts against the grain for many who have thought about natural right. All too frequently Platonism allows for politically established forms of discrimination among people which we find offensive given our framework of legal egalitarianism—"all citizens are equal under the law." In Plato this anti-egalitarianism arises mainly from a not entirely justified reliance on observations. In his day slavery and the social position of most others were firmly entrenched in custom and law. There was little social and economic mobility. Thus it seemed only obvious that some people *could not* get off the ground in reaching the levels of excellence that could, in fact, be attained by others. It was concluded from this (and some other considerations) that there is a *natural* division of labor pertaining to all *from birth*.

Yet even Plato could be misinterpreted on this matter by placing too much emphasis on his ideal society. We might note that in that ideal system sex and race and other shabby grounds for discrimination could have no place. Individual differences—in intellectual, artistic and other capacities and talents—matter, as does circumstance—people simply do not have the chance to excel equally.

On the other hand *intellectual* elitism shines through in Plato whether the ideal form of society is taken symbolically or literally. For in the end Plato did believe that some people were naturally better than others simply because they were the ones reaching for the ideal good, the understanding of good as good, the nature of the good, the nature of justice. Those who did not have the chance to do so simply could not become as good as those who had. This view has its problems, one of them being that goodness comes from something outside oneself, something that one could reach only if well situated. But surely whether someone is a good human being cannot depend altogether on such accidental matters. That would be the height of injustice—to praise or blame a person on account of his uncontrollable situation in life.

In short, in Plato's case we are left with a complete theory of natural right that relies on outside factors too heavily, not on the person himself. While it is true that some people are born without any capacity to control their own fate—thus without a chance to reach human excellence—these people are very different indeed from most of us, including some of the worst situated. These people, with severe brain damage or incapacity, may best be considered human cripples in the most crucial respect: the distinctive human capacities, choice and reason, are missing or drastically impaired. Plato had the rudiments of an important point (to be better understood as science progressed and could identify and account for such severe differences among people), but he did not focus fully enough on these to avert tending toward a dangerous form of elitism, one which attributed automatic virtues to some people and thus made it appear justifiable for them to wrest power from others, always by citing their natural superiority. (There are many viewpoints today also that tend in this direction—on both sides of the prominent political spectrum.)

We come now to Aristotle, whose naturalism is both similar to and different from Plato's. First of all, Aristotle held that nature and reality as such were not to be understood as Plato would have it. Instead of two quite different realms of reality Aristotle argued that there is only one all-encompassing reality. It has different *aspects*—thus we find in Aristotle the distinction between necessary and accidental features of what there is in nature. But all is nature, with only its aspects distinguishable (maybe in some sense even separable, although that is debatable when we examine what Aristotle wrote about these matters).

Aristotle, unlike Plato, presented the bulk, as well as the most developed parts of his philosophy in treatises. His essays consisted of arguments, refutations, comparisons, and the like and not of imaginary exchanges between people of considerably diverse degrees of wisdom and power of argumentation. He was also, to put it simply, more down to earth and optimistic about man's circumstances: no idealized world is required for man to make sense of the difference between individual trees or chairs, for instance, and the nature or essence of these things. Interpretations vary on just how Aristotle believed the difference exhibits itself, how it is manifest in reality, and how we can learn of it. Some say he relied on some such notion as "intellectual intuition" in his effort to explain how we could learn of the nature of something apart from its particularity, its actual isolated existence. Others have it that we must understand Aristotle to have been pointing to something more akin to mental effort, initiation of the mental activity that can lead to distinguishing between certain features or aspects that something has in common with others, for some purposes leaving aside those features not shared. Thus *if* some person pays attention, he will learn what *kind* of things there are by discerning existent differences and similarities.

"Intellectual intuition" seems the more dubious of the theories because it calls for something ineffable, something unexplainable. People just have it or they do not; what they can do is either there or not there, *independent of them.* (This could lead to a form of elitism similar to Plato's: some will understand the best things merely by having the intellectual intuition to discern more carefully.) Although in Aristotle's works there are passages that incline toward elitism, this does not follow from his theory of knowlege acquisition.

In his metaphysical writings Aristotle held that whatever there is must be of one kind or another: things simply *could not be* anything and everything whatever, undifferentiated and unspecific. This is not a remark about how *we* come to take things *(subjectively* as it were) but about *what there is and must be.* Even before we learn what any specific thing is and what it is not, we are entitled to say, just from knowing that there are things, that things must be what they are and not what they are not. So here, as in Plato, is a theory about the basic facts of reality. What Aristotle identified as the three interrelated basic facts of reality also serve as basic guides to understanding *specific* facts of reality. In other words, the Law of Identity, the Law of Contradiction, and the Law of the Excluded Middle are principles of *being* as well as the governing (logical) rules for *learning about* being, for getting to know reality. When so taken, the Aristotelian view of how we come to learn about reality, how we identify the nature of things—the kinds and types of things there are—does not require that intellectual intuition be the avenue toward knowledge. (Incidentally, just in case someone thinks that all of this is obsolete, it is worth noting that Aristotelian views are holding strong on many fronts. For example, after all of the rhetoric about the need for seventeenth-century science to reject Aristotelianism, we can point to the fact that Aristotle was not rejected—it was Aristotelianism in the guise of medieval adherents who had meddled with his views to bring them in line with Christian dogma that was rejected. Since Einstein displaced Newton as the high prince of physics, Aristotle has been recognized as being in line with modern physics in many respects.)

What is more important for our purposes here than the *means* to knowledge, is that Aristotle's naturalism did not imply either a division between the ideal and the actual (or practical), or an absolutely, timelessly fixed character of the natural or best. Some matters, of course, can be identified as permanent enough for us to work with. Thus human nature, as long as people exist, would indeed be what it is—whatever it is. Reasoning on the basis of a clear understanding of human nature must, then, have the force of natural law.

Now Aristotle relied fully on his knowledge of human nature in his *Ethics* and *Politics* to identify the right course of conduct people must take. But about natural law and right he wrote only a few pages (as far as we *know*).[4] In these he tells us that while there is a firm nature that can support knowledge of the most general principles of human conduct, the application of these principles in diverse situations can require strenuous efforts of interpretation. Man is indeed a rational animal: he alone is known to have the capacity for thought, to reason logically about what there is around him. And this is true as well: to make his life fully human requires that each person make use of his/her reason as fully as he or she is capable. The specific results of one's doing this cannot be foretold, given the multitude of human circumstances and capabilities. One can, however, in the effort to find out, count on one's capacity for identifying the needed principles or virtues.

Thus with Aristotle, who was far more attentive than Plato to the need to *cope* with change rather than relegate it to an imperfect realm, we find natural law and natural right broadly based, with great allowance for specific interpretations in newly emerging situations. Yet this flexibility (which so many recent critics of Aristotle omit from consideration as they label his view as one equating "natural" and "fixed"[5]) does not eliminate standards of right and wrong. Only by keeping in view the basic nature of man can we make the right decisions and choices about what should be done in the circumstances we face. Thus for Aristotle civil society is to be governed by nature—the nature of the being whom it must house, namely man. It follows that all men are most at home in a *good* human community because they *could* activate many natural capacities (communication, criticism, etc.) therein while apart from society they would be unable to utilize that possibility. (And "outside society" could well include "side by side each other but without actual community life" as we might imagine it to be in a concentration camp. This explains the qualifier "good" in that sentence about human community life.) Since he thought man's rationality to flourish most in circumstances where language communication is open to people, Aristotle considered man a *social* animal. This is not to be taken to imply that any or all societies would be as good for people as some one, best community. (He examined numerous constitutions and compared these to a standard which he identified by reference to human nature.) This retains much of the spirit of Plato, for he too tried to establish a standard by which to differentiate the good from the less good and the bad. But in Aristotle this good is quite reachable since it isn't "put out of this world," so to speak.

We may conclude then that Aristotle's naturalism is closer to our common sense understanding of what that approach could mean, namely finding out how some kind of things will come off best, most in accordance with their nature, and trying for it wherever possible. Since people can choose to be virtuous or not, they, especially, have the choice to reach the best or worst in their circumstances. There was thus no "impossible dream" in Aristotle's vision of the goal of human existence, either personally or socially. Nor did he require that all people seek the single virtue of the philosophic life as did Plato, but allowed that each could be as excellent as possible given his individuality. That "best possible" being quite enough to excel *as a person.*

I said at the outset that we need to trace the idea of natural right as it developed to be able to see what problems it was meant to solve, what sort of questions it had been used to answer. And with each variety we would probably find considerable good sense as well as error. While much more tolerant of diversity and individuality, Aristotle still relied heavily on sampling existing circumstances. Was this something damaging in terms of satisfying anything we might need to solve problems in our age?

To address this matter briefly is not easy because it takes us into that complicated philosophical problem of just what truth is. Is it something along Platonic lines—a statement that should never require, could never admit of revision, change, modification? If so, it seems we end with serious paradoxes if not contradictions, for always, in all fields of knowledge, what we have learned earlier could use some modification upon further thought and further discoveries about things around us. Nor do many things stay put for us to arrive at a complete understanding of them; even nature undergoes gradual and sometimes drastic changes.

Or is truth subjective, totally dependent on time and space? Then, however, it would appear that we could not set store by anything identified before *this* moment and place in time—nothing but immediate experience could carry the weight of reliability, no one could claim with justice that he knows anything in any general way. The problem becomes where to stack *that* discovery: among the many changeable truths, or in a class of its own with one solid member, the only permanent truth we have gotten hold of? But if that one truth is knowable, is there not reason to believe that more might be available? The ultimate conclusion of this view is that we cannot rule out that chance, so the search for general knowledge could go on with some confidence of success, however limited or remote. In the positive argument of this book I will have to shed some light on how we can best make sense of the idea that some things we believe and say can be shown to be true, while we could have good reason to improve on these beliefs in the light of subsequent work and discoveries.

Before we go on to take an even briefer view of later natural right theorists of the classical era, it is worth noting that Aristotle had what might be considered a very perceptive, indeed, perhaps entirely correct and unimprovable idea of natural right in relationship to civil society. Clearly there is no evidence in his works of what we now know as a theory of human or natural rights (*à la* Locke and the Declaration of Independence). But he hints at a solution to one problem of modern natural rights doctrine. This is the issue of whether the view that these rights are absolute, binding on all whom they concern, in all cases, is intelligible. For surely we can imagine instances in the case of any particular human right, even the right to life, when it would be justifiable to ignore considerations of it. There are the typical cases of moral dilemmas on desert islands, sinking ships, or life rafts, or during major disasters such as earthquakes, fires, or floods, where it would be unimaginable that considerations of people's human rights could serve as the decisive guidelines to action.

Aristotle's solution is to admit to exceptions. But unlike some modern as well as earlier critics of natural rights, he does not thereby abandon his doctrine that there are principles right for human communities—absolutely right at that, although it would be unreasonable to expect that they must have application in all possible circumstances people might face, even in the emergency cases described. One can marvel at Aristotle's perceptiveness here, his keen appreciation of problems raised as decisive by some today, as well as his brilliant approach to their solution. One must indeed admire what Leo Strauss has called "the spirit of [Aristotle's] unrivaled sobriety."[6] In the face of despondency, not just about the bad circumstances produced by human folly of the recent and not too recent past, but about the human condition in general, this genius' sustained sanity, and his affirmative conception of man as such, will forever be spiritual fuel to mankind.

As has been obvious throughout the above, the ideas of natural law and natural right are closely related. In brief, while what is right is easily tied to law in a societal context, it is smoothly tied to natural law when more basic guidelines are sought. In theories of natural right the laws of nature, of the natures or beings of various kinds of things, must provide the best principles of right judgment about them. To put it another way, natural right is to natural law as truth is to fact—the first are aspects of beliefs, ideas, statements, while the latter are what exists, about which beliefs, ideas, or statements are entertained, thought, or uttered, respectively.

With Thomas Aquinas, who followed Aristotle's philosophy as closely as his theological commitments would permit, the focus was not on natural right but on natural law. For him nature's laws are unfailingly absolute and unalterable because decreed by God, and even more binding than Plato's standards which had, after all, perfect application in the ideal realm only. While Aquinas' natural law theory had great influence, especially in ecclesiastical doctrines, it was too infused with ideas about a deity that stood above nature to be characterizable as natural law *sui generis*. The idea, however diversely taken by philosophers from Plato and Aristotle to Cicero and others, had always meant to point to a court of last resort. But in Aquinas' system that court had been placed wherever God's will was. As such, nature could not command *for itself* the respect required for purposes of providing a standard of sound judgment in either scientific or human affairs (where the distinction is meant only to point up the moral element in the latter).

What is certain is that critics of natural right took ample advantage of the fact that Aquinas concentrated on the topic of natural law. His absolutism, which was quite unlike Aristotle's or even Plato's, was thereafter taken as paradigmatic of natural right doctrine. Critics thought that by showing Aquinas to have been mistaken in his absolutism, all considerations of natural law and right would have to be abandoned. This, however, is a clear instance of pleading one's case, of assailing some admittedly problematic feature of an entire tradition in the evolution of an idea, and by such narrow focus concluding that the idea *cannot* have merit.

We may now conclude the treatment of classical natural right theory. We saw with Plato the emergence of full attention to the problem natural right doctrine had been designed to solve. With Aristotle came modification of the Platonic doctrine by way of a reckoning with the un-idealized world we face—with, however, no ultimate loss to the point of natural right theory, the attempt to provide standards for judgment and conduct. And we noted that with medieval theological underpinnings the natural law and right tradition assumed dogmatic dimensions, rendering its purpose and promise beyond reach. (In this sense Aquinas, an Aristotelian, was in fact closer to Plato.) For anyone, be he a devout person of religious faith or an opponent of faith as a means to dealing with reality, can admit that resting political life on ideas we can only behold by the grace of God (through revelation, mystical experience, or the authority of scripture and its interpreters) gets us away from the very thing natural right doctrines could promise with some confidence: likely success in the effort to reach understanding of things when we consult nature by way of reason—both common to mankind as such (even with the obvious exceptions mentioned earlier, e.g., mental incapacity). Although these do not promise a guarantee of ultimate agreement among members of human communities, they do offer the chance for it. On the other hand, faith and authority invite just the problems that natural right doctrine attempted to solve, i.e., the problems of diversity with every opinion founded on equally inaccessible ground, in this case a ground at God's discretion to provide. Even if Aquinas himself had not intended this result, his theory allowed it quite clearly.

Modern Natural Rights: Hobbes and Locke

It may indeed be entirely inappropriate to hold Thomas Hobbes, the famous English materialist philosopher, to anything like a natural rights doctrine, except for the fact that he clearly advocated views with that name attached to them. What with strides in understanding the methodology of the physical sciences and the serious impact of Machiavelli's radical empiricist edicts concerning the study of political matters, Hobbes faced problems as well as horizons for solutions, leading to a view that is difficult to iron out. His viewpoint represents the merging of two, perhaps quite incompatible, lines of thought about political matters, and his philosophy has had too much influence on subsequent political theorists to be left out when natural rights are studied. What then is the Hobbesian position and how does it relate to the history of human rights?

Let us reiterate here that classical natural right theory aimed at justifying what one believes and says, as well as what one does, by reference to a standard all persons can consult. For Plato the means of consultation had to be dialectical reasoning, mainly because simply looking at the world and the behavior of people (the imperfect realm of the perceivable) produced only diversity. (For Socrates especially, as distinguished from Plato, reasoning started from the consultation of opinions, for, as Strauss characterizes Socrates' position, "the being of things, their What, comes first to sight, not in what we see of them, but in what is said about them or in opinions about them. . . . For every opinion is based on some awareness, on some perception with the mind's eye, of something.") For Aristotle there had to be consultation of facts from which the reasoning could proceed. For both Plato and Aristotle the consultation would consist primarily in rational analysis, although Aristotle expanded this idea to include the experimental study of nature.

Underlying this approach we find a conception of human nature that points up one of the important differences between classical and Hobbesian natural right theories. In Aristotle especially, man is thought of as possessing the *capacity for choice*. Even in Plato there had been this implication, although some aspects of his thought—e.g., his explanation of evil on the basis of ignorance (which could, after all, be entirely innocent) and his elitist tendency—militated against the idea. Ultimately, though, the widely admitted but unwelcome fact of diversity in what people judged right in similar circumstances would point to the absence of full scale environmental and/or constitutional determinism in human life. In the main then, classical natural right theory conceived of human beings as capable of free choice. Certainly Aristotle explained human virtue by reference to this capacity; his own account was comparable to the contemporary philosophical slogan, "ought implies can"—only if we are capable of alternative actions is it meaningful to say we ought to do or ought to have done some of them.

Classical natural right theory, then, took man to be a living being capable of choice and reason. And since it is the capacity to reason that set man apart from the rest of the animal world (although not completely, as later theologians and philosophers would argue), it is this capacity that had to be identified as being up to them to exercise. Choice and reason—man's distinguishing and distinctive aspects, the two mutually implying each other. (For, and I will argue this later, there cannot be a distinction between the rational and the irrational if no freedom is possible, as we generally admit in connection with the criminal law of almost any legal system, despite the fact that determinists are now fighting against this very feature of legal theory.)

Hobbes, in turn, denied both these features of classical natural right theory. He held that man is fully determined to do what he does by the passions inherent in his biophysical constitution. So he obviously rejected freedom of choice, and took man's reason to be a mere calculating system spurred into action by the passions. Once both choice and reason had been robbed of their essential role in human affairs, what semblance of natural right could be left in Hobbes' theory?

The idea was that by learning of the above facts, man could better adjust himself to them. As with so many modern determinists, Hobbes tried to bring together two concepts which ultimately lead to severe paradoxes, if not contradictions: man is unfree, propelled by his bodily constituents, *and* he knows it. As such, perplexing as this move obviously is, the conclusion usually drawn is that man ought to act on his knowledge. The difficulty is that if man's passions do unalterably drive his movements, as Hobbes insisted, what sense is there in expecting him to be governed by what he knows—knowledge being a function not of the passions but of reason? Moreover, recalling that "ought implies can," what sense could there be in declaring that man should or ought to, when in fact he will as he will be so governed?)

But one crucial feature of classical natural right theory had been retained: its insistence on the fruitfulness and power of knowledge of the nature of things, in this case *human* nature. This the classics as well as Hobbes believed to be extremely important; it was, as I mentioned before, the very point of their naturalism to find a common point of reference in settling disputes, answering questions, solving problems.

Hobbes maintained his biophysical determinism and argued that knowing the determinants of human behavior should serve us well in our attempt to answer the questions we encounter only too frequently, including those that face us in our political situation. I call Hobbes' determinism "biophysical" because for Hobbes everything would ultimately have to be understood as physical particles in motion. From this it follows that man is constituted as a system of physical particles in motion, with the result that his biological passions, mainly the drive for self-preservation, provide the basic force that spurs all human behavior. This view is in no significant way different from more recent deterministic theories, such as the instinctual drive theory of Freud, the behaviorism of B. F. Skinner, the social psychological theories which explain human behavior by reference to cultural pressures alone, and so on. Nor was Hobbes entirely original. The early Greek materialist philosopher Democritus of Abdera had laid firm foundations for Hobbes' idea in the claim that "By convention sweet is sweet, by convention bitter is bitter, by convention hot is hot, by convention cold is cold, by convention color is color. But in truth there are atoms and the void." Yet until Hobbes no one had developed a comprehensive and highly influential political theory from a fully materialistic philosophy. Machiavelli had made significant moves in that direction, of course, as did Francis Bacon, a contemporary of Hobbes. But none had been so comprehensive as he.

I shall not dwell on Hobbes' overall philosophy. We need to note his influence upon the philosophical/psychological theory known as associationism, his limited metaphysics whereby knowledge of real being or things as they actually are in reality is barred to man (thus a view that preempted the conclusion of the nineteenth-century German philosophical genius, Immanuel Kant), and his persistent emphasis on the principle of mechanics as useful in understanding all areas of reality. For us Hobbes' political theory must take precedence over all these lasting contributions. For in an important way, despite the theoretical difficulties inherent in them, Hobbes' political views give the first clearly recognizable underpinnings for modern human rights theory, the doctrine of natural rights.

Hobbes believed that outside civil society, with no legal system prevailing, it is right for each person to do whatever he will do. In a sense each person has a natural right to do anything, to act however or possess whatever he can, with no limits. This followed from Hobbes' belief that people are driven to act and will thus do what they can just as long as their passions urge them on. To hold then that there are limits on what they do aside from the limits imposed by the laws of (their biophysical) nature, such as certain moral laws of nature, is absurd.

Later, when mankind experiences the inevitable consequence of such unlimited "freedom" of conduct—namely persistent lack of peace, actual or impending physical conflict—the realization of this state of war will require the formation of civil society. While in that society the unlimited rights all people have in the state of nature will have to be given up, Hobbes saw that itself as quite consistent with the nature of the situation. From the fact of the initial unlimited range of freedom of action, mankind *must* proceed, by force of natural (psychophysical) law, to abandoning natural rights as a means of self-preservation. This leads for Hobbes to advocacy of absolute monarchy or statism. No freedom is to be found in civil society, only positive (legislated) law remains. Hobbes defends this by arguing that the law of nature, because of the warlike conditions inevitable when natural rights operate in "the state of nature," requires the absolute rule of heads of states (monarchs or legislators). Thus Hobbes offers us the para-doxical yet purportedly logical conclusion that civil society must submit to absolute statism because man has natural rights!

Again, as with most seriously advanced views, Hobbes' idea contains the germ of important truth. Briefly, it seems true enough that in the attempt to ensure peaceful social existence people must accept certain implications of their human nature for purposes of social conduct. Men are isolated, either in fact (i.e., on a desert island) or by default (i.e., simply side-by-side but with no choice to cooperate in living), in the state of original human conditions. Thus concerns about the principles of community life are irrelevant (except in the minds of those who are already preparing for such community life). Any moral principles cannot have reached the point of application *for human communities* in that sort of state, the state of original nature. (It does not matter now whether such original states ever existed or not—they are, nevertheless, a meaningful analytic device to understand the development of ideas about human conduct.) Hobbes may not have admitted all that moral theories require—e.g., human freedom of choice. But he did offer moral advice: establish laws in human communities to serve peace! And that advice has considerable merit. We will have to pay attention to these points when an up-to-date theory of human rights is offered later in this work.

Next to come under discussion is the natural rights theory of John Locke, perhaps the most influential political philosopher in the context of America's political history. Is Locke closer to Hobbes than to classical natural right theorists? If so, why? What justifies the general view that Locke was opposed to Hobbes' ideas? For surely a philosophy which argues for the *legal* recognition, protection, and preservation of natural rights to life, liberty, and property is at the opposite pole from a philosophy which holds that legal systems must abandon all considerations of such (natural) rights. Before these questions, what did Locke believe, what did he think to be the case concerning man's life in his communities, and why?

As with the earlier sketches the treatment given to all these issues will be brief. I can only hope to provide an accurate enough impression of Locke's views, one that does justice to his own expressed philosophy as well as to the discoveries later scholars have made about what he must have meant. But of course I am not after some kind of survey. The following will culminate in my own understanding and evaluation of Locke. But more than in the previous discussions, I will focus on some of the discussions of Locke's thoughts by recent commentators, who have taken him to have meant—even said—different things. That is because these commentators as well as I believe that understanding Locke contributes important material to an examination of the American political tradition. For instance, when someone accuses Locke of merely expressing the bias of his own socioeconomic class through his insistence on certain specific natural rights, he is at the same time saying that the basic features of the American political system are far from universally applicable; they simply serve to advance the narrow class interests of some, even at the tragic expense of members of other classes. Such a view must be contended with because it enjoys wide-scale popularity. It is now almost conventional wisdom to identify all ethical and political theories as expressions of "party sentiments."

One of the first matters to be noted about Locke is that he, unlike Hobbes, professed faith in God along with his adherence to natural law theory. As in the case of Aquinas, Locke held that there is no incompatibility between these two stances. Some of his critics, including Strauss, have decided to discount Locke's commitment to natural law theory on account of his double standard. For Locke, however, there appeared to be no difficulty about this because the laws of nature expressed God's commandments and reason could apprehend them even without full knowledge of God. (Yet this did put God, not nature, in the ultimate court of last resort, a point Strauss makes very forcefully.)

Locke maintained that man's nature involved him in the law of nature from the very start. In other words, even in the state of nature, which he, like Hobbes, invoked frequently either as a historical fact or an analytic device (i.e., an imaginary but quite possible state from which we can deduce important knowledge), man was subject to the law of nature, to natural (moral) law. But here we face an immediate difficulty with understanding Locke. Although he subscribed to the idea of natural law as including *moral principles of conduct,* he also argued for the view that these natural laws amount to something found in Hobbes, namely innate desires for self-preservation and happiness. Man's nature then implies the law of nature that self-preservation and happiness ought to be pursued.

Some passages in Locke point more in the direction of the Hobbesian view, namely that these desires *impel* man toward the goal of self-preservation; others tend to support the equally prominent interpretation that Locke believed self-preservation and happiness to be what is good for man and thought it each person's choice and responsibility to pursue these. For example, Strauss inclines toward the first, while the French political philosopher Raymond Polin[7] leans toward the second interpretation. Both scholars cite ample evidence for their contention in their several essays on the topic. It must be noted, however, that Strauss' thesis rests on a characteristic method of reading between the lines. Thus to demonstrate his case he invokes several rather esoteric distinctions which arise from his own theory of interpretation. He points to passages in Locke which indicate a belief in being "cautious" or even coy (i.e., showing unwillingness to make a clear and definite commitment), so as to avoid upsetting those who might not fully appreciate what he was saying. From this Strauss argues that Locke used two approaches, one in his specifically philosophical works, another in his propaganda tracts. And the main exposition of natural law doctrine appears in a work Strauss argues must be placed in the second group.

Another scholar, C. B. Macpherson, has charged Locke with predominant Hobbesian inclinations as well as with producing the rationale (read: "rationalization") for what he and Marxists in general call "bourgeois rights." Briefly, Macpherson finds the theory of natural rights unacceptable because "of their possessive individualist postulates." He arrives at this view by giving no benefit of doubt to Locke—allowing no chance for the interpretation Polin, for example, has provided. Macpherson believes that "[b]oth Hobbes and Locke . . . read back into the nature of man a contentious, competitive behavior drawn from their model of bourgeois society . . . a model in which . . . everyone was always seeking to transfer some of the powers of others to himself."[8] While this model is most prominent in Hobbes, Macpherson claims that Locke held it too since he accepted "the right of infinite accumulation," property rights not explicitly limited to people's needs. (Actually Locke did put a limit on property rights, but here again there are contradictory passages in his works. If we want to hold, as Strauss does, that Locke would not have allowed a contradiction which did not serve a specific purpose, then we need to analyze the contradiction away, somehow.)

Yet others have said that Locke rejected natural rights in favor of the democratic principle. Wilmore Kendall charges Locke with explicit collectivism[9] by pointing to passages where advocating the democratic process of reaching decisions in human communities seemed to allow for the overriding of natural rights. Thus it is evident that no unequivocal interpretation of Locke has been offered by his students and critics. Nor is it possible to provide one here. What is possible, however, is to sketch a possible interpretation, a kind of rational reconstruction that will do justice, in our context, to Locke's views *and* influence.

In essence Locke recognized the undeniable value of human happiness. Here he followed the classics. But he did not think it opportune or even right to advocate the conclusion of that realization—a moral point of view that amounts to egoism. This egoism would hold that each person, by virtue of his nature as a human being, must serve his best interest, although he is free (can choose) to neglect it. Since as a moral point of view this might have appeared to Locke to be far too radical and even dangerous, the undeniability of the value of human happiness and the flourishing of one's own life could best be expressed as an innate desire. After all, even if the popular view is that selfishness is condemnable, we cannot be faulted for having the innate desire to be happy.

Hobbes had already devised a philosophical system in terms of which man is *driven* by a passion for self-preservation. By attacking this feature of Hobbes' view, Locke cleared the way for supporting the pursuit of life, liberty, and property, all clearly required for happiness. From this merger between the Hobbesian and Lockean view emerged the difficult political philosophy we now know to be Locke's natural right doctrine.

Others of his general epoch also achieved the partial merger described above, especially supporters of what we now characterize classical liberal or free market economics. Adam Smith, for instance, described the operations of selfish desires as private *vices* but public *virtues:* through the widely condemned selfishness that most people exhibit (as well as decry and feel shame for) we could at least hope for and expect a widely acclaimed but privately neglected goal: public prosperity. It did not seem to disturb anyone that such a view implied a rather dichotomous conception of reality and man's place in it. (On the other hand, ever since Machiavelli such split thinking had been tolerated on many fronts: hosts of scientific materialists made declarations of theism, and philosophers such as Pierre Bayle, a famous encyclopedist, declared the dichotomous roles of reason and faith in man's life. Perhaps, then, we can understand these modes of thought, however much we would like to have our great philosophers be consistent.)

Whatever the ultimate *intentions* of Locke, the *meaning* of some of his political ideas can be ferreted out. It is clear that Locke considered pursuing one's success as a human being the right course for people to take—whether desire or natural (moral) law showed this to be so. It is also clear that he believed that it follows from this that each person has rights that take effect in the context of civil society, rights that are therefore natural (i.e., follow from the nature of the context) instead of merely conventional or decreed. What these rights are can be known by understanding how happiness could be achieved in the company of others. Natural rights, then, provided for Locke the guidelines by which people *in society* can attain their natural, i.e., moral, desires and goals. And he identified these as the rights to life, liberty and property—the first giving ground for the last two with the latter rendering the exercise of the former a possibility in the world as we know it.

In the end we must admit that Strauss' objections appear the most compelling against Locke. He cites Locke saying that no rule of law is "imprinted on the mind as a duty." Yet "men . . . must be allowed to pursue their happiness, nay, cannot be hindered." So Locke, Strauss argues, accepts that there is "an innate natural right, while there is no innate natural duty." Since Strauss identifies natural *duty* with natural *law*, he concludes that "Locke cannot have recognized any law of nature in the proper sense of the term."[10] The central impact of this criticism is, to put it bluntly, that Locke's political theory had no moral or ethical foundation. According to this interpretation it is clearly a modern natural right doctrine, closer to Hobbes' than to Plato's and Aristotle's.

There is a crucial point to be noted in connection with Strauss' criticism. "Duty" means, most generally and recognizably, an obligation or commitment to act so as to benefit *others*. Thus people's duties are what they ought to do *for others*—for their country, God, or parents. Even in cases where "duty" has no ethical or moral implications—at least in the *primary* sense—someone's duty is a function of what *he contracted or promised to do for others*. A policeman's duties are what he should do *for* citizens; a doctor's what he should do for his patients, a teacher's are obligations to his students, and so on. To summarize: duties exist toward others—in the primary sense, at least.

Natural law, on the other hand, consists of principles of human conduct in general. Admittedly, if man is a social being and if there are natural laws pertaining to his conduct, there will be implications from such laws for how he should conduct himself toward others. Some of these would be duties. But they need not be the primary or only content of such principles. It is to beg the question of the content of natural law to identify it at the outset as duties.

Strauss' main point seems to be even more intriguing. He says that in Locke "the individual, the ego, had become the center and origin of the moral world, since man—as distinguished from man's end—had become that center or origin."[11] Strauss find it unacceptable that man's end could be his own happiness. And since Locke really gave no aid to this view, Strauss does not consider it. Locke, after all, did say "That which is properly good or bad is nothing but barely pleasure or pain."[12] Strauss then takes Locke to be a subjectivist, since the latter believed that what constitutes pain and pleasure is different for different people. Strauss does not permit Locke, as he does Aristotle, the more generous interpretation, namely that basic laws of nature, natural right, may require different application for different people at different times. So he identifies Locke as a crass hedonist, admittedly with ample textual support for his judgment. As such, Locke's view of human nature was that it initially lacks value and each person must struggle to create that value. Strauss takes Locke to have believed that "the way toward happiness is a movement away from the state of nature, a movement away from nature: the negation of nature is the way toward happiness."[13] To put it another way, "suffering and defects, rather than merits or virtues, originate rights."[14]

There is no doubt that Locke was muddled on ethics, but so were the classics, Strauss' tendency to think otherwise notwithstanding. Some commentators point to this ambivalence in Locke as the result of internal conflict concerning elements of his ideas.[15] There is no clear-cut ethical theory for Locke; he was in some ways a religious conservative who relied on Christian tradition for ethics. Yet it does not follow that his theory of human rights departed *drastically* from classical natural right theory. The following, therefore, will be the most plausible rendition of the Lockean viewpoint, reconstructed to reflect how it was taken (historically) *qua* political position, leaving the ethics of it ambiguous.

Locke was indeed within the tradition of natural law and natural right theory as begun by Socrates, Plato, and Aristotle, although by no means a pure proponent of the same. He did accept that there are natural laws by which human life ought to be guided; each person ought to do what is naturally good and right. What exactly this would amount to is not clear from Locke, although he hinted at an uncomfortable subjectivist theory with allusions to psychological egoism/hedonism. Whatever that good is which man must pursue—be it the avoidance of pain or the pursuit of human happiness—each man must *choose* it for himself. It is therefore *naturally* right that each man should be free to live, act, and acquire property (these enabling him to pursue the good). Although egoistically inspired, the law of nature pertaining to civil society implies each person's natural duty to refrain from obstructing the efforts of other human beings to make and act on the choices that could lead to human good. In a way Locke considered the obligation we have toward others to be limited to helping or enabling them to make a choice toward human good. The risk here is obvious—people may not use their freedom to that end. But without freedom, virtue is impossible, even if vice is impossible as well.

The problem with Locke is that his psychological egoism/hedonism may not provide him with a solid enough (moral) justification for political liberty and natural rights; for freedom from obstruction in one's choice between good and evil only makes sense as a value if such choice is possible. Without that possibility there is no sense in having the freedom. To the extent that Locke allows for such an interpretation, he must be considered an incomplete and inconsistent defender of natural human rights.

Admittedly, the above is a reconstruction that will be disputed by some. Whether Locke would have accepted it either is not clear. But from what we have at our disposal, both in the way of Locke's own discussions and those of his able interpreters, the above summary seems to make the best sense. It also helps in comprehending his general influence on political affairs, especially the development of the American system. One could even conjecture that Locke's failure to advocate a fully consistent and elaborate moral theory made it possible for so many different groups of people to unite behind his political philosophy. Yet without a firm moral point of view, the victory won on the political front may be short lived, as it indeed turned out for America.

With Locke we reach the last major philosophical attempt to justify natural right in the political realm. Locke is not only the philosophical father of the American political tradition, he was also the last of its best philosophical supporters. Philosophers are not often credited in terms of moral or ethical accomplishment. Instead we hear of their brilliance, genius, and so on. But Locke should be known by us, even (or perhaps especially) in the face of the cynicism that has overtaken our intellectual and moral atmosphere, as a commendable human being who set out to treat philosophy as more than an exercise for well-to-do and puzzled gentlemen with considerable disregard for mundane human concerns. From his analysis of human knowledge to his authorship of the greatest work in support of human liberty, Locke directed his efforts toward making human life on earth as good as it could be. A dedication not widely regarded as possible or worthy of praise in our age, where only suffering, helplessness, disease, and assorted misfortunes seem to warrant any expression of concern and feeling for people—in our age of the cult of the anti-hero.

The Mounting Case against Natural Rights

After Locke, natural right, now to be called by its modern name "natural rights," enjoyed enormous popularity. People throughout the Western hemisphere, and later more widely, had been provided with a philosophical defense of something many have *believed* proper to human beings without being able to demonstrate it. Mankind's history is not very old and it is not surprising that we find increasingly better ways of both showing *and* doubting what is right.

The theory of natural rights was considered by many to be the best way to understand the relationship between human nature and life in a human community—how both might best be secured, helped, improved, and so forth. And this theory, despite its inadequacies—for it had some—was for a while acknowledged by many as quite true. Even though intellectuals, especially philosophers and social reformers, raised many doubts about it and decried it (with Bentham) as "nonsense upon stilts," too many actual human affairs could be understood quite well with this theory in hand. As with theories in the sciences, so with political theories, the test is how well it explains or manages to render intelligible what belongs within its field of concern. Locke did manage to make sense of things. (Which does not mean, either in this or other branches of human knowledge, that all aspects of the theory had been dealt with successfully, that nothing was left to work on. If it did mean that, later attempts to give it support would be superfluous.)

Critics of human rights and natural rights theory will quickly deny that it made sense of things for everyone, since eminent figures in the field of political thought rejected its tenets. We shall see if the point of this remark must be accepted. For now I would simply respond by noting that in most cases rejection of natural rights theory emerged in close conjunction with a rejection of the possibility of making sense either of the world in general or of moral and political matters in particular. So opposition to natural rights theory usually emerged not because it failed to make sense of political affairs but because critics disputed the possibility of making sense of such matters—i.e., because of doubtfulness about the possibility of moral and political issues being open to rational understanding.

Lest I give the impression by such remarks that the idea of human rights found no formidable defenders, I must note that many individuals gave it their full intellectual and moral/political support.[16] Perhaps in a different philosophical climate from ours *these* people would receive our utmost attention. But in our age the force of intellect bound for other purposes seems victorious. Undoubtedly there are many scholars and students of human affairs, including philosophers, legal theoreticians, and practitioners, many people with no discernible place in the history of ideas, and many ordinary struggling individuals throughout the world, who gave and still give their loyalty to the vision and possible reality of a world where the rights of persons are fully acknowledged. Indeed, this is evident from the fact that few modern constitutions omit some mention of human rights, even at a time when the most prominent philosophers of the Anglo-American world, where human rights theory has gained its fullest realization, reject the idea wholesale or distort it so that neither classical nor modern natural rights theorist would identify it as akin to his view.

Perhaps the best illustration of what I am saying here is the following pair of facts. On September 30, 1973, the *New York Times* carried this statement in a small, page 3, news item:

> Sixty-five American scientists, academics, intellectuals and civil-rights leaders, including eight Nobel Prize winners have protested to the Soviet Communist Party leader, Leonid I. Brezhnev, against violations of human rights in the Soviet Union.

Yet in October 1968 one of America's well-known academic philosophers, widely published in journals and admired for his political activism, concluded a paper on human rights with the following observation:

> As much as I value a respect for human beings, all human beings great and small, good and bad, stupid and reflective . . . it seems to me quite evident that we do not know that there are any universal human rights.[17]

In spite of popular recourse to the idea, natural human rights *theory* is forgotten.

In this section I shall review, summarily, the scenario in the history of philosophy which has given rise to this paradoxical state of affairs. In an age when people throughout the world fight for what they call their rights as people, when events such as Vietnam, Watergate, suppression of artistic, scientific, political, and other ideas, curtailment of travel, confiscation of properties, invasion of privacy, control of the use of medicine, vitamins, and drugs, and of the ownership of gold—virtually total powers by heads of states to run the life of every individual of a nation (as reported recently not about the Soviet Union but about the United States by some of its senators—how is it that today the dominant intellectual climate has nothing to offer but opposition to the theory of natural human rights?

This question is not a simple one to answer. What exactly would such an answer have to supply? Surely not some psychological diagnosis of those who lived during the years when the intellectual respectability of human rights theory was declining. Some of that may be of help, but it would, at the same time, be presumptuous. Who is to say, at this stage or any other, that certain ideas, theories, beliefs can be taken as sure signs of psychological well-being or dysfunction? Certainly not someone whose training is in philosophy, if anyone at all. (Psychology has a hard enough time discovering just what its subject matter is, despite the ambitions of some of those in the field.[18]) Some people will say that history itself changes people's minds, that there is some force outside us which compels us to think along certain lines, to say one thing is true as opposed to another just because time has advanced. Others have suggested that mankind's economic circumstances produce different ideologies, including political doctrines, which express the prevailing biases of people, depending upon their particular economic class. In the history and sociology of science it is now a prominent idea that views or theories develop because of the aesthetic inclinations of those who attend to the topic—meaning, in the final analysis, that subjective, largely *a*rational processes underlie scientific and other theoretical developments in mankind's intellectual history.

In short, there are views about the way we must understand the development of ideas as varied as there are people and schools of intellectuals concerned with the topic. Although I won't be debating the matter here of how ideas gain and lose their intellectual respectability, popularity, even validity, I will have some things to say about it later in the book. For now I will rest with observing that what people think does have the capacity to foster or stifle, even arrest the development, popularity, and application of theories to concrete affairs in any field of study. Or I should say that these powers are attendant not upon *what* people think, but on whether they do or do not think, and think well, about the issues involved. For now I shall merely outline what are widely regarded or known to be trends in Western philosophy giving rise to the rejection, at least by most intellectuals, of the theory of natural rights.

(Before proceeding, I should let the reader know that some of what follows will be a bit technical. While the present work is not directed to scholars in the field, the arguments against natural rights have some technical aspects which cannot be done justice with a *simple* translation into straightforward, ordinary parlance. That, in part, may turn out to be what's wrong with those arguments! Nevertheless those who proposed them will certainly insist that justice be done to their intentions. And that requires engaging in what is considered to be the familiar language of philosophical discourse used by the proponents of the critical point of view at hand. For those who are less interested in the criticism of human rights theory in general than in its constructive case it would be entirely appropriate to skip some of the present discussion. Later, however, it might be fruitful to return to the negative case to see if the constructive theory answers some of the criticism.)

Without much doubt the most serious philosophical blow to natural rights theory, as well as to moral philosophy in general, came from the following influential passage in David Hume's *Treatise of Human Nature:*

> In every system of morality which I have hitherto met with, I have always remarked that the author proceeds for some time in the ordinary way of reasoning, and establishes the being of a God, or makes observations concerning human affairs; when of a sudden I am surprised to find, that instead of the usual copulations of propositions, *is*, and *is not*, I meet with no proposition that is not connected with an *ought*, or an *ought not*. This change is imperceptible; but is, however, of the last consequence. For as this *ought*, or *ought not*, expresses some new relation or affirmation, 'tis necessary that it should be observed and explained; and at the same time that a reason should be given, for what seems altogether inconceivable, how this new relation can be a deduction from others, which are entirely different from it. But as authors do not commonly use this precaution, I shall presume to recommend it to the readers: and am persuaded, that this small attention would subvert all the vulgar systems of morality, and let us see that the distinction of vice and virtue is not founded merely on the relations of objects, nor is perceived by reason.[19]

On the face of it, and that is how it has usually been taken, Hume's famous passage, consistent with his overall theory, simply rejects the possibility that we could ever *know* what is morally good or right, wrong or evil ("vice and virtue"), at least if we take it that knowledge is what we arrive at mainly from thinking and reasoning about what we are aware of in reality. As with all other important passages in the history of human thought, this one has its share of diverse interpretations. After all, Hume lived some time ago and his use of terms such as "reason," "perceived," "objects," "vice," and "virtue" may have been intended to convey different ideas from what we now take them to convey. Still, whatever the ultimate conclusion about what Hume actually wanted to say, we know what most intellectuals have taken him to be saying.

Why did Hume believe that the connection of propositions by "is" or "is not," as in "The car *is* yellow," is drastically different from ones connected by "ought" and "ought not" (as well as "should" or "should not," and even "must" or "must not")? First of all, it seems quite obvious. When we say that something is here or there, colored or not, wide or narrow, we are talking about what exists in simple, straightforward ways, while when we say that something ought to be here or there, colored, and so on, we are talking about what, perhaps, should exist or exists in some complex fashion. No one can deny that this is clearly a difference of some significance.

It is also clear that Hume's theory of knowledge was at the base of his understanding of the difference. For without that obstacle some might have demonstrated enough similarity between the two kinds of propositions to explain why those with "ought" in the conclusion might be able to be derived from those with "is" in the premises or vice versa. The constructive portion of the present work will try to achieve something much like that sort of a solution to the problem of moral knowledge.

Hume, however, believed that human knowledge is restricted in such a way that whatever propositions containing "ought" might mean, it is impossible for us to know such things. He believed, to state his positive case, that the human mind could only know of *sensory impressions,* nothing else. Not even objects could be known by us; only the impressions could be known, although we may be compelled by a psychological disposition to *believe* there are objects. (Hume did not apply this restriction consistently to his discussions of other topics, not even to his own theory of morality, and, indeed, he had one that tried to overcome his own objections. But that is not what is crucial at this stage.)

It is quite obvious that whatever we mean when we use the kinds of propositions involving "ought," we do not mean to be talking about a field as narrow as is covered by the phrase "impressions of the senses." That this is so should be clear from the fact that Hume found it incredibly difficult to justify any general beliefs about facts, even of a scientific variety. Thus if someone were to maintain, with the appropriate qualifications, that he knows that objects thrown into the air will fall back to earth, Hume would deny him that right. We can only know that we had an experience of sense impressions (which we chose to *name* in such a way that it now comes out "something that was thrown up fell back down"), and that we may have had this experience on many occasions. But all this entitles us to conclude by force of reason, with logical validity in its support, is that we *have had* these experiences, one by one, over and over again. The rest of what we say may be something we *believe,* even *have to* believe, but by some kind of psychological inclination, not by any force of a rational justification. Hume does argue that this is what leads us to such beliefs, even to the belief that we know about general matters. (How Hume himself learned about these general matters of human psychology is not clear.)

Although Hume wrote the *Treatise* at twenty-six, his later work, *Enquiries Concerning Human Understanding and Concerning the Principles of Morals,*[20] reiterated his entire doctrine with hardly a change. In this latter work Hume asserted that "If we reason *a priori,* anything may appear able to produce anything. The falling of a pebble may, for aught we know, extinguish the sun; or the wish of a man control the planets in their orbits."[21] And he added in a footnote:

> That impious maxim of the ancient philosophy, *Ex nihilo, nihil fit,* by which the creation of matters was excluded, ceases to be a maxim, according to this philosophy. Not only the will of the supreme Being may create matter; but, for aught we know *a priori,* the will of any other being might create it, or any other cause, that the most whimsical imagination can assign.[22]

We have here, clearly, the most eloquent expression of that well-known remark of many a man, "Anything is possible."

What should be noted is that the *context* of Hume's discussion may have had a good deal to do with his extreme position, for his work was an energetic retort to certain views entertained and held by earlier thinkers. I am not talking about Locke here, for Locke himself was in most respects closer to Hume on epistemological matters than to the ancients. Hume was addressing the Cartesians and schoolmen, theologians mostly, who believed in reasoning about *everything* a priori. Everyone has heard of the famous caricature of medieval theologians worrying about how many angels could dance on the head of a pin. That issue arose out of a serious (within its context) philosophical problem, namely the fact that angels were conceived as bodiless, yet could supposedly be *counted.* At any rate, Hume's fervent style and substance had a good deal to do with an impatience about that and similar armchair reasoning.

It is also important to note that while Hume's philosophy leads straight to *strict* skepticism, Hume himself advocated a *mitigated* skepticism about all matters. As he remarked in the index to the *Enquiry,* "excessive scepticism [is] refuted by its uselessness and put to flight by the most trivial event in life, [but] Mitigated scepticism or academic philosophy [is] useful as a corrective and as producing caution and modesty; and as limiting understanding to proper objects." Yet he also added that "all reasoning which is not either abstract, about quantity and number, or experimental, about matters of fact, is sophistry and illusion."[23] And that exclusion would seem to include moral reasoning, ethics.

Enough cited from Hume. It does not matter much for us, nor did it for the history of ideas, that Hume developed a theory in which morality was seen to be based on some kind of natural sentiment, one which could be disciplined by reason somehow. But Hume never made clear how this was to be reconciled with his pronouncements on the impossibility of reasoning about moral matters. Scholars since have worried about this, and many have provided insights about how Hume *might have resolved* the paradox.

What is crucial in our context is that David Hume's philosophy resurrected several pre-Socratic philosophical ideas, including thoroughgoing skepticism, the possibility that anything could happen as far as we could know, and the impossibility of the human mind knowing nature as such. Most important and lasting has been Hume's dichotomization of statements about what *is* the case and what *ought to be* the case, what is now known as the fact/value distinction. Hume almost single-handedly undermined all efforts to justify knowledge not derived *exclusively* from the data available from our senses. And anywhere we look today, in all the struggling sciences (sociology, economics, psychology, political science), in spite of dissimilarities with the physical sciences, the effort to produce evidence and argument based exclusively on observation attests to Hume's considerable influence. There had been others who hinted at the priority of relying on the senses—Francis Bacon, for example, was certainly one of those who considered the experimental, data-gathering method the only admissible and sufficient one for science. But it was Hume who provided this method with a full-scale philosophical system, a justification based on critical analysis of the very idea of knowledge. Hardly any other thinker had comparable impact on later philosophers or the ensuing intellectual and cultural era. As everyone likes to mention, the only philosopher considered to be of equal significance to Hume, Immanuel Kant, reported that he was awakened from his "dogmatic slumbers" by reading David Hume.

At this point I shall begin a more systematic presentation of Hume's argument, cast in modern terminology. There are many Humeans and neo-Humeans within the contemporary philosophical community, individuals who have added to and subtracted from Hume's ideas but who have never really given up the belief that human knowledge must consist of something much like what Hume maintained.

As mentioned above, this section can be skipped by those not interested in the critical history of human rights theory. It is certainly not everyone's job to concern himself with the battles that need to be fought on philosophical fronts. But it would not be doing justice to the topic of human rights theory to omit a consideration of its greatest challenge, one we are about to take up. Since in this work I do not plan to respond to each of the many criticisms of human rights theory separately, I shall merely outline the main features of the case against human rights. At first this will consist of presenting the argument against the possibility of moral knowledge. Later human rights will be brought into focus.

The case most often used against the view that we can identify the human rights all people have rests on Hume's distinction cited above. We may state this case as follows: what is believed or said about a person's rights (because he is a *human* being, thus his *human rights)* cannot be justifiably considered either true or false. Those who hold this view have explained claims or beliefs such as "The human rights of members of the black community are violated in South Africa" to be, variously, expressions of sentiments or feelings,[24] imperatives based on anything but *knowledge* of right and wrong,[25] performances involving the goading or urging or boosting of certain kinds of actions (or the discouraging or disparaging of the same),[26] and similar explicitly arational or nonrational undertakings. Central to the view, however, is not the specific counteranalysis of such statements, but the belief that whatever they are, they *cannot* ever be true or false.

While the view at issue is basic to virtually all those who reject statements about people's human rights, there are slightly different versions of it. So as to be sure that justice is done to exponents of this skeptical view on ethics and politics, here in outline are various renditions of the basic point made:

1.   Statements which pertain to values, e.g., "It is good to tell the truth," cannot be confirmed or verified in any rationally acceptable ways. (The latter usually means "by exclusive reference to sensory experience.")[24]

2.   Such statements cannot be proven true or false by a combination of deductive and inductive arguments, i.e., as (many believe) scientific conclusions are established.[28]

3.   Such statements are neither analytic nor synthetic—roughly, they are not true by definition or because the evidence justifies them. Thus they do not fall within the two general classes of statements capable of being true or false.[29]

5.   Such statements are "known" to be true by a different sort of knowledge from that which we have of most things, especially anything we could *all* discover and communicate about. Thus their truth is "known" by something called intuition, revelation, or mystical awareness, and we are confused to believe that they could be true or false as this can best be understood by people.[30]

6.   Such statements contain a copula (e.g., "ought to" or "should")

which signifies a relationship between things, events, or people for which no referent can be found in (empirical) reality. ("The car *rolls on* its wheels" versus "The person *should pay* his debts.")[31]

7.   Agreement about such statements cannot be reached by following certain accepted methods of settling disputes, ones, for instance, used by electricians or mathematicians when they are considering some question or problem.[32]

Not all of these positions exclude one another; some are frequently offered as reasons for holding others. In the final analysis all of them seem to come down to one: since statements pertaining to values do not say something about what *is* the case but only about what ought to be done or ought to be the case, such statements cannot ever express what one *knows*. Only what *is* can be an object or the subject matter of puzzle-solving, knowledge, or general statements; what ought to be or be done is never such an object or subject matter.

This basically negative philosophical position, the view that *knowledge* of right and wrong is *impossible,* still has our culture in its almost total grip. Not that everyone believes it. Now as in each era we find those who contend otherwise.[33] But the skepticism expressed above in brief outline is reiterated each day, in and out of intellectual circles. How often does one hear the idea that a scientific view requires that values be discounted? The value-free position concerning an understanding of human affairs has the support of virtually all of the social scientists who staff colleges, universities, governmental commissions, research foundations, and any other institution that has as its purpose the discovery of truth, the understanding of reality, even when it includes the reality of human life. How often is it announced that commitment to moral and political principles is at best a harmless bias, but mostly a dangerous prejudice that must distort the truth in any area of human understanding? "To each his own" and "None of us can judge our fellow men" are widespread popular versions of the same skepticism.

I will reserve criticism of this skeptical point of view until later, when the positive theory of this book is put to scrutiny. At this point several other significant arguments that have a bearing upon human rights in some critical manner must be outlined. First of all we have to consider the idea that perhaps we can never know the nature of man, and thus we can never identify human rights. For if human nature is impossible to identify—or if no such idea as the nature of something can be meaningful, so that human nature does not exist such that we could know it—then rights that people have because they are human beings, i.e., by virtue of their humanity, human nature, cannot be identified.[34]

The argument here is again to be traced to David Hume, although perhaps not as directly. Hume confined what is open to knowledge to sense impressions and the memories or copies of these we have in our minds. As far as reason is concerned we could not say whether anything exists beyond these sense impressions. We believe that there exist things, objects, events, relationships, and so on in reality, but all this must be considered rationally unprovable belief, a kind of animal instinct, the healthy but basically unfounded anticipation that these impressions have a source in reality. In page after page of devastating criticism Hume argued in this way that reason is impotent to know the world. Even with his most unique capacity, man was said by Hume to be unable to know anything but what is, in its essentials, already imprinted on his mind by (something we believe to be) nature.

If Hume's concept of knowledge is taken seriously, which it certainly has been and still is by many philosophers, clearly the nature of something cannot be known. Whatever is the correct understanding of the idea of "the nature of X," it must involve what items that make up the world share (at least sometimes) with other items. Human nature is something people, individually but in common with others, possess. But for Hume we could hardly know individual things. Even if we, as later philosophers did, admit that perhaps Hume went too far and we can know more than sense impressions, including, at times, objects and other items in reality, we can only conclude that we know these items one by one. As such we can never conclude about them that there is something they share with other things, especially not something as significant as *essential* features, qualities, or aspects. With Hume and neo-Humeans we may observe that people will believe in such common natures. After they have seen many individual objects that they have named apples, they will believe that other objects which resemble what they previously called apples are apples also. And so with many, many other things in the world. But all this tells us is that people are luckily equipped with what might be called valuable horse sense.

As Hume tells us plainly enough, and as hundreds of philosophers reiterate day in and out in classes throughout the world,

the only objects of the abstract science or of demonstration are quantity and number, and . . . all attempts to extend this more perfect species of knowledge beyond these bounds are mere sophistry and illusion.

In other words, we can never *know* abstract principles outside the sphere of fully deductive realms of study such as mathematics and formal logic. And to know the nature of something is to know a principle such as "Whatever is an apple must have properties a, b, c, or some specific combination such as that." This sort of statement cannot ever constitute knowledge for Hume, not at least "knowledge" that is anything other than induced by custom of mind, something that could never be confirmed by reason. The Humean view of such items as apples or human beings would maintain that what *is* may *not be.* As modern Humeans tell it, it is always *conceivable* that our belief that something is the case is false *always!* And if this be so, then we cannot ever *rightly* say we *know* anything at all (other than conclusions of deductive sciences).

In somewhat plainer terms, the basic complaint is that since there is a possibility of some kind—a logical possibility—that things will be different tomorrow, we are logically forbidden from concluding that they will be what they now are. Again this follows from the belief Hume held that only sense impressions give knowledge, and since tomorrow has given us no sense impressions yet, we cannot know a thing about tomorrow. The mere fact of time seems to serve as a barrier to truth, as if time, as such, by itself only a system of measurement, without anything actually happening, could act as a dramatic force to change things.

It should be clear that equipped with this foundation one must reject the prospect of knowing the nature of anything. For if we could know human nature, then we could also know that the next human being we meet will share something with all other human beings (or at least share with them certain capacities, however unused they might be) and if they do not share this something or somethings, there must be a special explanation. After Hume some philosophers tried to rejuvenate the concept of the nature of X, but most failed. And twentieth-century philosophers, in the main, have followed suit—with somewhat different arguments from Hume's, yet basically relying on similar considerations.

Something must be said about Hume's criticism that will caution us in our understanding of him. Hume's idea of a *rational* conclusion, of "this more perfect knowledge" he said could only be gained in mathematics and logic, was restricted. But since important thinkers before Hume held that we could gain just that kind of knowledge of *everything,* his criticism may have had force against them. If I were to claim that the knowledge we have of mathematical matters must *in all respects* be imitated in knowledge we have of, say, economic or historical matters, or concerning cooking, road building, and so on, I would likely be making a mistake. What I know when I know a mathematical fact is probably going to be different in some respects from what I know when I know a fact about economics, history, cooking, or road building. To restrict knowledge to one kind of knowledge, namely the kind we gain when we study mathematics, can be quite invalid. For we are not entitled, as a matter of logical reasoning, to prejudge the kind of knowledge we may have of various things.[35]

In a way Hume accepted the restriction some perpetrated upon the issue of what human knowledge is. If it is the case that mathematical knowledge *must* serve as the model for all other, then perhaps Hume is right. The problem is that the concept of knowledge itself had always been the most troublesome idea in philosophy. For the most part philosophers attempted to find something they simply had to accept, something so basic that they had to admit that this everyone knows. (But this was to confuse certainty with knowledge; everyone may indeed feel certain about some things.) Some philosophers believed that the truth of some ideas is surely undeniable. Others were convinced that some feelings or experiences could not be denied without grave disservice to sanity. So the former basically accepted undeniable ideas as the model for knowledge, while the latter accepted the feelings or experiences as such. But both accepted that whatever could serve as knowledge par excellence, one must *be certain* about it, it must be somehow immediately obvious, closed to doubt, not just to reasonable doubt but to a shadow of a doubt.

We may take it that David Hume found unacceptable the beliefs of those who thought we know some basic principles for certain because our thoughts about them seem unshakable. He denied Descartes' view that we have some innate, firm yet meaningful ideas (of reality) that we know to be true without the shadow of a doubt. So he attempted to find something else that might fit the requirement—and settled on sense impressions as so immediately evident that to doubt them would be impossible. In this way we might best understand Hume, without further ado, by viewing his philosophy from two perspectives: critical and constructive. Quite clearly he had found grave errors in the views of those whom he criticized, and then found it necessary to offer a counterview.

There is a rather interesting way these two approaches to human knowledge may be understood. We have on the one hand those who believe that knowledge can be gained by just thinking but not looking—as it is said, "by unaided reason." And then we have those who claim that all we need to do is look, never think; understanding is to be gained from pure observation. The armchair thinker versus the data gatherer.

After Hume, the German philosopher Immanuel Kant offered a massive philosophy aimed at rescuing us from total skepticism.[36] Even Hume did not like the conclusions his philosophical speculations had led him to. He liked to suggest a mitigated skepticism, and when he turned to such topics as theism and miracles, he showed that he had ample confidence (in at least his own mind) to distinguish between what people could indeed know about the world (natural laws, events, scientific principles, and so forth) and what was entirely unreasonable to believe (miracles, theism, and so forth.)

But philosophically speaking Hume argued that only skepticism is acceptable. And Kant did not want to accept this, although in the final analysis he did little to counter skepticism. He ended by agreeing with Hume that the nature of things, what they really are (in reality) cannot be known. He said, however, that what we can tell from experiencing the world through our senses is enough—that is all science needs. Certain basic structural features of the human mind equip us to organize our experience so as to serve our purpose. Anything else, such as free will or the existence of God, must be taken on faith. We can never demonstrate either God's existence or his nonexistence, but we must *assume* that man is free and that God exists, otherwise we could never make sense of morality.

Kant became influential in philosophy with his belief in those basic structural features of the human mind. Hume's contention that we believe in objects and the future and scientific principles merely because custom forces us to was widely abandoned and Kant's notion of what he called "the necessary categories of the understanding" was accepted. At least for a while. Later philosophers gave that up also but proposed that convenience and convention force us to see things in certain ways. While these views all have their complex versions, dispersed even today within the academic philosophical community—and thus hardly expressible to everyone's satisfaction in a mere overview—few seem to have escaped the Humean conclusion about the impossibility of identifying the nature of anything and the impossibility of knowledge of right and wrong. When it comes to matters not specifically related to human beings and their institutions, the part about knowing the nature of things is often dropped. In science most people accept the possibility of knowing the nature of something (e.g., electrons, cells, mammals, ulcers), at least with what is often called a statistical certainty, probabilistically. And in matters of conduct it is also accepted that *if* we have selected certain goals or purposes, we can ascertain the right and wrong (read: "efficient") ways of trying to achieve them.

What remains, nevertheless, opposed by almost all intellectuals—scientists, philosophers, scholars in the humane fields, and so on,—as well as tacitly rejected by most laymen, is the possibility of identifying human nature and knowing right and wrong pertaining to human conduct (private and public/political) in the broadest or ultimate sense, i.e., when it comes to knowing which goals or purposes ought to be pursued. With few exceptions the skepticism Hume taught concerning everything (but *emphasized* concerning morals or ethics) has remained most pervasively influential in the study of human beings and what they ought to do and avoid doing in personal or public life.

I am *not* saying that no one knows human nature and no one knows right from wrong. What I am saying is that most intellectual leaders in contemporary culture believe that none could know any such thing, and that to say otherwise is "mere sophistry and illusion." (We will see if this conclusion is justified in later sections.)

Contemporary Notions of Human Rights—Such as They Are

At the outset we must note that the idea of a human right is somewhat different from that of a natural right. Today any discussion of rights is usually of human, not natural rights. The concept of a natural right(s) seems unacceptable to most people who do have occasional use for something akin to that concept because, as mentioned earlier, the idea that man has a nature, that "human being" is definable, has fallen into disrepute; the concept is considered obsolete and refuted by most philosophers. And when it comes to these sorts of issues, philosophers have considerable impact on the general intellectual community. It is in philosophy courses that one studies epistemology, theories of knowledge. In these courses one usually hears that such notions as human nature, the nature of justice, or the nature of anything, are long dead, and one encounters numerous variations of the Humean argument we looked at earlier.

Yet the idea of natural rights, in spite of varying interpretations, has unquestionably had great impact on world political affairs. People have struck back at oppression, tyranny, and other forms of human inhumanity with that idea in mind as intellectual support. The American and French revolutions, as well as many others across the globe, made ample use of something like the idea of natural rights. Nor have intellectuals in general refrained from making political pronouncements about rights, even while denying that any rational support could be given for them. The switch from natural to human rights is not significant philosophically, i.e., those who find the former unacceptable will reject the latter also. But the move is understandable given people's casting about for support for political affairs, yet facing general dismay with the notion that there is something specific we may call human *nature*.

The problem centered on by critics was that earlier ideas of the nature of something seemed to require that these natures be forever fixed, unchanging, timelessly absolute. And it is rather implausible to suggest that anyone could identify the nature of man (or anything else) *forever*, that we can tell what human nature is and will forever be. Yet the alternative, that there is no valid idea as to the nature of something (simply because it may change, or with further discoveries we might need to change our idea of it), is equally implausible. The former notion implies omniscient dogmatism (we know all and absolutely about the nature of X), while the latter implies dogmatic skepticism (we know that we could not know the nature of X).

At any rate, in the wake of the downfall of the idea of human nature in philosophical, and later, educated circles, the important concept of natural rights was rechristened "human rights." Here is still accepted, implicitly, some universal characteristic that allows for calling a group of entities the

same, but without commitment to any theory about why this is possible—e.g., because they all possess human nature! Human rights is the
looser version of the concept natural rights. Typically, since it has become a
widely used concept (with the above qualifications as to commitment), it
has also lost any semblance of precision in its application. Similarly justice, peace, virtue, and other good characteristics turn out to be very
different under the inspection of different people, especially of divergent
ideologies. Yet such ideas do not die completely—something about good
things requires their partial acknowledgment even by the worst or the most
doubting amongst us. So human rights too persist, changing a good deal
from mouth to mouth, from legal system to legal system.

In philosophically influential circles several varieties of the idea of
human rights may still be found. Hardly any resemble what Locke was
talking about and what the Declaration of Independence made mention of.
One has the suspicion that if it were not for the historical heritage of
natural rights, these things we now call human rights would have some
other name. Indeed, most listed in the United Nations Declaration of
Human Rights are really human preferences, desires, goals, aspirations,
even privileges. Thus today we are supposed to have the *human right* to
"equal pay for equal work," "a just and favourable remuneration ensuring for himself and his family an existence worthy of human dignity,
and supplemented, if necessary, by other means of social protection," "a
standard of living adequate for the health and well-being of himself and of
his family, including food, clothing, housing, and the right to security in
the event of unemployment, sickness, disability, widowhood, old age, or
other lack of livelihood in circumstances beyond his control," "to freely
participate in the cultural life of the community," "to education [which]
shall be free, at least in the elementary and fundamental stages," and so
on.[37]

In line with the earlier natural rights theory, which sought to ground
universally applicable judgments, this is incongruous. Can it be argued
that, just by virtue of being a human being, I am entitled to all of these
things from my fellow human beings? Perhaps they cannot afford it, or
have better things to do with their talents than devote them to my
education, or with their wealth than to sacrifice it to my social security or
old age! And if they do not actually have better things to which to direct
their efforts, yet *believe* they do, am I simply entitled to take from them
what I "have a right to" (like, prefer, desire)? Or do I go to the local poli-
tician and persuade him to get a bill enacted that authorizes the police to
take what is "mine" by right from these individuals who won't give me my
education, my food, my welfare, all of which I might indeed have lost "in
circumstances beyond my control"? Why does *that* make any difference?

After all, if these things are mine by right, why can't I just take them as I could if someone stole my typewriter and I found it on him? And what about the natural right to liberty and property which *everyone* possesses? Do these not conflict with my right to education or clothing? If I have none of the latter, but they do, who gets what? And why? (Should we opt for such an impossible imperative? Will it not simply lead to open warfare?)

The fact is that in the context of natural rights theory these questions make sense. But in the context of the most widely agreed to contemporary conceptions of human rights these questions make no sense at all. As Professor Margaret Macdonald tells it, "Assertions about natural rights, then, are assertions of what ought to be as the result of human choice. They fall within [the] class . . . of . . . ethical assertions or expressions of value. And these assertions or expressions include all those which result from human choice and preference, in art and personal relations, e.g., as well as in morals and politics." And she adds that "To assert that 'Freedom is better than slavery' or 'All men are of equal worth' is not to state a fact but to *choose a side*. It announces *This is where I stand.*"[38]

Looked at this way, all the rights listed by the United Nations do in fact exist as rights. No one can deny that we all *prefer* at least most of those things we have a right to! Most also prefer a decent standard of living, housing, security in unemployment, favorable remuneration for work, and on and on. If all we are entitled to say about natural or human rights is that they express our preferences and choices, then anything and everything could be a natural right—for anything and everything may be (and probably is) preferred or chosen, wished for, desired, by someone.

Professor Macdonald's ideas have not gone unchallenged. Nevertheless, they are widely accepted in our culture, and are representative of somewhat different versions of the same basic notion, namely that human rights or natural rights either consist of or must depend upon expressions of preferences and desires.

Marxists, for instance, believe that human rights are social principles (privileges?) preferred by different classes of people. The propertied desire to keep and control what they have, so they advocate property rights; the poor wish to obtain what others have, so they advocate welfare rights; the intellectuals have a mind to give free expression to their ideas, so they advocate the right of free speech, and so on down the line, even to the leaders of nations who advocate the right of executive power. (To Marx any talk of rights possessed by people equally, unalienably, absolutely, and universally would have to await the communist epoch when all persons will have reached a common nature, total equality and perfection. Until then people are in a state of incompletion and imperfection, incapable of justifying equal human rights. Only after the various revolutionary stages will human beings become *fully human,* at which time rights would become human instead of class rights.)

Again some more recent human rights theorists have argued that they must be defined in terms of some *desired ideal* of what human communities should be.[39] Here again the ideal in terms of which the rights are to be defined emerges from human desire, preference, or choice and cannot be identified as true or correct. So the resulting rights cannot be considered true principles upon which societies ought to be constructed, principles around which a good human community must be organized. For as long as their source is a desire or choice without a standard of right and wrong, these rights are not objective but arbitrary, even if widely accepted.

Still other ideas about human rights have gained some currency. Thus some have argued that human rights are the expression of the general will, the public interest, national destiny, or the social good. Accordingly, human rights mean those principles by which everyone must act to serve the interest of the whole[40]—society, nation, race, God, or some other trans-cendant good. This particular version is exemplified in a decision the United States Supreme Court handed down invalidating a law enacted by referendum in California pertaining to the right of people to sell their property to whomever they choose. Justice White explained that the California law (Art. I, Sec. 26) enacted via Proposition 14 (in 1964) "authorized private discrimination," even though only "encouraging, rather than commanding" it. He added:

> The right to discriminate, including the right to discriminate on racial grounds, was now embodied in the state's basic charter, immune from legislative, executive, or judicial regulation at any level of the state government.

And that is exactly what is entailed in the notion of a right—its *exercise,* wisely or unwisely, is immune from others' interference. Justice White made this clear in the following observation as well:

> Those practicing racial discrimination need no longer rely solely on their personal choice. They could now invoke express constitutional authority, free from censure or interference of any kind from official sources.

Indeed this *is* how rights used to be understood. Thus those publishing communist political tracts and dirty books, those advocating that the government be dismantled and other sorts of objectionable ideas are also "free from censure or interference of any kind from official sources" in a country where the right of free speech is protected by law. But Justice White and the Court seemed to believe that only those activities should be provided protection from censure that accord with what someone in authority has decided is virtuous and decent. Racial discrimination is obviously wrong. But so is advocacy of the destruction of a constitutional government in favor of a dictatorship. The original notion of the natural right to freedom was that people in a human community are free to do wrong within their own spheres, *with what is their own*—print wrong ideas, buy dirty literature, and even select to trade only with those who belong to one (favored) race. That is the liberty which human rights guarantee, even in the face of public condemnation. According to Justice White and, now, U. S. law, one has no rights to do what the "public" considers wrong. (That is, what those in power identify as wrong, sometimes with and other times without public or the majority's explicit or tacit support.)

The reader may protest that this is an isolated case, that only opponents of racial discrimination are willing to abolish human rights so as to force people to act according to their moral views. In fact virtually all political factions in the United States are willing to do this. For example, in the same election during which conservatives in California campaigned ferociously for the passage of Proposition 14, Californians approved another measure which outlawed pay TV. Obviously some who voted *for* the one measure—for property rights—voted *against* the other—against property rights. For to go into business is to exercise the same right as to sell one's land and house, the right to use and dispose of one's own belongings freely, provided none is forced to cooperate in the endeavor. Moreover the recent hurrahs received by the Supreme Court for its ruling that none has the right to show films that the local community disapproves of came from conservatives,[41] those people who have been well known to advocate the "American way of life" of free enterprise, liberty, and so on.

Another version of this same conception of human rights is similar, although it need not deny that activities not in accord with the government's idea of virtue may be undertaken. This view goes back to pre-Socratic ideas of right and wrong, and holds that human rights are completely dependent on what the legislature says, what is enacted into law. This is a view which has once again emerged as a forceful contender. Also, there are no political boundaries between those who hold it. The well-known conservative author, variously involved in legal theorizing, psychiatry, social theory, and the like in his many articles and books, Ernest van den Haag, believes that there are only legal rights. He contends that the idea of human nature is useless since so many people entertain different versions of it. (Here we meet again the argument that disagreement proves the falsehood of claims pertaining to the subject matter of the disagreement.) So natural rights has to be discarded as a valid political idea; only legal rights are left. On the opposite political side from conservatism also, we find several thinkers who consider natural rights nothing more than the rights identified in legal statutes throughout the world's legal systems.

Professors Alf Ross, Kai Nielsen, and others have put forward theories to this effect.[42]

All these come under the general view today called legal positivism.[43] It is a theory of the nature of law that holds, basically, that provisions of law, even the basic (constitutional) principles, must be *posited* (put forth by us as an act of choice that cannot, in the end be justified). Thus the famous notion incorporated in the Declaration of Independence that there are rights had by nature (endowed by a creator), which cannot be denied rationally, with justification, falls by the wayside not only at the hands of Bentham, Hume, Marx and others, but also at the hands of some of our most distinguished current legal theorists. The only rights which exist and can be known are ones "we" have *decided* to incorporate into a body of law. And they are rights only because "we" have decided on their inclusion.[44]

This then is the current state of affairs. I have not offered all of the theories and I have omitted some that actually give support to the concept of natural human rights. This only in the case where such support seriously departs from the naturalist tradition, as well as where it simply echoes ideas already related. I also considered it unnecessary to dwell upon theories which propose that there are human rights *if* there are other rights. In his paper "Are there any natural rights?"[45] H. L. A. Hart argued this case. But since it is a conditional argument it cannot establish the existence of natural rights without first demonstrating that other rights exist. And this Hart does not do. Still others, e.g., Gregory Vlastos, have made efforts to argue for certain varieties of human rights, for instance, so called *prima facie* rights, but these are precisely to be distinguished from human natural rights by their prima facie character—they are not absolute within a system of justice but must yield to moral considerations when the latter are *"stronger."*[46] That, in turn, leads to the problem of deciding what count as stronger considerations than the rights of human beings in matters of political organizations and law. (Later I will discuss this and other views in more detail.)

For now there is only one other issue to be considered, namely the total rejection of human rights and other normative principles by those who argue that man is completely determined by his environment or instincts, so the question of right and wrong cannot arise for him either in or out of political circumstances.

Determinism versus Human Rights

In the earlier discussion of the theory of Thomas Hobbes it was evident that talk about human rights in inconsistent with the belief that what people do is entirely out of their control, that no one is or could be free to choose his behavior. I did not mention, however, that David Hume also held a deterministic view of human behavior. Hume thought that we can be free only to the extent that (we mean by this that) our will chooses from among alternatives open to us. But he qualified this position by holding that the human will is determined by the history of its possessor. Hume has been classified as a "soft determinist," to be distinguished from a "hard determinist" because the latter does not admit the existence of anything like a will, either free or determined. In Hume the determination is indirect, while in the hard deterministic theory it is direct—what happens to us directly determines what we do, how we behave.

Today these two versions of determinism are quite prominent in the social, psychological, and economic sciences. In psychology, for instance, we have the theory of B. F. Skinner, who may be called a hard determinist. He believes that it is the environmental circumstances that directly cause the behavior of human beings, although he offers a rather complicated account of how this happens.[47] In the same field we find Freudian theorists who also believe that all of what people do is out of their control. But they believe that the determination is accomplished indirectly via such factors as instincts, drives, unconscious motives, wishes, and, in the case of the neo-Freudians, social factors.[48]

In summary form this is what we are told by those who embrace some version of the idea that people have no control over their lives, that they are completely governed or controlled by factors other than themselves. Thus it makes no sense to talk about what is right or wrong, morally *or* politically. What will be, will be, regardless of anything we might choose. Man is, in terms of this view, passive. He cannot help himself, nothing is up to him. According to Skinner, who takes up the issue explicitly, human rights is just another of the many useless prescientific notions we have (somehow?) inherited.

Paradoxically many of these "scientists" advocate that they *ought to* be granted the authority and power to administer certain types of controls upon the rest of mankind, especially those who may not have turned out to "behave well."[49] Current developments in behavioral modification theory and psychosurgery attest to this interest in requiring cures for those who are thought to be sick, mentally ill. While some opposition to this exists throughout society—most prominently through the writings of Drs. Thomas S. Szasz[50] and Peter Breggin[51]—the idea is gaining more and more prominence.[52] Congress is involved in examining what regulations government should exert over such practices. Others think that worries about these techniques are generating unjustified restrictions for those who know just how to improve human behavior.

The determinism assumed by these social engineers is, of course, inconsistent with their advocacy that we *ought to* accept their views. There cannot be any sense to the idea of "ought to" from within this point of view.

Why this is so will be discussed at greater length in the upcoming investigation of human nature. One should keep in mind, however, that scientists do not discover that man is unfree—they usually take this as something they should start with, something that should constitute a basic assumption of being scientific. But that idea is grounded not on science itself but on a view about science, generally advanced by philosophically eager scientists. Biologists, psychologists, sociologists, economists, or political scientists often believe that to be scientific about their own subject matter they must accept that it is really nothing basically different from the subject matter of older, more advanced sciences such as astronomy, physics, and chemistry. But to become scientific this way is to turn things upside down, to start with assumptions that will color all the conclusions the scientists will draw about their subject, to restrict at the outset the means by which to study their own field. This is not science but dogmatism, a fact many of the social scientists are beginning to realize.

Despite some reorientation, we still find many scientists asking for a fully controlled society supposedly warranted by science. By this move the coffin is slowly being nailed shut on the idea of human rights by people whose productivity and freedom had for years been protected by that very idea. The question before us is, should that coffin be shut? Will the idea be buried alive?

CHAPTER 2

*With reasonable men, I will reason; with humane men I
will plead; but to tyrants I will give no quarter, nor
waste arguments where they will certainly be lost.*
William Lloyd Garrison

The Idea of
Human Rights

What Are Human Rights?

WE have examined both the development and the recent demise of the idea of natural/human rights. Now the positive theory of this work will begin. The reader cannot be expected to start by accepting the very thing that needs proof, namely that human rights exist. A preliminary step in that proof, however, is to explain what human rights would be if any of them could be identified. That is, we need to know first what it is that the present work aims to establish.

Whatever people might want to demonstrate, whether it is that there are electrons, flying saucers, viruses, and so on, it is impossible to start from *nothing* at all. Plato first posed the puzzle about this. In the *Meno* dialogue he asked how we might discover what something is if we do not already know. For where might we begin to look without the knowledge? Yet if we already knew what it is, why would we need to discover it anyway? So heads you lose, tails I win. But we really do not face this kind of problem unless we think of knowledge as coming in big solid chunks. In fact it comes gradually and it has a history. That is why I discussed at some length the history of human rights theory.

Let me reiterate the main points of the earlier section so that we can get a clear idea of what the task of the present discussion amounts to. I have discussed how "natural" and "rights" relate to each other. Briefly, natural rights have to do with being right by virtue of nature and not just custom or convention. For example, if there is a natural right each of us has to his own life, we know that we have this right because by reasoning from what we know about nature, we can justify the claim. Nature, not dogma nor authority, is the final source of the truth of a claim to have something by right. It could turn out that there is nothing we can defend by reference to nature. But it is important to recognize that the idea of natural rights goes hand in hand with the view that at least some of our claims to knowledge can be justified by a close examination of some features of nature—e.g., the nature of man.

The term "right" is not as easy to explain. There is good indication, however, that a "natural right" has been used to refer to some condition, situation, or conduct that is right, as opposed to being neutral or wrong, for human beings. For example, if we have the natural right to be free, then being free is right, not wrong for us by nature. Here again the justification is by reference to nature; something is right "by virtue of the nature of the thing." In this case by virtue of human nature. And the idea of the nature of something is, what makes something what it is, the crucial, essential features of being something. As an example, the nature of man in human rights theory was generally thought to be captured by the phrase "rational animal"— which is to say, for something to be a human being it would have to be true that it is both an animal and capable of rationality.

So now we can summarize the above points this way. A *natural* right was supposed to be a right someone has because of the nature of the case, including of course his own nature. And it was a natural *right* because by virtue of the nature of the case something could be shown to be right or good for something, namely human beings. Thus the natural right to be free was both natural and right for anything with a *human* nature.

The idea of a human right is actually just an abbreviation of the idea of a natural human right. Historically, especially in England and the United States, the political ideas associated with natural rights had a serious impact. The Declaration of Independence, for example, and most national constitutions today make explicit reference to such rights. But the more this idea came into use, the less rigorously did those using it adhere to its philosophical basis. The idea of natural rights rested on a fairly definite, although controversial, philosophical foundation called *naturalism.* This view held that what is morally right or wrong is something we can know just as we know anything else about nature. Not long after natural rights theory was born, however, naturalism itself came under severe criticism. After a while most philosophers rejected naturalism for various reasons, some sound and others flimsy. With this turn of events there no longer seemed to be any validity to the idea of natural rights. But since they had gained widescale popular acceptance and become part of existing legal systems, they could not easily be abandoned. What happened then was a small shift in emphasis.

Natural rights had to do with the rights all people have by virtue of their nature, but to accommodate the critics' opposition to naturalism, the term "natural" was dropped in favor of "human." Today, therefore, we find hardly any reference to natural rights in the philosophical literature. Instead those who discuss political theory talk about human (or individual or man's or personal) rights, not natural rights. This allows for greater leeway concerning the source of such rights, what they mean, how we know what they are, how we would have to justify the claim that they exist and we have them.

Although in popular discourse little attention is thus paid to the naturalistic origins of rights, one really cannot deny the connection between human and natural rights. The link is obvious in the history and in the theoretical basis of the two. A *human* right is explained as something due a person in a social context because of his membership in the class of humanity, because he is a human being. So still one's human nature leads to his possession of such a right. It is simple to evade this when "natural" is dropped, but to make clear sense of human rights we need to reintroduce the idea "natural," with revisions to meet the valid objections of naturalism's critics. For now we need to go further in seeing what human rights would be.

Many people talk about *having* a human right. It sounds like a right is something that could be given away, but this is misleading. A human right cannot be given up, except in the sense that it is given up when one dies or loses his humanity some other way—becomes a "human" vegetable or the like. (The latter case presents special problems which will have to be examined later.) Instead we might more fruitfully understand "having" a human right along the lines of having a good figure or having the relationship of child or parent. That is, a right cannot be thought of as some object or property, but is more like a relationship or condition. Thus the right to be free, for example, is best understood to mean: we are (morally, naturally) entitled to relate to others on a voluntary basis, not by coercion.

In current use of the concept, "human rights" is often thought to be entirely parasitic or dependent upon the idea of a legal right. Some argue that there cannot be rights other than those granted by some rights-granting authority. This means that our human rights are no more than entitlements to something if and when the legal authorities *will in fact* enforce or protect them. But if the law will not respond that way, we have no such rights.

The difference between human rights and legal rights, however, is that while one can have legal rights that others do not share, this could not be true about one's human rights. It is true that entitlement enters the picture in the latter case as well. But it is a natural entitlement, i.e., if each person has a human right to life, this does mean that each ought to be entitled to live without others' invervention. But what ought to be is not always the case! So while we may indeed have this human right, it could also be true that what we are entitled to is simply unobserved, evaded, ignored, or denied to us by those wielding legal power.

So the crucial difference between a legal entitlement and a moral/natural/political one is this: we are entitled to something by virtue of some legal edict in the case of the former, but by virtue of our humanity or human nature in the latter. In the case of legal entitlements it is possible that we should not be so entitled, even if the lawmakers decided that we should. They could be wrong. But about human rights there is no decision involved; we need to discover them, but no decision can establish a human right. In fact it is by reference to human rights that we check our legislated rights. Natural rights were introduced to serve as the basic standards, the organizing principles, of a political community. By reference to them a good (natural, right) legal system could be established; by ignoring them no one could say what would result.

Let us briefly look at what might lead people to believe that human and legal rights are one and the same. First, human rights have always been relevant to political theories and the solution of man's political problems. It is in the context of examining what could be sound political principles (e.g., constitutional provisions) that human rights arise. And the political and legal are easily assimilated; a concept which has its place in political theory is easily divorced from its foundation and taken to be an exclusively legal concept. And human rights have served as the foundations, even if only in print, of legal systems. The Bill of Rights, the United Nations Declaration of Human Rights, and even the constitution of the Union of Soviet Socialist Republics make explicit reference to human rights or their equivalents.

But in all these it is important to note the actual place occupied by human rights. In ordinary discussions human rights serve to connect moral and legal conduct. For example, when black people protest that their human rights are being violated they do not just mean that some positive, enacted law has been broken. Rather they want to call attention to the fact that it is possible to be lawful and yet violate human rights. By calling attention to human rights they point out that this violation should not be the case. In a word, where there is a human right, there ought to be (legal) provisions for its protection and preservation. This is not to say that human and legal rights are the same, but that the latter *ought to* coincide with the former as best as that can be achieved. Positive laws are what people institute (posit), and the political theory of human rights argues that such laws ought to give practical, detailed expression to human rights—i.e., that those laws are best which embody what is right for people because they are human beings.

If this were not the case, it would make no sense to claim that black people or women or minorities or some individuals have human rights that are, nevertheless, being violated, even though no actual law is being broken. But just this is being claimed by many, all over the world, and what is said on such occasions is easily understood. So even before we accept that human rights do exist, we can see that *if* they do, they are not equivalent to the laws that entitle people to do various things, enjoy certain conditions, be free to act, and so on. The important point for the present purpose is that human rights could as a matter of history be related to or be quite different from positive (legislated, politically identified) law. That is why in the history of political theory human rights have been tied to *natural* law as a firm foundation.

Having said this much, let me specify what I will take to be human rights, that is, *what* I will try to argue they are, what I will claim and defend do in fact *exist*, and what I will show we *can identify*. If someone has a human right to X or to do Y, then (a) he or she is a human being, and (b) it is because of this fact alone that certain conditions or circumstances are both possible and right for him in a social context. To put it another way, there is a class of entities we can identify as human beings, and in a social context they ought to enjoy certain conditions just because they are human beings. A human right to something is like any other right except that the entitlement is fundamentally due to (justified by reference to) the fact that the possessor of a human right is a human being.

An important matter emerges from considering the above. If there are human rights, it is only because one is a human being that anyone has them. As a result, those who advocate human rights can rationally ask only for such conditions as are indeed justifiable simply by reference to membership in the human community, to being a human being. There is thus a significant difference between human rights and other entitlements. The importance of this has been recognized and accepted by many, but it has also led to some distortions. Seeing the respect paid to whatever a person is due in virtue of his/her humanity, some are led to tie all of their demands and requests to human rights. Even where it is obvious that the demand is related to factors unique to them as individuals or as members of sub-groups—students, postal workers, doctors, lawyers, the wealthy, the poor, laborers, business leaders, blonds, blacks, men, women, and so forth. But if there are human rights, they do not pertain to what a person is entitled to by virtue of his/her membership in the class of entities designated by the concept "human" living in a human community. No more is rationally justifiable.

This provision of the theory of human rights goes some way toward securing what was so eagerly desired by John Rawls in his widely discussed book *A Theory of Justice* (Harvard University Press, 1971). Rawls argued that a valid idea of justice can be formulated only if we conceive of rational people seeking to identify justice from the point of view of a "veil of ignorance." By this he meant that no considerations of personal identity—of one's particular attributes and situation in the world—can justifiably enter into the formulation of the principles that ought to govern a human community. It is clear that by focusing only on what is essential about being a human being, i.e., on human nature, in an attempt to arrive at the principles of social organization, this requirement is well satisfied by the tradition of human rights theory. (I will later come to some crucial differences between Rawls' idea of a good human community and the theory advanced in this work. For now let me just mention that Rawls seems to be after a *nonmoral, ethically neutral* point of initial reference from which to develop a theory of justice. But human rights have moral significance from the start. It is thus a requirement that they refer to conditions that should and could be secured by choice, at will, voluntarily, by all those who are members of the human community. By the time a theory of human conduct reaches the point of answering questions about the nature of a good human community it must already have travelled past many ethical considerations, e.g., the nature of a good human conduct in general.)

I close this section with a final reminder about the social nature of human rights. The conditions at issue are right for people within society—it is only for people who are in a social context that they need be identified. By oneself, alone, in isolation from others, e.g., on some inaccessible island, considerations of human rights have no point; they *can* arise but only potentially or hypothetically. Granted that people ought to be free, for example; but the kind of freedom political theory identifies does not have a bearing where no potential limitation on one's freedom could arise. No others can be threats; there is no need for a moral standard by which such freedom might be required and made more likely. Locke saw this when he realized that although in order to identify the natural basis for rights we need to examine the state of nature, man's state before entering human community, such rights have no actual application there. Although there is this lack of applicability, it is a mistake to think that we need not abstract individuals from their social situations to gain an understanding of the basis for the rights they have in community.

How Do We Know There Are Human Rights?

The next preliminary matter to be handled is the question "What would it be to know or to have identified a human right?" If it is true that human rights would be moral conditions of society, conditions that are right for people in a human community because they are human, we can answer the above question as follows: "It would be to know those conditions . . . that are right for people in society because they are human beings." To know the right social conditions for human beings depends on a number of other possibilities. Is it possible to know what the right conditions of human life are as such? Is it possible to know what is right, good, wrong, or evil? Can we know the nature of human beings? And is knowledge itself possible? In a reasonably complete approach, all these must be answered, at least with viable success, in order to go at our task with some promise of a solution.

Specifically, we need to do the following: show that human beings are distinguishable from other sorts of things, i.e., that human nature can be identified; show what it takes and whether it is possible to tell that some specific entity is a human being, especially in difficult cases where we find unusual problems; then we need to identify a standard of human excellence in terms of which we can consider how to judge a human political community, i.e., identify which conditions *should* obtain in one. This last is where we get to human rights, or fail to do so, as the case may be.

To state the central questions another way, familiar to all of philosophy: (1) the concept of human being must be definable; (2) how we can employ this definition successfully needs to be explained; and (3) the morally good life needs to be identified. All this because human rights involve what it is to be human, what it takes to identify something as a human being, and what is right for people and right for them in a social context—what it is to be a good person and to be a good human community.

But all of this presupposes that we can *know* the answers to these questions, i.e., an answer to the question: "What is knowledge?" No answer would mean no further investigation along the lines set out in this essay. So the first task will have to be a closer investigation of what knowledge is. Some people would put before us even more basic issues: "Is knowledge possible at all?" and, maybe, "What is it for something to be anything?" With this last we have come to metaphysics. I will hardly touch on it, but I must introduce some aspects of this issue because, frankly, no problem in philosophy can be handled without having identified some basic, metaphysical facts. These are what provide the ground of argument in the final analysis. There must be a ground of argument, otherwise all conclusions would simply rest on quicksand. And why should anyone accept conclusions that are as unstable and unsupported as that?

My thinking on the issue of metaphysical first principles is drawn from Aristotle and Ayn Rand. To present and defend my ideas in summary fashion is risky. Nevertheless, as pointed out above, these foundations must at least be indicated. To return to the above question: what is it for something to be, to exist? Taken in the only meaningful way possible and answering it as sensibly as can be done here, the response is the simple statement of fact that *to be is to be something with an identity*. To be something, as such, is *to be distinguishable* from other things, specifiable by those able to know reality. To ask: "Is anything distinguishable at all; are there entities in the first place?" really is more an idle wonder than a sensible question, since asking it also answers it. We know, even if we never bother to think of it explicitly, that existence exists. Every thought, perception, belief, feeling, and so forth attests to that much. Then there must be distinguishable things, beings, events, etc.; otherwise we couldn't even distinguish that question from others.

Now having recognized this much, as most would, certain rules can also be identified. Our first clue, provided by the above, to answering any question is that as we make our attempt to do so we must not accept anything that contradicts the basic notions just offered, or contradicts other facts we know about existence. That is because any breach of these two fundamental facts would ultimately lead to believing in meaninglessness, in some idea that things are this and not this, all at once, that one thing is itself and not itself at the same time in the same way, that both what we say and its denial are true, even though both cannot be true and still be understandable, distinguishable, and identifiable by us, who can, as a matter of fact, know a good deal about reality. The proposition that the above characterization is all wrong, that something is at once what it is and also nothing in particular, that all things are jumbled into one, an infinite number of chaotic somethings and nothings—this proposition itself is unintelligible. We could affirm or deny nothing, and even that we could not affirm or deny meaningfully if the above basic facts are rejected. Of course people can *say* that this is false, but then they usually add that nothing makes sense anyway. And it is right that if they deny what have been advanced here as basic facts, nothing can make sense to them. The obvious stumbling block is that even *their* observations could not be made sense of if they were correct.

For now this much about the basic facts and principles that will guide our inquiry will have to do. I will return to the issue of knowledge later. We now need to get on to some of the more direct issues surrounding human rights theory. How might we learn of the existence of human rights? Or, more importantly, what would have to be done to achieve a demonstration of their existence, for we can learn of the existence of various facts of life in different ways, but we cannot prove their existence in just any way.

By "know" I mean at least that knowledge of human rights is not drastically different from how we know all sorts of things—to add or divide, to get to Chicago, what mother said last night, where the river meets the ocean, who did the flowers at the wedding, what caused George's bloody nose, where Sue went wrong in her marriage, what Ted should do in his life, which of the buildings has the more beautiful architecture, as well as what people should do to live a good human life. I say "not drastically different" because I will not assume out of hand that all the above are known in exactly the same way; but since all of the above, if we do know any of them, involve the requirement that we provide evidence, reasons, arguments, justifications, understanding, experience, trustworthy testimony (or some collection of these), they *are* known the *same* way, i.e., via the human cognitive apparatus, our minds—with all the aid that can make a difference.

I will attempt to show that what human rights are and whether any exist can be known in the same sorts of ways we can know reality on other fronts. When I undertake to show that someone has the human right to something or to do something, I am prepared to offer evidence, argument, justification, and so on, just as when trying to establish other facts, to show that statements about them are true, what they assert to be the case is, indeed, the case. In particular instances we might have to show that X belongs to Harry Jones (property rights), Y is for me to decide and act on (the right to liberty), Z ought to be left free to live his life (the right to life)—always by producing a justifications or by relying on certain justifiable principles which have been shown to be true.

The point is to see if this sort of an undertaking could be carried out, if the nature and existence of human natural rights can be established. With this aim, it would ordinarily make sense to start with the preliminary points and discuss moral knowledge, political knowledge, the issue of definition of concepts and, in particular, of human nature, and only then come to discuss human rights. Though the order is logically unobjectionable, it does not suit the goal of *communicating* the present case. What will make more sense here is to begin by establishing standards of value within the moral and political realms to see what justifies a claim that some act is morally and/or politically wrong. Then we can trace back and determine the possibility of offering such a standard in the first place, when we consider critical inquiries which have zeroed in on that issue.

If none of this could be achieved some might still say that we can know what a human right is and whether any exist, but only if we understand knowledge as something uncheckable, unsupportable, unprovable, or indefensible. Such claims to still "know" something must end by attributing special powers to those who make them. Since from that sort of thing we cannot expect to demonstrate a rational legal and social system, the basic principles of a good human community cannot be safely left to such "knowledge." Only the sort of knowledge is admissible that any person without severe brain damage, with the capacity for reasoning and experiencing life, could gain. Admittedly, many may not choose to pursue that knowledge, but at least they would not be barred from it as they would have to be if the knowledge consisted in intuition, revelation or the like, namely less than universally available, ineffable means of reaching truth.

If human rights cannot be identified by us, they have no place in politics. I have tried in this chapter to indicate the crucial issues to be dealt with in any endeavor to so identify human rights, and I have set the stage by outlining some principles basic to any inquiry about reality. Next I will focus on the moral underpinnings of the theory of human rights to be developed in this work.

CHAPTER 3

Values, and order, and meaning are indeed created by men, by men's choices. But that does not mean that they are created in their entirety by each man at each point in time; it does not mean that they are created in just any way at all, arbitrarily. For all of us, they have their foundation in human nature; and for each of us they have a further foundation in the life he has already lived, the growing-up he has already done, the language he has already learned, the person he has become.

Hanna Fenichel Pitkin

Human Virtues and Excellence

An Overview

MOST defenders of the free society heard from today rest their views on the argument from skepticism. This argument has it that freedom should be protected and preserved because, since no one can know when another person has done something wrong, imposing one's judgment on another always runs the risk of being misdirected. As Dr. Milton Friedman once expressed the idea: if one *knows* that another is sinning, one would be wrong not to stop it. But if we cannot know when another is sinning, then the obvious course is to leave him alone. Thus skepticism is offered as a defense for political freedom.

Too many attempts to defend the Western democratic, free or semi-free constitutional systems rest on skepticism. Another favored argument, often linked to the Founding Fathers, is tied to denigrating humanity so as to construe all power as dangerous. C. P. Snow illustrates this well:

"I should not like to see any group of men in charge—not me or my friends or anyone else. Any man who has lived at all knows the follies and wickedness he's capable of. If he does not know it, he is not fit to govern others. And if he does know it, he knows also that neither he nor any man ought to be allowed to decide a single human fate. I am not speaking of you specifically, you understand: I should say exactly the same of myself."
"You do not think highly of men, Mr. Eliot."
"I am one," I said. [*(The Light and the Dark*, 1947]

I will not defend the free society along these lines. This is because, first of all, we *can* know quite well that someone is doing wrong ("sinning"), and yet we could know also that this alone does not entitle us to do anything *to* him. From "John is sinning" and "George knows it," nothing follows about what George ought to do or not do to John. Other premises are needed. Nor does it follow from one's confidence in man that anyone should rule another—quite the opposite would seem to be suggested.

Moreover, historically the skeptical argument has not even been persuasive—almost the entire classical liberal tradition relied on it to defend the free society (as Friedman, Hayek, Popper *et al.* rely on it these days), yet Mill and others in this tradition turned socialist in later years, presumably when they saw the need for a commitment to some values. Perhaps because when they learned that John was sinning, they believed that this had implications for some action against John's freedom to sin.

Another reason for rejecting this argument is that liberty is clearly not a virtue in itself. As a condition of a political community, liberty makes possible the choice to take on tasks, to act by one's judgment, to cooperate or compete with others in various endeavors. When others leave a person autonomous (physically and without the threat of physical obstruction), he is then free to act. That freedom, on its own, is only a condition of something, of something valuable arising from what will be done. It is not itself the good to be done.

The argument in this work will consist, first, in justifying a standard of moral evaluation, answering questions pertaining to what is required to establish the truth of some assertion that something or other (person, institution, and so on) is morally good. This serious problem will not be treated in full, although I will have indicated at each stage of the argument where one would have to develop it to make the case as conclusively as possible.

In the quest for a standard we must take some detours. For instance, most philosophers reject the idea of the nature of man, contending that it is impossible to identify the essential characteristic(s) of anything. Discussion of this will be brief in this chapter, although later I will show why and how it is possible to define concepts—that is to say, what justifies the view that the nature of things can be known, that we can identify defining characteristics of some entities. All I will do later in this chapter is to sketch a definition of the concept "human being." This will involve a short defense of the view that human beings are metaphysically free and that their freedom lies in their capacity to choose to think. That is, that they are the kinds of entities that can *cause* some of what they do; and that, specifically, they can cause their consciousness to function or can fail to do this, all on their own.

From these considerations it will be possible to return, with a foundation in hand, to the issue of standards of moral judgment. I will argue that a person is morally good just when he does cause his consciousness to function properly and to the fullest (i.e., to the degree that it is possible *for him* in line with his own capacities) and just when his actions are the result of these choices (where, again, he *can* achieve this). A morally good human being, then, will be the one who does the best he can do both as an individual and as the *kind* of entity he is, a rational being. Once this has been developed, it will become possible to show why only a free society can accommodate human beings in living their lives as morally responsible individuals. So, contrary to those who defend liberty because we allegedly cannot know what is good, the present defense argues that it is because of what is good, namely each person's choices to live rationally, that liberty is good, and human rights should be protected and preserved. And contrary to its opponents, the free society, including its economic system—capitalism—rests on a rational moral foundation, not on innate selfish instincts or trust that a deity will reward those who work hard in life.

In Search of a Standard

The main problem with morality has always been that people have disagreed about the means of establishing whether a moral judgment is true or false. (This is of course a *philosophical* problem with morality. The more general problem of morality is simply that there is too little of it around!) Most people believe that in ordinary life and even more so in the sciences it is a relatively straightforward matter to obtain knowledge. But concerning what is right or wrong in human affairs it is widely believed to be impossible to obtain *knowledge*. I have already noted how David Hume advanced an idea of human knowledge in terms of which one can only know that which can be observed—contacted by the human senses. Thus there could be no standard of truth concerning moral judgments. And subsequent thinkers have tended to go even further.

Most philosophers of the early twentieth century held that whereas in science the truth of statements and theories can be established by applying the principle of verification, i.e., checking whether statements referred to facts observable by the senses, in ethics, politics and aesthetics this could not be achieved; all we can do at best is express or prescribe or foster emotions, desires, wishes, preferences, and so on. Even philosophers generally committed to the importance of morality and each person's nature as a moral agent, e.g., existentialists, believe that we *can not* identify standards by which the truth of moral judgments could be established. These latter philosophers conclude that human beings face a fundamental paradox in life—they are all morally responsible for what they choose to do, but there is no way for them to know which actions are right and which wrong.

In such an atmosphere of moral agnosticism (and subjectivism), where the bulk of important philosophical writings have advanced arguments to show the impossibility of justifying moral judgments, developing a case for standards of right conduct is an ambitious task. The burden of proof is laid upon those who claim that this is possible, while opponents generally feel that their skeptical objections require no detailed justification. Yet, as we shall see throughout this work, there is no fully developed and conclusive argument for moral skepticism. The original theory of knowledge in terms of which moral judgments could not be shown to be true (or false) has had to be abandoned almost entirely. The idea that in science there are *easily* specified ways by which to obtain knowledge of reality has come under widescale attack. The theory that verification by sensory contact with reality *will* do the job is false—science necessarily, as all rational enterprises, employs theory in its claims about what exists in reality, so mere passive observation will not enable one to tell if the scientific claims are true. Many ideas which were introduced by philosophers to distinguish between different kinds and types of judgments and statements are mistaken and have been so identified by contemporary thinkers. The old but still prevalent idea that on the one hand there are theoretical and on the other practical judgments (or conceptual versus empirical, a priori versus a posteriori, or analytic versus synthetic) has been shown to be very difficult to uphold. And indeed it is more likely that all of our sound claims, judgments, statements, and so forth consist of a proper mixture of theory and observation.

Our problem here is to identify a standard of truth by which we can distinguish between moral judgments that are correct and those that are not. Within areas where considerations of human conduct are not at issue standards of truth are established gradually, as the field of inquiry develops. Philosophers dealing with the theory of knowledge aim, in their constructive endeavors, to specify the minimum standards or requirements to be met for attainment of knowledge. Beyond these it is the people within the special fields who must specify the detailed standards appropriate to attaining knowledge of the kind or type of entities they study—by adherence (explicitly or not) to the minimum or basic standards of knowledge and learning applicable in their special realm. (Epistemologists are not by profession physicists, chemists, biologists, psychologists, nor are they taking everyone's place in the task of identifying right and wrong in specific circumstances. They aim, when they do, at the essentials of knowledge.)

In trying to identify the standards appropriate to moral issues, we need to identify the need for or function, if any, of morality or moral judgments. (I say "the" function, although many of my colleagues are at this point abandoning me. It is one of the widely accepted philosophical conclusions today that nothing could have just one or one specifiable set of functions. In the chapter where I turn to answering critics I offer grounds for rejecting that conclusion.) Our basic question, then, concerns what it is that moral judgments do, what objective function they have, what they judge, what it is that moral statements state. Only by answering these sorts of questions will it be possible to learn of the standards that are suited for establishing whether specific judgments are true, false, probable, likely, unlikely, impossible, and so forth.

Let's start by observing that moral judgments concern people and their affairs, institutions, and so on. They are about human beings as such, not as parents, professionals, Negroes, and the like. As the latter one can have traits and carry out actions that are open to moral appraisal, because in each he is, whatever else he is, *a human being*. Yet the moral judgment pertains to someone and some action in view of the fact that he/she is a human being.

Why is this so? To answer we need to consider the issue of what function morality has, the role it plays in life. We know well enough that when moral evaluations or judgments are made the focus is on what is good or right. But in moral matters the adjective "morally" is attached to "good" and "right." To find out why "morally" must mean "by virtue of being a human being" or "in one's capacity as a human being," and, in the case of "right," why "morally" must mean "by virtue of being the action of a human being" or "as the actions (institutions, and so on) of human beings," we must first understand the more general idea of "good" or "right." In short, we need to know what in general is meant by saying of something that it is good or right—what are we identifying about something when we observe that it is good or right?

In other than moral contexts, when something is good, excellent, bad, or deficient, *what* is it that something *is* by being such, by having such characteristics? What is it about good knives that is good about them, good shoes that makes them good (or constitutes their goodness)? What is it about good hikes, football games, coffee beans that makes them so? Why is one tree a good specimen of its kind, another a poor one? (I leave for later a discussion of whether asking for *the* good about such things is defensible.)

In these and similar cases (most involving many complications that cannot be managed within our scope) we evaluate something in terms of what it might be at its best. But "its best" is just what is difficult to make fully clear, although we find it quite easy to tell when a knife is good, what are good shoes, hikes, football games, coffee beans, and so on, especially when we are experts about these things. A well-trained botanist can identify a good specimen of an oak tree, as can a competent butcher identify a good knife. Why is it that competent people can do these things? What is it that they know?

In all these and similar cases it is necessary to know what *kind* of thing we are talking about, so as to be able to tell whether we have a good, mediocre, or poor variety at hand. Someone who does not know what fencing matches must be, what the essence of a fencing match is, would not be able to referee such matches, perhaps not even enjoy them. (As a newcomer to the United States, I could not tell a good from a bad football game except from what Americans said and how the crowds acted. Yet having grown up around a family of fencers, I could tell immediately if someone was a good fencer, even whether he had the talent to become one.) In short, to be able to evaluate something it is necessary first to know what kind of thing it is.

Quite often the nature of something is identified by reference to its goals or purposes. With artifacts such as knives we know what *kind* of thing they are because we also know of their purpose in our lives. And we know how good a knife is by knowing how well it satisfies its purpose. With things found in nature matters are a bit more complicated. Coffee beans are the kind of thing they are independently of what we use them for, but our evaluation of coffee beans does not depend on our purposes with them. On the other hand botanists can distinguish a good, i.e., healthy, from a bad sapling or tree even if they serve no human purpose.

In all of these cases we find complexities that could not even be hinted at here. The important one to mention is that when we evaluate things around us we often have reason to use a mixture of standards—we may make reference to what we know of health and disease in plants *or* to our purpose for them. Often these coincide but sometimes they do not, e.g., when a good specimen of some animal is judged good not by its health but by how well it can serve some experimental purpose in medicine. (But notice in this case: the specification is well explained first so that we understand why an ordinarily poor specimen is now considered good.) The point that is important for us, in spite of some complexities, is that good and right—i.e., is it a good sapling? is it growing right?—pertain to what kind of thing something is *and* how well it fulfills or is likely to fulfill some purpose or end that it has. And it can have this goal as a matter of its natural development (as the kind of thing it is) or because of what people have in mind for it in their own lives. (We can also evaluate something in terms of how well it serves other needs—e.g., whether the carrot is good enough for the rabbit.)

In all these cases judgments of good and right can be seen to relate to living beings and their goals. Inanimate objects, unless they are being considered in their relationship to some living entity, are neither good nor bad. This is because such objects do not face the main alternative that renders values meaningful, life or death. It makes no sense to consider eruptions on the surface of the sun either good or bad, except as they may relate to some life. A beautiful diamond is one because of its relationship to the (aesthetic) values of human beings—there are no *intrinsically* beautiful or good or right things, only things that are good, right, or beautiful in relation to living entities *for* which things can be good, right, and beautiful in terms of purposes or goals.

But do people themselves have goals or purposes? This is not to ask whether they set for themselves goals and purposes. The question is whether as people you and I have a specifiable, *universal* goal or purpose in life. We know that people strive for all sorts of things. Moreover, they often set themselves goals that flatly contradict others' goals; thus some intend to build, others to destroy bridges, some want to achieve power at any cost, others honor even if it costs them all the power they might have achieved. More often people's goals are simply different—some want vacations in Paris, others plan for long sessions at the piano to complete their composition. Some want to become professors, others businessmen, and yet others movie stars, pilots, and drama critics. The question we are now up against is whether human beings, on the order of trees and birds, might have goals or purposes appropriate to them because of what they are, by their very nature.

Several problems will have to be faced in order to answer this question correctly. But first of all we need to realize that only if this is a meaningful question can there be some hope that morality is a natural, objective aspect of human life. Unless we can find this kind of role for morality, it must either be discarded as a myth, or be handed over to the mystics who have tried to claim it as their domain in virtually all human epochs.

One reason that this approach to morality has not met with great success in the recent past is that most people have come to believe that science prohibits talk about goals or purposes. Thus to refer to the *end* of the sapling as a healthy tree is thought to be scientifically odd. Yet this is a matter that is quite unsettled within science. During recent attempts to reduce all fields of science to mechanics, reference to ends or goals did seem unjustified. But reductionism is not a successful approach to the study of nature. The idea that there can be natural ends of goals that living things strive to fulfill has not been dispensed with. The question is how the existence of natural ends or goals can make the role or function of morality in human life clear for us.

When we consider whether people as such have a purpose or goal in living, the sort of goal in question is not one that is simply set by someone, accepted, or desired in the way one might set for himself the goal of climbing the highest mountain in the world. Such a goal may indeed turn out to be consistent with the kind I have in mind. But clearly these sorts of goals have to do with individual talent, circumstance, and other features not shared by all people as people. It would not be possible to defend any such (idiosyncratic) goal as the one appropriate for all people, for how could something be everyone's goal if only here and there could people possibly achieve it? The philosophical idea that helps us here is expressed in the slogan "ought implies can"—one can only be said to have the responsibility or obligation or duty to do what it is possible for him to do. So I am here attempting to find a goal that *could* be achieved by *any* human being. Only then could it be everyone's goal as a human being, i.e., as I will put it later, everyone's proper or moral purpose.

The task of identifying this sort of goal has been undertaken by many philosophers, most notably Aristotle.[1] Within the Aristotelian philosophical tradition many have tried to defend, reformulate, or update his ideas on this matter. The objection to this effort has been enormous also. Part of the impetus for rejecting the idea of what in the Aristotelian tradition may be called natural goals or purposes has come from certain views about science. I mentioned before that with Machiavelli and Hobbes, as well as many early materialist philosophers, all influenced by the sensational advances in the physical sciences, the notion that human beings could (uniquely) choose their actions fell into disrepute. Thus even today many believe that a scientific frame of reference implies: human beings cannot choose what they will do. Correlatively, science is widely believed to exclude the very idea of moral goals in human life.

I will not detail the recent discussions about why the idea of free choice is quite unobjectionable from a scientific point of view. Suffice it to say that objections to the idea have usually been based on the assumption that the only kinds of things that exist in the universe are material objects in motion governed by mechanical laws, loosely modeled on Newton's laws of mechanics. In addition to the logical fault with *assuming* the nature of one's subject matter, this view is no longer even found adequate to understanding the behavior of the physical realm. To demand a priori that it be imposed on discussions and studies of human affairs is unjustifiable; the possibility that human beings have freedom of choice cannot be precluded. Nor does such freedom entail the denial of universal causality or the denial that all things must have a cause. Human freedom in this basic sense, i.e., pertaining to man as distinct from other living entities, means that human beings can initiate some of what they do, that they are creative, capable of original behavior, and that they constitute (or could if they so chose) one group of causes in the universe we know.[2] Still, showing that such freedom is consistent with scientific requirements does not establish its existence.[3]

To answer the question of whether man is free—or can be free, for the point here is not that everyone always actually utilizes this freedom—we have to consider the following: what conditions would have to exist so that human beings would not be free? Either everything that people do would be caused by something over which they have no control, over which they have no determination of their own, or everything they do would happen randomly, with no cause at all. The free will issue, properly conceived, pertains to whether human beings can cause what they do—whether you and I and all those around us not crucially incapacitated are justifiably identified as responsible for the actions we undertake, for at least some of the alternatives we have selected to pursue in such matters as what we do for a career, whom we associate with, how we treat ourselves and others around us, what ideas we accept and act on, or reject, or take no position on. In short, human beings are free if they can cause some of what happens in the world.

The initial problem is often posed: can we answer whether people are free in this sense? Here again, I will not argue against general skepticism, the view that we cannot know anything. So if the question is meaningful, if we can understand what it would be for people to be free, to be in the position to initiate some of what they do, then we can answer the question. What we need to find out is what would indicate that people can be free in this sense.

Here it is important to realize that this question is not about something we are not involved in. In short, the issue of whether human beings can be free is very much self-referential, one directly pertinent not just to the person who asks it but to the *activity* of asking it. And this fact is crucial to answering the question. For if people cannot be free, if the answer about human freedom is in the negative, then the answer cannot be freely given; it is either forced upon one or it just occurs with no cause whatever. If the answer is in the affirmative, if people can be free, then the answer could be *produced* by the person who asks it; that person could be an active contributor to what the response will be.

For instance, I can try out what it means to say that I am *not* free in the above sense. One of the implications of such a view would be that whatever I do, however carefully or sloppily I consider this issue, my answer will not be my responsibility but the responsibility either of some cause other than myself or of nothing. My own involvement in the production of an answer to this question would have to be characterized in one of three possible ways: (1) My genes were once set so as to produce the answer I will give; (2) my environment, acting on my organism, produced the answer I will give, or (3) the answer I will give is a random, uncaused occurance in the universe. If I cannot freely answer, one of these is true.

One problem with this result is that the activity of discovering the right answer to the question is outside our own control. But by a "right" answer what we must mean is one that accords with canons of sound reasoning, consistency of meaning, attentiveness to the relevant facts, the absence of prejudice, subjectivity, bias, carelessness, and all those matters that often result in wrong answers to questions. If indeed everyone produces right answers by chance or causal chain, then no one is in a position to check whether the answers are right, to marshal the relevant methods and materials and see whether the conclusion is justified. Then we simply cannot *know* what the right answer is. When a person knows something it must be that he could, if asked and given enough time, prove what he claims to know. (By this one need not mean "prove beyond a shadow of a doubt," for doubts are often present even with knowledge—people would need to be very healthy psychologically, very confident of their memory, and so forth, to do away with all doubt.)

So if the answer to the question about freedom is that we can never be free, then we cannot come up with right answers that we can *know* to be right, that we can check and test for adequacy. The crucial point is that this implication must apply also to the answer about whether we are free: a negative answer implies that we cannot know whether that answer is right! In other words, if we are not free, we are not *free to know*—we cannot identify that we are not free nor identify anything else for that matter. This is the decisive point against the denial of human free choice, namely that without admitting its possibility, the possibility of meaningfully considering arguments for or against anything (including free choice) is also denied.

This is an important argument and worth recapping: to deny human free choice means that rational evaluation of arguments must be given up in favor of either accounting for assertions by reference to factors over which people have no control, or saying assertions cannot be accounted for, i.e., they are random, unexplainable events. Then human reasoning—moving, i.e., causing one's mind to move, from premises to conclusions, finding out what is the case and checking whether we carried out the process correctly—is impossible. It is impossible, moreover, concerning the issue of the existence of free choice itself. The argument given above is not the (usual) type whereby some premises are established and the conclusion deduced—that human beings can choose some actions(s); instead it shows that denying the possibility of free choice, denying that people can initiate some of what they do, renders it impossible that *we could establish the truth of any premise whatever.*

Thus the most crucial problem of the denial of free choice obtains in the area of reasoning about reality, in the realm of the achievement of knowledge. From precisely this error in the rejection of freedom of choice we detect in what fundamental respect human beings can be free, for it shows the intimate connection between freedom of choice and human reason, between choice and rationality. What emerges here is that human freedom consists fundamentally in every person's capacity to choose to be conscious as the kind of conscious being a person is, namely a *conceptually* conscious, a thinking entity. People can be free in that they can (choose to) initiate their own thinking.

The importance of this is that morality and politics—which pertain to our actions in personal and community affairs—presuppose human freedom in some of what we can do. Thus in an effort to understand what it would amount to for someone to be morally good, to live a morally good life or to have done a morally good deed, the first item to be noted is that people would have to be capable of (at least some important) free choices.

And wherever we can identify that such choices are possible, it is in that realm of human life that we can justifiably bring to bear moral considerations. Since morality presupposes the capacity for free choice, it is only where this capacity exists and where it is required (e.g., human actions, relationships, institutions, policies) that there could be room for morality.

It will now be possible to continue the search for a proper purpose or goal that each human being has simply by virtue of being human. While morality presupposes freedom of choice, that alone is not enough to render it part of human life: if *any* choice we make is as good as any other, then none *could* be identified as good or bad for purposes of achieving it. But if this were all we could mean by "morally good or bad," then contradictory (kinds of) acts and contradictory purposes could be morally good or bad, rendering morality entirely incoherent and impossible. There can be no standard of moral good if any goal selected may be as sound as any other.

Only if a specifically human goal can be identified—one shared by all people just by virtue of being the kind of thing that they are—could an identifiable standard for moral valuation be found. If there is nothing on that order that human beings ought to achieve, no *summum bonum*, then the idea that they ought to achieve it could not be meaningful. Again, ought implies can—the responsibility to be and act morally (good) implies that there exists a distinction between being (and action) that is or leads to moral goodness, and being (and action) that does not. That is why those philosophers, e.g., existentialists, who have denied that there is a goal or purpose for human beings as such have also denied that moral judgments could be true or false.[4] And those who deny such purpose but still wish to insist on the meaningfulness of moral judgments and morality itself have generally concluded that human life is dismal, futile, even totally absurd.

I will turn now to some work done by Eric Mack, a philosopher who has not accepted those conclusions but has developed a convincing argument that human beings do have goals as such, and that it is therefore possible to establish the truth of moral judgments. He sets out in the paper we will consider to argue that conclusions about what human beings ought to do (normative statements) can be demonstrated. Moreover, he shows that the premises from which such conclusions follow are not themselves statements about what human beings ought to do or be. This is crucial because of a provision of logic which requires that an argument cannot assume its conclusion. So in proving normative conclusions, unless some premises could be found—i.e., some facts could be known—that do not already state what people should do, the entire theory would be circular and prove nothing. Mack is therefore after a position or "formulation in which the normative conclusion follows quite strictly and soundly from the non-normative premises."[5]

Let's now consider Mack's argument—I quote its central steps. It begins with the conditional statement that

If there is some need or requirement which explains (plays a role in explaining) the existence of some thing (object, activity, process, etc.), then that thing functions well if and only if its use or enactment satisfies the need or requirement which explains the existence of that thing.

With respect to each living thing, it is the fact that remaining in existence as a living thing (not merely as a collection of dead cells) requires the successful completion of numerous processes that explains the existence of valuation.

If a standard for goal-directed action is complied with as a result of choices made by the acting entity, then the (normally) resulting good is a moral good, and the actions (specifically the choices) of the agent are morally good.

Whether or not this standard (or any alleged standard) for goal directed actions is complied with is a matter of choice for human beings.

From which it follows that

The morally good, with respect to each human being, is the successful performance, and the result of the successful performance, of those actions that sustain his existence as a living thing.[6]

What Mack shows here, fully elaborated in his original paper, is that "the end of the objective function of a man's valuation is the sustenance of his life." (By "man's valuations" is meant the choices of actions, things, and so on, explicit or implicit, he makes in living his life.) Underlying the first premise (above) we find two statements which simply define "functioning well": "Anything which in functioning satisfies its (or its users') goal is functioning well," and "The function of a thing is its use or enactment in regards to the satisfaction of the requirement which explains the existence of that thing, if there is such a requirement."[7] Mack explains the second statement by noting that while a heart may, e.g., function well in some circumstances for timekeeping, it functions well *as a heart* "on the basis of how well it satisfies the requirement which explains its existence . . . how well it supplies the cells with nutrients and oxygen."[8]

The idea developed by Mack is one that Aristotle first proposed. Aristotle is often taken to have believed that everything in nature existed with some inherent purpose or goal, which is false for most things and gave rise to serious problems in the early stages of science. In any case, when it came to human beings he argued that the proper goal of each person is his own success as a human being, his own happiness. (We are talking, of course, about people who have not been incapacitated by factors outside their own control. Those who cannot exercise choice—e.g., vegetables, newborn babies, and so on—must be considered either within the category of borderline cases or of *potential* persons.) The happiness discussed by Aristotle is far broader than what people usually mean by the term "happiness." It is closer to what Ayn Rand has characterized as "a noncontradictory state of joy."[9] The main feature of this state is not pleasure, fun, or excitement. Instead it is a self-acknowledgement of worth, a sense of being a successful living entity of the kind human beings are.

To consider this thesis further, we will have to take another close look at human nature. We need to know what kind of entity is involved in order to know what processes or actions sustain its existence. So, what is man's nature? In other words, what is it about human beings that entitles us to class them into one group of living entities, to distinguish them from others? Of what does our humanity consist?

Many in the recent history of philosophy have denied that man has a nature. They believe that there is nothing essentially human, nothing that each person as a person must have as a characteristic, trait, property, feature, or aspect. Most philosophers believe that in the final analysis our classification of entities in different groups is arbitrary, or a matter of habit or convenience. There cannot be a rational justification for such classifications, least of all when we turn to human beings. For now let me relate Laszlo Versenyi's succinct observations on this topic:

> If human nature is unknowable then so is human good and it is impossible to talk about human excellence in general. Indeed it is impossible to talk about man as such, since man as such could not even be identified. Barring all knowledge of human nature—that which makes a man a man—the word man would mean nothing and we could not even conceive of man as a definite being distinguishable from all other beings. Consequently anything we might say about man would be necessarily meaningless, including the statement that human nature as such is unknowable to man. Thus the postulate of the strict unknowability of man is self-contradictory. To the extent that we talk about man we obviously hold that his nature is, in some respects at least, knowable.[10]

I shall later discuss objections to defining concepts, to identifying the nature of things. At this point I will assume that we can define things and provide a brief argument for a given definition of the concept "human being."

The factors that justify our classification "human beings" for entities who otherwise share none of each other's particular components are that each can choose and can reason. Man, unlike all other animals, even those suspected of some minimal degree of conceptual capacity, can think. Each person, in maturity, can formulate and use concepts, and each can reason by their use. People can identify different individual or particular items in reality as members or units of a class, as *kinds* of things, events, actions, institutions, and so on. They may differ from other animals in other respects as well, but even in their possession of a thumb, complex vocal cords, and so on, they are not alone. And those aspects which are unique to them, e.g., making tools, appreciating art, using artifacts, and so on, they owe to their capacity to reason. Without the capacity for rational thought none of the other unique elements of human life could occur. Man, as Aristotle perceived, is a rational animal, a living being capable of conceptual awareness.

Man's rationality must involve, as seen earlier, the capacity to choose. Conceptual awareness could not occur without the freedom to engage in such action, without man's *power* to initiate the act of *forming* concepts. Concepts (ideas, theories, plans, reflections,) do not exist independent of a mind that thinks. Ideas are produced by people; they cannot be *found* "out there." While sensory and perceptual awareness may be produced in animals by those features of the world that possess sensible qualities, there is nothing in nature that produces concepts; there is nothing in nature that forces generalizations, classifications, theories, and ideas upon us. (This is a plain fact. One can detect it simply enough by considering how many people in identical situations do not have ideas on certain issues that others have thought through thoroughly.)

Human rationality involves the possibility of forming one's ideas correctly or incorrectly, of having a sound or unsound rationale for what one believes. It thus involves the possibility of being right or wrong in what one believes, in how one classifies, categorizes, and abstracts various aspects of nature. In the earlier discussion of free will these issues emerged clearly enough, so by this point what human nature is has been detailed sufficiently: man is the kind of living entity that can think and choose. Rand has found the very apt phrase, "a being of volitional consciousness," to capture the meaning of "rational animal." Despite all the attempts by commentators upon the human condition (from behaviorists, mystics, existentialists, and many others who usually end by denouncing humanity as basically evil or impotent or insignificant) this idea of human nature is the best that can be formulated in terms of our present knowledge. Whether the latter is adequate will be considered in the later section on definition.

I turned to a consideration of human nature after we saw that the idea of a proper goal of human beings is defensible along Aristotelian lines.[11] Aristotle identified man as the rational animal, and both Aristotle and Mack construe his proper goal to be his own happiness—his success in life as a human being. What "as a human being" means, in turn, required a discussion of human nature: being an animal with the capacity to choose to think is what renders persons distinctive, unique among animals, members of the class we designate by the term "human."

The *sort* of success that living a human life can involve is tied logically to what kind of thing a person is. The happiness of a human being is not, therefore, a state of sensory pleasure, although such pleasures are also necessary for a successful human life, since man is not *only* a rational being but an animal with the biological capacity and need for sensory experiences as well. Instead the happiness or successful life of a person must involve considerations that *depend* upon his conceptual capacities. Man must, in order for him to be a success, satisfy the requirements of his unique capacities. He must be a success *as* a rational animal. He must choose to live in such a way that he achieves the goals that are rational for him, individually but also as a human being. The former will vary depending on *who* he is. The latter are uniform and pertain to *what* he is, to his humanity—his goal as a human being must be to do best what is his unique capacity: live rationally.

One way to test whether the above is true is by attempting to deny it. This would be to admit that one has a proper goal as a man, but it is not whatever will make him a success at living a human life. But clearly this cannot be. Whatever else might also be a proper goal for each of us, success at living a human life must be our natural, universal proper goal. A person may be a success at many tasks, may have achieved innumerable goals, and could be the best at his profession, hobby, sport, or whatever. But if we are still justified in concluding that he is a failure as a human being, as we sometimes do, then we are also justified in claiming that he has not achieved the goal that is proper to all people. In fact, a careful investigation shows that only those achievements are ultimately worthwhile that do not conflict with a person's goal as a human being. Not that everyone echoes this idea; there are enough cynics in each age to preach the contrary. But there is evidence in even less rigorous discussions of human affairs to support the idea that happiness, the state arising from reflective approval of and joy about one's life, is a goal more precious than any other. Such approval, of course, must be backed with support, evidence of achievement. And the evidence can only be offered as such and assessed if a standard is available. As with all other living entities, man's goal is to live successfully in a way appropriate to him. But unlike other animals, this success must be achieved by conscious effort commensurate to each person's own case. An individual achieves his purpose or proper goal if he succeeds in living his life well, and he fails if by his own lack of effort he misses out on this. (Matters out of one's control clearly cannot be considered as contributory to one's failure. One cannot *fail* at something that is impossible to *achieve.)* After all this, following Mack's discussion, we need to consider what will amount to living well. Granted that the goal is living well, and that this is what is involved in achieving happiness, what does living well come to?

To live, a person needs knowledge. To gain it he has to think: what to eat, how best to survive cold winters, what career to select—these and similar tasks require knowledge, understanding, skills, familiarity with the human situation, history, and all of what enters into living. This, in turn, requires first and foremost the effort and action necessary to gain knowledge, namely thinking. Thinking, or rationally attending to the world, is something that we have found a person must do and sustain by choice. The process of rational thought—not, of course, daydreaming, idle "streaming of the consciousness," and other undirected mental functions that draw on ideas and are, therefore, often assimilated to thinking—must be initiated. To that extent some degree of rationality is required for even the most mundane of human lives. In childhood most people start off enjoying thinking, figuring out the world around them, asking questions, and exploring. Some are obstructed in their efforts, and yet others fail to carry them through. To attain even a minuscule degree of competence in living a person has to focus his mind, otherwise he will either meet with disaster at every turn (except when "lucky") or become a total dependent, a literal ward of others (e.g., in our times, which make this such a readily available alternative, a ward of the state).

When Socrates explained that "virtue is knowledge" he was hinting at the idea I have been trying to develop in this section. This is that, as human beings, all of us are morally good to the extent that we make the personal, individual effort to gain the knowledge needed to live a successful life, to maintain our existence as human beings, to achieve our happiness. Thus, our happiness depends upon how rational we are; how well we *sustain* the crucial activity open to our choice or neglect—thinking. The rest follows from that.

What remains now is the task of specifying how this standard of morality may be applied in each person's particular, individual life. Thus far the standard has only been identified in terms by which it is *possible* to judge (one's own or others') conduct as morally good or bad or mediocre, and by which we can evaluate people, actions, institutions, and whatever is the creation of humankind as these relate to man's life *qua* man. (Of course, many of these creations can be evaluated in terms of standards unrelated to morality—conduct may be graceful, displeasing; institutions may be cohesive, stable, large, powerful; people can be tall, old, fast, rich. To ascertain which statements are true, which false, which likely true, and so on concerning these aspects of human affairs and creations is not our concern.) The measure of moral goodness (or virtue or excellence) consists in the contribution of someone's choice to his existence as a living thing. Or in Mack's terms, "The morally good, with respect to each human being, is the successful performance, and the result of the successful performance, of those actions that sustain his existence as a living thing."[12] And we have seen, also, that the crucial action that each person can choose to perform is the initiation and sustenance of his own thinking—an activity that is necessary to sustain his life.

In the process of developing this point I have defended the view that human beings are capable of free choice and that it is in their activity as thinking beings that this freedom can be identified most fundamentally. Thus the two central conditions for a standard of moral judgment have been met: the identification of the freedom to choose and of a purpose that is everyone's natural goal *qua* human being. Accordingly, when we attempt to learn of what is morally good, it is this standard that we must employ; the question in each case will be whether the chosen act contributes to the sustenance of the (human) life of the person choosing it.

As with all standards, use requires application in actual circumstances. That is, the standard identified is not only appropriate to ascertaining the truth of a moral judgment—the ascription of moral achievement, responsibility, irresponsibility, or virtue—but is also important in determining what a person needs to do to accomplish his own moral excellence in his particular situation. This is no different from trying to find out what one needs to do to satisfy any other standard in particular circumstances; in the present instance the issue is far more general than in most others—matters of morality are everyone's business, whereas, e.g., satisfying proper medical standards or standards of good driving are not.

In the next section I will outline the conditions that need to be satisfied for applying moral standards in particular cases. And I will also attempt to answer some of the well-known objections to the ethical point of view presented in this section, usually characterized as the ethics of egoism or the morality of rational selfishness. This moral point of view has not had a good press, so there is ample opportunity for responding to its critics.

Moral Virtues as Means to a Good Human Life

There used to be a commercial on television which ended with a question to the effect: "Must it taste bad to be good for you?" Every time I heard the ad it occurred to me that one of the saddest features of many people's lives is that they accept moral codes which work in diametrical opposition to their own good. I am not an adherent of the philosophy of Friedrich Nietzsche, but when he observed that nihilism would reign in Europe for the next two centuries, he had his finger on something. Nietzsche put it this way:

> Why has the advent of nihilism become necessary? Because the values we have had hitherto thus draw their final consequence; because nihilism represents the ultimate logical conclusion of our great values and ideals—because we must experience nihilism before we can find out what value these "values" really had.—We require, at some time, new values.[13]

There can be little doubt that people everywhere have begun to sense something awry with most of the values they are taught by parents, ministers, politicians, television stories, and whoever else gets into the act of propagating moral codes these days. The clearest evidence of this dismay with "our great values and ideals" comes from psychologists. It is their clients who stand as character witnesses to the devastating consequences of trying to take a morality of altruism seriously. Central to virtually all varieties of Christian moral codes, and adopted by many agnostic, humanistic and atheist moralities as well, is the idea that the highest of all moral values is the willing sacrifice of everything one values, even one's own life, career, family, children—whatever is of importance. Self-sacrifice or acts of selflessness are taken by most moral teachers as mankind's greatest virtues. College commencement exercises and high school graduation addresses overflow with oratory about the student's duty to go out into the world to serve mankind, God, country, or the future. There is not a political speech that does not exhort the citizen to serve the public interest. Books abound on the evil of selfishness, even after philosophers have more or less given up defending the rationale of the morality of altruism.[14]

Although some philosophers have tried recently to revive the doctrine—e.g., Thomas Nagel attempts to defend it in *The Possibility of Altruism* (Oxford University Press, 1970)—most have focused mainly on discrediting egoism.[15] In this their charge is not only that ethical egoism is inadequate (which they often admit of other moralities also) but that it is flatly *impossible* as a candidate for a moral framework. In this most of the philosophers have been followers of Immanuel Kant, the famous eighteenth-century German philosopher.[16]

Kant's idea was basically that since each person can be counted on to pursue his own well-being as a matter of natural (scientific) necessity—as propounded by the students of human behavior of his day—there could be nothing praiseworthy, commendable, or noble about actions that aim for this goal. To achieve moral excellence one must act from a principle, and this principle must be universally applicable to human beings. But when one's desires or natural inclinations coincide with such a principle, one cannot really be morally good; the motivation is irrelevant for purposes of achieving moral worth. In short, Kant believed that one must be motivated to act in total disregard of, if not in actual opposition to, one's own best interest in order to be doing something morally correct. And although Nietzsche and others found this outlook basically reprehensible,[17] and others have shown it to be based on defective arguments,[18] even today the bulk of philosophers find themselves drawn to it. Moreover, it was wholly consistent with the professed morality of the Western world from Plato onward.

Thus if the reader finds the ideas of the present work strange, that is quite understandable. While in America people have managed to more or less live in disregard of sheer moral propaganda, when they put on the moralist hat—go to church, make speeches, discuss politics, teach their children, evaluate themselves—they tend to embrace a basically altruist morality. The central thesis of this ethic is, as indicated earlier, that one's choices and actions ought to be directed toward the goal of furthering the interests of others (e.g., God, the state, one's racial group, nation). John F. Kennedy's famous slogan that one ought not ask what one's country can do for oneself but what one can do for one's country expresses the sentiment here quite well, as does the idea that we are all our brothers' keepers! Those are two characteristic slogans of the altruistic ethics.

Since this book is not devoted primarily to explaining an ethical position in full, I will attempt to indicate the concrete meaning of ethical egoism only at a basic level, and then I will concentrate on some of the more prevalent criticisms of this ethical position. In these initial comments I want to warn the reader that, in spite of the first section, the meaning of "morally good" may not be familiar to him as explained herein. Most prominent moralities have been inclined to entail suffering, sacrifice, pain, abstinence, and whatever else took from one's life, always, of course, in order to meet someone else's needs—God, society, the nation—and in some cases, to thus insure some future reward. At the same time these moralities seemed to acknowledge that you and I simply cannot *live* by them, so they allowed for built-in imperfections such as original sin (Roman Catholic), the idea that we are but at a prehistoric stage of man and thus understandably defective (Marxist), or the inherent absurdity of human life (existentialist).

The position proposed in this work, as is evident in the previous section, differs from all of those just mentioned. One might consider it revolutionary, but that would be to pretend that these ideas had not been thought of before. Yet from the Greeks all through history to our own times, there have always been people who rejected the morality of altruism. Virtually all of the great creative geniuses—artists, scientists, philosophers—pursued values independently of or only secondarily related to whether their actions were to benefit some mystical or "humanitarian" goal. Even when they advocated some variety of altruism, as in novels, poems, and plays, this had more to do with custom than with practically implemented conviction. (After all, *advocating* ethical egoism, over and above accepting and practicing it, does come close to flaunting one's own virtues and goodness—something not quite consistent in a person who is secure in his moral worth.)

Perhaps the widescale popularity of altruism among intellectuals is partly explainable by the close ties, historically, between church, state, and intellectual establishment. Not that all intellectuals actually practice altruism. They are first of all unable to do so consistently; in addition, many find it unnecessary or irrelevant to implement their own professed ideals in their personal conduct. But most do advocate altruism through the values projected in their scholarly tracts, novels, plays, philosophies, political choices, or other means of explicit or implicit declaration of alliances. Religion and the State gain perpetuity, in turn. (Observe that the first business of every dictator as well as religious leader has been to persuade the people that their duty is not to themselves but to some higher cause—God, das Volk, der Vaterland, der Führer, the coming revolution, the new man, the great society, and on and on.)

I must confess that I have not fully examined why some people—among them many who are unwilling to live with those doctrines themselves—seem readily inclined to advocate altruistic doctrines. (One cannot help wondering about John Kenneth Galbraith's advocacy of socialism in the face of his love for the luxury of the Swiss Alps during high season. When one believes that sacrifice by those who are more well off will save the world, surely the fact that it is not required by law cannot be an obstacle to living by that principle, as restrictive laws *are* obstacles to the freedom to live for one's best interest.) Others have dealt with the question of why altruism is popular—e.g., Ludwig von Mises in *The Anti-Capitalist Mentality* (D. Van Nostrand Company, 1956), Helmut Schoeck in his classic study *Envy* (Harcourt, Brace and World, 1970), and Ayn Rand in her essay "The Age of Envy" *(The Objectivist,* 1969). My concern here will be with explaining some of the practical, concrete implications of the ethics of egoism.

In our earlier discussion of the standard of moral judgment we noted that choices and acts are good or right when they lead to success in living. Contrary to Kant, it is easily observed that people do *not* serve their own interests automatically. Nor is the satisfaction of desires to be equated with serving one's best interest, as anyone who has ever tried to lose weight or discontinue some desired practice knows well. What then does it mean for someone to live his life well? The purpose of applying moral standards is not so much to judge others and have others judge you, but to enable each person to plan his own life, to carry out actions rationally.

The most straightforward answer to this question is that each person must identify what living well will be within his own situation. A moral point of view, one that is discussed, defended, criticized, and so on by philosophers and other theoreticians, simply is not sufficient to yield specific instructions as to what a person ought to do. A general claim may be defended, in this case, that each person ought to pursue his own happiness. But because people have only a few characteristics in common, and even these they experience in different degrees and situations, there is not much that one can say (without the same knowledge that person has) about what each person should do.

The most universally applicable moral advice it is possible to give is that every person ought to make the effort needed to identify what will produce for him a happy life. The primary requirement for that is the use of one's mind—thoughtfulness, careful attention to one's own situation, history, prospects, talents, likes and dislikes, and the like. It would be entirely presumptuous for me to give advice about what is the right thing to do, since there is little that one can know about a reader from my position. (When we come to politics the matter will be different, since we all have more political circumstances in common than the general condition of being human. But *morality applies more broadly than politics.*)

A request for explaining the meaning of a moral principle—in this case the principle of ethical egoism—is usually after a set of moral virtues that would be characteristic of someone who lives by the main principle at hand. Indeed, there are basic kinds of activities all of us are likely to have to perform, situations everyone is going to face in life, and the question concerns what implications egoism has for purposes of coping with these.

In terms of egoist ethics the central virtue each human being can acquire and sustain is rationality. This virtue is actually more basic than the specific *tenets* of egoism, for even identifying these tenets requires that someone be rational, that someone think the matter through and identify the proper (moral) ideal.

Outside of rationality or, more appropriately, in consequence of one's rationality, egoist ethics would involve some more specific virtues, a hierarchy of principles usually called a moral code. This code would refer to such general principles of conduct as honesty, integrity, generosity, magnanimity, courage, honor, pride, independence, justice, and so on.[19] Thus a rational or moral person would follow a policy of honesty in communication with others (and in dealing with himself), recognizing that denying the facts of reality would in most cases put him into conflict with himself, with his own goal of coping with life successfully. Honesty is a principle and, as other principles, once corrupted, it does not function well. Integrity, also, is a rational or moral individual's recognition that defaulting on morality in living one's life cancels out what is required to deal with reality successfully, namely a rational, consistent approach to life. Courage involves the acknowledgment that values may have to be defended against threats, narrow desires, and assaults from those who would want one to sacrifice them for something of lesser or no value. It can be seen that the specific virtues that emerge within the context of an egoistic ethical code are complex, sometimes well known, at other times somewhat unusual, as with productivity and pride. Yet without making the effort to create or work for what one wants and needs, one can survive only by becoming a parasite or a thief. And without acknowledgement of one's own moral achievements one does an injustice to morality and to oneself; there is nothing quite so anti-rational as false humility or self-demeanor.

The vices identifiable in an egoistic moral framework are basically characteristics and principles of conduct that are irrational, which indicate an unwillingness to address oneself to the requirements of living a good life. Corresponding to the fundamental virtue—rationality—is the central vice—*evasion,* the mental act of unfocusing, of disengaging oneself from attention to life. The other vices stemming from evasion would include self-abasement, fraud, dishonesty, compromise of moral principle, and hypocrisy.

Beyond these broad ideas and ideals concerning how a moral individual would act, what his values would be within the context of the egoistic framework, there is little more that can be said in these general terms. Instead of attempting to create artificial examples[20] by which to illustrate the working implications of this ethical position I will turn to the consideration of critical objections. Appreciate some of the ramifications of the present point of view.

But before facing the critics I want to explain that the point of discussing these issues must not be lost. It is my aim, of course, to defend the free society as right by reference to its capacity to accommodate, on the community or political level, the moral implications of ethical egoism. The doctrine of human rights I will defend follows directly from egoistic ethics as these pertain to community life. Thus in order to provide a comprehensive argument for the free society it is necessary to give at least the main features of the defense of each of its premises, including that human beings should aspire to live their lives well. Only if these premises are defensible can the idea that each person should be free to have the right to live, act, and pursue his happiness be defended adequately.

Although the last portion of this book is devoted to answering some broad critical objections, it will not do to wait to answer some of the better known criticisms of the present moral point of view. One of the objections raised against egoism is that it does not meet the qualifications of a moral point of view: moralities, it is claimed, must pertain (only) to human interactions, not to sustaining one's own well-being. For example, in his book, *Anarchy, Freedom and the Law* (Prentice-Hall, 1973) Richard Taylor tells us that "A man alone in the world could not possibly commit any wrong. His actions might be skillful or clumsy, sagacious or foolish, beneficial or injurious to himself; but they could not be morally right or morally wrong. These ideas just do not apply here."[21]

But because morality is not often thought of in terms of what people do with their private lives, it does not follow that we should accept that line of thinking. Taylor says that a man *alone in the world* would have no business with morality; he could not be said to be either good or evil. It is true that if we have an entity that is entirely alone, with no possibility of being classified as a certain kind of entity, then it is impossible to identify the standard of conduct right for it. But then we could not call this a man either, and Taylor's point would be impossible to express. As long as we in fact conceive of *a human being* alone in the world, there is no reason why we can not also conceive that this human being is not doing what he should, i.e., he is not making use of his capacities, he is not aiming to sustain himself, he is living in violation of the requirements of a good human life—so he is immoral. Taylor says that sagacity and prudence may characterize such an individual, but that this has no moral implications. Yet he never considers characteristics, with their implications, such as integrity, honor, courage, dedication, or productivity (all similar to sagaciousness or prudence) and the virtues versus vices of the entire Greek tradition. Even the Christian tradition focused on duties and obligations without quite ignoring considerations of virtue and vice.

What Taylor has done, it turns out, and he is by no means alone here, is to make morality a purely community, even political, affair. His example to illustrate his case, namely that "The idea of theft is without meaning apart from the idea of property,"[22] indicates this well enough. Theft is indeed a wrongdoing that could only occur within a social situation. Yet surely there are evils other than theft! A person who has no respect for himself, who lacks courage, who neglects his life and values, who degrades himself or wastes himself on trivia may be *morally* condemned, although he has hurt or endangered no one but himself. One can with full justice have contempt for such an individual; indeed this is what best accords with the idea of morality developed in these pages.

In one of his many anti-egoist papers Kurt Baier argues that egoism is not a bona fide morality because "like law and custom, morality is an essentially coordinative institution."[23] Baier too means by "morality" what is meant by "mores," "customs," or "taboos," even laws. In primitive societies these usually serve the function of law and no distinction between morality and law is evident. But these are tribal groups where the importance of the individual has not been fully acknowledged.

In more developed civilizations, with more available knowledge, the distinction between morality and politics makes good sense. Morality, as it pertains to private conduct, can be universal and yet allow for development along different lines, thus fostering a pluralistic culture where individuality can coexist with cooperativeness and competition. Political principles, on the other hand, involve explicit requirements of generality and uniformity: *everyone's legal equality* should be enforced because without uniform compliance the coordinative function of law to secure the *common* good would be undermined.[24] But why must law aim for coordination? Because it deals with conduct that pertains to interaction exclusively. And unless *everyone* abides by the proper rules of interaction, conflicts will arise and the benefits of social life are jeopardized for everyone—the common good, the *condition* of morality in society, is endangered. Morality, however, does not aim at the *common* good. Its purpose is the good of man (i.e., human beings), and man is what he is in individual instances, never in some universal incarnation. But I shall come back to politics later. The burden of the above has been to respond to claims that morality serves social purposes alone and does not apply in guiding personal affairs.

Another objection to ethical egoism comes from those who argue that morality is a code of principles that guides one to do the right thing when tempted by self-interest. Thus a moral problem consists of having to choose between acts that promote one's self-interest and those that aim at some other (morally proper) goal. In this objection we can detect once again the influence of Kant. And when morality is conceived along these lines, it is clear that ethical egoism is diametrically opposed to any possible candidates.

There are, of course, instances in life when one is torn between conflicting goals. This is especially true for those people who rarely if ever *think* about their own values, and very likely give no thought to the issue of what is their highest value, most important goal. When they feel inclined to do conflicting things, it thus becomes difficult to decide. And if they accept the general culture's most prominent values, the choice does most often come down to doing either something *they* want or something *others* want of them.

However, the issue of conflicting goals also arises in connection with choosing between what one desires to do and what one believes is important or right to do. And in this case the characterization given by critics of egoism often fails to apply. An egoist might well have a strong desire to give up on some task he has undertaken because he feels tired or wants to play golf or just be rid of his task. But continuing it need not be some *duty to others*, some social responsibility, or self-sacrifice. It could well be something that is, in fact, in his own best interest. For instance, the temptation to sleep late arises each morning and must be met with some resistance, not because some selfless duty must be fulfilled but because getting to work late or missing one's classes can ruin what is possibly a very selfish project. When an artist struggles to complete a painting, his may be a moral struggle without it being the case that completing his work is a duty to any others.

The last moral problem situation—where one must choose between goals, one urged by what one desires, the other by what one has judged to be right—has often been characterized as the conflict between narrow and enlightened self-interest. This way of construing the situation is not help-ful without specifying the standard for enlightenment and narrowness. And without identifying the proper goals of a person, it is impossible to know whether one or another course of action will (more likely than not—for we are not talking about final *guarantees*) attain what is in his interest.

There are other objections to egoism that rest on a narrow conception of what is meant by "self" or "ego." It will be recalled that most contem-porary philosophers do not accept the idea of human nature, believing that no criterion can be found for specifying limits of the applicability of the concept "human being." To put the matter more traditionally, they do not believe we can know the nature of things, what things are "in themselves." This doctrine harks back to Kant and others who have been influenced by empiricism. Instead of offering a definition of "human being" and thus a clear direction for what "self" means, these philosophers tend to leave the idea of "self" or "ego" unanalyzed, which leads them to accept any "intuitive" or "ordinary" view of the self as fully adequate.

When so conceived, it does begin to seem like there is a self which is nothing but some randomly wishing, desiring, wanting, believing, impres-sionable, isolated, narrow, indefinite thing. Self-interest then gets a short shrift by being taken as whatever someone happens at the moment to desire, and morality becomes the tool by which others restrain the wild beast. Ethics must then appear to be in conflict with self-interest. These thinkers do not acknowledge that what one wishes, and so forth, can obstruct self-interest, because they do not identify carefully what it is for something to be in the interest of a person, a human being, *a self of this sort.*

What is in a person's interest? Not just anything that "turns him on." *(If* "interest" is taken as "benefit" or welfare," not as "object of desire or curiosity." And surely it is not these that are meant in ethical egoism.) Just what does constitute a person's welfare, his/her *rational* self-interest? To answer that question one must know a good deal of the person involved, as well as the kind of thing we are talking about. *Rational self-interest* can only be identified if there is a standard. And such a standard is possible by reference to the *kind* of selfhood in question. While there are many thinkers who take a person to be a mere bundle of passions—a view whereby morality is impossible because of the absence of free choice—this is not the view advanced here or by others who defend ethical (as opposed to psychological or innate) egoism. We are talking about the self-interest of *human* beings!

I am particularly intrigued by objections to ethical egoism that imagine situations in which the course of action that would emerge from such a framework *could* not lead to moral conduct. The charge is simply that ethical egoists could not as such be in the position to act morally in some situations—one would have to both perform and not perform the same action in order to be moral. Thus, some argue, the examples show that ethical egoism is self-contradictory.

Kurt Baier's example is so bizarre that it is worth relating it in full. To test the possibility of ethical egoism Baier suggests that we consider the following hypothetical case:

> Let B and K be candidates for the presidency of a certain country and let it be granted that it is in the interest of either to be elected, but that only one can succeed. It would then be in the interest of B but against the interest of K if B were elected, and vice versa, and therefore in the interest of B but against the interest of K if K were liquidated, and vice versa. But from this it would follow that B ought to liquidate K, that it is wrong for B not to do so, that B has not "done his duty" until he has liquidated K, and vice versa. Similarly K, knowing that his own liquidation is in the interest of B and therefore anticipating B's attempts to secure it, ought to take steps to foil B's endeavors. It would be wrong for him not to do so. He would "not have done his duty" until he had made sure of stopping B. It follows that if K prevents B from liquidating him, his act must be said to be both wrong and not wrong—wrong because it is the prevention of what B ought to do, his duty, and wrong for B not to do it; not wrong because it is what K ought to do, his duty, and wrong for K not to do it. But one and the same act (logically) cannot be both morally wrong and not morally wrong.[25]

In this contrived example, the most important question is left unanswered: namely, just what *is* in the interest of B and of K under the circumstance that both want to be but only one can be president? Baier never addresses himself to the issue of what standard is to be used to identify what is in one's self-interest. The unexamined, unscrutinized goals of these men to be president are "granted" to be in their respective interests. Why? No answer is offered. Baier never discusses whether they *ought* to regard becoming president as their self-interest, and thus take it as the only guiding goal for the rest of their activities—which, incidentally, reportedly involve "liquidating" each other. Instead he ends up saying that "This [the above conclusion] is obviously absurd. For morality is designed to apply in just such cases, namely, those where interests conflict. But if the point of view of morality were that of self-interest, then there could never be *moral* solutions of conflicts of interest."[26] In fact the example only shows that Baier misunderstands what is properly meant by "self-interest"; only then could there be no solution to the conflict.

An important point needs to be made about this case and those like it which permeate philosophy and ethics textbooks. *If* there are circumstances when people's best interests come into conflict, need it be concluded that these cannot be accommodated by a code of ethics aimed at guiding each to achieve *his own* best interest? First we must assume that those involved are in the context morally impeccable i.e., we are not concerned with conflicts between those who put themselves in quandaries by way of moral improprieties. (This assumption is generally acknowledged to be necessary—*any* moralist must admit that good and bad people or actions *can* come into conflict with each other, so we need good people or conduct to test the issue.) As human beings it would be in the best interest of such people to achieve a rational solution to their problem, to resolve their conflict by rational means, through a careful consideration of alternatives, and so on. Rational self-interest means just this.

So when a scarce good is desired, everything else being equal, sometimes the (rational) means of deciding who shall have it must be an election or a competition, flipping the coin, exchange of values, and so on. Since there is only one presidency to be had, if in fact it is in the best interest of each candidate to pursue the presidency when only one is available, they can realize that the best solution of their conflicting desires or wants may be achieved by elections. (As it happens, this is how such conflicts of interest between decent people are usually resolved.) The alternative assumed by Baier is clearly not something that would be in the self-interest of those involved—liquidating people leads one to an unhappy future, agonies of mind and body, a future of legal reprisal and constant fear, to say the least. It is only if we accept that it *can* be in the *best* interest of human beings to undertake their affairs in society by murdering off their competition that Baier's problem arises. But when properly interpreted, the best interest of a human being *cannot* be served by such means, except in dire circumstances. This is the next point to be made.

Let us admit, finally, that there might be occasions when not everyone's best interest can and will be achieved. I pose this only as a conceivable case, or one that is possible to imagine under emergency circumstances. Usually when such a possible case is fully explained, the solution that is in the best possible interest of each of those involved also emerges. Such cases require careful thought of course, for they are puzzling precisely because they are unusual and unprecedented. Take as an example: fifteen morally good people, each of them rationally concerned with his own best interest but not, of course, hostile to the similar interests of others (who are after all his own kind—human—and for whom, by rational analysis, the same moral code applies), are faced with shipwreck and a lifeboat that will only hold ten. In the situation there is clearly no possibility of saving everyone. Thus it cannot be that everyone's (in principle, generalizable) self-interest is to get into the boat—an *impossible* goal cannot be in one's best interest!

Knowing of their plight, and being in the (admittedly odd) position of discussing the situation, what would the fifteen rational egoists do? I am aware of the artificiality of trying to solve the problem while sitting at a typewriter or reading this book—yet many people will have known similar circumstances and most will have read of people who have faced them with courage. The first thing that rational egoists would do is get clear on their situation. For example, they would need to make sure that everyone is indeed able to take on a long lifeboat trip, for if any of them is not it would be irrational for him to pretend. He would be found out as soon as his imminent death became evident and the agony of living through the just punishment the others would administer would not be worth the lie. (I say "just" punishment because it is rational for people to secure from others adherence to a code that will best serve everyone's self-interests, not just someone's desires or wants. The point here is that the dynamics of solving problems with others requires rational planning on the part of each person, leading at times to the institution of procedures all will be compelled to adhere to. This will be important when we begin to consider political issues.)

At any rate, each of the fifteen is fully prepared to benefit from gaining the chance to be among those taking the trip, but not each of them *can* go. The rational procedure would be to devise a fair and impartial selection process. Although one may not expect the losers to *feel* well afterwards, *if* their rationality has been sustained they will see that objectively nothing is gained by throwing a fit. Under such circumstances one would hardly have the chance to debate the matter, but we are talking about fifteen rational egoists who are dedicated to serving their respective best interests and who, therefore, would attempt to think of the best solution available. Bringing in feelings, fits, and irrationality as decisive would distort the case. Such cases as the above are obviously rare. In any case the point has been that they do admit of *rational* solution if those involved are willing to abide by that standard.

There is an objection to egoism that arises quite often from a type of discussion that anyone will find familiar who has ever conducted an argument with contemporary philosophers. (I will return to this objection later when I consider why some kinds of objections simply cannot be answered without some serious digging beneath the question itself.) The approach involves citing some incident where our "moral intuitions" indicate that one interpretation must be given whereas the theory being proposed, in this case ethical egoism, indicates a contradictory answer. As an example, I ask the reader to remember, if that is applicable, how the famous movie *Casablanca* ends. The general impression of that ending is clearly one that favors altruism: Humphrey Bogart selflessly sends away the person he loves to travel with another man. Moreover, Ingrid Bergman agrees to this decision; thus we apparently have *Casablanca,* a movie that has had me in tears, ending in an orgy of selflessness. As some would say, our "moral intuitions" dictate both that Bogart was right and that his was an altruistic act.

Yet the story does not support this conclusion unless one chooses to use "intuition" by which to *understand* human affairs. This term is generally used to mean something like common sense impressions, characterizations we are accustomed to on an unreflective level of awareness. (Some philosophers and mystics use the term to try to distinguish a certain type of knowledge that does not involve thinking, reasoning, evidence, and so on, but few have managed to come even close to making sense of this alleged variety of knowledge.) In the case of *Casablanca*, as in most cases where perfectly decent and thoughtful people appear to relinquish their self-interest, what we have is a clear acknowledgement *of the enormous value of freedom* (in this case from Nazism) *to the main characters*. In its behalf even love must take second place.

The psychological benefits derivable from implementing ethical egoism can add a great deal to an appreciation of the meaning of "self-interest." All this may seem unreal in a world where people operate mostly from range-of-the-moment desires and feelings—as when housewives scream for price controls, then find themselves without food three months later, truckers demand government aid to secure whatever is needed to stay on the road, only to find that from then on the Washington bureaucrats have control over their lives, and people insult each other in anger and lose a best friend in the process. Although in the face of such incidents the moral point of view advanced here may seem unrealistic or inappropriate, it is not *therefore* impossible to live by. But more importantly, it is better than any alternative that has been proposed, even and especially for settling conflicts, surely something in one's best interest almost always.

One of Baier's and others' problems is that they evaluate egoism as if it were a closed system, with no possibility of improvement and modification. Yet they will have to admit that altruism, the extreme negation of egoism and the most popular morality around, has deadly flaws which render it an impossible code to live by for any conscientious believer in it. On altruistic grounds the lifeboat case is simply impossible to solve. If every one of the fifteen people ought to promote the interest of the others, where that interest may conflict with his own, there is nothing to solve—everyone ought to jump into the sea! Even if any real solution were offered, that X will stay but Y will not, X would have to give his place to Y, *ad infinitum*.

Unless compared to the way in which different moral codes serve the goal of leading a human life, the significance of the ethical egoist's framework cannot really be appreciated. In some ways it is a demanding moral point of view, as some have called it, idealistic. Ethical egoism does require conduct such that people must be as fully aware as possible of their situation and alternatives so that they can guide themselves toward their own happiness with skill and competence. This moral point of view also understands man to be a far more capable being than most others do. It is in direct opposition to views which deny that there could be a valid moral point of view for human beings. There are those who fault egoism for being unrealistic about the capacity of human beings to achieve happiness. Yet even if many people *will not* choose to strive for their own happiness, this does not demonstrate that they *could not* do so, nor yet that they should not. Nor is everyone's happiness equivalent, so when some people believe that their own happiness involves full enjoyment of the arts, they are wrong to believe that because others may not be capable of their *kind* of enjoyment, happiness is impossible for those people.

After these defensive remarks it will help now to explore some of the details of egoism. This can be done by confronting the rational egoist doctrine with questions it certainly should answer. For one, what would evil amount to within this ethical position? Even more crucial is the question about the connection between reason and happiness. What can rational thinking do to produce happiness? It cannot guarantee against harm; that much is obvious. Nor is it the case that rational choices and action must produce what under more favorable conditions *could have been* a better state of affairs. A captain of a ship might do the best, most rational thing possible and yet, through ignorance for which he cannot be held responsible, be instrumental in the loss of many lives. Good people cannot perform miracles, either in matters of concern to themselves alone or when attempting to perform their responsibilities to others (arising from their commitments or natural obligations). Nor can they always see what must be done so clearly, with omniscience as to render impossible retrospective improvements. (Thus, for example, we distinguish with good reason between regret and sorrow—responses to mishaps we have been party to but were not responsible for—and guilt, remorse, and other forms of self-abnegation, arising from our negligence and omission.)

At this point we can perhaps quite dispassionately discuss the nature of evil. What has been said thus far already implies the sensible view of that fact of human life. What does need to be made clear is that evil rarely occurs as it is depicted in most television series. (Actually soap operas do a fairer job of it, even if their standards of evil are rarely precise and consistent.) Most evil is depicted through characterizations that have the guilty parties enter and leave with thorough malice, viciousness, sinister motives, brutality, and the like. These are your "mean people" whom TV detectives hunt down, Westerns put under black hats, and war films place in the enemy camp. Such pat characterizations contribute to the myth that evil must be malicious, that the persons who are evil would admit it and revel in it (or have some phony psychological compulsion to do it).

But it simply is not so in "day-to-day" evil. Evil is mostly banal,[27] subtle, evasive, "innocent," sincere, naive, unpremeditated: when husbands lie to wives "because of love," when parents nag their children "out of concern," when employers harass employees "because of nerves," when employees steal pencils "because the firm is so rich," when you drive too fast "because—well, for the hell of it," and so forth. Evasions met with from bureaucrats, teachers, scholars, barbers, from people everywhere who know that other things could have been done or who could have found out—these comprise the major share of evil in the world. The compromises people often make for obscure and undefined "higher" purposes, doubletalk that fakes knowledge and hides ignorance, and on and on. If evil is seen in this light, rather than in terms of the cliff-hanger moral dilemmas philosophers often cite to illustrate virtue and vice, then the present account is indeed best suited to provide one with an approach to understanding morality *and* immorality.

At any rate let me proceed now with an investigation of the connection between rational, moral conduct and happiness, the proper goal of such conduct and of each person's life. What I want to clarify is that rationality is a policy, not a gate ticket to happiness. Clearly it would be silly to condemn any moral code for not protecting someone, e.g., against physical disease. (Although some codes do produce plenty of mental agony and even dysfunction, since trying to live by them inevitably leads to pervasive dilemmas, value conflicts, and guilt). Nor is it right to expect permanent good fortune from living a morally good life, except in the sense that one's self-esteem will be intact as a result, however many mishaps may be met with in life. (It is interesting to note in this connection how often people rave about some new ritual or practice they have taken up—vegetarianism, transcendental meditation, jogging, a new diet—as the way to happiness for everyone, chiefly because at the outset it produces for them a state of elation. One may wonder how much this is due to the actual ritual or to the choice they have made to do something, anything, about improving their lives.)

More needs to be said now about the policy of rationality as a characterization of moral excellence and the means to happiness. After years of irrationality, to start out being rational about one's life may really do little. Instituting this policy in one's marriage after fifteen years of negligence and evasion or self-deception or however many ways marriages can be botched up, will not make the relationship suddenly burst with joy. Nor can intermittent rationality, living by some virtues (being sincere, but dishonest; kind but a coward; a decent father but a negligent businessman, and so on) achieve the happiness that a moral life makes possible. This same is true of politics—thus the absurdity of piecemeal solutions to fundamental problems in a nation's political affairs.

In short then, I am not arguing that doing the right things will either guarantee the best conceivable consequences for one's life, or take immediate effect after years of irrationality in one's life. Living rationally—in full conceptual focus on one's life as a human being, asking questions, and doing all in one's power and circumstances to answer them where answers are crucial to a person's individual life—merely makes it most likely that one will be happy, will have a successful life, and know and experience it as such.

Let me now point to certain matters about the manner in which objections to an ethical theory must be approached. Often the validity of a definition of moral goodness is established by examining whether all of what is *ordinarily regarded* as good can be accounted for in terms of the definition in question. Thus people will ask: if we understand goodness to consist of such and such a way of life, can we make sense of the "intuition" or *common belief* that Albert Schweitzer or Martin Luther King, Winston Churchill or Jesus was a good human being? Can we take moral virtue to consist primarily of choosing to be rational when confronted with the actual lives of widely admired persons?

A point to be heeded here is that many people can be and are just wrong about what is good, right, morally worthwhile. This much is uncontroversial—not everyone with different views can be correct about what is morally right, for then we have to accept that reality admits of contradictory facts, of "A and not-A." (We know from our brief discussion of certain basic, metaphysical facts that this cannot be.) As people use language everywhere, clearly the concept "good" is used with considerable confusion in the moral context. Many contradictory claims are accepted, many conflicting uses are in evidence. Without heeding this warning, one can always produce examples which the definition being offered will not cover, where paradoxes will emerge. Nor can we jump, in considering the examples, from testing the definition against a Christian conception of what is morally good conduct, to a hedonist's or Hindu's idea of moral virtue. Many people use the idea of good, including those who are in fact evil! A sound view of morality surely cannot be faulted for not living up to the "common sense" idea of virtue entertained by evil persons, especially those who deceive themselves about their own moral nature.

In this connection it will help also to recognize that many people subscribe to a moral point of view that has nothing to do with human nature, where the idea of what is right and wrong derives not from an understanding of the nature of the entity that is to live by the moral code involved but from some supernatural entity's (alleged or reported) notions of what human beings ought to do. As mentioned earlier, we are interested in identifying a moral point of view that is rationally defensible, i.e., for which justification lies in arguments, facts, and so on, that anyone with healthy conceptual capacities who chooses to attend to the problem can understand and assess—not one where it takes grace, intuition, or revelation to grasp what is at issue. But it bears noting here that many "moral notions," and often the idea of morality, do emerge from or are associated with religion and mysticism. Relatedly, customs and mores are often cited as evidence of the existence of different, and hence the relativeness of moralities. In fact, however, these are not moralities, but practices dependent on factors unique to regions, heritage, climate, ignorance of science (i.e., myth and error), and so forth. To take so-called moral matters from these contexts and stack them up against a genuine moral doctrine, one that is designed to suit human beings as such and has nothing ethnocentric about it, is logically unjustifiable.

Still another objection comes from people who wish to condemn any ethical doctrine that will benefit man, simply because they have a view of man as destructive of the essentially good things in nature. In the upcoming discussion of animal rights I will present an example of a modern philosopher endorsing a morality—he calls it an extreme form of altruism (and he is right)—that would serve the good of animals at human expense. Ecologists, too, often implicitly embrace such a viewpoint, particularly when they mix up their doctrine with some varieties of Eastern mysticism.

There have been philosophers who have argued quite seriously that relying on reason is morally inferior to following our animal instincts, our sentiments or feelings. David Hume, among others, believed that man should yield not to the judgment of his reason but to his sentiments, although Hume's concept of "reason" in this context meant something different from what has been meant throughout this work. He had in mind the reason of the rationalists—pure, speculative reason, from which the most bizarre problems and conclusions had been derived. Still, many philosophers today understand "reason" to mean some kind of dry calculation with no awareness of human reality. So they have decried rationality, as do the counterculture advocates. At any rate, without attending to the questions rationally—as meant in this work—these matters cannot be handled at all, which is just the point here.

In addition to the above broadly based objections to the positions and arguments advanced in this discussion, some more technical ones are worth addressing before we move on. One such fine point may be put as follows: it has been argued here that the moral choices that make someone a good person are the initiation and the sustenance of rationality, of one's conceptually conscious processes. But would one not need to know before making the choice to initiate it that rationality is productive of human good? And would that not require rational consideration?

Let me put the matter a different way. A good person is such in choosing to be rational about his life. As Rand puts the matter, "moral perfection is an *unbreached rationality.*"[28] This rationality has to be chosen, otherwise one cannot be responsible for being rational. One must have caused one's own rationality, otherwise there is no moral pertinence to this action at all or to any other actions following from it. But how can such a person be good by that choice if he could not know beforehand that it will lead him toward the goal that is proper for human beings, namely a good life, happiness, his own best interest? Unless this question can be answered, we are left with the view that people simply do or do not make this "choice"—when they do, they will more than less likely be happy, and vice versa. What is *morally* good about it in that case?

It should be obvious that this is a crucial issue, and that its complete treatment would deserve a long book with close and detailed attention to matters of human psychology.[29] What I will do is hint at the answer and indicate in which direction one would have to go to explore it fully.

Earlier we saw that human freedom cannot be denied without giving rise to serious contradictions. The argument showed that such a denial leads to a self-referential inconsistency, that the denial itself cannot be justified because that depends on the possibility of human freedom, the lack of bias that makes an objective assessment of the issue (actually) possible. This argument shows that human beings *can* be free but does not tell us much more. It does point to the fact that it is fundamentally in their rational capacities that individuals can be free. That clue allows us to outline an explanation of the choice to be rational, an explanation which will not prove man's moral nature; it will only indicate the answer to the present question about the nature of moral choice, how it comes about in one's life, and so forth.

Briefly then, let me note that people have conscious capacities such as sensation, perception, the experience of pain and pleasure. This we share with animals, whatever their precise mechanisms may be. The way, therefore, to conceptualize the emergence of moral choice is by considering a child's development. Before even the perceptual level of consciousness develops significantly in infants they can experience pain and pleasure. Their avoidance or approach in the appropriate circumstances, i.e., when exposed to painful or pleasurable circumstances, is initially a matter of reflex action, is simple and does not involve complex planning.

It can be observed that children will tend toward what causes pleasure, provided nothing intervenes in a destructive way. They will gradually have sufficient clues as to what kinds of experiences are enjoyable, which are more than less enjoyable, which require some pain or struggle for attainment, and so on. Thus in their development as human beings it will become possible for them to conceptualize their immediate situations and to select from among different pleasureable items, as well as to tolerate some painful ones if they understand that these are required to obtain certain pleasures. Once their conceptual capacity is added to their lower conscious awareness—once children can reflect upon what they feel and perceive—they are in a position to choose between focusing on different feelings, and on this or that object of perception.

It is very likely that moral consciousness begins to develop at this stage. That is to say, it is when they develop the conceptual facility to assess different experiences and, as it were, go for these or those, that they acquire character. (We cannot sensibly talk about the *character* of a baby, but we can of an older child.) Of course during years of dependence upon parents and other adults a child's choices will be important only in limited areas. But even here a child has many opportunities to choose what is or is not good for him.

At later, more mature stages an increasing number of matters will be "up to a person." His range of possible influence concerning his own life will grow, again, provided there is no drastic intervention. (With serious psychological interference the struggles may be more severe and opportunities for influencing one's own life may be delayed.) By this stage the capacity to plan, to make long-range conceptual determination of one's life, increases and the issue of whether the person is making the effort to think through the problems and tasks and opportunities he faces makes clear sense.

Now one reason that the question about whether one can morally characterize the early choices appears to be compelling is that it assumes that a person can only make *one* start toward rationality in his life. But this is clearly not the case. A person's freedom ranges over the part of life when his health permits reasonably normal conceptual activities. Rationality can be sustained for a while and then abandoned. A person can choose to think about some issues but not about others, even though the opportunity to do so existed. The human mind does not go blank because it is not fully employed.

The early actions of a child do not permanently determine what sort of character he will have. It is the child himself, during the evolution of his life, each day, each moment when he is unobstructed, who makes the determinations. Of course, as Aristotle noted long ago, patterns can and do develop; yet recoveries from earlier failings and errors, as well as benefits from sustained effort, contribute to these patterns. For the child, as far as we can tell, and others have developed this issue in greater depth, there is ample opportunity to act on his world rationally. By the time we grow to maturity, if we have made the most of circumstances, we will have a wealth of knowledge, and an understanding of relevant alternatives. In any case we will be free enough to make lasting commitments or resolutions concerning whether we will attend to the world fully, diligently, rationally, carefully, or will refrain from this by allowing others to direct us. The choice to be rational is one for which we have many opportunities in life. Facing it in more mature years will also involve becoming aware of the consequences of its neglect!

There are now several more issues to be considered. I want to address myself to a challenge often put to those who advance philosophical positions. The question is most often raised in terms of whether the position makes a conceptual or an empirical claim. The challenge conveys commitment to a philosophical point of view, of course, about what kinds of claims to knowledge there can be. Conceptual knowledge, or knowledge of the meaning of concepts, is supposed to be distinguished from empirical knowledge, or knowledge of facts. Another way of putting this is to ask, "Has this theory been developed by observation, or by analysis of concepts; is it based on evidence, or on the meaning of our concepts?" From the present point of view this distinction is somewhat artificial, so although the question is popular, it is problematic because it makes use of certain philosophical concepts that are often accepted uncritically.

What is not clear is just what the challenge means. Are there any *strictly* empirical theories? In all seriousness this means, "Are there any theories which are based on statements, observations, ideas, explanations, and so on, all of which can be reduced without remainder to references to sense experiences, to sensory inputs?" The answer is "No." There simply are no such theories. Francis Bacon and B. F. Skinner are wrong: one cannot even open one's mouth about a subject if all that will count as meaningful is something that passes this test. David Hume, who tried it, realized this.

We might be more generous than this, however, and accept that what is being asked for is something like "a theory developed primarily from observations, scientifically respectable methods, facts about the world, reasonably good estimates of quantity, and so on." Taken thus, the present discussion of the concepts "moral excellence" or "virtue" or "good" is an empirical theory of what is good for human beings as human beings. The starting point was Mack's discussion of *natural functions*. I have made all sorts of mention of the actual, *factual results* of irrationality and rationality in human life; I have talked briefly about happiness, which is something we can *experience;* I might also add that the theory gains considerable support from various psychological *discoveries* to the effect that anxiety, neurosis, even psychosis is often caused by someone's failure or inability to think clearly about his world and life. I admit that the measurements are not the same as those we use in physics or even economics; it does not follow from this that nothing has been observed, isolated, recorded, and so forth. It bears reiteration that it is illegitimate to ask for the same standards of precision in all fields of study.

But how should we respond to the second part of the question? Has this been a conceptual investigation? As indicated, most philosophers mean by this, have the issues been dealt with entirely by reliance on the analysis of concepts? It is assumed that by starting with the concepts at hand, those widely used in the language, factual knowledge is unnecessary. That is to say, when someone wishes, e.g., to understand what it is to be a bachelor, there is no need to go out and check with bachelors. We take the term as it is used, see what its component concepts are—male, adult, unmarried—and conclude that being a bachelor means being a male, adult, unmarried individual.

The problem with this view that there can be something like purely conceptual analysis is that all concepts must at one time be formulated. And although by now many of them are clearly enough understood not to require an investigation of the facts that gave rise to them, e.g., the actual difference between married adult males and unmarried ones, some are not. When we consider these, we cannot rely on existing, prominent usage. Especially not when moral concepts are at hand. A line in *King Lear* well explains the futility of pure conceptual analysis in matters pertaining to morality: "Wisdom and goodness to the vile seem vile."

The next issue I want to touch on is also important within the context of contemporary moral philosophy. This is the idea that morality is, after all, extremely elusive, hard to get a hold on, something strange in reality, out of the ordinary, natural states of affairs known to us. This view is often expressed by saying that morality is an autonomous or sovereign realm, standing all by itself. Even though the Humean view about morality's inaccessibility to reasoned consideration—i.e., that right and wrong in human affairs cannot be identified rationally—is no longer powerful, others have tried to defend something close to this idea.

Beardsmore argues, e.g., that although we can make a rational case for some of our conduct, the rationality of that case can only go as far as the moral viewpoint we were taught or otherwise accepted. We can reason about conduct, institutions, policies of states, and so on, but only *from within some moral framework*. Catholics can come to agreement with Catholics, Buddhists with Buddhists, stoics with stoics, Japanese Samurais with Japanese Samurais.[30] There can be coincidental agreement between members of different moralities, but they are incapable of resolving moral disagreements, even if they do their level best. Beardsmore tells us that in "ethical disputes nothing comparable [to scientific ones] need be true. Often these are not decidable, even in principle, simply because the disputants cannot even agree over what criteria to apply. They each have reasons for their judgments that they make, but neither admits the relevance of the other's reasons. The argument has reached a deadlock."[31]

Jon Wheatley defends a similar idea. For him basic moral positions are "stands," or indefeasible principles, which means that they *cannot* be justified. "The pacifist's stand (and it is a stand) is that there is an (indefeasible) principle proscribing killing."[32] The idea that the indefeasibility of this claim must itself be defended, i.e., that a pacifist, to demonstrate the correctness of his view, must *show* that one cannot rationally deny it, is not considered by Wheatley. Nor does Beardsmore defend the view that "the disputants *cannot* even agree over what criteria to apply."[33] Both seem to think that people are helpless in their adherence to moral positions and cannot open these positions up to criticism and change their commitments or convictions when shown to be wrong about the issue at hand. (Admittedly one cannot go on considering any and every objection, leaving room for nothing else in life. But when tough problems arise there is good reason to seek out a *sound* solution, which may not be one that is consistent with one's previously accepted moral standpoint.)

I am not saying that even philosophers actually act as if this view of people's believing helplessly were correct. Philosophers, for instance, are not satisfied when they learn that another's conclusions follow rationally from some *accepted* premise; they want to see the argument taken as far back as is rationally possible. And although they will differ about what this point is, most of them take it that their starting point is the rational one, the right one, even if this point amounts to denying that a starting place *can* be reached. And the same holds about people in general—those who profess to deny reason in morality *blame* others for not denying morality as well, for being so unreasonable as to ask for reason!

Yet there clearly *is* something about morality that sets it apart from other areas of concern. Hardly anyone can deny, for example, that questions about ethics are raised only in connection with people. But this too is in the realm of nature. The fact is, morality pertains only to free action, and to the best of our knowledge no animal other than man is capable of this. Responsibility, duty, obligation, or the failure to meet them are not applied to other than human beings except in an anthropomorphic sense, never meant seriously. Dogs are not put in jail, nor are they punished seriously—only beaten to be conditioned, or patted to be encouraged. It is only with human beings that judgments and actions are found to be free, open to choice, self-initiated. In light of this fact we can make sense of morality, for it is only with respect to free actions that such concepts as "right" and "wrong" are intelligible. Livers and hearts may not function well, but only people can do *wrong*, only they can act immorally.

As such, morality *is* autonomous—uniquely pertinent in human affairs. Physics, chemistry, biology and many other fields can be studied without regard to values. These are indeed value-free sciences since what they study does not possess the capacity to choose, to make value judgments, to act in accordance with principles of right and wrong. But the sciences that study man cannot evade the fact that values are relevant to his existence, that he can choose between the right and wrong ways of doing things. For the people in these infant sciences to proclaim their rejection of values is to engage in systematic ignorance and evasion; if man is just the sort of natural entity in relation to which values are essential, then studying him without regard to values is simply wrongheaded.

There is then a sense in which morality is autonomous: only people are open to moral evaluation. But this autonomy of morality does *not* arise because moral concerns are unnatural, supernatural, or otherwise mysterious. The feeling of wonder, amazement and awe that sometimes accompanies man's awareness of man, that which overwhelms one with the realization that no other beings known to us can be self-conscious and contemplative about their own being, does not require (and clearly does not warrant) the conclusion that something weird is going on, something incomprehensible or ineffable. Those who draw this conclusion generally start by accepting that nature cannot admit of anything but the sort of things and events we study in physics and chemistry—so the reality of human freedom and responsibility must for them either be dismissed (behaviorism, materialism, physicalism, determinism) or ascribed to mystery or absurdity (religion, mysticism, existentialism). It's the view that divinity or unnaturality follows from the recognition of our nature as moral agents that sends so many social scientists scurrying off to deny the reality of the human mind and of human freedom and dignity!

What I have tried to do in this chapter is develop a moral framework that is rationally defensible, one that accords with a consistent and factually adequate regard of man as a living entity with a specific nature. I set out to show that each person should pursue his own happiness and that he can do this by choosing to think and act rationally. I considered some standard objections to the morality of rational self-interest, mainly where people have argued that egoism could not even begin to make sense as a moral point of view. I also explored some of the implications and details of the moral theory at hand, some of the virtues entailed by its moral code, although I certainly left much to be discussed in a more comprehensive treatment. (Also, I should admit that I have put an emphasis on virtues that are not generally included within other moral viewpoints. Thus generosity, kindness, mercy, compassion and other virtues, appropriate in human life within various contexts, were not considered; instead I have focused on the more general virtues of integrity, productivity, independence, and, mainly, rationality itself, from which the rest would have to be derived for various specific areas of human conduct.) I went on to iron out some of the more problematic aspects of this view, and finally considered how all this meshes with the widely made observation of the uniqueness of morality in human life.

My next task will be to integrate these ideas with the political theory of human rights. Perhaps some will question the wisdom of devoting so much space to a discussion of morality, especially when the discussion could not be fully completed. Yet it should be quite understandable. Values are man's most basic concern—art, commerce, play, politics, each person's individual affairs, indeed the entire world revolves around values. Human life is difficult and exciting because of this, because their attainment brings us happiness and their loss sorrow; because their destroyers make life less than it could be and those who create them, who defend them and preserve them, give life its grandeur and beauty. We must all deal with tomorrow and tomorrow awaits us with alternatives. Will we select the right ones or will we fail even to make the effort needed to learn which the right ones are? Will we deny our capacity to make sound choices because many have failed to make them and others have been rendered incapable either by callous fellow human beings or by accidents of nature? Will we declare the world absurd because people's absurd conduct and occasional misfortune have made portions of it full of misery? Will we, in short, take up the task of attending to our existence in the unique and distinct way that human beings can—rationally?

The kind of society that I will try to defend in the next chapter has been condemned by many for not heeding the fact of man's moral nature—by allowing for rampant brutality, for lack of virtue and nobility in human affairs. People from different political perspectives, Marxists, fascists, modern liberals, or conservatives, have all charged the free society with callousness. They have tried to sell us the idea that in freedom men will be beasts, that they will be alienated from their own essential nature or concentrate on crass pleasure with no heed to the requirements of human excellence. I will show that this is not so.

My aim, then, will be to demonstrate that, given the moral framework that was developed in this chapter, given that each person is responsible to achieve his own happiness, the society that is suited for him is one in which his individual liberty is fully secured—i.e., protected and preserved to the maximum degree possible given the knowledge available to those within a given human community. Contrary to what the critics claim, it is only in such a free society that the moral agency, the freedom and the dignity, of each person can be respected. Thus only in that kind of a community can the moral life flourish. That life, of course, cannot be conceived of as guaranteed by political conditions, by acts of government, even by the most sensible and true theories of philosophers. That life must be the creation of individual human beings alone or in each other's company. No one can write a book by which people can and will be made good. That is impossible, and those who promise it are misleading the world, while those who ask for it are waiting for solutions from inappropriate sources—outside of their own creative souls.

My hope is that the upcoming considerations will help at least those who want to contribute to the prospects of a human community in which the moral life is possible, even if that means that such a community must accept the fact that free agents may abuse their liberty within their own lives. If there is to be a chance for the good life the risk of a bad one must also be accepted. There is no escape from that.

CHAPTER 4

The interdependence of words and the world, the determining and limiting role of concepts on what is perceived as reality, will generally be most intensive with respect to human, social, cultural, and political things.
                                                            H. F. Pitkin

Human Rights and Good Human Communities

The Rationale for Human Rights—Preliminaries

A rationale is a theory that provides rational justification for some statement. I mean "rational justification" in its broadest sense, i.e., a complete and consistent argument that establishes the truth of some claim or set of claims. I do not mean a "logical" argument which shows the validity of a conclusion based on certain unexamined ideas, feelings, or preconceptions. Since many contemporary philosophers deny that the foundations of a theory can be established as true, they do not use "rational" in the above sense but rather in the narrow sense of using logic to derive certain conclusions from wherever one starts. But there is nothing ipso facto rational about using logical arguments—the maddest of human beings invoke *some* logic. By denying that foundations for various theories can be secured nonarbitrarily, contemporary "defenders" of reason are actually undermining reason.[1]

A rationale for human rights would provide justification for the conclusion that there are human rights and that these rights are of such and such a nature, i.e., that there are in fact certain identifiable human rights. If such a rationale is successful it ought to convince those aware of it of the truth of the theory being considered. (Skeptical objections to the above points have already been discussed, and some will be handled in the final chapter of this book.)

In the present discussion my purpose is to provide the above rationale. Some progress toward this end has already been made by the previous account of moral excellence. I have argued that human nature consists in the fact that each individual has the capacity to choose to be rational, to attend to and understand reality by way of his form of (conceptual) consciousness. Moral virtue lies in a person's initiation and sustenance of the activity of rational thought, that which underlies or fails to support his actions. This is because rational conduct is most capable of making one's life successful. From these considerations we must now turn to politics.

Politics is a branch of ethics. Politics, of course, does *not* mean either political science, or what these days passes for politics, namely being an unprincipled, compromising, amoral, or immoral practitioner of power-seeking. While ethics investigates and evaluates all human conduct, politics studies the basic principles of human community life. Often this is expressed by saying that politics investigates the nature of the general or *common good.* However, that idea is not simple and most often is completely abused, leaving one with the impression that it is not possibly intelligible, i.e., that there could be nothing that is generally good for human beings in a community. (One need only consider in this connection the myriad programs politicians justify in terms of such notions as "the public interest," "the national good," "the common good," and so forth. What with the obvious fact before us that these programs usually serve the interests of one or another group of people at the expense of the rest, the claim that they serve the general or common good *must* be false.)

By the concept of general good I mean whatever is indeed good for human beings generally, as such, solely because they are human beings in a community of other human beings. I will say at the outset—there are certainly few things that will count as good in this sense.[2] In and out of society we all have different purposes to achieve, and some of these are without a doubt good for those who take them on, without being good for others in the slightest. There is one good, however, as I argued in the last chapter, that is general: our moral excellence. *We should all* strive to be good human beings. Whatever else we ought to do—and there will be many different tasks required of different individuals to achieve a morally good life—this one goal we all have in common. To the extent that the prospects of reaching this overriding goal are enhanced by living in human communities, those communities are good. To the extent that the principles by which a community is organized impede a person's chances to achieve that goal, that community fails to be a good one. At times, indeed, a community is organized along such obstructive principles that it could be one's moral obligation to work for its destruction and for the creation of a different one embodying principles that enable pursuit of one's own moral goals. (It is to this problem that both John Locke and the designers of the Declaration of Independence addressed themselves when they advocated that government *should be* overthrown in certain circumstances. As a concrete example, it is not difficult to see that citizens of the Third Reich ought to have, and some had, worked for its destruction.)

When I discussed earlier what a human right would be if any could be identified, I said that it would be a condition that is right for people in society by virture of the fact that they are human beings. Ayn Rand makes this point quite clear when she says:

"Rights" are a moral concept—the concept that provides a logical transition from the principles guiding an individuals's actions to the principles guiding his relationship with others—the concept that preserves and protects individual morality in a social context—the link between the moral code of a man and the legal code of a society, between ethics and politics. *Individual rights are the means of subordinating society to moral law.*[3]

Rand, certainly a modern thinker, identifies individual human rights in the great tradition of classical natural law and natural right theories. As such, she provides the link we found missing in Hobbes and Locke, who only hinted that human rights are political principles that identify what is right or good for people in society.

These rights specify what social conditions are good or right for people by virtue of their humanity, and thus guide us in our effort to learn what people ought to do, how they should conduct themselves, in a *social* context. The sense in which "right for" is meant here is the moral/political sense, not, for instance, the medical, educational, economic, biological, or some other sense about which we do not all, simply as human beings, have any responsibility or choice. Human rights specify conditions which all of us ought to provide for each other. (Doctors, teachers, businessmen, laborers, and people in other areas of creative and productive work *can* provide what is right for us in specific areas—but because of what they have done with their lives, not because they are human beings.)

It is important to see that human rights are moral principles, although they are ones which apply to people within a social context—they have the purpose of guiding people in conduct that pertains to dealing with others. Because of this qualification we consider the moral principles which comprise human rights under the rubric of political theory. And to live in accordance with these principles will most often require some measures in addition to keeping them in mind! Since the principles pertain to conduct in a social context, toward others, in accepting them we need to consider what it would take to ensure their widescale observance. In matters of personal, private conduct one can prepare *oneself* for the future requirement to do the right thing. One can, for example, cultivate good habits and policies, make resolutions, prepare reminders, even institute "schedules" which will serve to bring about the goals one has chosen to pursue. Failure to act in accordance with these will not, however, harm others (unless they are dependent upon the person which may or may not be warranted). Unless others are unavoidably involved, personal, or private immoral activities—and there certainly are many—will only hurt those who are party to them voluntarily, of their own accord.

The above is not so concerning conduct that must necessarily involve other people. It is therefore best that in a human community the limits of each individual's sphere of action be identified for all to see and understand, so that actions which constitute the infringement of another's sphere can be more readily identified and the harmful consequences remedied. Indeed, the difference between actions that are immoral but private and those that are immoral but public must in part be that the former produce their own punishment, while the latter require the meting out of punishment (retribution, penalties). Here the point is to distinguish between wrong actions that must harm another but may benefit the agent and to enable us to decide on a proper recourse.

The above may seem a bit too abstract, perhaps because we commonly talk about these issues in terms of rights—e.g., "I have the right to do as I please, without regard to right and wrong." What we mean by this is that I *ought to be free* to do as I please so long as the actions pertain to me, not that I am morally justified in doing as I please. Thus a person might in fact be entirely irresponsible in his personal life, but that is his right—it is, so to speak, "his business." This kind of familiar discussion, however, presupposes that human rights exist, and we are just at the point where that is exactly what remains to be proven. But we must recall what we are trying to find out what is meant by the statement that human rights exist, for a number of philosophers have debated the issue of what such existence would involve, what it means to say that human rights exist. As a negative example, Professor Henry Aiken tells us that trying to answer this question *"simpliciter,* out of any context of inquiry or concern [will] entangle you in a murky swamp of speculation about the nature of being *qua* being, or reality as reality." And he tells us that "such speculations . . . turn out invariably to be disguised queries about the meanings, or better, the uses and roles in our discourses of the words 'being', 'existence', and 'reality'."[4]

To avoid any suspicion of murkiness it will help to make clear again: "Are there human rights? Do they exist?" would be answered with "Yes" *just in case* it is true that some conditions are right for people for purposes of social conduct because they are human beings, or just in case it is true that some principles of conduct apply to the organization of human communities so as to render those communities good, i.e., conducive to the achievement of human excellence. So if what is and will be said here is true, then human rights exist, and if these statements are false, then human rights do not exist.

A point of clarification: the sense in which human rights might exist is the sense in which there can be principles of combustion or photosynthesis, even when nothing is in fact burning or photosynthesizing. The conditions that human rights specify are right for people or not right for people. If the former, then there are human rights, even when no one acknowledges them or conducts himself by their provisions. (Though of course many people can conduct themselves in accordance with their provisions even without acknowledging them, just as people can maintain a balanced diet without knowing it.)

Are there human rights? If we can identify at least one, if we can show that one such right exists, the task of this chapter will be accomplished. That alone will show that there are such rights and that we can know this, which is what so many have denied.

The Human Right to Political Liberty

As a possible human right let me state a candidate as follows:

Each and every person ought to have the maximum freedom of choice and action in the pursuit of his own aspirations, in the conduct of his life.

This statement expresses, somewhat elaborately, the human right to political liberty. Its rational justification (defense, proof, and so on) will establish the existence of a human right. The form of that justification will emerge presently, but as a moral judgment pertaining to conduct in a human community, its justification must accord with those standards laid down in the previous chapter.

One point needs to be made before we can go on to justify liberty as a human right. First, we need to keep in mind that others *can abstain* from interference—meaning, if it is interference *on their part* it is up to them. Thus it is not interference when someone is thrown against another by a tornado. Clearly there are cases when we can identify a combination of interference (what could be avoided by the agent) and some other force that makes its consequences greater. Such issues are grappled with by insurance and tort lawyers. The fundamental point is that the interference I am talking about makes sense only in the context of an understanding of man as a being that can cause some of his actions, as an agent.

At this point let us recall the basic moral principle that people ought to choose to live rationally, that this is the means to man's proper goal—a rewarding, successful, i.e., happy existence. An implication of this principle is that any situation which enables their doing so is better for people than any which presents obstacles. Whenever other human beings are part of one's world it is therefore better that they do not act so as to obstruct one's moral agency—i.e., one's potential for choosing to do what is right or good, to live rationally. (This means that without interference the opportunity to live in accordance with one's own choices would be more extensive. It does not mean that without obstruction one would necessarily make the morally appropriate choices to live rationally. The issue, I emphasize again, is that of having the option, not of guaranteeing the best alternative such an option makes possible.)

Now to say all this is pointless—although not meaningless—outside a social context, when we think of man in isolation and consider what moral principles apply under such circumstances. (I have already answered those who deny that morality has application in that kind of case, that is, to assume that morality *must* be *other*-oriented.) Whatever living alone will involve, it will not require knowledge of the principles of human interaction. The identification of human rights makes a point! It does not just state a fact—it satisfies a moral purpose: the statement which I proposed in order to identify the human right to be free tells us how all people ought to act toward each other to make it possible for each to aspire to moral excellence. Someone who would obstruct such aspirations, even knowingly or unknowingly threaten them, demonstrates his unwillingness or inability to live by principles *which serve his moral purpose in a social context.* For some this might mean simply that they are mistaken to remain in a human community. If it could be shown that one's own moral aspirations entailed acting so that others' would be obstructed, then one ought to remove oneself from a social context. (Many people want it both ways—enjoy the benefits of social life, e.g., economic opportunities and companionship, but refuse to observe the principles of conduct which render this possible, e.g., violate others' human rights.) Many anarchists believe that human rights ought to be respected, but that this is impossible via the establishment and administration of a legal system—the contention being that that process would necessarily violate people's human rights. To follow up on this conviction, such anarchists would have to leave society, even if its members were attempting to implement human rights. For they could only inconsistently force others to abandon efforts to organize a moral human community.

Given, then, that their purpose is to live a good life and that they are in the company of others, everyone should enjoy maximum liberty. That is to say, for anyone whose moral purpose involves the experience and company of other human beings, the principle I have identified as the human right to political liberty will provide (at least) one fundamental guiding rule by which to do so successfully. Thus, in the context of life in human community, the human right to the maximum possible liberty is what *ought to be* adhered to and protected as well as preserved. This, to repeat, because this principle is *right* for human beings to observe as they live with others.

One may ask at this point: have we merely established a conditional truth by having shown that, given that one has the purpose of living a good life among others, this principle must be the guide? It is of course conceivable that a life among others would be inappropriate. Although (as Aristotle argued) man is a social animal and his happiness can only be realized as fully as possible in the company of others, we cannot deny out of hand that there could be some whose happiness would not include the benefits that can accrue from the company of others. But it is highly unlikely that living as a hermit would be good for someone who had the opportunity to live among others who observe the principle just defended. The fact should be noted, however, that this opportunity is rare. Perhaps no human community enjoys the protection and preservation of human liberty, although many give lipservice and some, like the United States, allow for it sporadically. In view of this fact, renouncing community life is not tantamount to rejecting that it is right to live with others in political liberty. It is only to a society with indeed the maximum possible implementation of these principles that full allegiance of its members can be expected. For different people loss of some liberty could spell more or less threat: in a country where freedom of expression is widely upheld but freedom of trade curtailed, some may accept, others reject "the system." If those with white skin enjoy acknowledgment of their liberty while those with black skin do not, the latter will probably reject "the system" more readily. Nevertheless, refusal to accept it may not at once justify a call for its revolutionary abolition. Later I will consider the right of revolution in greater detail when I take up implications of the present theory of human rights. But for purposes of preemptive clarification it will help to keep the above points in mind.

Thus far it seems clear that for political purposes, i.e., to organize a human community in accordance with what is morally good for people, the human right to political liberty is basic. Many less general principles follow from this broad one. But human rights, in this case the right to be free to pursue actions pertaining to one's life, are the most general principles *in a social context*. For less general purposes than the organization of a good human community less general principles of conduct may be applicable—kindness, courtesy, hospitality, generosity, benevolence, prudence, thrift, frugality, modesty, and so on, may all figure into one's conduct, both private and public. These, however, are appropriate in relation to some people on some occasions, while human rights in a social context *pertain to conduct involving anyone or everyone*, with all other principles relevant to human relationships subordinate to them.

Before continuing, let me summarize the meaning of the human right to liberty. Regarding any person's life, he ought to be treated so that he is free to (choose to) judge and act as he will.[5] In more familiar language: coercion is immoral, regardless of who perpetrates it in a human community, private citizens ("criminals") or officials of the legal system ("government"). The reason for the above is that only by acknowledgment, protection, and preservation of this freedom is a morally good life possible for people in each other's company, for human nature requires that the good human life be something that a person achieves for himself. Thus, just being human warrants the acknowledgment and implementation of human rights—it is right for human beings to live this way in a social context.

Here it is worth injecting the observation that the present theory of rights contains a feature unmatched in most other political theories. This is the clear justification of the legal foundations of a good human community in terms of an ethical doctrine concerned at the fundamental level with the potential excellence of *individual* human beings. This feature, known vaguely as the individualistic aspect of the American political tradition, sets the present doctrine apart from most, including Platonist, Hegelian, Marxist, Rawlsian, and so forth, because other systems generally begin from a preconception of what would constitute a desirable *social* ideal, what a human *community* might be like at its best.[6] And that ideal generally requires the development of political conditions that accommodate what can happen only rarely, if ever, namely the presence of perfect human beings and no one else within a community. If indeed all people were born perfect, and with perfect knowledge, these ideals might be what would best constitute the legal organization of a society. A community of fully rational, absolutely just, honest, productive human beings—all of whom simply could not falter from constant virtue—is not one for which our legal system should be designed! That cannot even serve as a model, since the laws of such a system could not adequately deal with the plain fact of evil.

It should be noticed that most of these political theories require serious transformation in human *nature* before their ideal system can be implemented. This is because they require a sort of entity for which individual characteristics are entirely insignificant, where *only* being essential man matters. Marx needed to postulate "new man," as does B. F. Skinner. Hegel too looked forward to the ultimate realization of man's basic potential to reach his essence—in the ideal state, of course. None of the major statist political philosophers—Plato, Hobbes, Hegel, Marx *et al*—liked man! They all wanted a basic change in human nature itself and used the model of such a changed man to criticize existing human affairs. This itself points up the essential disregard for individual human beings in these theories, since they could not take seriously that, for the kind of thing man is, perfection is a matter of self-achievement, not species modification.

Because individual characteristics *are* significant, agents of a legal system, the government, cannot plan the perfection of the individuals of a society. Such perfection involves the particular features of the moral agents making moral decisions. The legal principles of a free society have to be based on those characteristics of persons that are had in common—on human nature. (These, contrary to what some ordinary language philosophers hold, need not be clearly revealed in all uses of the concept "person," nor need they be perceivable, sensible characteristics—one might have to identify them by a process of thinking, not just looking![7])

Only if the law is based on common aspects of persons can it be just, equal, universally implemented, and so on. On the other hand, the extra-legal principles of an ethical system, i.e., virtues pertinent to personal, private, individual conduct, have varied relevance; they have a different impact on different people's lives, depending on who they are and what they do. Personal moral values are *valid* for all people but have different *applications* for various individuals and groups, whereas the (proper) social principles which justify a legal system must be uniformly applicable by virtue of each social participant's membership in the human race. While the basic principles of community conduct—embodied in law—apply to everyone participating in community life, some people have no occasion to demonstrate either virtue or vice pertaining to some sorts of activities, so that courage or loyalty or some other virtue can have very little to do with their lives.

None of this implies the relativization of ethics—that one individual cannot know what is morally proper for another[8] or that different people (in different cultures, for instance) should abide by basically different principles of conduct. It only means that people are individuals with varying talents, aspirations, and histories, who can therefore be different rational animals with the capacity to choose. Friends, spouses, colleagues, and others near someone would have a good idea of what he should do, even if the person himself is negligent in learning of such facts. And governments could, in principle, find out what everyone should do—although just learning what that is would be a full time occupation. But to implement the appropriate edicts with equality and efficiency would be impossible: those doing the implementing would necessarily enjoy unequal status. Thus gambling laws prohibit taking private risks, yet the enforcement itself is a risk-taking endeavor.

For a free system there is a recognition of the need for political solutions as well as moral ones, but not a confusion between these. The present theory does not, as Stanley Cavell expressed it, "politicalize morality." The purpose of politics is to make the moral life possible, not to replace it with paternalism or a revolution in human nature itself. This regard for the individual is evident, e.g., in this theory's appreciation of the value of a pricing system in the market place, instead of a forced distribution system. In the former, variations in costs and prices exist by virtue of differences in the people who deliver and purchase goods and services, whereas opponents of the free market system generally complain about lack of equality in pay, working conditions, prices, wages, and so on within the market place. Individualism, taken seriously, implies diversity and difference, but not inequality. To identify such variations as inequality would imply that equality could be achieved in these areas, thus disregarding what is itself a fact of human nature: individualized circumstances, development, and so forth.

F. A. Hayek, the Austrian economist and student of Ludwig von Mises, stresses a point about the free market, the economic corollary of a free society. He has observed that the idea of a free society implies the recognition that many individual decisions can produce a systematic approach to the development of a culture—much better than centralized decisions might.[9] Unfortunately Hayek thought that the term "rationalism" best characterized the philosophical approach which gave backing to the centralized social system,[10] that the Enlightenment led many thinkers to propose centralized solutions to the problems of human beings in a society. Actually, rationalism itself has no clear implications for political theory; all it emphasizes is that problems can be solved. And this can support the idea that individuals can be rational *agents*, whereas dictators and governments (e.g., wage/price boards) cannot.

While in justifying a political system we must start from the more pervasive field of ethics, it may then seem unusual that it is law, the standards of political action and organization, rather than morality that has universal and equal application. However, in community life law pertains to everyone in a specific, narrow ("limited") respect, although without exception, whereas in life the correct ethical code has relevance to everything, including to how one ought to employ community standards, how one ought to act vis-à-vis the law. It is with reference to membership in a community that law has relevance and thus is universal; but it is with reference to living one's life that morality is of the utmost significance, even though its application will of course vary in accordance with enormous differences in people as the individuals that they are. To the extent that the principles of community life ought to pertain to everyone, they can only apply to aspects of human life we share, i.e., our nature as moral agents and the prerequisite for actualizing the capacity for morality, namely human liberty and its corollaries.

One of the recurrent criticisms of human rights has centered around the traditional claim that they are universal, absolute, and inalienable. Although I will return to this issue at a later point when considering specific objections to the thesis of the present work, for now I will simply make clear what it is about human rights that renders them such, i.e., what is the correct meaning of these terms when used in *this* connection.

Pointing out that human rights are universal means that all those who are human beings have these rights. They are all, universally, without (important, relevant) exception, the kind of entities for whom it is right to live in a human community where the conditions for moral life are acknowledged and secured. Everyone is entitled, by virtue of what is good for him by nature, to be treated in accordance with the principles at issue. The point of asserting the universality of such rights is, most often, to differentiate them from what have been called special rights, those which individuals may have by virtue of membership in some special group. For example, the rights of members of a club to use some facility; the rights of union members; the rights of stockholders in a corporation, and so on. None of these are universal human rights, even though they are rights of human beings. The universality of human rights is entailed by their being rights anyone in the class of human beings possesses simply because of that class membership and what that implies about community life. It is this point that can sensibly be made by employing the concept "universal" in the present context.

What about the absoluteness of human rights? Many philosophers have taken their characterization as such as a severe liability. But all it means is that *within the realm where such principles apply,* namely the realm of community life (designed to serve the moral purposes of everyone), they hold without exception, in any and all circumstances. I will have more to say about the implications that follow from this feature of human rights, e.g., what happens when it is simply impossible to secure the moral interests of everyone, as in some emergencies. Yet in interactions within the context of a human community, the human right identified above, for example, implies: each person ought indeed to be free to choose his course of conduct and none may (ought to) abridge it. This is to make clear that whatever noble purpose one may have for violating another's human rights, one ought not do so. Some believe, for example, that when the "nation's security" is at stake, the privacy of communication between a psychiatrist and his client is no longer covered by the human right to liberty or property. Or that when others are poor, the property rights of the rich do not apply. Or when a very sordid film is being shown the liberty of the owner and producer, as well as the liberty of the viewer, must be suspended. And we could continue. It is to make clear that these contentions are false that it is often argued that human rights are absolute, that the principles hold without exception for purposes of living in a human community.

In connection with the idea of "absolute" human rights it must be noted that the claim that it *must* refer to something final, timeless, or unchangeable about the principle in question is false. That charge will be cleared up when we consider the conception of knowledge that is being invoked in this work. For now it should be clarified that "absolutely true" or "absolutely applicable" does not mean true forever in this form, unrevisable, unchangeable, but only means that, *given what is known* of the subject matter, no rationally justified exception is conceivable.[11] And this is true of principles in the sciences, also. So the absolute human right to be free assures one that acting within one's own rights is always and equally defensible against others' interference, even when the particular action one takes may not be morally justifiable. It is the objection against others' aggression that is *always* justifiable in the social context.

What about the supposed inalienability of human rights? That pertains to whether someone could ever lose or give up his human rights, in the fashion that one can obviously lose or give up some special rights, say, to the use of the college library or to the receipt of benefits from a union. The idea is that no choice, either on the part of the person or of someone else, can deprive anyone of what is by nature his right. The obvious problem that comes to mind is: what happens when someone is put into prison, if it is not that his rights are being alienated? The answer is that if someone is punished for having violated another's rights—and this, directly or indirectly, is the only possible justification for punishment—this must be construed as the logical (moral) consequence of his own choices and actions. As Herbert Morris makes clear in his stimulating article "Persons and Punishment,"[12] every criminal (in the sense I have indicated above) ought to experience what is by right his, the consequence of his having violated the rights of another. In effect, the criminal is jailed by his own choice, in that he is jailed in line with the logical consequences of his own choice. Just as changing one's mind about a contract after signing it does not alter its implications, so not desiring going to jail does not change the objective consequences of one's actions. Thus freedom of choice is exactly what is being protected and preserved by sending a criminal to jail—that is what the choice to violate others' rights leads to, and each person should be free to experience the consequences of that choice.

Another problem case that is often raised in connection with the inalienability of human rights is whether one might not alienate his human rights by voluntarily entering into slavery. But this idea has no meaning; i.e., voluntary slavery is a contradiction in terms. A slave is, by definition, one who is controlled (fully or partially) against his choice and will. Yet it is argued that people could sell themselves into slavery by, say, asking ahead of time for payment that will relieve the suffering of a loved one, offering, for sale, themselves.

This kind of "sale" is indeed a strange one, because one party to the sale no longer exists after its conclusion! It is not something the seller has, but the seller himself that is sold, without remainder. But the conceptualization of this kind of "sale" is impossible; thus it cannot be communicated into law, into any form of implementable principle. Were the seller to vanish, i.e., "logically" vanish—be no longer his own agent but "the property" of another—the necessary conditions for a trade would not exist. It appears then that strictly speaking one cannot alienate one's human rights by "selling oneself into slavery," although one can, of course, pay a high price (e.g., lifelong service) for something. That would simply be a case of hiring oneself out for certain services, a trade that could be challenged in court or some other institution devised to arbitrate contracts. So long as the "slave" complied he would not be one, since he would not be subjugated—i.e., nonvoluntarily pressed into service. Once he resisted and challenged his case, he would have his human rights protected as anyone else, given that the society is one where human rights are acknowledged and implemented. If this were not the case, we could conclude that the society fails to adhere to the principles that a good human community requires. In neither case would it be accurate to say that someone's human rights could be alienated, only that they may have been violated, even systematically, by the legal system itself, as they certainly were and still are in many societies.

Political Liberty, Human Life, and Property Rights

In virtually any field of study there is the danger of treating some topic, as some are wont to say, too abstractly. The problem is that while identifying certain principles which apply throughout the range of the topic involved, it is difficult to keep bringing up the specific instances which will have to be understood in terms of the principle identified. Thus in the present discussion I have defended the claim that every person ought to be free to choose to conduct himself in his own life, but just how should we apply this principle to specific cases? Each case will, of course, exhibit its own complexities. Even citing some examples may not satisfactorily show the manner in which the principle is correctly applied. Examples occur in precise contexts; they have a history. It is virtually impossible, without distortion, to exhibit them for inspection in a setting such as the present one. Yet it is insufficient to deal with cases one by one, as if they were all part of a disjointed, unconnected universe of chaos; that is the point of having principles! Thus some relationship between the principles at issue and concrete states of affairs must be illustrated.

The most useful way to embark upon such illustrations will be to cite cases most people are familiar with. This way they can check out whether the context has been adequately put before them to serve the purpose of showing the application of the principles at issue. In the later portions of this book I will present a number of widely known, concrete political/social events and problems. By way of explaining these, the principles I have called human rights can be seen at work; or, alternatively, where they have been evaded and rejected, it will be possible to detect the consequences that ensue.

We can now return to the principle defended earlier and trace out some of its implications. First I will explore the meaning of the two crucial terms used in the statement of the principle, namely "life" and "freedom." By understanding these within the present context, it will be possible to trace out the implication of the human right to political liberty quite precisely. The discussion will then lead to the controversial issue of the human right to property (or private property rights). Exploring the reasons in support of this right will involve consideration of some common ideas on the history of capitalism. I will also examine why there exists a common prejudice against wealth and for poverty, such that the poor are generally thought to be deserving, the rich criminal. My central goal in this section is to show that pursuing wealth is good.

To repeat, here is what the principle at issue states:

> Each and every person ought to have the maximum freedom of choice and action in the pursuit of his own aspirations, in the conduct of his life.

Obviously one of the crucial concepts in this statement is "life." For in order to be able to apply the statement to specific cases, it is necessary that we can make clear what someone's ("his") life is.

Now the most obvious point to be made here is that life is a biological phenomenon. To live, something must have the capacity to cease living—it can die. While at certain levels it may not be simple to tell the difference between biological and chemical processes, in the bulk of cases no such problem exists, not at least for our purposes. And in such cases life is distinguished by reference to the fact that entities that are alive must generate behavior that will sustain their existence. Life, then, may be defined as the self-generated process of behavior that leads to the continued existence of some entity in a given form, namely so that it may persist in sustaining its own (kind of) existence. Most thinkers will hesitate to offer a clear definition of the concept "life." This is due, partly, to an awareness of the continual growth of our understanding of the phenomenon, and many believe that we cannot offer a definition of a concept unless we have understood everything about it.

Ayn Rand has shown why a definition can not require omniscience or finished inquiry about some topic.[13] Many other philosophers have recently identified the fallacy in that sort of demand, but most have not attempted to offer a clear alternative.[14] Rand, however, has. She has also ventured to offer a sound, up-to-date definition of the concept of life: "Life is a process of self-sustaining and self-generated action." This manages to capture the crucial, distinguishing aspects of the phenomenon of life, so that we can isolate it from among the other phenomena we encounter in reality. That, of course, is exactly what purpose a definition serves—to organize our awareness of reality, based on our gradual perception and understanding of its various facets.

The statement of the principle I have called the human right to political liberty mentions "his life," i.e., the life of some individual human being. As such, we are here making reference to the self-sustaining and self-generated activities of the kind of entities that human beings are.[15] As indicated earlier, human nature characterizes a living entity with the capacity to choose rational activity, and thus action. In identifying the kind of self-sustaining and self-generated action involved in the life of human beings we must recognize that man has the capacity to choose between living and dying. Persons, uniquely among living things, must *choose* to do that which will sustain life. That is to say, the self-sustaining, self-generated activity that is a human being's life must be initiated or chosen by the individual himself—at least at the more mature stages of his existence, once he is no longer a *dependent*. And, because of this characteristic, human beings must also choose to sustain their lives more or less well.

These facts, in turn, give rise to a further clarification needed to understand the principle of political liberty. Since a person requires knowledge to sustain his life, the choice at issue in the right to political liberty is just the choice we have been talking about in connection with morality. Each man must be free to choose to gain the knowledge and perform the actions required for his life,—i.e., if his life is to have the opportunity to be a good one, if he is to have the option between moral and immoral conduct, an option open to him by nature. The choice to learn, to judge, to evaluate, to appraise, to decide what he ought to do in order to live his life must be each person's own, otherwise he simply has no opportunity to excel or fail at the task. His moral aspirations cannot be fulfilled (or left unfulfilled) if he is not the source of his own actions, if they are imposed or forced upon him by others.

This brings up for consideration the concept of freedom or liberty. The meaning of the concept "free" in the principle at issue is (must be) restricted to absence of the restraint, interference, obstruction, intervention, and so on that human beings can perpetrate. Obviously we use the concept of freedom in other senses as well. We say, "I cannot get free of this tree branch that fell on my leg," or "I want to be free of this awful headache." Freedom from want, from dissatisfaction, from illness or other sorts of conditions can sometimes be achieved by getting people off our backs, so to speak. In other cases, however, these conditions have nonhuman origin and then are not involved in the freedom to which our principle makes reference.

Taken in the context of the present discussion, the freedom at issue is freedom to choose and act without having these obstructed by other people; the intervention at issue, in turn, is mainly physical or quasi-physical. Thus simply dissuading a person from doing some action is not to eliminate his freedom, since by virtue of the fact of man's fundamental capacity to choose his actions, each of us is ultimately free to reject others' advice. Even if we are what is called "gullible" or suggestible," the fact remains that it is crucially up to us that we will *yield* to persuasion, advice or suggestion. (I am aware, of course, of the millions of people who believe otherwise. I have already offered an argument for freedom of choice.[16])

While we now have some idea of what it means that everyone ought to live in maximum liberty, we are far from being able to identify what this would amount to in concrete circumstances. Some people believe that the freedom to choose to act involves freedom to do anything to anyone. Now this is clearly enough precluded from the present theory—for that would mean that not each person is free. Others will claim that freedom of choice must involve any action that does not *directly* involve another person. And by this they may mean another person's physical body. Thus when a person writes a song and another makes free use of *it* without the writer's consent, this is taken to be a proper exercise of freedom of choice. Then again it is frequently proclaimed that freedom of choice involves making use of anything one can lay a hand on, doing anything anywhere on the face of the earth. Thus some people believe that when an airline charges a fare for transporting a person from one place to another, that constitutes a limitation on the passenger's freedom of action! After all, if everyone ought to be free, that must mean free to take a seat on an airline without the imposition of a charge. Many people think that freedom of action is curtailed if one is forbidden to speak at a radio station, in some lecture hall, or on television.

It is evident, therefore, that the meaning of freedom of choice and action needs to be specified more clearly. For it is certain that the principle could not be true if *by acting on it,* most people would simply clash with others. In short, if by attempting to act on the principle, some people would be unable to even start out, then the principle cannot be correct. For here again we must remember that "ought implies can." If we want to show that each person *ought to* live in maximum freedom, we must also show that there is such freedom each person *could* enjoy. In other words the truth of our principle requires the *possibility of acting on it.*

No doubt if some people act in *violation* of the principle, then others will not be able to act on it. Thus if some are not free to live their lives because others impose force on them, the victims will not be able to act freely. But this does not prove that they *ought* not be free, for we have already noted that it is possible for others to *refrain* from imposing force. Thus the fact that they choose to act in violation of the principle does not mean that the principle could not be acted on—all it proves is that people *can* violate moral and political principles. And that is certainly no news to anyone!

What is thus important is whether by acting *in accordance* with the principle each person *could* be free to choose and act in pursuit of a good life (or a bad one, if that is what his choice amounts to, so long as this does not impose force on others). If despite strict observance of the principle, people would *inadvertantly* impose force upon each other, then the principle cannot be true. For then the statement that each person ought to be free would conflict with the consequence that only some people can be free. But since ought implies can, if each ought to be free and not each can be, then it cannot be true that each ought to be.

We must therefore see whether we can show that each person could be free to choose and act in the conduct of his own life without obviating the same freedom for others. The first clue in this inquiry will be the implications of the definition of human life as the self-sustenance and self-generation of initiated actions.

First to be noticed is that self-sustenance requires certain items, objects in nature that will sustain human life. People must initiate the actions that will lead them to identify and secure for themselves those things. From this alone we can learn the first pertinent fact: there must be some place where actions to sustain one's life will occur, and there must be some things that will sustain one's life. Thus the freedom of choice and action involved in maintenance of one's life cannot exist without the freedom to act in some place and in relationship to some things.

What this tells us is *crucial*. It cannot be true that each person has the human right to freedom of choice and action in conducting his own life, if it is not also true that each person has the human right to acquire place and things required for living. The moral life of each person implies the human right to liberty. The corollary of this right is that each person ought to be free to acquire things in nature. As Rand has explained this point, "Just as man can't exist without his body, so no rights can exist without the right to translate one's right into reality—to think, to work and to keep the result—which means the right to property."[17] Rand goes on:

> Without property rights, no other rights are possible. Since man has to sustain his life by his own effort, the man who has no right to the product of his effort has no means to sustain his life. The man who produces while others dispose of his produce, is a slave.[18]

This general but crucial fact is denied by most social and political theorists of our time. Locke, who developed the best case of his time for property rights, is widely dismissed as a mere mouthpiece of a biased propertied class. Whatever his motives, the position he outlined is still unrefuted. It is well expressed in the following passage:

> Though the earth and all inferior creatures be common to all men, yet every man has a property in his own person: this nobody has a right to but himself. The labor of his body, and the work of his hands, we may say are properly his. Whatever, then, he removes out of the state that nature hath provided and left it in, he hath mixed his labor with, and joined to it something that is his own, and thereby makes it his property. It being by him removed from the common state nature hath placed it in, it hath by his labor something annexed to it that excludes the common right of other men. For this labor being the unquestionable property of the laborer, no man but he can have a right to what that is once joined to, at least when there is enough and as good left in common for others.[19]

There are, unfortunately, many problems with Locke's view. For instance, it is not clear what he means by "labor." As John Hospers puts it, "Assuming that mixing his labor with something is relevant to his acquiring property rights of that something, how is one to determine what kind of labor, how much labor, the influence of this labor on others (e.g., whether welcome to them or not), is to count as making him the rightful owner of the thing in question because of the expenditure of this labor?"[20] In the following I will attempt to provide an alternative defense of property rights, one in which these difficulties might be resolved.

Historically, at least, the idea of a society organized in terms of the rights of individual human beings was closely linked with the idea of private property, capitalism, free enterprise, laissez-faire. Certainly the connection is not widely approved; many have denied it, and to date most people believe in the prospect of human rights without—even in disregard and violation of—property rights. John Maynard Keynes emphasized this in his book *The End of Laissez-Faire* (Hogarth Press, 1927), as have thousands of apologists for the welfare state. Nonetheless it seems worthwhile to attempt a demonstration of such an interdependence (now that the Soviets and their allies have begun to recognize it too!).

First we need to understand what is meant by the idea of property rights. There is much confusion about this, in part because nearly everyone who has been concerned with the issue has tried to show that nothing of the sort exists, i.e., that individuals should not be free to own goods and services, only collective bodies or states should, and that the institution of private property is therefore evil. From hard core Marxists to so-called nonideological welfare-state liberals—even including some modern conservatives—many intellectuals consider the institution of private property to be a weapon of class warfare, a provisional and limited legal device established by governments, or at best a crude means by which individual greed might be exploited for the benefit of social welfare. Property rights, in turn, are acknowledged via full legal recognition and protection only here and there in the world.

Even in the United States, where critics still confuse the mighty leviathan of the semi-welfare state with the capitalism of a free economic system, the right to own things is severely circumscribed by provisions for unlimited taxation, extensive public ownership (read: "government control of goods and services"), regulation of business of all sizes and kinds, and other strictures which favor the semi-democratic collectivism that exists, over the liberty of the individual to acquire and trade items and services voluntarily. Such intellectual leaders as John Kenneth Galbraith and Michael Harrington (of course many others could be mentioned) clearly favor the socialization of all wealth. Laissez-faire economics—the idea that government must (ought to) "let" business be conducted by traders, unhampered by politicians—is ridiculed. Yet the illusion permeates the air that free speech, free assembly, free artistic expression, and other liberties can be respected while the government increasingly controls all the productivity, trade and labor of human beings.

Many people associate private property with a picture of capitalism which is entirely distorted and obviously odious. This image of capitalism takes its foundation to (necessarily) be fierce, brutal, unlimited war (competition) among people, and, moreover, to be gained from only by those referred to by Marxist oriented commentators as the "propertied" class. As such, it is associated with what is called "social Darwinism," the belief that the principle of "the survival of the (physically) fittest" does and ought to govern the development of society, including individuals' chances for survival.[21] This idea is generally associated with the social philosophy of Herbert Spencer. Actually it is a simplification and distortion of Spencer's viewpoint, but the latter comes close enough in its explicit language to serve as a scapegoat. Thus *all* capitalistic notions are commonly assimilated to this crude picture—more akin in the end to the caricatures of, e.g., Charles Dickens' industrialists, than to the actual, historical entrepreneurs and businessmen who comprise the bulk of the capitalists in industrial nations. Accordingly, capitalism is seen as a system where anything and everything is permitted (by law and morality) in order to gain power and riches, and capitalists are envisioned as robber barons, warmongers, and other unseemly sorts who are entitled by the system to subvert both morality and law for their own (greedy) ends.

The language in which these notions are expressed may be more subtle, the theoretical analysis less "moralistic" and more "scientific." (Marx himself vacillated between the two in his *Das Kapital* with no attempt to demonstrate the viability of either for his own critical purposes.) The end product is the same in both cases: a free economy breeds evil; only a controlled system, where private ownership of items and services is limited or prohibited and the system kept in check by "rational" organizers from state office buildings, could achieve justice and welfare. From official textbooks in high schools and universities to television situation comedies and documentaries—and even newscasters' hip rendition of the daily news—the entire culture reflects this view of the situation. At its root, presumably, lies the idea of property, the individual's right to own things, to produce and trade them freely.

Even some advocates of a free market accept the view that "capitalism" means what it has come to mean at the hands of its critics and enemies. Thus they claim that capitalism could exist under a fascist or socialist political system, inasmuch as under these some people (bureaucrats) control massive capital. What with the bad press the term "capitalism" has received in the past century, one can sympathize with this strategy—why fight language that has bad connotations if you can perhaps change from one word to another and still defend what is of actual value, the free market? As a matter of fact, however, the concept "capital" is clearly wedded to "private property," and by accepting attacks on the former the value of the latter is undermined. Nor does the idea of "capitalism" succeed in being meaningful by allowing that fascist and socialist states can subsume a capitalist economy. It is the character of a fascist state to permit paper (legal) title to items and services while retaining full governmental power to regulate and distribute the actual items and services some are said to own (in law); and ownership in socialism is prohibited in all but the narrow area of something loosely called "personal" property. How the term "capitalism" could still apply is entirely mysterious!

It must be acknowledged that as capitalism emerged in human history it amounted to a mixed system involving elements of mercantilism, feudalism and capitalism. Those who held land and other valued items had not always acquired them by way of production and trade but by inheritance from others to whom the items were often bestowed by monarchs, the church, or other state or state-affiliated groups. Although this can explain some of the confusion about the precise nature of capitalism, the characterization even of early (mixed) capitalist economies is generally distorted. Few analysts understand that it was the *political* conditions by which freedom of production and trade became a real possibility for individuals and groups involved in making a decent life for themselves that constituted the *essence* of capitalism. Admittedly the eighteenth and nineteenth centuries were dominated by social and political philosophies that emphasized the economic aspects of society. Even John Locke's (in part) ethically inspired political philosophy did much homage to prevailing economic views of human behavior. This, however, was due to the prestige of (Newtonian) mechanics and science in general, not to the actual predominance of economic features.

In this connection I must mention that twentieth-century social science, including retrospective historical analysis of political and social conditions, is still dominated by (mechanistic) methodologies that assume human action to be fully determined by outside forces or inner drives. Thus even with updated knowledge of what more than less free market conditions and the concomitant political conditions did for the welfare of the citizens in industrial societies, the prevailing myth condemns capitalism, mainly because those observing the past rarely if ever consider how terrible the lot of most would have been without the elements of liberty that came to characterize the industrial nations. By keeping in mind only the hardship that existed side by side with the rise of capitalism historians have managed to omit from consideration *what might have happened* without a relatively free market, how badly the majority of the population might have lived without the opportunity to work for "capitalists."

Another problem worth noting here is that many people believe that there are *set* classes of people such that the capitalists comprise one, the workers another and the petty bourgeois yet a different one—variations depending upon how complicated one's Marxist "revisionism" has come to be. I want to warn that these segmentations of human communities are misleading. For example, we may have a society with sick people and healthy people, but it is an error to assume that those among the sick will stay among the sick, while the healthy will keep their position stable. It is only by way of a rather contorted Marxian analysis that people come to accept that a "worker" or "capitalist" must remain in his position forever. Thus the language of capital versus labor is born and the image of a society of warring factions gains wider and wider acceptance with little regard for either the historical realities (which contradict the view that members of one "class" must stay put) or the possibilities that implementation of a free society would open up. In the case of the latter everyone is a potential capitalist, a productive agent with the opportunity to create, acquire, and trade for valuable items and services, including money. There is, then, no separation between labor and capital; there is only a distinction between what people do—work productively—and what people achieve—wealth. A more realistic division reflecting a continuum (involving better or worse judgment and production) instead of two exclusive groups (or three or four) should emerge within the context of a dynamic, not static, human community.

Let me now return to the most crucial feature of the sort of human community I have been defending, namely the institution of private property. What is the nature of such an institution; what in fact, does it amount to? There are attempts in many a social or political theory to explain the nature of private property, but most of them avoid what I shall try to do here, namely, offer a moral justification of the system that includes the institution of private property as one of its essential features. So I want to look at the problem freshly.

The first question is this: What might justify the statement "A owns X"? Putting it another way, how could we prove the statement "X is mine (yours, ours, his, theirs)," where X is not a person or something on the order of my team, town, arm, dream, mother, and so on? What, at minimum, can we expect if it is indeed true that someone owns something? Let me start with a great clue. Norman Malcolm tells the following story about the philosopher Ludwig Wittgenstein:

When in very good spirits he would jest in a delightful manner. This took the form of

> deliberately absurd or extravagant remarks uttered in a tone, and with a mien, of affected seriousness. On one walk he "gave" to me each tree that we passed, with the reservation that I was not to cut it down or do anything to it, or prevent the previous owners from doing anything to it: with those reservations it was henceforth *mine*.[22]

Clearly Wittgenstein was here indicating, by contrast, what it means to own something, what owning something must be. The "reservation" cited is absurd precisely because it would render it meaningless to say that the tree then belongs to someone.

Indeed, if something does *belong* to a person, *he* will have the say about its use or disposal, while others will not. He, not others, *ought* to (be the one who will) have that say. But here we see clearly that we must have justification for such a statement of what ought to be done, who ought to do or not do something.

But any justification encounters a difficulty right off. Many people treat wealth (belongings, property) as if it simply *happened*. (To some it "happens," to others it does not!) Thus virtually all the currently popular discussions of poverty and riches—ranging from the loose, albeit finely expressed words of Galbraith to the carefully constructed arguments of professional philosophers such as John Rawls and Nicholas Resher—start by offering schemes for distributing the wealth that exists in a community. They hardly ever concern themselves, however, with the issue of *why* this or that person has wealth, nor why some person(s) ought to be given or seize the power to distribute wealth. In short, there is ample wisdom on schemes of distribution, but a paucity of thought on how anyone could be justified in engaging in that process.

It is the neglected issue of what justifies ownership and control of objects that theories of property rights have been meant to solve. Of course I am not saying that proposed theories have been flawless. Hospers' query shows this clearly enough concerning the views of the most famous property rights theorist, John Locke. On the other hand, opponents of the idea—those who argue that no one has any such rights or that people have them only with respect to a specified measure of selected goods—have done little to show why the use of goods and services ought to be directed by some body called the government or state. When attempts are made, they usually amount to the elaboration of a point which is unquestioned, namely, that the government may do anything it sees fit and/or can get away with, or that such bodies politic may do so because many people sanction it.

One reason that there is so much concern with distribution and its goal, and so little with justifying it as a means, is perhaps well stated in this passage from Herbert Spencer:

> The kinship of pity to love is shown among other ways in this, that it idealizes its object. Sympathy with one in suffering suppresses, for the time being, rememberance of his

transgressions. The feeling which vents itself in "poor fellow!" on seeing one in agony, excludes the thought of "bad fellow," which might at another time arise. Naturally, then, if the wretched are unknown or but vaguely known, all the demerits they may have are ignored; and thus it happens that when the miseries of the poor are dilated upon, they are thought of as the miseries of the deserving poor, instead of being thought of as the miseries of undeserving poor, which in large measure they should be. Those whose hardships are set forth in pamphlets and proclaimed in sermons and speeches which echo throughout society, are assumed to be all worthy souls, grievously wronged; and none of them are thought of as bearing the penalties of their own misdeeds.[23]

No doubt suggestions such as Spencer's as to an alternative conception will be met with scorn or suspicion. His characterization of the predominant attitude is well borne out by the evidence. For example, few prominent social critics chide the poor for wrongdoings, or would even entertain the notion. The courts are castigated for prejudice and lack of compassion toward those with little material means, whereas the wealthy are roundly condemned for any and every indiscretion and crime.

This is paradoxical, first of all, because in the one instance material well-being is considered a genuine and valid desire, even need, something which those who are poor ought to enjoy, while in the second it is considered a liability, at best, and a crime in itself, at worst. Secondly, the poor are thought to get into trouble only because they are poor—which they should not be, so what they do is excusable; the rich, in turn, are thought to do wrong *because* they have or pursue wealth, but this does not excuse them. Yet both cases are explained without regard for the individuals as persons with the responsibility to make moral decisions that resist simple acquiescence to emotions, upbringing, economic circumstances, and so on. In short, the bulk of our culture's critical commentators discriminate on the basis of material conditions, and in favor of those who have little. (In spite of the commonly revered idea that other than material wealth is what will make one's life happy—and more conducive to spiritual well-being.)

The entire approach whereby class membership (itself a muddled notion) is taken to determine a person's moral and legal culpability for misdeeds reeks of thoughtlessness.[24] Even if it could be shown that many of the poor have genuine excuses for misconduct and few of the rich do—a highly unlikely prospect—such data can have nothing to do with how one ought to approach individual cases, for the same reason that frequency of misconduct among members of some race, nationality, or ethnic group ought to have nothing to do with how one should then treat an individual of a particular background. But, of course, class consciousness—class discrimination, class hostility, ridicule and injustice—is now closer to being acceptable and tolerated, even encouraged (by quota systems, for example).

Once it is accepted that poverty equals suffering, and suffering is bad, it is but a stone's throw (easy but not necessarily legitimate) to the idea that anyone should make every attempt to alleviate poverty—even if it involves the violation of human rights. As a result even the most ardent supporters of free trade (enterprise) and capitalism (private property rights) tend to mitigate their support of political liberty when it comes to applying it to the liberty to acquire and own wealth. At certain stages, they say, the law should support the violation of human rights—when, for instance, the destitute, the sick, and crippled, the needy, and others who are thought to be deserving would seem to gain from it. Then of course, as with all principles that are systematically disregarded, the snowballs start rolling. Next we violate human rights to help the artists, the unemployed, the scientifically significant, the beautiful, to further moon missions, science and industry and, of course, education, symphony orchestras, public broadcasting ventures, and on and on. At the end of the road looms a total state. Recall what John Ehrlichman (one of those associated with the federal government's most powerful center, the White House, and with the authorization of what might include burglary,) said about whether "national security" justifies violating the privacy of the therapist/client relationship. He said that such powers belong to the presidency. And when Senators Ervin and Talmadge protested that our legal tradition holds a man king in his own castle, Ehrlichman remarked with acute precision: "I am afraid that has been considerably eroded over the years, has it not?"[25] Indeed it has—what with "Blue Laws," trade restrictions, "no-knock laws," censorship ordinances, and numerous similarly legalized violations of human rights, the case is simple to demonstrate. (How outrageous it was to see the Watergate Committee senators, many having voted "yea" on laws in this category, aghast at Ehrlichman's remarks.)

In noble words there are few who do not pay homage to liberty, justice, fairness, honesty, privacy, and the like. But implementation of a principle requires consistent, sustained commitment, not lip service. Part of the reason for a lack of such commitment may be that people are genuinely confused, they do not know the relationship between liberty and private property. Unfortunately the case for these is often kept out of circulation. Not because it is weaker than opposing cases, although considering the kind of ideas that are taken seriously these days, weakness itself could not have much to do with the neglect, even if the case were a bit problematic. Rather than being weak, it is perhaps less thoroughly argued by traditional theorists than the case for other rights. Those like myself, however, who contend that the case can be had, that we ought to be free to acquire, own, use, and dispose of items and services—from trees to pharmaceutical formulas to musical compositions, to just simple time—will hopefully resist capitulation. That could only spell doom for our personal integrity and well-being, as well as the best kind of life possible to people in human communities.

I have thus far been dwelling on some confusions which lie in the way of or distract attention from understanding the notion of property. But we need to return to the question: what justifies the statement "A owns X"? For even if no one were to reject in principle and action the institution of private property, in particular cases conflicts can arise concerning who owns what; these ought to be resolved by applying a theory (a political system) with the provision that private property rights foster the prospects for human good in a community. Obvious examples of such conflicts are claims in connection with homesteading, staking out mines, catching fish, using water, polluting air, inventing some device, writing novels, and so forth. Far more complex situations of claims and counterclaims give rise, of course, to more complex justifications for what belongs to whom. So we need to see how, in general, one must justify such claims.

One favorite pseudoconcept that will not do is that everything or even something belongs to everyone, to all at one and the same time. It won't do for several reasons, but mainly because the idea must lead to the absurdity Wittgenstein's "gift" to Norman Malcolm illustrates. It simply makes no sense whatever to say that I own the moon vehicle that the astronauts used, or that you and I and all of us own Lake Erie—however much collectivists *wish* to make such notions seem sensible. Just how someone or some of us could own these items may not be crystal clear at all times; for one, we need to discover ways of ownership as different types of things become available for it. (One reason, incidentally, that Marx could renounce private property in that in his future communist society there would be such abundance that everyone could have anything he needed and wanted—i.e., everything would be what economists call a "free" good, such as clean air used to be.) It simply will not help to dismiss the task of learning how something might be owned with the announcement (or Congressional *declaration,* as in the case of the electro-magnetic spectrum in 1927) that all of us or "the public" or the nation owns it. Saying it does not make it meaningful, for that requires that it can be implemented in actual, dynamic, complex human societies. It is like trying to square circles; it will not work. The reason is clear if we consider the purpose of ownership, as already explained.

What might work is to consider the matter in a simple form. A person roaming around in the wilds of prehistoric times may not know what ownership is. He may have done nothing to institute or protect the practice of ownership. But after a while we can learn how it *should* be discussed, even in connection with his prehistoric situation. Imagine that as he roams he *decides,* at some point, to make use of some object—a branch or stone or bird of paradise (if we transport him to Hawaii). It does not work, so he drops the thing, but another one he picks up does do the job he *wants* done. That job may be anything at all—scratching himself, building a fire, covering himself, quenching his thirst; it makes no difference. So now, our "wild" human being—for that is what we are talking about, not apes or giraffes—*takes* this item, pockets it, or at least puts it under his arm. Then he wanders some more and returns to the enclave where he has made a shelter. He puts down this thing he decided to employ for his purposes, and he goes to sleep.

Another of our pals comes along and from some distance spots our sleeping friend, as well as the item just brought into the dwelling. This newcomer too *wants* to employ the item. Sneaking up carefully, he *takes* it and disappears. Upon awaking the original user takes notice and tracks down the silent visitor. Again, knowing the danger of risking too much, he waits, and when dark sets in he retakes the item, or at least a good enough replacement of it, returns to his cave or whatever, and starts *thinking* about how to avoid such trouble the next time. That is, provided he is acting as he should! He may, of course, evade the fact that this has lost him considerable time and effort, has shortened his productive life.

At any rate, we want to know what happened in the above case. Perhaps the way the case is set up will seem objectionable. For this looks suspiciously like the "state of nature" discussions many philosophers have used before and many others have, in turn, found unrealistic. There *is* a problem with talking about cases so far removed from our times, as well as with describing them in a way that does justice to the fact that they occurred prior to the use of those concepts we are likely to employ to think about them, concepts with only a recent history.

Nevertheless, as Locke was among the first to realize, understanding what human nature requires in a social context may presuppose an analysis of human nature and conduct independent of that context. Only extreme empiricists will maintain that we cannot do this, since our evidence for what man is comes from encountering him *in* society. But we are not extreme empiricists and it is not true that their approach will best handle our attempts to gain knowledge. So we can distinguish between man among men and man on his own. This is because we can isolate man *in thought,* not unlike the way we can isolate electrons, shapes, colors, and days in thought, despite the fact that all these occur in reality in the company of and attached to other things. Where would mathematics, geometry, or physics be if it were required that the objects they study be regarded in a strict empirical-naturalist-realist fashion, only as we find them before we have come upon them with our ability to make distinctions and sometimes even to separate them from their natural surroundings?

So it seems important to start with such simple cases, not because history records them or they actually occurred, but because they could have occurred, quite like the example above would have it. And it is a simple enough case. We need not handle questions such as where these people come from, have they a tribe or country of their own, obligations that may have tainted the situation, and the like. We have before us the essentials of something that could have happened, and now we must understand it in terms of certain general ideas we have previously found valid for discussing human life.

Earlier I argued that people ought to (choose to) use reason for purposes of discovering how to live and how to do so with as much success as possible. Our wanderer seems to be living up-to this moral requirement. He did use his mind; he decided (chose) to make use of some item in nature so as to live, to do what was needed or what he wanted to do in order to contribute to the achievement of the general goal that has been identified as proper for all human beings. He made the mental effort to identify some object and use it for his purposes. Perhaps he erred in what he thought would result from his action; but it was the best he could do, so he did it. At this point the concern is not whether there are instances of such decisions of acquisition that may turn out to have adverse consequences—even if not merely via honest error but through outright negligence, e.g., when one acquires some uninspected food item. (By the morality of ethical egoism, if the purposes are either erroneously conceived or thoughtless and wrong-headed, it is more than less likely that the person will experience adverse consequences.) Our concern is whether the kind of activity we know as acquiring and holding items—i.e., the institution of private property—is good for people in general, *qua* institution, not *qua* all the possibilities it allows for, including abuse.

And we see that human beings can, if they keep up their policy of rationality, achieve self-beneficial purposes by the choice to obtain and keep items. The action to obtain items and to use and dispose of them can be good for man. One's choices in relation to such options as exist in nature and in society regarding acquisition can be better or worse (one can even be negligent in not choosing to take advantage of certain opportunities—thereby evidencing irresponsibility in the satisfaction of one's proper goal of success in life). As such, actions that contribute to acquiring things are one kind of action among those that constitute living a morally good life. (It should be noted that what will contribute to self-sustenance is not exclusively "work by the sweat of one's brow." As the saying goes, "man does not live by bread alone"; thus production, trade, creativity, and the like are included in *acquisition* for the purposes of living a successful human life.) Interference with these constitutes the obliteration of a person's moral capacity, and it is in the interest of every person to secure measures against such interference.

Our simple case illustrates that human well being requires that individuals choose to obtain what can benefit them. *Acquiring valuables is good.* Obviously when we import the conception of the above simple case into the complicated and historically dynamic case of contemporary human communities, the description will be far more complex, involving knotty and often baffling interrelations of first owners—people who acquire some item yet unclaimed by others—and *n*th owners—people who acquire items offered in trade, bequeathed, or otherwise provided for selection by those in the community—and groups of *n*th owners—corporations, families, partnerships, and so forth. The matter of entrepreneurship (thoughtful selection of courses of conduct by which value may be generated) becomes more significant and widely crucial in a complex society, but the basic moral principles that call for and should govern those involved do not change because of complexity. (Here note the error of the labor theory of value and property rights, incidentally. As James Sadowsky explains, "the owner of property performs an entrepreneurial function. He must predict the future valuations that he and others will make and act or not act accordingly. He is 'rewarded' primarily, not for his work but for his good judgment."[26] The point about entrepreneurship is a moral one: it is rational selfishness which justifies the private property system. Conservatives like Irving Kristol (in his "Capitalism, Socialism and Nihilism," *Public Interest,* Spring 1973) should consider the following: a person who values doing business ought to (and will if he has foresight) value the conditions of doing business, and the conditions of living well, namely morality. Thus, as Kristol's critic Roger Donway explains, "There is . . .no point in a trade whose very terms destroy those preconditions. And for that reason, a trader cannot set any price on the suicide of his soul."[27] It may be that people do commit moral suicide in free markets—as under other economic and political arrangements—and might even trade away their freedom, as some people in business do when they foster governmental interference. But that is not the consequence of living by the ethical code upon which the principles of a free society and free market rest. It is quite the opposite of that.)

From the above considerations it is best to conclude that to create property, to acquire items for use and holding that contribute to one's well-being and happiness, is good. From this it follows that the conditions that make this possible are also good. We have thus far been dealing with only one owner, except in some of the parenthetical remarks which served to make the points more familiar to what we are concerned with in contemporary human communities. To see the implications for such expanded cases we need more work.

In our example we had two people, both of whom made the choice to use and control something; but the first individual had already acted when the second made his decision. When we considered that the first person would, indeed should, have thought of a way to protect against constant trouble with another taking what he chose to possess (from unpossessed nature), we noted that he would thus have abided by the correct moral point of view. Let us see whether the second person also acted as he should have. The purpose of choosing to possess the item in question would be to enhance one's welfare and happiness. This is true for both people. Does the second one in fact achieve that purpose—one we grant that he ought to make attempts to achieve—by taking the item from the other? It is not good enough to argue that the choice to take the item is wrong because it con- stitutes theft. "Theft" is a characterization that assumes that it is true that someone ought to have exclusive use and control over some items, i.e., it presupposes the institution of private property. But we are now trying to establish that this institution is justifiable, we are trying to show that "A owns X" is on occasion true. In which case someone other than A taking possession of X without A's agreement would be theft (barring mitigating circumstances that could arise, of course). Yet if both "A owns X" and "Not-A owns X" can be true at the same time—i.e., both the first and second person ought to have exclusive possession of the item in question—then, recalling Wittgenstein's absurd case, ownership is impossible. From "ought implies can," we must conclude that if both those claims could be true, then no one ought to acquire anything, since no one *can* own anything. Our case must fall apart unless we can defend that, once "A owns X" is true, "Not-A owns X" must be false, i.e., someone other than A ought not possess X (unless, of course, voluntarily acquired, which is implicit throughout this discussion).

To defend this we must show that if another person owns something, then one's welfare or happiness will less likely benefit from taking than from not taking it (and pursuing some alternative, e.g., buying, creating, substituting for the item in question). It is clear that if "crime pays," one finds it difficult to imagine how it could be shown that it would be bad for the offender. The act of crime—in this primitive case a "natural" (moral) crime, not a legal one—cancels out the alternative of not committing it. We thus get into the difficult area of identifying what might have been: what the offender does not know he cannot miss. If he does not know what he might have gained by honest work or trade, he will not miss it, not at least consciously. But these considerations are crucial for our purposes—it is not enough just to focus upon what can and would happen by taking the item—we must examine what could be better by not taking it and doing something else. There are several reasons which support the institution of ownership from the point of view of someone who has the option to take from another or produce on his own (including by trade, of course).

First of all, the opportunity for cooperative contact with others will be lost with the act of taking from another what he has honestly and/or voluntarily acquired (i.e., chosen to use and control from nature or from willing traders or bequeathers). Second, as a human being each person benefits from consistent thinking and acting, since the form of awareness of reality suited for people is best maintained when those are performed consistently. By taking from another in the fashion being considered, one is acting as if the institution of ownership were wrong for that other person, while at the same time right for oneself. If "A owns X" *must* be false, then if A is the same kind of being as Not-A, then "Not-A owns X" cannot be true either—inasmuch as both are fundamentally justified by reference to those aspects of the case that A and Not-A share, namely their human nature. Taking from A, Not-A is endorsing a contradictory statement (belief or view) about human life which must, so to speak, subvert his thinking about reality. (Which is not to say that people cannot do this—contradictions can be *thought* and *said*, mainly because, while they cannot exist, being said *in time* the elements which contradict each other *can* be kept conceptually apart.) So the offender, even if never pursued, will at least suffer some confusion between what is real and what is not real—akin to what pathological liars face in their personal lives. And since this confusion is bad for a person, it ought to be avoided.

Next we must consider that although people must have items and services by which to secure the well-being and happiness that is their proper goal, nature as well as the market contain these in an amount that is at each period of time limited. With many people around some process of "rationing" is necessary, one which should not leave the rationing in the hands of a select group; that is to say, a scheme of forced distribution puts other people in an unjustified position of rule over oneself (or vice versa). The basis of distribution that does not require a rule/ruled relationship among people is the principle of prior acquisition (choice, decision, discovery, invention) of the item or service that can have value for someone (just for himself or to others as well, through trade).

What we have now is that ownership is a morally appropriate institution for human beings in general. And its prevention by people, who could refrain from doing so, is wrong. In certain cases it could turn out through "luck" that some thief—for we have now established that the offender is a thief (or unjustified intruder when acting unintentionally, even by accident)—never suffers any adverse consequences. But it is clear from the moral conclusions already established that to rely on *his* own work (and/or trade, creativity, ingenuity, etc.) is better for the person than to live off the work of others (who are not willing to share), i.e., to steal or confiscate. It may *appear* that thieves are well off when they have succeeded in their theft. But this is because few people consider what might have happened instead of theft, what thieves might have had the opportunity, and ought to have chosen, to achieve. Too many defenders of parasitism make it appear that human beings cannot help the circumstances they face, that theft is (always, for them) the only alternative to turn to. (I am not talking about cases where honest production has become virtually impossible through prior and unremedied violation of human rights.) Yet even in the most dire situation a potential thief could *ask* for help—he might actually get on the phone and call people he does not even know, or make a flat-out trade with someone, sell his future assets, and so on. These alternatives—and they come to mind by the hundreds in each example—can only be brushed aside by denying ·that the individual involved has the capacity for choice, to activate his own mind and limbs, to explore alternatives to theft and act on them. But in fact this is what thieves ought to have done instead of what they did do!

Now in earlier arguments for property rights also, the starting point was often that people need things to live and to live well. Hobbes interpreted this in a rather mechanistic way by saying that we are all driven—by passions, the fear of death, and the instinct to survive—to do things, take what there is in nature, use it, and so on. Locke was not so clearly an exponent of this kind of theory of human action, although as Strauss indicates (even if too persistently) Locke too relied on some type of natural or innate desire to explain the value of property.[28] Few defended private property *rights*, and when they did, it was not with any *moral* justification.

The above is likely the consequence of a predominantly (and popularly acceptable) deterministic analysis of the kind of case I described earlier and treated in terms of a moral principle. When one wishes to justify a human action or policy or institution, this is different from offering some kind of mechanistic or semiphysiological, semipsychological, semihistoricist explanation of it. And if the intellectual defense of property rights rests in the end on such a deterministic analysis, it certainly lacks *moral* support. Even while Locke and others tried to associate the institution with other conditions necessary for morality—political liberty, for instance—they did not see their way through to justifying acts of acquisition, the creation of property, as something good and right for man. They only attempted to provide a justification for *the liberty* which would make such acts possible.

The prominent *moral* point of view in most cultures, even during the rise of political liberty in the age of revolutions and capitalism, has usually been some form of altruism, the doctrine that each person ought to choose to do good *for others* (i.e., this is seen as the *basic* moral virtue, with duties, obligations, love, and kindness as central to the moral codes in point). In such a climate "selfishness" and greed are central vices, and a *moral* justification of the choice to acquire things, of private property or ownership, becomes laughable or highly suspect to most people. Some defenders of the present point of view have always existed—some have argued that one is morally responsible to strive for happiness in his life. But those who believed, either in some misguided sincerity (I should *like* to consider it), or through self-deception, or with exploitation in mind, that all men must live for the good of others, went to work fast indeed, just when the idea of private property rights was in its formative stages. Capitalism is *the* most misrepresented, harangued, and despised political economy ever, if numbers make a difference. Nevertheless, in some ways it is also the most revered one, not by so-called superpatriots or capitalists (read: "businessmen or the wealthy"), but by millions who have deliberately chosen to live where it is the dominant political/economic way of life.

I do not think it unfair to say that whatever one might think of the philosopher/novelist Ayn Rand, she is perhaps the first widely read (chiefly outside of academia) thinker who has defended capitalism as morally right because human beings can work (trade, create, risk) for their own good only when and where it prevails. (Some, of course, might say this is a false belief, even after we have gotten this far. But no one can deny that Rand does advocate capitalism on moral grounds, i.e., that it is a system that is good for human beings, morally good for them, to choose for themselves.)

Nevertheless, it sometimes is important to shed additional light on the topic from so called value-free (efficiency) frameworks, the vantage point of economically oriented defenders of the free market. I will not go into this defense, but will point out its inadequacies in the face of the *moral* theories commonly pressed into service to condemn capitalism. One cannot ultimately justify a basic human institution—a socioeconomic system—by reference to such criteria as "workable," "useful," "efficient," and so forth. Man's nature as a moral agent requires justification for his actions, institutions, and policies on the basis of what is right and good. Only *then* can we determine what will work best to achieve it, what is most efficient or useful for that purpose! This is not to lessen the worth or scientific validity of the conclusion that capitalism is the most efficient system of economic organization—i.e., that free trade is how people can best and most efficiently attain ends that are desired (as well as morally justifiable, where this issue arises). The good (the objectively good, not just anyone's idea of it) is indeed best pursued in freedom.

And this is where a purely economic defense can have nothing to say. Freedom will not be a good political condition, e.g., for those who want to enslave people, for *that* purpose, more specifically. Political liberty, the equal right of free choice and action in one's conduct, including in one's economic conduct, is useless for purposes of forcing others to do one's producing, inventing, creating, and so on. Thus any who have such purposes will not consider the free market useful, workable, efficient. This despite the economist's claim that the free market does everything most efficiently.

The kinds of issues taken up in this chapter show how the present theory gives support to human rights and the right to private property. I have identified human rights and given reasons why they ought to be protected and preserved. It may appear that the argument in the latter case is of the value-free variety, the one just mentioned. But this is not so. The institution of private property is not just useful, but useful for a primary moral purpose—i.e., the pursuit of each individual's happiness. When "property" is broadly understood, as used here, it is right for everyone!

Let me now conclude the topic of human rights. I have defended the right to liberty, and a corollary right to property—one which is the primary practical expression of the former political right—both of which should be accepted once the right to liberty is understood as the principle that each person ought to be free to choose to think and act to conduct his life successfully, to be happy.

The justification of the human right to political liberty has been in terms of a theory of morality presented earlier. But I want to point out now that any moral point of view which accepts the definition of man I have stated (i.e., as essentially free and rational) would be compatible with the human right to liberty. Even more strongly, it must be the case that to be moral in any way requires the protection of that right. Of course this does not mean that any moral point of view could give adequate justification for political liberty. But if all moral conduct must be chosen, and if each person should conduct himself morally, then no person should be obstructed in his freedom to choose. In this sense any moral point of view is compatible with human liberty of choice and action. To the extent that anyone is dutybound to act to serve goals other than those related to personal happiness, in a free society none could be prevented from doing so. But, of course, no one would be permitted to coerce others to this end.

In addition, one good way of making such pursuits possible is by ensuring that each person can clearly delimit his sphere of action, i.e., by protecting his ability to do with his property and himself as he chooses—again provided he leaves others and their goods intact. Communists, fascists, and all others will then be able to advocate, Christians pray, lovers love, transcendental meditators transcend—except all on their own time, in their own territory, and at their own cost, or through voluntarily attainable means.

But it is clear that alternative moral philosophies which are compatible or even require it cannot give support to political liberty all on their own. They are mistaken to the extent that they deny that each person should choose to live his own life to the best of his ability, with success.

Some other principle that they might profess as equally or even more crucial will conflict with this one, and thus undermine the support given to political liberty and to private property. This is why the intellectual defense of the free society has for the most part been relatively weak: the result of contradictory premises, one derivable from that identified here, the other from its opposite, (in the main) has been vacillation between integrity and compromise of liberty. Thus when one believes that it is the first duty of each person to serve society or others or the public interest or God or future generations, the prospects of depriving others of their liberties in pursuit of some "noble" goal will appear too minor a wrong to forego.

The present moral point of view holds that the only social or common good that is justifiable is political liberty and what it implies. Only this is good for each one in a social context because of what he or she is—a human being. This is the only rationally justifiable, truly *common* good. The good or just society is one in which the human right to political liberty is protected and preserved. Living in society is beneficial because everyone cannot do everything; so it is in their interest for people to opt to cooperate, trade, compete, and otherwise productively interact with each other. Because of this fact they can justifiably insist that anyone not so cooperative, i.e., willing to violate human rights, be checked, that they not profit from such acts, even be punished, penalized for doing so when this can be proven.

Of course in a civilized, sophisticated society the violation of human rights as well as their respect and exercise can be manifested in multitudinous ways. But taking such complexity into account is not unique to law. Principles, definitions, categories, classifications, and so forth are all identified means by which people can organize a complicated yet ultimately intelligible world. To do so, in turn, effectively, competently and with commitment to the goal of knowledge, understanding, and happiness, requires of a person first of all a diligent and sustained effort to think. The choice to exert this effort, to initiate acts of rationality, is the basic and most morally worthwhile choice anyone can make. If not made, nor carried out as a policy, however, a person's life and the culture in which this is pervasive will reflect it. Not always fatally—people can live in limbo, linger on midway, closer to and further from the best they are (or would have been) capable of doing. Nor is it widely agreed what would be the results of each person's choice to deal with the world rationally, always, throughout waking life. What appears to be a sensible, warranted characterization of this ultimately Greek ideal is related eloquently by Leo Straus:

The good life simply, is the life in which the requirements of man's natural inclinations are fulfilled in the proper order to the highest possible degree, the life of a man who is awake to the highest possible degree, the life of a man in whose soul nothing lies waste.[29]

And fully understood, the implication of this ideal for community life may best be understood as follows:

[P]olitical freedom, and especially that political freedom that justifies itself by the pursuit of human excellence, is not a gift of heaven; it becomes actual only through the efforts of many generations, and its preservation always requires the highest degree of vigilance.[30]

There is no guarantee that people will take advantage of what is good for them, even of a good social system, should one ever be established. After all, political liberty is what a good system must protect precisely because people can *choose* to live a good human life. They can thus refrain from so choosing; they can misuse their freedom and lead lives without others' miseries inflicted on them but plenty inflicted by themselves. Yet the probability of people taking advantage of what is good for them is greatest when political circumstances (e.g., the legal system) themselves prevent the consequences of self-inflicted, even unavoidable misery from being imposed upon others, to be assumed and paid for by those with their own goals to pursue. (This is not to say that help should not be given, or even that it cannot be something *morally* due another; but it is to say that political authority should not be legitimized to enforce such charity.) A political system with the appropriate legal provisions identified in accordance with the principles of human rights will encourage the development of moral life, since it cannot reward an immoral one; it cannot even foster it except by error and abuse, and by the consent of those who want to carry that burden.

We are now entitled to conclude that there are human rights and that they ought to constitute the foundations of a human community's legal system. The particular means by which natural rights, the moral basis of a good legal system, relate to the specific features of a working legal code will not be considered here except by implication. Suffice it to note that the positivist claims about the nature of law are rejected by the present analysis—laws cannot be valid without some recourse to correct moral principles; order itself is not sufficient for law; justice too must be attempted by a legal code in order to have validity. But one will have to look elsewhere for a good defense of the natural law position against positivist attacks.[31] My present task is to discuss the idea of government that is consistent with the theory of rights presented thus far.

CHAPTER 5

The violation of a written *law moves us to indignation but the violation of unwritten law cannot arouse us* institutionally. *We have come, corporately as a people, to hold the proposition that justice equals statute.*
                                        Frederick D. Wilhelmsen

Government
and Human Rights

The Anarchist Thesis

IN the discussion of the nature and justification of human rights we found that the principles which constitute the rights in question ought to be instituted within a human community. We saw that such institution would involve adherence to a legal system applicable to all members of a community, founded on the principles in question. In the face of the evident possibility of their violation, some means should be established by which the moral interest of members of a community is protected and preserved, that is, by which political liberty and its maintenance can be ensured.

Before I embark on outlining the sort of means by which this purpose is best achieved, it will be necessary to consider some arguments to the effect that even a legal system designed to protect and preserve human rights may not ever employ coercion. The arguments which purport to show this emerge from what are generally called anarchist doctrines. "Anarchy" means "no rule." More broadly, the term indicates a doctrine or system in opposition to the establishment of government. Once the arguments of certain anarchists have been met, the constructive portions of the present topic will be developed.

My aim here is not to discuss all types of anarchism. I am not sure some of them are intelligible—for example, leftist and Marxist-oriented anarchists advocate that all property be held communally or collectively but that no government should exist to keep people from running away with some of it! Anarchocommunism is, at best, a vision; it depends on the idea or faith that humanity will someday develop into a *different species,* one whose members will do everything "right," automatically, in an environment of full abundance, with no scarcity. If that were possible then, indeed, the purpose of government and law could no longer make sense—there would certainly be no need to protect and preserve human rights and legal justice: it would happen anyway, automatically.

So one reason for not discussing this form of society is that from what I can understand, there is no room for human beings in it. Clearly my aim has been to solve a problem facing people now, to argue for a society that is right for human beings, not for some species that may or may not evolve once people have vanished from the universe. I will later make some response to Marxist criticism of human rights theory, but it is not worth discussing the Marxist variety of utopian anarchism. (It is utopian in the sense that what it promises for some type of creatures is not something that can be held out to human beings with any expectation that the promise might be fulfilled. At any rate, there is no rational reason to anticipate the realization of Marxist communism while there are *human beings* who ought to find the best form of community life for themselves.)

The sort of anarchism worth discussing in our context is one that argues against the institution or establishment of governments on the ground that this would be immoral. Three different versions of this argument have recently (re)emerged. The first concludes that the fact that people are moral agents renders it morally impossible to authorize others to perform tasks which a government must perform. The second argues that governments *must* violate human rights. The third contends that the moral principle that each of us ought to choose to further our own interest precludes that some agency protecting human rights should be established, since acting to further one's interest must sometimes lead to the violation of other people's rights. With each of these I will deal only briefly.

The first argument was developed by Robert Paul Wolff in his book *In Defense of Anarchism* (Harper and Row, 1970). It is a rather complex position developed along the lines of some theses of the important eighteenth-century German philosopher Immanuel Kant. I shall simply outline the position.

The idea is that man is a moral agent because he is both capable of choice and rational. The former renders him responsible for his actions, the latter puts him in a position of being able to abide by or neglect moral principles. So far the position resembles the one I have presented considerably, although in details there are serious differences. For example, for Wolff it is not clear whether the process of reasoning—thinking—is what is fundamentally open to choice. It is more likely that he believes that choice consists only in *selection* from among alternative courses of overt-action. But this difference will not be crucial in the present context.

From the fact of man's moral agency Wolff deduces that each person is morally autonomous just in case everything he does is the direct consequence of his own judgment. Any course of action done as a result of a command constitutes a relinquishing of one's moral authority and autonomy. One simply *cannot* delegate either of these to others. At best, one's moral autonomy and authority may be abnegated (not exercised), never delegated, for the latter is an active denial of one's moral nature. It undermines human nature at its roots.

Now, as several commentators have already observed, once Wolff's idea of autonomy and its necessity for morality is granted, it is a smooth ride toward the denial of the possibility of government and political authority. If only individuals may determine what they ought to do, *and* if delegating to another the right to issue commands or edicts which will circumscribe what one should do cannot be but a denial of one's moral nature, then *any* administration of a legal system *must* be morally objectionable. Thus Wolff recognizes no form of government, no legal arrangement for the organization of social life, as even remotely capable of moral justification. He specifically rejects any form of democracy as a means by which law might be established and administered.

One reason Wolff's thesis is important for us is that it expresses a position which might be taken to follow from one put forth in these pages. And there are similarities, as mentioned before, that are worth noting. I have argued that it is indeed individual human beings whose choices and actions are good or evil, right or wrong. How might it be possible, then to rightfully leave to others even a limited number of decisions in however narrow area of human life? On the face of it Wolff's argument would seem to preclude the moral justifiability of any form of legal authority, authority that can have a bearing on the conduct of one's own life.

In response let me explain first that Wolff's argument might be valid against any form of legal authorization to prescribe conduct having no bearing on the lives of others, private conduct that does not unavoidably involve others. Thus even so-called representative democracy falls short of moral justifiability when it comes to such issues. Usually what is known as representative democracy is unlimited in its jurisdictional authority over the actions of the members of some human community. This differentiates such a democracy from one where the democratic method is restricted to limited purposes—e.g., the selection of administrators—and a majority does not have the authority to change (or have changed) the basic constitutional principles of a legal system.

But in response to Wolff's wider thesis, when government is viewed as a hired agent, on the analogy of a doctor, psychologist, teacher, or one's "power of attorney," it does not necessarily imply that its commands deprive a person of his moral autonomy and authority. In such a form of government the administrators have a job to perform that may involve some but not any *type* of command. Thus the kind that a policeman of such a system may issue—i.e., is explicitly authorized to issue—is limited to commands that protect and preserve human rights. A policeman under a legal system which implements the principles of human rights is authorized to issue only defensive commands. So long as a citizen does not choose to act in such a way that he involves another unavoidably (whether intentionally *or* inadvertently), or so long as someone or some group does not choose to act (or embark upon policies, organize institutions, and so on) in ways that are reasonably identifiable as constituting a clear and present danger to others, the administrators of the legal system are usurping their authority by commanding them or forcing compliance with their orders. In short, governmental authority can be morally proper only when strictly limited to the protection and preservation of human rights. As such, the government is bound to act morally, in the capacity of a hired guard and respondent to criminal injustice.

Wolff cannot object to someone who obtains help in his attempt to retain his moral autonomy, i.e., his *authority* to choose his own course of conduct, to exercise control over his own actions. Should others act so as to pose a clear threat to or actually obstruct this authority, protection is justified. And the government of a community that is organized along the lines of the principles identified earlier in this work would carry out this protection fully authorized, itself guided by the principles. It is for this reason that Wolff's defense of anarchism does not undercut the efforts of those who aim to devise a legal system and its administration in accordance with human rights. It is precisely for purposes of *protection* of individual moral autonomy that such a system would be devised. As Jeffrey H. Reiman explains in his able critical commentary on Wolff's book, *In Defense of Political Philosophy* (Harper and Row, 1972) the task of political philosophy "lies in determining the real connections between the things human beings value—such as moral autonomy—and the forms of political association—the systems of political authority—which sustain or thwart those things." The aim of my work is to identify these connections and thus meet the formidable challenge of Wolff's defense of anarchism.

The second version of anarchism is similar to Wolff's in that it once again charges the theory of government with proposing a morally intolerable institution. The most prominent proponent of this variety of anarchism is Murray N. Rothbard, the libertarian economist, student of the late Ludwig von Mises, and author of several important treatises on economics and political theory. Rothbard's position is different from Wolff's in two respects. First, he argues his case against government from the conclusions of the present book concerning the basic principles of a human community, namely the theory of human natural rights. Rothbard is one of the few exponents of *individualist* anarchism or, as he sometimes calls it, anarchocapitalism.[1] (Of course Rothbard has many adherents and disciples. But he is the most well known and diligent exponent of the form of anarchism which has its roots in natural law/rights theories and can claim along its intellectual lineage such thinkers as Lysander Spooner, Josiah Warren, and Benjamin Tucker, all of them individualists and anarchists according to at least some of what they have written.[2]) Second, Rothbard, in contrast to Wolff, advances an alternative mode of social organization, one without a government (which he opposes). He proposes what might loosely be called a system of laissez-faire defense agencies as a means by which individuals might take steps to protect and preserve their rights. These two elements of Rothbard's anarchism are, of course, closely

related; his second point—that some form of social organization is necessary—is required by his first. It does *not* follo, however, that if he is wrong
about the immorality of government, nothing of his second point remains
valuable for purposes of understanding the kind of society that is organized
in line with the principles of human rights.

My concern will be with what Rothbard takes to follow from his first
point. He summarizes it as follows:

> Morally, which for me is the prime consideration, it seems to me unquestionable that,
> given the libertarian premise of nonaggression [i.e., human rights theory], anarchism
> wins hands down [over the theory of government]. For if, as all libertarians believe, no
> one may morally initiate physical force against the person or property of another, then
> limited government has built within it two fatal principles of impermissible aggression.
> First, it presumes to establish a compulsory monopoly of defense (police, courts, law)
> service over some given geographical area. So that individual property-owners who prefer
> to subscribe to another defense company within that area are not allowed to do so. Second,
> the limited government obtains its revenues by the aggression—the robbery—of taxa-
> tion, a compulsory levy on the inhabitants of the geographical area. All governments,
> however limited they may be otherwise, commit at least these two fundamental crimes
> against liberty and private property.[3]

("Libertarianism is the label that has been applied to the theory of society
or political philosophy that identifies the initiation of force against others
as the one form of human interaction that is impermissible in a human
community under all circumstances. I have not used the label thus far
because many libertarians base their acceptance of this basic prohibition on
something other than a theory of human rights. Some take the principle to
be self-evidently true. Others view it as an efficient device for social organization without giving it a foundation based on a moral point of view. But I
will henceforth use the term "libertarianism" to indicate the theory of
human community proposed in this work.)

In considering Rothbard's remarks I will not concern myself with his
second "fatal principle." The means by which an agency or hired administrator would obtain payment from those it would serve in the capacity of
protecting and preserving human rights must always be circumscribed by
the principles that are to be protected. If all forms of taxation violate
human rights, than any agency charged with this responsibility would
have to obtain revenues by other means. Nor is it possible to prejudge the
many ways that firms delivering a service for customers can obtain
payment.[4] Admittedly governments have usually relied on taxation, and
taxation taken as usual must involve the violation of human rights,
although there can be exceptions—namely when the taxed have freely delegated to some people the authority to levy a specified fee upon them (but
none other). In this instance, taxation could be coercive only vis-à-vis those
who disagree with the means by which the charges are determined and

levied. This group may be quite large, but not *all* those who are taxed are thereby coerced.

At any rate, the second point is not central. As to the first "fatal principle," it seems clear that Rothbard is begging the question. To call the monopoly that a government has over a given geographical area "compulsory" is to prejudge the manner in which such a monopoly is or could be established. Here again, of course, history tends to support Rothbard, although it is a simplification to believe that most governments are *imposed* upon *all* those within their range of jurisdiction. Many people simply acquiesce when some rise to power; others give their wholehearted support, and some, of course, partake in the governing. In most Western semidemocracies the politically active and interested majority supports the state. Compulsion pertains mainly to the active opponents. None of this makes it any more justified, only somewhat more understandable. To the extent that there is a meaning to the concept "people," it is quite true that most people "get the governments they deserve" in places where some semblance of democracy reigns. Supporters of the free society deceive themselves if they think that there is much opposition to the institution, as opposed to some particular practices, of coercive government. There is very little opposition to it *on principle*.

Nor would it be quite fair to call all ruling bodies of various states in history "governments." The concept "government" is relatively new in history and should not simply be equated with "state." These points aside, we must acknowledge that Rothbard is here making something other than a historical claim about what governments have done. His contention is more general: there *could* not be a government that is not compulsory. He is arguing that governments are inherently coercive or compulsory—these are features that government has "built within it." Which is to say that according to Rothbard the concept "government" can only be defined by including in the definition provisions for compulsion or aggression.

What Rothbard has here is therefore an impossibility proof, that no one could construct a definition of government, and accordingly conceive of a comparable human community served by a government, that avoided compulsion. His reason is that any government must serve some given geographical area, which already renders it compulsory because some property owners who would prefer service from some other agency would not then be allowed to obtain it. But is this true? Would a government *have* to disallow secession?

The problem here is complicated. We are talking about abstract matters whose practical consequences and manifestations would not be simple to specify. After all, any change from one form of political system to another would face the difficulty of transition. But at this point we are concerned with whether (*in principle*) a government could be instituted that would not exhibit the fatal principle of coercion which Rothbard says all governments *must*. Once we discover whether this could be accomplished, we can proceed to the concrete situations people face in their own times. (This ordering of priorities is not unique to political theory. Medical students must first learn their theory and then start work on actual cases which come in all varieties and complexities not specifically mentioned in the theoretical discussions.)

To answer Rothbard's challenge we need to ask what type of service protectors and preservers of human rights would offer and deliver. Only by identifying the kind of work that a hired servant or agent must (can legitimately) perform can we evaluate the various means by which it might and might not be performed properly. We know that the protection of human rights involves, among other things, defending people against aggression or protecting them when such aggression can be foreseen with reasonable certainty, when the presence of such aggression, or its imminence, can be communicated to the hired agent. The agent in turn must be located somewhere—in some region of or near the area being serviced. Bluntly put, this agent—"the government"—must be some *place* and cannot be omnipresent in the place where those whom it services live and work. Concretely, policemen, e.g., have to get from their location to wherever the aggression is taking place or appears to be imminent.

Now, given Rothbard's proposal for various competing defense agencies, if between the location of "the government" and the person(s) being serviced we have some territory that is not protected by the same agency—i.e., falls outside the jurisdiction of the government—the government is not authorized to proceed to the area where it is needed. Because of property rights it would require permission to cross. But there could be no assurance that such permission would be forthcoming, not unless some overlap of jurisdiction existed, in which case the problem does not arise: we have what comes close to a case of federalism, with some arrangement similar to what we know as the relationship between federal, state, county, and municipal governments.

So it appears that *the nature of the service* implies some type of geographical homogeneity among the areas to be serviced by the agent that is hired to protect human rights. The same goes for preserving human rights. In this case the courts which would hear cases of dispute would have to be accessible to those who have employed them. By breaking up the area served by each court and each police unit, the identification of the violation of human rights and the corresponding enforcement of the remedies would be rendered impossible; that is, without violating the rights of those not party to the relationship between citizen and government, the government (Rothbard's defense agency) could not function for the citizenry.

What this indicates is that the kind of service which governments—or agents of (lawful) protection and preservation of human rights—deliver must be obtained in a particular form. That is the nature of the particular trade relationship. One can call this a defense agency system if one likes, but it would still be true that the only moral means by which people could delegate to others the authority to protect and preserve their human rights is by uniting into homogeneous human communities, with one legal system per community, administered by a given "firm" or government. This is not unlike the fact that if the services of an ice skating rink are obtained, one cannot complain that his freedom is abridged because the ice is not delivered into the living room. Different commodities and services require different forms of delivery.

An important point is that they also call for different forms of discontinuation. One's freedom is not abridged when in the middle of a movie he does not receive half his money back upon demand. The trade simply excludes that type of move. Nor can one decide not to take the trip on American Airlines after the plane has taken off—while, of course, with a taxi one can disembark at any time. The point of all this is that the nature of competition is different when purchasing services like the administration of a legal system based on human rights, from what it is when purchasing such services as bowling instructions. And this pertains also to the way in which one can discontinue one's relationship to a government. One need only consider hundreds of different types of relationships where one party purchases and the other delivers a good or service: the circumstances of beginning, middle, and end will all have to do with the nature of the good or service in question.

Rothbard's complaint that governments govern over a given geographical area seems, then, to be a complaint about any valid self-defense. That those in the area will be coercively tied to the government with jurisdiction cannot be taken as self-evident. To see whether violation of any rights would be involved requires that we investigate the most rational means by which the relationship between the parties to the trade in question can ensue. Is there a monopoly here? Well, if only one free society exists and there are no others to choose from, we do indeed have a monopoly. But if, e.g., both the United States and Canada were free societies, both with governments to protect and preserve human rights, both with moral means of selecting the administrators, then no monopoly would exist. Any citizen could *(a)* secede from the United States and live in isolation, perhaps start developing an enclave with its own administration of justice, so long as this did not begin to interfere with the relationship between the citizens of the United States and their government; or *(b)* could sell his goods and/or take his business to Canada, once the relationship between him and the United States government has been *justly severed.*

It seems then that although a government of a free society might be a monopoly—no other such government might be available—it need not be so, nor need it be compulsory at that. On the other hand, not being compulsory does not entail infinite flexibility of action on the part of the citizens. The government has as much right to expect the citizen's end of the trade to be held up as the citizen has with its government. For example, if the nature of the relationship called for (something like) at least a four-year contract, one would not be able to just up and leave without paying damages; nor could one simply hire some other government if the services of that agent would have to be delivered in violation of the property rights of one's neighbors.

It seems that Rothbard's objections are not valid. There is no impermissible aggression necessarily involved in so-called "monopoly government" merely because it has exclusive jurisdiction over some area. Obviously we have seen more than our share of compulsion with existing governments and those that have pervaded history. But it does not follow that all governments must, of necessity, be coercive. Most simply act beyond their proper role.

None of this is to say that some of what Rothbard advocates in the way of private police, security guards, arbitration agencies and the like could not be utilized in a free society. The only point to be made against him concerns the judgment about government's "fatal principles" of impermissible aggression. It is false that government must be coercive, although it may be true that a free society has plenty of room for diverse forms of self-protection. After all, security guards, arbitration agencies, and the like are with us in the present political system, already managing to coexist with governments that are hardly limited to the protection of human rights. It should be clear from that alone that in a society where the functions of government would be strictly circumscribed by the provisions of a legal system based on human rights, plenty of work would be left to private agencies. Yet there must (ought to) exist a court of last resort—a court bound, so to speak, by the law of the land—to be defined and enforced by a legal system's administrators in accordance with a system based on human rights.

The central point to be made in answer to Rothbard and those who agree with him is this: it follows from the principles of human rights that action ought to be taken to institute their systematic protection and defense. If "government" is the concept best suited to designate such agencies, then it is morally justified for people to establish (hire) a proper government. It may be that those administering the laws will do a bad job, in which case one is morally obligated to alter or abolish (fire) those involved, provided terms are met for such disassociation. In some cases, where the administrators try to prevent this—and thus subvert their essential function to serve people—revolution is warranted. (More of that later.)

Obviously this point is initially a moral one. There is perhaps a sense of unreality associated with these considerations because today such choices are not with us often enough, nor are they properly characterized when made by some. But we must understand the principles by which they would be justified so that we know their implications for current conduct vis-à-vis the issue of political reform. What I am saying against Rothbard is that it is in their interest and people are entitled to establish moral governments, ones that protect and preserve human rights (only). Furthermore, this can involve various kinds of arrangements, limited only by the principles to be preserved. But at the stage of such action—should it ever be taken pure and simple, and however it might emerge from the present context—this is a moral issue, not a legal one, since we are here talking about the *establishment* of a legal system, not its existing precepts.

Now we come to those who opt for anarchism because they believe that systems designed to protect everyone's human rights contradict the moral principles I defended earlier, namely that each ought to choose to do the best for himself as a person. The idea is that a consistent individualist, acting in terms of ethical egoism, must reject the notion that his actions ought to be guided by considerations of others' rights. That would be to violate one's ethics—to act on a principle other than ethical egoism. To yield to the legal principles protecting human rights would be to concern oneself with what is in the interest of *others*.

This argument is supported by examples such as the following: suppose I encounter a drunk in a dark alley, sprawled on the ground; he is loaded with cash and my interest would at this time be well served if I had this cash (or cash in this amount); I know the chap is unable to prevent my taking the loot, nor is he able to report me. No one else is around; in short, I know I am safe. Is it not clear that I ought to take the money? The argument ends with the conclusion that it is.

This, then, is the general claim: it is in one's self-interest at times to act in terms of what the principles of human rights prohibit. Therefore, human rights are morally unjustified as principles of a good human community. Basically the example and its general conclusion indicate the *rejection of politics;* this doctrine may therefore be classified as a version of anarchism. Crucially, no mention is made of the context of the case—a community of human beings, consistent with ethical egoism, all aiming to achieve human happiness. This larger consideration, and what follows from this purpose for the identification and implementation of principles of community organization, do not enter the argument.

But one *should* consider the matter from such a context. To act rationally toward others we need to know something about them. We should acknowledge that others are free agents, in the metaphysical sense of being capable of genuine choices, and can thus choose to acquire things on their own, without immorally interfering with others in the process. This enables us to learn also that people ought to be able to use and dispose of what they have chosen to acquire, that this option is good for them. It is also a justifiable inference that they ought to choose to act so as to protect and preserve what they have acquired. All this enables us to act vis-à-vis others in the most rational way—we can and should count on justified resistance to any attempt to prevent this from happening. Even if people do not actually resist, it is still rational to count on justified resistance.

The *rational* course of action in line with egoism is to establish principles of community life that reflect this knowledge. Knowing that people are free to be irrational, to evade that something belongs to another, one should make the needed preparations for such irrationality should one become unavoidably involved. This would include developing a legal system in terms of which such actions are repelled, punished—legally prohibited. That in turn commits all those who are part of the system to act accordingly.

Now if we reconsider the example in this wider context, what is the case? Once we know that in society people are justified in protecting themselves against those who will not abide by the principle that one thing belongs to this person (group, organization, and so on), another to that, the drunk fellow's money will no longer be morally accessible to the potential criminal. Granted I may not be caught. Granted that even if the drunk and his pals catch up with me I can fight back successfully. Yet in the context of a voluntary association with others for mutual benefit, one ought to live by taking only what no one has claimed or someone is willing to part with under mutually agreed upon conditions. It is to prevent the damage that occurs when this principle is violated without proper recourse (deserved punishment, restitution, etc.) that political principles are identified and legal systems are developed around them. Or, to put it more precisely, it is for this reason that they ought to be so identified and developed. And if this is so, then to take the drunk's money is to violate the principles of human rights *and* ethical egoism, the latter being the moral grounds for the truth (and establishment in law) of the former.

Yet there is a point to the criticism, namely that there can be instances where consideration of political principles is morally impossible. I will come to this later when I take up some broader criticisms of human rights theory. For now I ask only for anticipation of my remarks on emergency cases where regard for political principles is (morally) impossible. In such cases, again, ought implies can. Certain emergency cases do not then count as violating human rights, but indicate the requirement in special contexts to consider some actions outside the purview of community life, specifically those that are removed from it either by physical or moral circumstances. But none of that militates against the soundness of human rights theory for purposes of defining the principles for organizing human communities in the interest of human beings. If this can be done it should be; if it is impossible then it makes no sense to say either that it should or that it should not be—principles of organization cannot be relevant.

For now I want to recall in outline what I have tried to show in this section. Three versions of anarchism have been cited and I have attempted to argue against all of them that government *can* be a valid and morally justifiable avenue of securing the protection and preservation of human rights. First, when they protect the moral autonomy of persons; second, when they protect the properties of persons; and finally, when they serve to implement the moral principles applicable to the conduct of individuals in a human community.

In each case I have offered rejoinders with a (given) theory of government in the background, namely the idea that a good version of that institution is best for the protection and preservation of the self-interest of individuals who choose to live in a good human community. I have alluded to this idea sometimes obliquely, at other times in detail. I should admit that I myself have doubts about the advisability of using the term "government" for what I have in mind in talking about the institution or agency of protection. R. A. Childs, Jr., an advocate at least on occasion of Rothbard's approach, has argued persuasively that Occam's Razor would seem to require the introduction of a different term—after all, "government" is so widely applicable to morally unjustified institutions, agencies, actions, and policies that talking about good government may appear to be an outright contradiction in terms.[5]

Yet I see this issue to be one of competing alternatives, of better versus worse answers to the question of political organization. I might illustrate this by the example of the institution of marriage: one must admit that many marriages are indeed hopelessly bad. Some are not so bad, and only here and there can one spot a good marriage. But by taking a statistical approach, one might argue that most marriages are surely less than even remotely good. That, however, does not prove that none that are good *can* be had, nor, of course, that most marriages are not better for those involved than if these individuals chose some other form of life, singlehood or whatnot. These are comparative issues at times.

And the situation with government is similar. None can argue that most are good or perfect. None can deny that a great many should be changed (as one might say that a person would be better off in another relationship, even another marriage). But all this does not show their *inherent* disvalue. So while calling the perfect marriage a marriage in the face of so many horrible cases may seem to debase the relationship, that would only be so if one were committed to a rather strict nominalism/empiricism—a view that words can only name or describe visible experiences, never versions or characteristics perhaps only conceptualized and not yet achieved in reality. Mr. Childs notwithstanding, Occam's Razor does not seem to be violated by my use of the concept "government" as I talk of the morally justifiable employment of some agents for the protection and preservation of human rights. Even if I acknowledge, with sadness, the misapplication of that concept, its abuse and historical burdensomeness.

At this point I will state more comprehensively the justification for such an institution. Then I will explore the relationship between government and human rights more closely, and indicate in a general fashion the manner in which the present theory can be employed to make sense of the dynamic existence of a human community where people are born into the system moment by moment, with their direct participation in the system clearly circumscribed by existing conditions at their birth, childhood, maturation, and so on. In the next chapter I will come to some existing concrete problems.

The Purpose of Government in a Good Human Community

From earliest recorded intellectual history people have concerned themselves with the nature of government, at least in some form. In the philosophy of Plato, for example, the ideal society had as its central purpose the achievement of justice. Here "justice" meant something different from what we generally mean by or associate with this term—the correct adjudication of human conflicts (verdicts, punishments, laws). Plato meant by "justice" what would now more appropriately be meant by "common good." As we saw earlier, the ideal society of Plato was probably meant not to be implemented, but to be used as a model. Moreover, Plato's main character in the *Republic*, Socrates, introduced the ideal society in order to better explain the nature of goodness in respect to individual human beings. Accordingly, the main feature of the ideal society turned out to be perfect harmony. Justice amounted to every person's fittingness within the society, in line with his talents, capacities, and the needs of the society. There was to be no conflict between the good of the individual and the good of society in an ideal system. Within the individual also, there had to be a harmony of the three main elements of the human soul, reason, passion, and drive, for someone to be good.

The point to be made here, however, is that Plato formulated a view of society and its principles of organization with the common good in mind. Thus the goodness of both individuals and their communities was to be the purpose of a proper social organization. The same basic idea, but with considerable difference in detail, can be found in Aristotle:

Anybody concerned about good law keeps an eye on the virtue and vice of the citizen. And it is plain that the community *(polis)*, if it is so-called truly and not just in name, must make virtue its business. For the association is otherwise an alliance, different merely with respect to place from alliances of distant parties, and law is a compact, as Lykophron the sophist said, "a guarantee of mutual rights" *(engyetes alleois ton dikaion)*, but it is not able to make the citizens good or just [*Politics* III, 9, 1280b5-12].[6]

Aristotle, then, viewed the polis as having as its purpose the making of good human beings, "to make citizens good or just." But there is a possible confusion here, just as in the literal acceptance of Plato's ideal society. In Aristotle the polis *is* the human community that has embarked on achieving happiness. This is at least true as he explained it in the first part of his book on political matters. In Book III of the *Politics*, however, Aristotle began to talk of the polis as the government of a human community, or at least as if the polis contained as one of its essential features the administration of laws. What appears confused in Aristotle is that the purpose of the human community is the same as the purpose of its government. He rejects that "law is a compact . . . a guarantee of mutual rights" in favor of the idea that government itself "must make virtue its business." i.e., paternalism. Yet even in this Aristotle may merely be ambiguous, for by making virtue its business, the law might simply focus on guaranteeing mutual rights. This follows when we realize that the law can only make virtue its business by protecting each person in his liberty to choose; without choice there can be no virtue or vice. Since Aristotle was aware of this, we may be justified in thinking that he was closer to the mutual guarantee of rights idea than he himself believed.

In general, all political theories have had an idea of the common good, although it has been understood on the basis of ideas of man, deities, and so on, not successfully justified by rational standards. What the common good has been taken to be has varied a great deal, so much so that employing the idea itself may not be very useful by now.

Yet within the present conception of society a government would in some respect have as its purpose to serve the common good. The theory being defended here is not entirely independent of traditional efforts to solve problems faced in human community life. To the extent that the role or function of government ought to be the administration of the legal system of a good human community—conceived along the lines of human rights theory—it is, in a specific sense, designed to serve the *common* good. To make clear just what this amounts to in the present context, one must consider what role a government has, given that an individual can live his life best in political liberty, where he is free to choose to act so as to achieve his moral purpose, happiness. It is in the sense that this purpose might be served by a government that it would be appropriate to hold that governments are established to promote the common good—i.e., what is indeed universally and necessarily good for every person in society.

People, then, ought to organize a community along well-publicized principles of social interaction which will contribute to their common good. The protection and preservation of the community in question will result in what I have (with some reluctance) called a government. In this connection it is worthwhile to recall the wording of the Declaration of Independence, a formidable statement of at least some of the ideas I am attempting to justify in the present work:

> We hold these truths to be self-evident, that all men are created equal, that they are endowed by their creator with certain unalienable rights, that among these are life, liberty and the pursuit of happiness. That to secure these rights, governments are instituted among men, deriving their just powers from the consent of the governed.

Although its authors may have been mistaken to take these truths to be self-evident—one may suppose that if they were they would be widely implemented and there would be no need to justify or prove them here—once we acknowledge that these human rights exist, we have a responsibility (we ought) to make provisions for their protection and preservation. Any political theory has its ideological implications—i.e., a program of action that follows from an integrated set of principles. A sound political theory is impotent without them: merely believing these principles, having them as facts that make no difference in one's actual conduct, achieves no purpose at all, especially not for those the principles are supposed to serve.

In accordance with the theory of human rights, government ought to serve a definite purpose, namely to deliver a service: "to secure these rights." Government, then, is the agency people should institute so as to have their rights protected and preserved, to administer the adjudication of disputes in line with the ablest interpretation of human rights—at its best. At its worst it purports to do something like this but in fact hides behind this morally justified goal so as to secure other things, usually the special goals of some people, and certainly not the goals of all of the people.

Now unlike bakers, florists, auto manufacturers, artists, psychologists, philosophers, and other producers and creators, governments are employed for purposes of delivering a rather special service, namely to make justifiable use of physical force and its threat or imminence. David Kelley makes this point well:

> The use of coercion against criminals and foreign aggressors is a service, one provided by the government to its citizens. As such it may be considered an economic good. But it differs from all other economic goods in just the [following] respect. . . . When its use is morally improper, it does violate individual rights. Coercion, in this world, must some-

times be exercised. Given the existence of criminals, and the constant possibility that some men will prefer criminal to honest means and ends, the existence of a power to prevent and punish this by force has a certain value. Its value is restricted, however, by the moral principle forbidding its use against persons who have not themselves used force against others.[7]

The conclusion, as Kelley continues:

Coercion, therefore, and coercion alone, falls under the proviso mentioned earlier: since it has the potential for violating rights if used improperly, its use cannot be determined by the value preferences people happen to hold, whether right or wrong; and so cannot be determined by market forces. [The] use of coercion must be determined solely by rules derived from the appropriate moral principles; and it must operate in accordance with such rules without taking into consideration any individual or collective desires to the contrary.[8]

In his article Kelley offers several reasons for rejecting the anarcho-capitalist theory, both as Rothbard develops it and as it has been propounded by David Friedman,[9] and in doing so he points up several features of proper government. He is especially concerned to show that the idea that the service government offers could be sold in the way in which all other services are sold is impossible. This because the existence of the free market, where trade ensues, presupposes the existence of the institution of government; thus pricing and supply and demand can only exist once government exists to ensure the necessary conditions.

It is not my purpose now to discuss and criticize more arguments for or against anarchocapitalism. The anarchist case purporting to show that government must act immorally has been dealt with already. In these last few paragraphs I have been concerned to point out that the service government provides is different from others, those not involving force. When governments abuse their (proper) function, when they act outside its limits, their actions, policies, branches, officers, and so on will of virtual necessity be unavoidably harmful to anyone involved. First, of course, the integrity of government will be undermined. Second, the abusive conduct will almost inevitably lead to institutionalized or systematic perversion of the principles of good government. One need but consider how so-called emergency policies, first excused by reference to some goal which is taken to justify going beyond what government ought to do, almost always remain part and parcel of the institution. (In 1973 Senator Frank Church and some of his colleagues published a research project showing that since the early days of Franklin Roosevelt's administration the United States has had a government fully geared to emergency operations! Each emergency policy, implemented as a temporary measure and often in violation of expressed constitutional principle, became part of the status quo. With the recent so-called "crisis of governmental authority," some wonder how it is that so many things could go wrong with what government is doing. The answer that becomes more obvious with each inspection is that government has extended itself, often even with the tacit acquiescence of the majority, all out of proportion to its proper function, even in terms of the somewhat inconsistent, though still relatively superior, standards of the United States constitution.

Of course, all tools human beings devise to serve justifiable purposes can be abused and subverted. With the instrument of government, the moral purpose of which is to secure human rights, this is no less true. Nevertheless, it is also true that when a government becomes subversive of its proper goal, the scars left will be far more pervasive than when other human creations are abused: a government deals with all of the people, at least potentially, and with how the future structure of a human community will develop. It is therefore all the more important to achieve a clear definition of the government's function and to insist on total integrity, the lack of any compromise in performance of that function.

Basically, the government of a free society would have a rather minimal role in people's lives. Whereas today virtually every news item deals with some element of government, in a free society this would not be the case. One might say, even if somewhat mundanely, government ought not be construed as the end all and be all of human life in a community—for the simple reason that it cannot be and still be of value. It is, in fact, unrealistic—utopian—to expect governments to perform functions for which they have no wherewithal, let alone moral justification. The nature of an entity determines what it can and ought to do; going beyond it must end in disaster. While many philosophers find this principle to be troublesome—with worries about whether man can identify the nature of something, whether it is not at least conceivable that something can act beyond what its nature would allow us to infer—it is simply a function of the most pervasive law of reality, the law of identity as it applies to actions of entities. Elephants cannot write symphonies, pigeons cannot commit logical fallacies, lightbulbs cannot wish to turn on—and governments cannot make the world (people) good. All they are suited to do, at their best, is to protect human rights so that the people, who must choose to become good, can do so.

All this may seem very "unrealistic" in the light of most of the ideas that permeate our world. There are myriad varieties of popular proposals (many with aims which are not themselves bad) which involve further and further encroachments on human liberty. But one feature of a rational realism is to do the best to identify what (really) ought to be done to improve one's life, the conditions within which it is being lived. The fact that the idea of political liberty has already been presented in one form or another, better or worse, throughout recent intellectual history, and has subsequently fallen into disrepute through default, does not validate the contention of some that today we must discard it, that it is obsolete, unsuited to the difficult problems we face. As will become clear, most of those problems are the direct consequences of having evaded the principles advocated in this work, not, as some are wont to charge, of their having been tried and found lacking.

Sometimes it is important for people to acknowledge that drastic departures from the status quo are the only means by which to achieve even minimal prospects for improvement of the possibilities of human life. Realization of the propriety of directing political action toward implementation of the principles of the present theory will be the only avenue toward genuine solution of human problems on the social/political front. When this is accomplished (gradually, as such things must be after many years of having steered on the wrong course, with only occasional adherence to wisdom), individuals can elect to turn to their own problems, alone or in cooperation with others, leaving their government to carry out its proper function.

I have offered here the major features of a government of a free society, one based on human rights. I have not said how we might have to interpret the various elements of the present theory in the process of undertaking the change from where we now are to where we ought to be concerning political matters. I will touch on that issue in a later chapter. In the next two sections I conclude the discussion of human rights theory for the time being. First I will consider some problems related to the theory versus other views of political communities and governments. Then I will turn to some of the administrative aspects of a community organized along the lines advocated.

Human Rights versus Enemies of Liberty

There is always a bit of arrogance in advocating a system of politics and morality, if only because most people today dispute the possibility of finding out whether any such system is correct. In addition, advocating a system of politics because it promotes the good and interest of individuals, including my own of course the advocates own, has been considered a grave liability. Presumably one must be for something only if it makes no difference to one's own good whether it will be achieved. I am convinced, however, that my interest as a human being coincides with the interests of others, although that really is unimportant except as a fact about the theory which I have found right. For purposes of improving (at least the chances of) my own community life, it is important to identify those interests people have in common. Those that are unique to me, as an individual with a particular identity of my own, are not relevant here, although they are, of course, significant in other contexts of my life.

Part of my view is that without the *ability* to grasp the validity and soundness of the theory of human rights, people cannot be asked to subscribe to it. If people, just as they are, with a reasonable facility in the language spoken in a community, *cannot* understand some idea, that idea is useless for purposes of political organization. Of course, even if they can do something, including understand and agree upon an idea's validity and truth, they may not choose to. But that is a different issue from not being *able* to do so.

Human rights theorists, in the main, are unique in political philosophy because their views do not imply special capabilities (or rights) for themselves. As Locke noted long ago, one need but "consult one's reason" to grasp these truths. The idea behind this is sound—namely, that a conscientious, rational investigation of the basic aspects of human life and the circumstances of community existence would lead a person to conclude that there are indeed human rights and we ought to make provisions for their incorporation in the legal system. These rights are not divinely or specially "communicated" or granted to select parties (even if a creator established them, ultimately); they can be discerned by rational attention. If they do, indeed, exist. (If not, *that* will be discovered, and ought to be acted upon. The only unacceptable notion is that we *cannot* know the truth about these matters, an idea promulgated widely these days.)

When we consider most political theories advocated today, it is difficult to remain dispassionate. Almost all of them (except pacifism and anarchism) proclaim special powers for some as against others. Marxists have designated the workers as *the* worthy class, and brought about the mass oppression and slaughter of millions who did not belong to this class. (No doubt the so-called Western Marxists will protest forever that their "correct" interpretation of Marx would never have produced such horrors. But this is wishful thinking.) National socialists identified Aryans as the specially privileged master-race with unlimited authority over the life and property of others. The religious sects and caste systems of India and Pakistan are well known. American racists and their more powerful comrades in South Africa make similar "benevolent" assignments of elitist "rights" to themselves. B. F. Skinner's political/scientific/technological system proclaims the members of Skinner's own profession, behavioral technologists, as the possessors of the wisdom and knowledge qualifying them to govern the rest of mankind (with only the best of intentions, of course). The list of such elitist is very long.

Whenever a political theory advocates the use of force against people who have not provoked it with their own aggressive actions, some people, usually the advocates included, are accorded the authority to order others around, sometimes as far as the gas chamber. American liberals, incidentally, are most notorious for their advocacy of the distribution of wealth, while their conservative counterparts prefer to force people to shut down theaters or radical political seminars, but neither group favors the extension of paternalism to areas its members dominate. By the present theory nothing like this is justifiable.

There are many varieties of statism, some tending toward what we vaguely call the right wing, others toward the left. In America and elsewhere in the West we find few prominent people advocating either of the extreme versions of left and right. More often however both liberals and conservatives—the words used here having even less precise meaning but still indicating directions widely perceived in contemporary American politics—mix their principles, some favoring more liberty pertaining to one sort of activities, others advocating freedom of conduct concerning opposite areas.[10]

Of course outside the mainstream of both the liberal and conservative approach we find various sophisticated efforts to provide a rational(ized) reconciliation of freedom and coercion. Thus in the two centuries since Hegel's massive efforts to combine the forces of Reason (Absolute Spirit in its inevitable process through history) with the liberal idea of the conditions of liberty—each understood in peculiar ways, of course, for purposes of the synthesis—a good deal of academic speculation has concerned itself with a reinterpretation of prominent social and political ideas. Most important among them for actual political affairs has been Marx's analysis of freedom.

For Marx, basically, freedom is a condition that society strives for. Accordingly the ideal of liberty is not actually violated by manifestations of coercion and tyranny, because for Marx the foundation of human development consisted in a process called the historical dialectic. In essence this meant that contradictions were part and parcel of reality itself, whereas in the original (and only meaningful) sense of the term, only the human mind could entertain contradictions (when, e.g., someone believes that there exist mutually exclusive states of affairs). Borrowing from Hegel, but with serious reservations (which robbed Marx of the Hegelian foundations of the idea of the dialectic), Marx conceived of mankind as moving toward the realm of "absolute freedom"—which meant total absence of economic scarcity in human life. In such a situation anyone and everyone could obtain and do anything without adverse consequences for or losses to what others wanted to obtain and do. (Of course, capitalism, with its immense power for production, was required to produce such a situation!)

It should be mentioned that contemporary socialists and Marxists are in much disagreement about whether or to what extent Marx believed in freedom of choice—i.e., that individuals are capable of making initial choices, causing some of their behavior. There is evidence in Marx's writings that he accepted some measure of the type of freedom I have argued for in the present work, but it is not clear that this can be reconciled with his equally firm acceptance of the Hegelian idea of historical necessity. More than likely Marx would have wanted it both ways, for by accepting "the march of history" thesis he could promise the inevitability of communism to the workers, while by accepting some measure of genuine choice on the part of the workers he could make sense of the idea that they ought to help history here and there. Without some degree of genuine choice, the notion that anyone *ought to* help makes no sense.

Contemporary Marxists have different ideas on this. Sartre, for instance, who calls himself a Marxist, rejects the all-embracing determinism he finds in Marx. The American Marxist Andrew McLaughlin has recently outlined a view close to Hegel and Marx as dialecticians. As he put it, "The basic point is that societies *do* in fact socialize their members in ways that cause those people to want what society needs them to want."[11] From this he argues, in what can only be a rather convoluted way, that "if we take freedom to be highly valuable, then we can try to socialize people so that they can be autonomous." A large part of this thesis (as is the case also with B. F. Skinner in *Beyond Freedom and Dignity*) is to show that society is necessarily manipulative. In particular, to show that capitalism in manipulative, McLaughlin cites the example of the Selective Service, which has always used the force of law to "induce" people to enter certain professions and schools whose attendees are exempt from military service. Just how that shows that *capitalism* is manipulative is quite clear—in no way at all. It does show that any *government* that is not systematically committed to protecting and preserving human rights will be manipulative.

Of course McLaughlin wants to argue further (a popular thesis) that capitalism creates wants and needs by advertising. Thus it socializes people in behalf of big businesses and other capitalistic parties. Yet, aside from the fact that the idea that "consumer behavior in the market place is highly conditioned" is without scientific foundation (although some scientist may have proposed it), even if this is true one may wonder, what of it? Why should one accept McLaughlin's socialization? Or Skinner's or Galbraith's? Frankly, if socialized I must be, I'd rather have it happen from the disorganized, haphazard groups we find in market places than from such determined idealogues as the above.

Other contemporary Marxists do not share McLaughlin's idea about freedom and socialization. Michael P. Lerner, one of the youngest and most prolific contemporary Marxists, tells us that ". . . I do think that events of the future are not inevitable, but depend on many contingent circumstances. Not the least of these is what you, the reader, decide to do with your life. . . ." That the reader is capable of deciding what to do with his or her life is just what is denied by McLaughlin when he claims that we are all socialized—conditioned by society—to do what we will. Lerner, however, appears to accept the view that we are, right now, free to choose.[12] This, of course, is just what I have argued. But it would make a shambles out of Marx's ideas about class-determined states of consciousness about the inherent irreconcilability of different viewpoints that emerge from each economic and social historical context.

What we must note is that despite these disagreements most Marxists advocate some form of statism, the dictatorship of the workers, at least while mankind awaits the emergence of the automatically "good" human being that this inevitable historical process will ultimately produce. Even Lerner predicts that eventuality. And while Sartre, Fromm, Marcuse *et al.* rarely put forth historical predictions, they too argue for some form of historical emergence. For example, Marcuse's idea that man will eventually reach his essential being is identical to Marx's own view on this issue. We cannot really expect that any Marxist would drop something so potent as the vision of a future where all human problems are solved. It, like heaven in Christianity, can serve as a powerful incentive (socializer) to get people moving.

With this rather unclear doctrine it is possible to be for both freedom and coercion. Since "true" freedom can be achieved only when mankind evolves into a different type of being—a "new man"—the coercion that occurs in the process of reaching that epoch is seen to be historically necessitated. Marx's views are not at all clear and consistent about these matters. In his youth he seemed to be unconcerned with a *political* solution to man's temporary state of alienation from his own society and activities, whereas in later years he hoped at first for the revolutionary ascent to "new man" (communism), and then for the gradualistic development of the utopia of anarchistic communism. Yet his main line of thought has left an enormous imprint. Thus whether Marxist or not, most leftist-oriented thinkers hold that the good society must be made maximally egalitarian.

Equality, for the designers of the American constitutional system of law and government, meant primarily *equal protection* and preservation of the rights of each person in a society. This because each person is entitled to develop *his own* moral character, regardless of the individual manifestation of his humanity (be he tall, short, black, white, in possession of an IQ of 85 or 185, woman or man, and so on). After the Marxist movement this was not enough for intellectual speculators. Equality came to mean: alike in *all* respects. That, of course, is simply unrealistic—people are alike in just one central respect: each *could* achieve moral stature within his own capacities, but this could turn out differently for each. Perhaps because of the acknowledged value of science, with its emphasis on measurement, many believe that unless one can *see* the equality among all people, it simply could not be construed as real. "True" equality would therefore have to be achieved by a coercive (e.g., scientifically, technologically, or otherwise imposed) process of equalization. Since this can only be done if the equality in question is manipulable, it becomes imperative that everyone be made *materially* equal. Matter, after all, is eminently visible and physically controllable. (Which does not exclude mental equalization for the many who believe that mind is totally reducible to physical components; thus brain-tinkering, e.g., psychosurgery, is not excluded from the possible means of equalization!)

The concern with justice within the social realm is thus no longer confined to such (civil) libertarian issues as due process, *equal administration* of law based on the political theory of traditional natural law/rights, all of which presuppose the idea of man as a moral agent. Instead *distributive* justice *(à la* Resher, Rawls *et al.)* has become of prime, even exclusive concern: the issue is how to distribute what there is in the vicinity of people (apparently with focus only on *good* things) so that all will get an equal share, regardless of the sources of the benefits in question, i.e., individual human effort and voluntary choice. And once again we find that those who would engineer the social transformation from evident (observable) inequality to equality must have a special place and status in the political hierarchy.

Interestingly, some of those who are most often linked to the American political tradition opened the road to this development. John Stuart Mill tried to justify individual freedom by reference to what it would do for society in general. He also envisioned mankind in constant *species* ascendance, thereby paralleling Marx in crucial respects. Subsequent Millians (Utilitarians) held that freedom might be a dispensable obstacle to swifter achievement of the greatest happiness of the greatest number. Mill himself turned toward socialism in his later years, and his defense of human freedom in *On Liberty* is an unfortunate mixture of brilliant analysis of the dynamics of uncoerced human action, the need for intellectual liberty in behalf of scientific progress and truth, and the moral contention that all this is desirable because society or mankind as a whole will benefit. Such reasoning has led to fervent controversies about whether the rights of individuals might not be ignored so that society might be better off—ending, ultimately, with abandonment of a *serious* concern with human rights throughout the Anglo/American intellectual arena. In theory, proponents of the doctrine that conduct should be geared to provide for the welfare of society at large do not come into conflict with human rights. They just have no place in such views. Given their popular appeal, however, and that of legal systems constructed in line with them (or doing at least lip service to them), some attention is usually paid by such theorists to how their views square with human rights.

Such highly practical questions as "What should be done about smog, pollution of lakes and rivers, ill health, poverty, and so forth?" might perhaps be answered by Utilitarians with ease if it were not for the impact of human rights theories. While it is a simple matter to ridicule those who oppose water fluoridation as a Communist conspiracy, it is more difficult to deal with serious conclusions from dentists that forcing everyone to drink fluoridated water has unavoidably hurt *some* people. The benefit sought (legislated) for the bulk. And we can go through all of the governmental programs for which people's monies and time are confiscated, and find that they are excused or advocated by reference to some greater good for the greater number—sometimes a number that will be realized only in the future.

In all these arguments, hints, and appeals, the idea of human rights has a small role indeed. This is evidenced clearly when we ask *who* it is that will determine and effect the greatest good—administer the distribution of wealth, goods, time, labor and so on available in a given society. Even if it is rarely explicit or emphasized, most of these views insist that some group of (wise) persons will be assigned the role of carrying out the rational management of society. Of course it is usually maintained they will be *granted* this power. But the meaning of the *democratic* method or the propriety of that provision is rarely analyzed. (One may be puzzled as to why democracy is so important for these purposes; why are even some of the most ardent Marxists in the West pointing to this feature of their system instead of simply declaring for a dictatorship of the proletariat? Why is it that Michael Harrington, the late Norman Thomas, promoters of Chile's President Allende—why do all of them assure us initially that their system will be and ought to be ushered in democratically? The answer is most likely: because democracy is the last homage to be paid to human rights. If each person's human rights are not protected and preserved, at least the rights of the majority [of the politically concerned] will appear to be; they, at least, will be free to exercise some choice. Thus a remnant of the theory of rights is retained, at least in appearance, in those theories that actually advocate a political system in which no such rights are recognized.)

Of course not even democracy is of significance to all who argue for political systems which deny human rights. Herbert Marcuse has constructed a complicated rationale for discarding even the choice of the majority. He maintains that capitalists have managed to bamboozle the public (through advertising catering to and even creating phony needs and wants) into thinking they are free and capable of choice. It is only an illusion that people are free to buy on an open market and that voters are choosing from among candidates selected by a democratic process expressing the true wants of the rank and file citizenry. There is for Marcuse no genuine electorate, even in the largely diluted sense of a two-party system. This hoax, then, invalidates any objection to revolutionary actions based on the belief that the majority oppose revolution. (B. F. Skinner too proposes that when some people believe that "the survival of the culture is at stake," they may begin to take those actions needed to save it, presumably with no responsibility to consult with the rest.)

The most ambitious attempt to offer a reconciliation of sorts between the tradition of natural rights and the concern to make all people equal is the political theory of John Rawls. This work deserves some attention because, although those who hold views similar to mine vary widely in their assessment of its merits as a philosophical production, it has taken the philosophical (as well as the broader intellectual) community by storm. Hardly anyone concerned with political matters has held out and refused to discuss it. So while I agree with R. M. Hare that Rawls' ideas give one a feeling "all the time that they were slipping through [one's] fingers," and that the book is "extremely repetitious . . . seldom clear whether the repetitions really are *repetitions,* or modifications of previously expressed views,"[13] a brief mention of the book, *A Theory of Justice,* is required, if only to indicate its central problems and why its conclusions should not be accepted.

In the maze of arguments, intuitions (Rawls' term), and assumptions that are largely undefended, Rawls' thesis comes to this: *(a)* Everyone ought to be born absolutely equal (in natural assets and what they make possible for a person); but *(b)* unfortunately *there are* many differences among people in their natural talents and their circumstances for enjoying them; so *(c)* "we" must distribute throughout the entire population whatever benefits are acquired from the natural assets and beneficent circumstances of individuals (since all these are "common assets"). As Rawls puts it, "Those who have been favored by nature, whoever they are, may gain from their good fortune only on terms that improve the situation of those who have lost out. . . . No one deserves his greater natural capacity nor merits a more favorable starting place in society." He does not actually suggest that "one should eliminate these distinctions. There is another way to deal with them. The basic structure can be arranged so that these contingencies work for the good of the least fortunate."[14] The structure would make sure—by efficient direction, one must assume—that wealth would increase by preserving the amount of liberty needed to induce the productive people to keep working. But it would also ensure that that production would not leave the unproductive less well off than they had been prior to further self-enrichment of the producers. Thus everyone's liberty is limited by the provision that the least "favored" benefit from what is done with that liberty.

For Rawls, as for many others in the history of political theory, the value of equality—that people ought to be equal in all respects that can be of benefit to them—is central. This may be said about the present theory also, except that the meaning of "be of benefit to them" is far narrower than for Rawls. Since as moral agents human beings cannot benefit from coercion, even if coerced to take help, Rawls' scheme of distribution must do violence to their well-being. The crucial point to be stressed here is that Rawls does not attempt to rationally, systematically justify the ultimate value of equality—he takes it as an unquestionable common intuition, a widely adhered to belief that equality of this sort is the proper guiding value of human life and a just legal system. As Robert Nozick observes, Rawls gives

no cogent argument to (help) establish that differences in holdings arising from differences in natural assets should be eliminated or minimized. . . . Clearly if the shaping [of people's original position] is designed to nullify differences in holdings due to differences in natural assets, we need an argument for this goal, and we are back to our unsuccessful quest for the route to the conclusion that such differences in holdings ought to be nullified.[15]

Rawls may be right to point out that people would generally wish for a greater degree of and more widely manifest well-being, that more people would be happier, wealthier (and, we might add, wiser). But from this he has not demonstrated the conclusion that some of us could or should *impose* that desirable state of affairs on the world, that the liberty and moral dignity of individuals should therefore be violated.

Let me quote from Nozick at length, for it would be pointless to rephrase what he has said so clearly and succinctly concerning these crucial aspects of Rawls' theory.

Why ought people's holdings to be equal, in the absense of special moral reason to deviate from equality? (Why think there *ought* to be *any* particular pattern in holdings?) Why is equality the rest (or rectilinear motion) position of the system, deviation from which may be caused only by moral forces? Many "arguments" for equality merely *assert* that differences between persons are arbitrary and must be justified. Often writers state a presumption in favor of equality, in some form such as: Differences in treatment of persons need to be justified. [E.g., Isaiah Berlin: "No reason need be given for . . . an equal distribution of benefits—for that is 'natural'—self-evidently right and just, and needs no justification, since it is in some sense conceived as being self-justified."] The most favored situation for this sort of assumption is one in which there is one person (or group) treating everyone, and having *no* right or entitlement to bestow the particular treatment as they wish or even whim. But if I go to one movie theater rather than another adjacent to it, need I justify my different treatment of the two theater owners? Isn't it enough that I felt like going to one of them? That differences in treatment need to be justified *does* fit contemporary *governments*. Here there is a centralized process treating all, with no entitlement to bestow treatment according to whim. The major portion of distribution in a free society does not, however, come through the actions of the government, nor does failure to overturn the result of the localized individual exchanges constitute "state action." When there is no *one* doing the treating, and all are entitled to bestow their holdings as they wish, it is not clear why the maxim that differences in treatment must be justified, should be thought to have extensive application.[16]

There is, in short, no reason to believe that benefits ought to be distributed. Only in the case of agencies such as the government, designed specifically to serve all in the only way it can succeed—in providing protection and preservation of human rights—does the principle of equality make sense. (In private life a father may have the responsibility to bequeath his wealth to his children in equal proportions. But Rawls never justifies any conception of the state on the model of a family—and just as well, since the state, unlike parents, produces nothing and has no justifiable parental functions!)

Rawls does explain why he does not accept the idea that someone might be entitled to gain by his natural assets: "The assertion that a man deserves [i.e., it is just for him to possess and enjoy] the superior character that enables him to make the effort to cultivate his abilities is . . . problematic; for his character depends in large part upon fortunate family and social circumstances for which he can claim no credit."[17] He does not specify the extent of this "large part," nor does he give a proof for this flat-out denial of moral agency and achievement (as well as failure and loss) as the correct idea of human nature and life. Rawls is advancing the notion that whatever people have (do, fail to do, et cetera) is dependent upon external factors of their lives, that even their character is not up to them. (Although a plausible case can be made for this about many aspects of people's lives, perhaps even personality or style, character is clearly a moral quality, and therefore logically tied to choices; so Rawls' doctrine ends in the denial of the possibility of morality, which is devastating for his attempt to provide a *moral* justification of egalitarianism.) Indeed, Nozick offers the following, which gives support to the above:

> This line of argument can succeed in blocking the introduction of persons' autonomous choices and actions (and their results) only by attributing *everything* noteworthy about the person completely to (certain sorts of) "external" factors. So denigrating a person's autonomy and prime responsibility for his actions is a risky line to take for a theory that otherwise wishes to buttress the dignity and self-respect of autonomous beings; especially for a theory that founds so much (including a theory of the good) upon persons' choices. One doubts that the unexalted picture of human beings Rawls' theory presupposes and rests upon can be made to fit together with the view of human dignity it is designed to lead to and embody.[18]

Indeed, it cannot! (Again shades of Skinner, since the latter also wishes to establish a higher "dignity" by denying our very capacity to choose and achieve anything on our own.)

Rawls' theory is novel only in its assumptions and steps, not in its general conclusions. Most members of the intelligentsia hold to the egalitarian ideal. And who can deny that even today most government oratory, if not actual policy, is aimed at the satisfaction of demands made in behalf of the "least favored" or " disadvantaged" people in our society, especially in economic matters? On that front we find in Rawls a standard egalitarian ideal.

Yet there is no reason to believe that material wealth is the only good and thus the one to be shared, nor that giving it to people after appropriating it from others is an improvement of the former's lives. There is reason to believe that a parasitical dependence on others' achievements cannot bring health and welfare to people. Instead it is likely to foster a kind of limbo, of moral ambivalence, from which there is no reason to emerge, although it yields nothing particularly glorious or dignifying to one's life.

It does deserve mention that some have objected to an insufficiency of egalitarianism in Rawls' theory, contending that he is too egoistic, too concerned with people's self-interest. And indeed he makes allusions to such notions as self-interest, rights, liberty, and so forth. This in his effort to achieve the reconciliation mentioned before. But in the end, as with all attempts to sacrifice moral principles to something thought to be more important than morality—in this case full equality—there is little of these principles left when the doctrine is assessed.

I will not concern myself further with Rawls' views because I find it difficult if not useless to argue against intuitions. My own theory has been advanced in line with what I believe anyone *can* recognize as standards appropriate to a rational inquiry. Whatever errors or omissions there may be here, I do not advocate that anything but a rational treatment justifies accepting my conclusions. And relying on intuitions, i.e., widely accepted or experienced beliefs, hunches, feelings, and impressions concerning what is right, wrong, good, or evil in human life ought to be avoided as much as possible in one's personal life, but must be kept out of political matters. For here we are dealing with each other, not with one author and one reader who can leave each other be if they so prefer. Rawls' principles are intended, as are mine, to lead to political action. His, however, would be necessarily coercive, in which case especially one must insist on something more accessible and assessable than intuitions as justification. (Nor will it do to say that others, even in scientific theories, rely on some unquestionable premises, axioms, and so on. First, these are truly unquestion*able* only when to discard them must mean that nothing makes sense, which is untrue of intuitions. Second, axiomatic principles are far less plentiful in any rational enterprise than in Rawls'. Finally, scientific theories have no coercive implications for people.)

Some will dismiss his theory of justice as a heretical pipedream: pipedream it is, but heretical certainly not. The book has been criticized primarily for being internally inconsistent, often for not having gone far enough, only here and there for producing outrageous, immoral conclusions. Which is understandable in light of the fact that our present legal system is replete with measures which rest the lives, properties, feats and personal happiness of individuals on considerations of others' interests and necessity.

When this happens, when any remnants of greatness, human achievement and self-satisfaction are penalized so that not just the culture but the law itself enslaves great men, then one can begin to appreciate why many commentators describe America as despondent, culturally; why the nation that was once the hope and aspiration of millions of human beings (who sought liberty, not biological, environmental, or financial equality) must be reminded by oppressed Soviet intellectuals of the political principles that once were identified as its legal foundation.

Richard Weaver wrote a work well known to students of American political and cultural thought called *Ideas Have Consequences* (Phoenix, 1959). That title captures an important truth more often evaded than challenged. The following example should not come as a surprise to scrutinizers of political ideologies, as Dotson Rader made clear about his own when addressing William Buckley on his television program, Firing Line:

> You're continually trying to find rationality behind what people do politically—particularly what the Left does politically. The thrust of the Left is against reason. It's anti-rational. That's why it's anarchistic and nihilistic. It's antirational. . . . The motivation behind, say, the desire for those abstractions doesn't come intellectually. It comes emotionally. It comes out of the gut. And that's why attacking the Left for this and attacking the Left for that is a very rational argument, but it doesn't work.[19]

It is noteworthy that the thesis of the present book, wherein the free society is shown to be defensible from a general philosophical framework that identifies man as a being distinguished by as well as morally responsible for rationality, comes under direct attack from people such as Rader. They are more keenly aware than conservatives like Buckley of the crucial connection between the idea (and reality) of man as a *rational* being and the nature of the society appropriate for him. And they receive plenty of support in their attack on the foundation of political liberty. From its philosophers to its sociologists, psychologists, and historians of science, the bulk of intellectuals have renounced human reason, not just in matters of political theory but in science and philosophy as well.

One might think that orthodox Marxism, at least, holds out for science and rationality! But even there anti-rationalism prevails. The Hungarian Marxist Agnes Heller put the lid on the coffin of reason-in-Marxist thought:

> *Faith* in this invincibility [of human substance] is inseparable from Marxism. We use the term "faith" for as long as alienation exists, as long as the alternative of the continuation of alienated society persists (and even the alternative of further alienation), as long as the

alternative of accumulation of negative values is viable—the invincibility of the human is and remains a faith. But this faith is *inseparable* from Marxism, since it is *inseparable from the perspective of communism, from the standpoint of the proletariat, of the new materialism.* Should it turn out that our faith in the invincibility of the human substance, in the absoluteness of the progressive build up of values were hopeless, Marxism would lose its validity. As Marxists, who have made our decision for communism, who have recognized the *possibility* of communism within *existing* societies, who struggle for the realization of the alternative, this *dynamis—we believe in the invincibility of the human substance.*[20]

This, presented in a philosophy journal, amply bears out Rader's observation. It is a tragedy that liberty may be destroyed by people whose intellectual paraphernelia produces, in the end, no more than what comes from the gut, and from a faith in human invincibility. Any culture must have a great deal more than that to make its way to success. The performance of the anti-rationalists is elegant and even brilliant although made in behalf of a thesis about human *impotence*—in the bold and dismal tradition of Immanuel Kant.

But I will leave off these reflections of doom. As I said earlier, it is difficult to remain dispassionate when considering many contemporary trends. What needs to be discussed now is the alternative to these political doctrines, these varieties on statist themes we have been perusing, citing, describing.

What does a theory of human rights have to offer in a dynamic human community? What could there be if consideration and respect were given to such a system? That is to say, admitting that we might have done better by *consistently* adopting the ideas and ideals of a free human community, by incorporating the principles of human rights into the legal systems of our human communities more rather than less, what of this now? This is not an inquiry about what will happen, nor about whether hopefulness should be one's blind commitment, but about what service knowledge of human rights may provide, given the wrong turns and likely continued wrong directions of our political affairs.

Human Rights and Political Authority

I have argued that the development of government can only be morally justified if its function is to protect and preserve human rights. I should now make this clearer. For thus far I may have left the impression that my theory of government involves a *social contract* of sorts. In some sense this is right, except for the plain but important fact that the concept "contract" is misapplied: contracts emerge in a legal context. They are agreements with legal force, meaningful only where a legal system exists and is enforceable, i.e., one may enter into contracts which do not violate the basic tenets of such a system and expect, even demand, that these be upheld by the agents authorized to do so. But the context in and the means by which a government ought to be instituted are precontractual, what we could call natural or moral. There is no legal system and agency for any contractual relationship to take form. The question is then, what (kind of) means should be employed to establish a legal system and its administration, the government?

Although these may seem to be questions that fall short of being relevant to present social circumstances, they must be answered prior to attending to particular cases in terms of our theory. Clearly, governments did not *in fact* emerge by way of explicit agreements or anything of that sort in the bulk of cases in human history. Yet we can identify how they ought to have been established, i.e., the most general principles of conduct that govern the proper establishment of such an agency. This is no different from our ability to tell with certainty that black people should not have become part of American society by means of enslavement and forced immigration but by ways proper for purposes of joining a human community, if at all. We know that compulsory membership in a human community is wrong, and that both entry and departure should conform to principles of human conduct. (This does not apply to criminals, of course, where the principles must be applied to cover what should be done with those who violate or threaten the rights of innocent citizens.)

In general, then, how ought a proper government be established? In the simplest terms: by choice or freely given consent. But that alone will not illuminate the issue. Is this just a new version of the social contract theory, a theory both historically and logically indefensible? As with most seriously advanced political ideas, the social contract theory had an important insight, and that insight must be part of a valid account of the right approach to forming a civil society, a legal system with a means for its protection and preservation. Yet the difference between the contract theory and what is being proposed here is crucial. Let me point to it first by analogy. Consider that there is an important difference between establishing a romantic relationship by falling in love and uniting in marriage. Both should involve the consent of the participants, but the former is a far more subtle, tacit, even unself-conscious development of a relationship, while the latter is necessarily overt, explicit, technically circumscribed. Love, friendship, professional and other personal ties all involve better and worse means of establishment, but these are characteristically (though not exclusively) extralegal, gradual, evolutionary, and personal. Marriage, partnership, and contract, on the other hand, are possible only within the framework of a legal system which explicitly defines and upholds their terms.

The analogies above are not designed to prove the point, only to illuminate the difference between different means of establishing human relationships. The more personal ones *ought* to be free of compulsion, of course, and in this they resemble the more legalistic. But the former *bring about* a union, *establish* a relationship, while the latter are designed to *maintain* it, to *protect* against the always real possibility that people will change their minds. Without proper protection (terms of dissolution, etc.) others can experience suffering and loss (beyond emotional disappointment) that irrational, unjustified elements of the change of mind should not inflict upon those who have been promised cooperation and united effort. It is into the former category of personal relationships that the establishment of an organized human community must fall, even though, contrary to Hobbes, there exist better and worse means by which that can be done. Hobbes thought that necessity (the passion for avoiding death) would push individuals into social units, thus forcing upon all a social contract, a device by which peace would be maintained. He too saw what constitutes a reason for the establishment of civil society, namely that it is good for people, but this good he thought would be pursued of necessity, not be choice.

Because people are free agents, however, necessity will not impel them to establish a *civil* society. Some may not choose to be part of a community at all, even though it is right for them. Others may freely consent to an organized existence that in fact damages their best interest. The point is that care ought to be taken in the establishment—as well as maintenance and support—of an organized human community, care that will render it a civil(ized) society, not a barbaric state or an unprincipled, chaotic group or tribe.

In other personal relationships the parties ought to practice virtues in coming to form them—love, for instance, requires honesty, self-knowledge, independence, pride, and so on. A friendship, as Aristotle so brilliantly and eloquently identified, requires good people, ones who have cultivated virtues, moral character. Professional ties can also be undermined by a failure of character—lack of integrity, productivity, and so forth. As with these, so with the establishment of an organized human community—to build up to them well is not a matter of random, accidental conduct, purposeless and flighty or frivolous behavior. As such, both types of relationship can be submitted to moral scrutiny. If this were not so, if moral elements did not enter in, we could not make sense of such perfectly intelligible facts as phony friendships, misguided love affairs, ill-conceived governments, and so on.

First, in all human relationships there are certain basic ingredients which must be satisfied for them to be realized properly. They can all be varied considerably, but some basic features must be incorporated—sometimes tacitly, at other times with conscious deliberation. And all these features are closely tied to specific purposes, goals and values, which can involve only some people, in some places, in some epochs, and so forth. The kind of relationship that people embark upon in creating a human community, however subtly and gradually they might do this (or would have done it, had they done it properly), has its own standards of propriety: the human rights I have been working to identify and explain in this work. The rights and wrongs of the means by which the most general of human associations possible, namely a community of human beings as such, with no other purpose except the general one to live human life well, are the rights and wrongs we are able to identify by reference to the principles of human rights.

It is true enough that when a community would just get under way there is no enforcement of these rights and wrongs. But in the process of establishing such a community, the question of what ought to guide its existence, its development—of what its basic principles of organization ought to be—also involves the question of how people ought to enter into it. The protection of people's moral interests by way of maintaining laws based on the principles of human rights would make no sense if without such protection and maintenance one would have no rational grounds for observing them. In the earlier discussion of the "primitive" case those reasons were pinpointed already—i.e., why it is that everyone ought to conduct himself without violating the rights of others. What this implies for the present topic is that in the establishment of a government that serves to protect human rights these rights themselves should serve as the guiding principles—just as in the maintenance of its laws the same principles of conduct ought to serve as standards of proper (police, court, punitive) procedure.

So just what would be involved in establishing a government in line with human rights? What would those so engaged be doing, and why would that be right?

The purpose of setting up government is to assign the function of self-protection within a community to specialists. In the criticism of anarchism this was explained already. The point of devising a legal system that is publicly (communitywide) perceivable is to "advertise" the proper means by which to participate in a human community, (and to administer and insure just retaliation for offenders). Unless the opportunity exists to learn of these means, especially their detailed implications within various specialized areas of conduct (updated in line with the development of new areas by those so authorized, e.g., a legislature), violators cannot be held responsible for their transgressions. Yet this does not imply that all those in the vicinity must declare their loyalty to the laws. The following points should make clear why this is so.

The establishment of a proper government does not require the full consent of all of those who might be subject to the laws of a free society. The protection and preservation of one's moral (self) interests does not require the sanction and consent of those who violate or threaten to violate them; self-defense cannot wait for cooperation. Thus it is false that only full consent can authorize the kind of actions which a properly established government undertakes. Criminals would certainly withhold that consent in many cases (except where they are ready to atone). If full consent were a prerequisite, civil society could not be established and maintained. Then we would have to conclude that such a society *should* not be pursued: ought implies can. But we know that a good government, even once put into operation, will not please everyone! Moreover, it should not do so, lest it stop being a good government. It should, however, serve everyone's moral (self) interest, including the (true) interest of those who would oppose it and deny its authority.

On the other hand, none of this justifies the turn Hegel took at this stage of the analysis: that everyone must be made to conform to the will of the state! Secession, for example, or emigration, is always a proper option in view of the human right to liberty, however unwisely that liberty may be used by withdrawal from a good civil society. But Hegel's point is sound to the extent that, given the range of authority of government (the maintenance of peace and freedom—protection and preservation of human rights), those actions taken to pursue its proper purposes ought to be considered *prima facie* binding, i.e., binding unless demonstrably in violation of its purpose. To this point I will return later.

There are a number of ways open to those who have made the decision to establish a means for combating violations of and safeguarding their moral interests. A convention could accomplish this. With its admitted difficulties and improprieties, the constitutional conventions in America's history made the above procedural alternative an actual historical reality. Once the basic principles of community organization are identified—by those who convene and by others from whom they learn about such matters, including philosophers (e.g., Locke)—the convention would have as its proper goal the identification of the implications of those principles for their maintenance. These implications, together with the principles themselves, will constitute the foundation of the legal system. Even conduct during such a convention ought to be guided by the principles involved—thus persuasion, argument, rational discourse, but not coercion ought to be the method of approaching various problems that can and would most likely emerge.

One of the central issues that would have to be considered in such an (imagined) convention is the means of constituting the authority of legal administrators, officers of the law, and so on. Here it is crucial to note that the establishment of such authority will again have to be accomplished by adherence to human rights. Unless an individual or organization adheres to those principles in the process of being instituted (i.e., taking office) he cannot be trusted to uphold laws designed to protect them (i.e., the people) against violators. His integrity, in short, would be lost in the process, and thus also his authority would be undercut.

The point then is this: political or legal authority presupposes authorization of the government in accordance with the principles of a good human community. Those who assert this authority must be prepared, morally and logically speaking, to justify that they have been so authorized. Tradition, custom, happenstance, and whatever else can contribute to the dynamics of a civil society can only be kept in check, morally speaking, by constant demands upon those who choose to work in the field of legal administration and enforcement—the practice of taking an oath of office or loyalty on the part of those employed in government, however much it is abused and distorted in a statist society (where virtually everyone works for "the people" in government related services), pays homage to this point. The "just powers" of the officers of a government are powers that are morally justified. And the moral justification required in this context must, because of the nature of the enterprise, be by reference to the principles of human interaction as such—not to principles applicable in romance, friendship, professional cooperation, but to those that apply irrespective of special relationships, simply by virtue of being human. In short, if in accord with individual human rights (and by some due procedure) someone can show that he has the authority to act, judge and make decisions affecting others, he has political authority.

Now an important observation is that one may never have a culture where people acknowledge human rights in sufficient numbers to establish political authority by adherence to them. Not only must there be a well-conceived process of proper authorization of political agents; people must be aware of it and construe it as of prime value for purposes of social organization and life. Because "governments are [ought to be] instituted among men, deriving their just powers from the consent of the governed . . . , whenever any form of government becomes destructive of these ends, it is the right of the people to alter or to abolish it, and to institute new government, laying its foundation on such principles and organizing its powers in such form, as to them shall seem most likely to effect their safety and happiness." But all of this may not be what people believe, as is the case in our own time. Yet that does not mean that they *should* not believe it, any more than a thief's not believing what he wants is owned by another means that he should not believe it. However, that large numbers of people fail to realize, or actively deny, the proper conditions for political authority may make a discussion such as the present seem superfluous, especially when presented in the hypothetical fashion that has been evident here.

There is nevertheless a sound purpose for treating these matters in their general, uncluttered form before transposing them to the moral and political conditions of actual and contemporary states. I want to emphasize though that being "pure" in this fashion is not to be confused with being utopian. (No more than when medical students are concerned with health per se, even though they realize that the likelihood of encountering an optimally healthy specimen is small.) This is not "idealism" but a possible state of affairs—what people could do and could have done, even came quite close to doing here and there.

Let me turn to some other issues related to establishing a civil society. Devising the legal system must take consideration of those not yet capable of making decisions or not yet born into the area where the government will have to carry out its purposes. This is a very difficult problem, and much debate has ensued among human rights theorists as to whether it is possible to construct a system of laws that takes full cognizance of the forthcoming generation.

For now I will simply hint at the solution to this problem which emerges from the present theory. If the principles in accordance with which the system is established and which it is to protect and preserve are correct ones—if these are indeed the human rights of all individuals—then there should be no problem. For under such a system the rights of all people ought to be protected and preserved, including those who newly enter the system. Because these will be children in most cases, their rights will be safeguarded by the protection of their parents' rights and the freedom of their parents to act toward them only within the same strictures. Thus, e.g., parents, by creating human life, take on responsibilities which they have no right to abandon—in fact, all they might do is to hire teachers, nurse-maids, and so on, or give up their children if some others *volunteer* to take care of them. Once the children are grown and may be identified as *capable* of leading the life of an adult (not simply *willing* to do so, although that can be a clue to whether they are capable), they would be entitled to the protection of their rights as well as to leaving the area in favor of the juris-diction of some other government or the life of a hermit or nomad—pro-vided they can without violating the rights of those in the vicinity.

As long as the legal system conforms to human rights principles, no newcomer can have complaints—i.e., rational ground for concluding that his best interest as a human being in a social context is not protected and preserved. If the newcomer chooses to become a member in such a human community, he/she may then act in any fashion conforming with human rights. He is not forced to (is legally protected from being forced to) do anything other than that which accords with his own choice; if he violates human rights the punishment will be an expression of his own choice.

Of course there are many possible ramifications of this, as there must be in a dynamic system—some questions can be answered only as we learn more about the emerging conditions of people and territories where the system is chosen. But from the above we can begin to see how the theory we are considering is suited for purposes of both hindsight and foresight (within the reasonable boundaries of what we know about such matters today). In some formal respects my description of the right way to go about forming a legal system and establishing a government corresponds to the formation of the American republic. Where this is not the case, the judgment from our perspective must be: so much the worse for the formation of that system. And this is not idle talk: in fact violation of human rights—in the many instances and variations we are able to identify in America's history—accounts for many of the complaints people have with American culture. This despite the fact that most commentators choose to charge America's unique political tradition, and the corollary economic system known as capitalism, with the fault. From racial segregation, inflation, and interventionist foreign policies, to the rule of Congress by lobbyists, corruption of the federal regulatory agencies, and ecological problems—all such ills are commonly blamed on capitalism; which means: on the institution of private property; which means: on the focal place of human rights in the original constitution. But quite the opposite analysis is appropriate.

While I am not about to embark on a comprehensive discussion of all these charges—I am simply not knowledgeable enough about economics to manage the more bizarre ones pertaining to the evils of the free market, e.g.—in the next section I will examine some case histories. I should warn my reader, however, that I do not believe that the existence of human rights violations can *by itself explain* the consequences. It must be clear by now that all such explanations must, in the end, be traced to the choices of human beings, to people themselves. This is the only rational approach and the only one that can give rise to some hope for improvement of the situation. For human rights theory, unlike Marxism and other doctrines, does not have history as its helper. *People* must do the work, through and through. Individually, first, and in voluntary cooperation with each other, if that is possible, thereafter.

CHAPTER 6

Coercion *includes, besides preventing a person from doing what he chooses, making his choice less eligible by threats;* restraint *includes any action designed to make the exercise of choice impossible and so includes killing or enslaving a person. But neither coercion nor* retraint *includes* competition. *In terms of the distinction between "having a right to" and "being at liberty to," . . . all men have, consistently with the obligation to forbear from coercion, the liberty to satisfy if they can such at least of their desires as are not designed to coerce or injure others, even though in fact, owing to scarcity, one man's satisfaction causes another's frustration. In conditions of extreme scarcity this distinction between competition and coercion will not be worth drawing; natural rights are only of importance "where peace is possible" (Locke). Further, freedom (the absence of coercion) can be* valueless *to those victims of unrestricted competition too poor to make use of it; so it will be pedantic to point out to them that though starving they are free.*

H. L. A. Hart

The Realpolitik and Human Rights

Reason, Human Rights, and Change

THE point has already been made that although many are familiar with human rights as at least the nominal foundation of the American political system, the theory of human rights—what gives human rights their best support as aspects of reality—is not widely known, nor regarded in practice. For this reason I will spend some time in an attempt to bring the present theory to bear upon ongoing, concrete human affairs, This will serve to both illustrate and expand the theoretical points made thus far.

But a few issues must be raised first about how we can best go about applying theory to cases. Contrary to what some might and do believe, it is not always simple to apply ideas learned even from careful theoretical and analytical processes. True enough, the idea "chair," for instance—the concept of chair—is hardly cumbersome as invoked in practice. When someone asks me to bring in the chair from the next room it is easy enough to pick it out from other objects. Even when asked to bring in a chair (any chair) I am usually able to simply pick one of the chairs, if there are any around. But at this point I may already require a more complicated judgment. If I find several objects in the room that might be used as chairs, it may require more effort to sort things out so that I take back a chair and not a strangely constructed table. In cases involving human artifacts, with changing character and emerging inventions, frequent rethinking and re-application of concepts are called for. Even outside the context of human intervention and creation, we sometimes find it difficult to identify whether some particular thing is, for instance, this or that kind of flower, a tree or a bush, a river or a lake, a tornado or a hurricane. Some have argued that all these classifications are simply invented by human beings, quite arbitrarily at first, and carried on through generations, thus signifying nothing orderly *in nature,* only a propensity for people to organize (pigeonhole) their experiences. Much could be said about this, but the earlier discussions pertaining to metaphysical issues (fundamental facts, and so on) should make clear the problems in thinking that our classifications, categorizations, or conceptualizations could do us any good without a firm basis that is considerably more than arbitrary (chancy or random). I will not dwell on that issue here. The point is to discuss how the idea of human rights, identified and validated earlier, may be employed in attempts to make sense of contemporary political affairs.

A second preliminary point about our application of concepts and theories is that just because we have an idea of something, in this case human rights, it does not follow that we already do or need to know everything to which it might apply. There are many items in reality whose existence or significance is open to discovery, and the question about how one might come into their ownership, for example, presents the need for *ongoing* application of property rights. Discovery of the electromagnetic spectrum opened up a new variety of ownership. Since no one had previously known that such items as frequencies existed in nature, no one had asked how someone might own (rent, buy, sell, steal) this or that frequency. The concept of ownership is not, then, confined in its applicability to a certain fixed number of certain kinds of things. It might be feasible to solve pollution problems by establishing ownership in air, water, and so on, as legally enforceable features of a society. Until recently this concern faced no one. Since air and water were not scarce items everyone could use them freely and there was no point in making some parcel of air or water one's own, preventing its abuse, making the most of it as best one could. But today clean air and water are becoming scarce. No longer will it be without significance who uses what segment of air and how it is used. Application of property rights would require that we find out *how* a person could make portions of these items his own, use them, trade them, be penalized for ruining others', and so on. Many people raise objections against fully implementing the property rights system in economic affairs on grounds that technological changes make it impractical. That is to say, because new items emerge and familiar ones are modified, refined, or altered, they foresee (insurmountable) problems with implementing the principles of a system that involves property rights.

There are two major points to be made about this objection. First, human rights are not rules; the legal system organized in terms of them is not a game with (static) rules invented to limit the range of activities of the players. In most games decisions are made by invoking the rules, which some unilateral decision can change. Indeed, if the rules of chess were seriously altered, it is doubtful we would still be playing *chess*. At any rate, human rights are not rules which are laid down but standards, principles identified through an examination of the nature of the entity whose conduct they serve to guide. Two things follow from this fact. First, depending on new developments in the relationships people can engage in, the principles are open to wider and wider *application* with no need to change them. Second, should the *nature* of the entities involved change, then, and only then, is a change in the principles themselves required. Human nature has not changed for many thousands of years, although the perimeters of human actions, relationships and conditions of life have changed. It is a failure to notice this point—or an unwillingness to do so—that leads people to say such things as "We need to abandon our obsolete constitutional system of government in our modern era," or "The American system of law was suited for a predominantly agricultural society, but it is inapplicable for purposes of guiding conduct in an industrialized, technological age." (Not consistently, it is often remarked that the emerging nations of Africa and Asia cannot benefit from the political system of individualism *because* they are not yet industrialized!)

Second, the legal system based on human rights is not static in the way mechanical systems are. To propose that such a system is static is to fail to notice an important epistemological fact about principles in general: the knowledge of the nature of things and of the principles that do (or should) govern (or guide) their action does not constitute a final picture, a sort of passive grasp (or snapshot) of timeless and fixed existence. The philosophy of Plato first encouraged the conviction that knowledge must mean to have grasped some final, static, unchangeable idea (or perfect form). For centuries such an idea was by many taken to be the characteristic candidate for what I have called a definition (or the nature) of something. And if true, then if we ever do know anything it would mean that there could never be a change in the scope of our knowledge—otherwise we would simply be proven to have failed to grasp the truth of the matter. The evident growth of knowledge contradicts the Platonic view of what it must be.

The fact is that in philosophical circles, where these issues are discussed and political philosophies are debated, the issue of definitions is crucial to human rights theory and morality in general. Since the nature of anything, including human nature, has often been explained along Platonist lines, critics who saw the pitfalls of that view had a telling point against the rest of the position.[1] In the next chapter I will offer some ideas about a view of knowledge that can escape the wrath of skepticism. For now it is enough to note that it is mainly by understanding human rights as unalterably fixed, static rules of conduct that one can object to them as did Jeremy Bentham and other more contemporary critics, charging that they must lead to a rigid, stagnating legal system which cannot accommodate the changing conditions of human existence.

Before I proceed to consider some ongoing problems of society from the point of view of the present theory, another warning is due. A *theory* is often thought of as a static statement of some facts and relationships in reality. So it too is thought to be inherently restrictive, incapable of growth and development, requiring drastic revolutions, major turnovers, so as to accommodate change.[2] This only holds if one forces the idea of a theory to conform to the earlier mentioned conception of knowledge and understanding. No inherent conflict exists between the idea that principles govern reality (and ought to govern human conduct) and the idea that we can keep an open mind about the future, whether anything new will occur that will require revision of our ideas. The proposition that one *might* have to change one's mind is not a valid objection to what one has now concluded on a sound basis. After all, one might *not* have to change one's mind also; the objection amounts to no more than a declaration of ignorance about what the future will bring. And ignorance of the future is no ground for changing the conclusions that are rationally warranted. (Yet it is often no more than "what *might* happen" that underlies the objections to many substantive conclusions about the world and how one ought to cope with it.) Another fashion in which people express the same "objection" to some conclusion that is warranted by the best available case (theories, observations, evidence, arguments, comparisons, tests, and whatever else constitutes a good case in some field of knowledge, for this can vary with the nature of the subject matter being studied) is to say: "Why not opt for a different view anyway? Why not *assume* that there is a better one, even in the face of the best case we have?"

But to these approaches there is no answer, simply because they seek answers from nowhere, having refused to work with the best that human beings can now offer, namely a case that has emerged from a rational investigation of the subject matter at hand. The desire for something other than or more than a rational argument cannot be decisive for human beings intent upon dealing with the present problems of mankind in a framework of cooperation, objectivity, and cogency. The latter is the only approach that can be justified as suited for human purposes, even if some philosophers have tried to present rational arguments that the human mode of investigating reality is itself the main stumbling block to knowledge of reality, true knowledge, knowledge *unimpeded by rationality!*

Virtue, Vice Squads, and Human Rights

All along some readers probably think of the present theory and proposals as some kind of dreamy, romantic ideals—the idea of a good human life and a good political system is so far removed from what we find in our midst that no realist could possibly take it seriously. The presupposition is that realism requires renouncing values and ideals, because today the term often means something closer to pragmatism or expediency, facing each problem separately as it arises, refusing to "impose" one's values on the world, being tolerant of any and every proposal contrary to one's own. At the other end of the pole are those who misconstrue fighting for ideals to involve imposing one's values on others by force. It is these people who (necessarily) subvert human rights most frequently. The examples are many and I can mention only a few.

Those who advocate laws to limit or prohibit all kinds of activities believe (or tolerate) the idea that the freedom of human beings to conduct their own lives ought to be infringed upon whenever others do not choose what the advocates of the laws have concluded is right. These people want to forcibly prevent or regulate gambling, prostitution, selling matches on Sundays, selling wine after eleven P.M., taking too few or too many vitamins, entering one's child in the school one has judged best, advertising one's products on children's TV programs, traveling to Cuba, printing or reading dirty books, advocating repugnant or wrong political ideas, choosing whether one's earnings will go to moon shots or to keeping philharmonic orchestras in business, supporting one's own choice of scientific research or scholarly studies, making risqué jokes on television, smoking cigarettes, acquiring certain types of drugs, selling one's house on one's own conditions, forming labor unions and entering into exclusive contracts with businesses, marrying a mate of different racial or religious background, giving money to those one loves without being penalized for it by taxes (except if the government approves of the beneficiary), engaging in sexual practices of any kind alone or with consenting partners, and on and on—the list is tragically long, even in this, our so-called "free society." None of the above activities involve others who want no part of them—there are no unavoidable consequences for people who have other goals and purposes. Yet they are all regulated or forbidden outright.

The list does not even mention many of the activities one is forced to carry out. One must stand ready to join armies when some others decide that this should be so. (At this writing the actual implementation of this power to conscript is suspended, but Congress still has the authority to activate the draft.) One must obtain licenses to practice medicine, barbering, television repair, and thousands of other professions. One is forced to submit architectural plans to city politicians to make a determination about their merit. Children must be sent to school at a certain age. And of course, most pervasive of all, anyone who has an occupation must also do forced labor for the government to support the various projects others have decided ought to be carried out.

I am not about to consider the hundreds of proffered justifications cited in each of these instances. Some have already come up and others will be touched on—especially relating to a favorite conventional notion that as long as "people" want these things, they ought to be done, that is, the doctrine of collectivism. (The democratic theory of social good is just one example of this.) Nor will I now discuss whether we can really know when rights are being violated. The point here already presupposes that human rights exist, that we can learn what they are and therefore what constitutes the basic features of their violation. In the upcoming sections I will exhibit several areas and cases which would come under the category of unjustifiably prohibited or coerced conduct such as listed above.

Even here it is best to stay with general descriptions, and not speculate on the most detailed elements of each actual case as it would emerge when, for instance, investigated in a court room. That would not be possible without a great deal of knowledge of particular circumstances. I will take several commonly known areas where the government forces people to act as government officials ("the people") judge right and good, or where they prohibit conduct they judge wrong. Some will be of significance to many people (those whose rights are infringed upon most), while others are closer to the concerns of only a few. They all involve the violation of the human rights of individuals in American society (as well as other societies, but I will not be directly concerned with these).

In all of these instances the point of the following will be to indicate that it could have happened differently; it was essentially the choices of human beings that made it possible; and we should act differently now, as well as in the future, to the best of our available knowledge.

State Education and the Free Society

Aristotle explained the social nature of man by reference to his capacity to learn from others and the potential contribution of such learning to each person's happiness. Indeed, for Aristotle the purpose of community life lies mainly in the indispensability of a good human community to the achievement of the greatest possible degree of human self-sufficiency. A paradox, some people might think—after all, does not self-sufficiency mean independence of the contributions *others* might make to one's life? A sufficient self, Aristotle would have replied, is one that has achieved the greatest of its potential.[3] In society the potentials for everyone are far greater than in isolation.

Education is unequivocally important. It is a service of value to people, and one which can be provided only through creativity, productivity, labor, management, investment, risk, and a host of other human endeavors required in order to offer any valuable service and product in society. In this respect, at least, education is no different from anything else people want from each other so as to obtain some benefit. Shocking as this may sound to some, in a free society, organized consistently in accordance with human rights, education would be entirely depoliticalized, i.e., independent of government(s). It is precisely because of its importance that education should be kept as free as possible of any element of coercion. By treating it as a public enterprise education becomes one more area of human activity unavoidably characterized by severe limitations on personal and economic freedom, not to mention the more specific freedom of thought.

The most obvious of these limitations is that the activity must be supported from taxes, funding obtained by coercion. Moreover the venture must thereafter be subject to some kind of public control, which in effect means governmental control. Parents and children are forced into a system they have not chosen to participate in and about which they have little if any say. Since all must pay into the system—lest they forego their existing liberty of action (by serving in jails for tax evasion)—it is virtually impossible for them to avoid it. The only alternative to participation is to rely on private schools, incurring serious additional costs (double jeopardy). And even there state governments exert control via accreditation requirements, a process that clearly assumes superior knowledge by those close to the state of what constitutes the best educational method and content.

Let us ward off some initial challenges to this position which might render it impossible to consider seriously the criticism that public education involves violation of human rights. In line with a doctrine often attributed to Thomas Jefferson, many claim that a democracy depends upon providing citizens with basic knowledge so that all can be participants in the political system. It is regarded as such an important matter that "society as a whole" rather than parents ought to make the decision as to whether, when, and how the child ought to be educated. A modern twist on this objection is to point out that since everyone in society benefits from the education of its members—the emphasis is increased productivity rather than responsible citizenship—everyone ought to (be forced to) bear the costs associated with such improvement.

Several crucial issues are overlooked in arriving at the Jeffersonian conclusion. It is assumed that the state *can* provide this education and, moreover, can do so without harmful consequences to the citizens outweighing whatever the education itself *might* accomplish. Let us leave aside the obvious problems with educating people to be good citizens. More important is the assumption that the admitted value of education implies that it should be forcibly imposed on people. It might be worth recalling that Jefferson said, "I have sworn . . . eternal hostility to every form of tyranny over the mind of man."

The fact that education is of great benefit to most people could well support the belief that it ought to be provided for those who need and want it. When something is valuable to someone it is quite true that he ought to obtain it, but the means by which he ought to do so is not specified in the mere acknowledgement of this value. One ought to consider whether the various means by which this can be done *ought* to be employed. An extreme case should illustrate this: recently a forty-seven-year-old man with a rapidly failing heart checked into a New York hospital for a possible transplant operation, but there was no dying contributor with a suitable organ. Without another heart the man would be certain to die within a short period of time, while with it he would have a chance at perhaps many more years of life. The value to him of a new heart, then, is clear. Yet to suggest that this entitles the individual to hire someone to kill a "donor" is simply outrageous—to do so would be a severe violation of another's right to life.[4] And while that kind of suggestion is often given legal sanction in societies that aim for the good of Aryans, workers, the rich, the poor, or the ecologically useful, those are barbaric societies just for that reason—the rights of human beings are evaded in the process of reaching some good that may, on its own, without such violation of others' rights, have merit. Furthermore, there is no logical difference between taking another individuals's life for one's benefit and taking away another's property and liberty; there is only a difference in the degree of severity. The example cited is extreme but not. irrelevant to the point.

There are many other objections people will make (and have made) to the present thesis. Some are not worth debating—e.g., that we should not treat education as a business, as if there were something demeaning in doing so. A more important retort is that children are necessarily coerced anyway when sent to school, namely by their parents. So why object to state enforced education? This raises the issue of whose responsibility children are. But since parents (or appropriately selected guardians) chose the child, he/she is certainly not someone else's responsibility. And as children, as *dependents,* their welfare ought to be the concern of parents. (In case of criminal neglect coercion may be justified against the parents. But with the present educational system parents are coerced with no criminal neglect on their part having been established.)

To return now to the case at hand, education, let us consider the numerous ways in which states necessarily, unavoidably obstruct human liberty in managing it. The most obvious is that childless parents (and those who have chosen to limit the size of their families) must finance the well being of others' children, a fact which clearly imposes upon them unjust burdens, i.e., a responsibility they have not assumed either by explicit choice or by their actions. (For even if one has a child "by accident" that action imposes upon a person responsibilities that *ought to* have been acknowledged at the outset.) Conversely, the beneficiaries of the system are legally encouraged—even forced via compulsory education—to encroach upon the rights of others to obtain benefits for themselves (or their children). Of course those who consider the so-called population problem fail to notice that state education makes it simple for parents to relinquish one of the most severe responsibilities of parenthood today.

Many will protest that, in spite of these factors, it is not right that innocent children might not receive an education. But this merely reiterates the value of education without considering what are the right means of obtaining it. Certainly nothing in the legal system based on human rights would prohibit people from contributing to others' education, from organizing charities, from devising business ventures by means of which long-term loans could be made available to those who want to obtain an education. Nor is it a valid objection that such schemes would not emerge, given that the value of education is recognized.

People are also restrained in, at least, and often prevented from selecting the education they think suitable for their offspring or themselves.[5] This is first of all because of the public funding of the state system, whereby one's resources which might go toward selecting a different system are depleted. And second, even if one selects a nonstate institution, the latter too are regulated by the state, which again limits one's real choice of type of education.

Another immoral consequence of the involvement of state power arises from what is known as the "equal protection" clause of the Constitution. This clause is generally interpreted—by intellectuals, especially those with egalitarian political attitudes (which includes quite a few)—to require that all tax-supported services or projects be completely equal in substance and in their methods of dispensing the services.

It should be noted that in its most meaningful context such an equal protection provision would be fully justified: since government (if we take the Declaration of Independence seriously, and by the requirements of previous chapters) is established to secure the rights of all human beings, their human rights, it is important that all individuals have their rights equally well protected and preserved. Since only *human* rights—those which *all* human beings have—can be *equally* protected, it is arguable that the "equal protection" clause of the Constitution pertains to each person's entitlement to equal protection against private or public violation of his rights to life, liberty, and the pursuit of happiness.

Yet in recent years government has taken on all sorts of protection which has gone far afield of those rights which, being universal, can be equally protected. A poignant example is a recent communication from New York Republican Senator Jacob K. Javits, in response to my letter protesting proposed restrictions by the Food and Drug Administration on the purchase of vitamins (notice how far we are getting from starvation!). The following passage expresses the currently dominant approach with unusual candor:

While we protect the right of the individual to buy vitamins, we must at the same time safeguard him and those individuals who may not be aware of the dangers of potential over-use of vitamins against the possible hazards.[6]

No mention is made of how in the effort to safeguard people against *possible* hazards, people who *may not be aware* of the dangers of *potential* over-use (never mind all these empty qualifiers), the actual, real, existing human rights of millions of others will be violated.

The case is similar with education. And when the equal protection clause is invoked this must involve the forcible equalization of people in respects where they can not at all benefit from equality. For the egalitarians forget that while with respect to their rights all human beings are indeed equal—because of their membership in the class of entities with their particular *nature*—with respect to the kind of education that will be good for them this is just not so. The same, of course, goes for the amount of vitamins people need or the amount that can hurt them. (It is interesting that the FDA made the proposals about vitamins on the basis of controversial experiments, and scientists in the field of nutrition are up in arms about the results and the proposed ruling. But not, of course, about human rights!)

The consequences of the equal protection provision applied to education are, of course, deplorable. That provision must go hand-in-hand with the notion either that education can somehow be quantified in general terms, to apply in equal portions to all children—regardless of talents, interests, preparedness, intelligence, opportunities in the context of one's own future, etc.—or that all these differences can be overcome by varying amounts of education so that all benefit equally. The outcome in practice is that the system becomes geared to some mythical "average child," with the result that the majority receive an education ill-suited to individual characteristics. The payoff is well-documented in the recent literature: bored and often violently rebellious students, frustrated teachers, and effectively illiterate high school graduates.

Another consequence of statist educational systems is that hardly any room is left for genuine and careful experimentation with educational methods. There is a tendency to implement only the "establishment" theories. In the present age, when social scientists for the most part view human beings as passive respondents (either to their genetically inherent instincts or to their environment), the prominent educational methods accommodate these models. (Interestingly enough, the Montessori method, developed in private schools, seems to have the greatest promise thus far. But by its very nature it is unsuited for state implementation; it is based on the idea that children flourish best when treated as free agents, capable of choice.)

To all this some will respond with a weakened Jeffersonian argument: "But is not some mediocre education for all better than the risk of getting none if it would be left to the choices and activities of the individuals involved?" Of course—for some people it is no doubt good to get this much at least. Some might indeed get nothing if it were left up to their parents. It would be absurd to claim that no one benefits from the present educational system in America—or in the Soviet Union or in any other nation where the bulk of it is provided by the state.

But some people *can* benefit from falling off a roof. This of course says nothing about what they might have gained had they not fallen off. But even if that is outweighed by the gains from falling off, it is still illegitimate, logically, to conclude from this that now everyone *(a)* ought to fall off roofs or *(b)* ought to be thrown off.[7] So just because some children *can* benefit from the present system it does not follow that they would not gain from one which is basically different. As long as there is the *possibility* of benefiting from a system in which human rights are respected, such a system is better than one where human rights are violated.

But we are not just speaking of possibilities. The fact is that there is ample evidence that free human beings can do better at everything than slaves or semislaves. Concerning education in particular, there is a great deal of evidence that children *(a)* would be better off with the responsibility for their education left in the hands of their parents, *(b)* are clearly hurt by the education they now get (in comparison to their mental and emotional capacities), and *(c)* would cultivate a sense of responsibility if they could not take it for granted that others may be forced to support their goals and purposes in life.

A final point about education in particular is important to mention. The idea that public education is free is widely accepted, in spite of the fact that the state forces all to pay for it and all to attend state established or approved institutions. Public education is, of course, not free in more ways than one. While the country enjoys relative freedom, such forced labor to support it and forced participation as we experience with the educational system of the United States are generally considered insignificant. The relative political liberty of the country does not encourage emigration, and attracts enough people from abroad to offset the loss of "investment" in some who do leave! But in this connection it is good to keep in mind that recently when a number of Jews attempted to leave the Soviet Union the state imposed a tax upon them, arguing that these individuals had received a "free" education and now clearly *owed* the government. Similar measures were proposed in England during the late 1950s when many professionals wanted to emigrate to the United States. Should the tide turn in this country it is virtually inevitable that one's "free education"—to which everyone is now supposed to have a virtual natural right—would no longer be regarded as quite so costless and provided in the spirit of pure altruism that the argument in its support feigns.

Still, in the last analysis, the most important of all the above considerations is that education, while an admittedly good thing for most people, does not justify the violation of the rights of human beings. Even if the state could do it well, though it cannot; even if the state did not use it for purposes of establishing loyalty to its own leadership and policies, though it does; even if it did not stifle the development or the improvement of this particular human activity and theoretical field of inquiry, which it clearly does—even without all these obvious deficiencies, the education of any individual should not be achieved at the expense of violating human rights. It is in no way morally different from taking a gun, going next door, robbing the home, taking the money and hiring a teacher, then going to another home and taking the resident child at gunpoint to be "educated" by the teacher—even if the teacher is Socrates and the child the offspring of two of the most negligent people in the universe.

A great many other issues could be considered here in relation to the general topic of education. E. G. West's well-researched and argued thesis about the lack of any economic justification for introducing public education could be reiterated at length.[8] The circumstances involving the introduction of public education in Massachusetts so as to *prevent* the admission of black children into the available educational system, namely private schools, could be recounted. The initial aim of most of America's public school systems—to establish centers for official instruction in the most favored religion of some state—could be discussed. But these are topics on which others have elaborated at length.[9] The main point to be made in connection with the present topic is not only that there is a clear moral justification for taking government out of education, but there simply has never been any *evidence* to suppose that governments would improve on the educational circumstances of the people. While the moral case is the most significant in the final analysis, these other points should only go to show that a breach of morality is usually followed by disastrous consequences—the economic, sociological, psychological, and related cases against public education give ample support to the contention that it is bad for people.

The conclusion is well-expressed, not by a libertarian, but by a close friend of the Left, Ivan Illich:

Two centuries ago the United States led the world in a movement to disestablish the monopoly of a single church. Now we need the constitutional disestablishment of the monopoly of the school, and thereby of a system which legally combines prejudice with discrimination. The first article of a bill of rights for a modern humanist society would correspond to the first amendment to the U. S. Constitution: "The State shall make no law with respect to the establishment of education."[10]

While it is unlikely that a movement in this direction is soon to emerge—what with people divided into warring interest groups on practically every issue—it is in fact the *moral* responsibility of every person living in an organized human community to support measures that foster instead of hinder the development of the best alternatives. Granted not all of us can concern ourselves with every statist measure. But for those concerned with education, cognizant of its value for those who need and want it, the divorce of the state from educational activities ought to be a main, even if only long-range, goal.

In the process of adjusting the present legal and political system to the principles that are correct for human communities, many courses of action can be identified as suitable. Any measure leading in the direction of greater liberty and independence from the state deserves close examination and intelligent support. Such remedies as the voucher system suggested by Milton Friedman need to be examined very closely—sometimes remedies which still involve the state can lead to even greater state control because of the virtually inevitable entrenchment of governmental bureaucracy, an enterprise aimed not at profit and, thus efficiency, but power, and therefore longevity at any cost. Some people have, of course, decided to struggle by turning to the development of private educational alternatives, even if this means having to suffer unjust financial burdens in the process. For those with children this alternative could be appropriate, yet even these individuals owe it to themselves to give expression to their dismay with state-run education whenever this is possible and productive. Only by such a concerted effort is there a chance that the current debacle in education will be reversed.

Of course, even if no one takes these steps the fact remains that people ought to so long as education is indeed a value to human life. Nor will failure to act be inconsequential. In the case of governmentally conducted education the evidence should be quite obvious. But when the continued existence of some activity is so thoroughly dependent on the violation of rights this result ought not be surprising. It is only sad that not enough people recognize even this much about the situation—thus asking for even more state interference. Human education, however, is far more precious a thing than to be left up to experts in the administration of *force*. For that is precisely what governments are expert at—nothing else.

Censorship—No; Obscenity—That's Your Responsibility

These days reference to the First Amendment of the Constitution—once the most explicit statement of rights all of us possessed according to that document—ought to draw only cynical grins on people's faces. Frankly, in the American legal system there is no longer any *legal* barrier to censorship. Of course it is still a fact that censorship is less prevalent in this country than in most others. As with any long-developed free enterprise, the press, e.g., will not suddenly stop producing the legitimate wares of its trade simply because of the removal of official protection against those who might want to regulate its activities. But, as will become clear, there are many other areas where censorship prevails, although rarely recognized as such.

Following the five notorious rulings of the Supreme Court in the summer of 1973, the American legal system is left with the following principles by which the activities of all enterprises, including the press, shall be judged:

> It is sufficient to reiterate the well-settled principle that Congress may impose relevant conditions and requirements on those who use the channels of interstate commerce in order that those channels will not become the means of promoting or spreading evil, whether of a physical, moral or economic nature.

Justice Burger, who wrote this majority opinion in the case of the *United States* v. *Orito,* adds the following footnote:

> Congress can certainly regulate interstate commerce to the extent of forbidding and punishing the use of such commerce as an agency to promote immorality, dishonesty, or the spread of any evil or harm to the people of other states from the state of origin.

The rationale, protection of the populace from possible harm, is the same, of course, as that offered by Senator Javitz (quoted earlier). Because the press in this country has rarely been threatened with government intervention, censorship and debates about "free expression" have usually centered around the production and sale of obscene or pornographic materials. And it is usually accepted that it is the conservatives who, in their concern for preserving the good community by fostering the goodness of its members, would abrogate the rights mentioned in the First Amendment. Yet as Ayn Rand argues in her discussion of the Supreme Court's obscenity rulings, it only appears that the conservatives and liberals—both in American politics and on the Court—differ in their basic philosophical positions, and thus in their willingness to put aside basic liberties for certain purposes. Both camps hold the same premise—*the mind-body dichotomy*—but choose opposite sides of this lethal fallacy.

> The conservatives want freedom to act in the material realm; they tend to oppose government control of production, of industry, of trade, of business, of physical goods, of material wealth. But they advocate government control of man's spirit, i.e., man's consciousness; they advocate the State's right to impose censorship, to determine moral values, to create and enforce a governmental establishment of morality, to rule the intellect. The liberals want freedom to act in the spiritual realm; they oppose censorship, they oppose government control of ideas, of the arts, of the press, of education (note their concern with "academic freedom"). But they advocate government control of material

production, of business, of employment, of wages, of profits, of all physical property—they advocate it all the way down to total expropriation.

The conservatives see man as a body freely roaming the earth, building sand piles or factories—with an electronic computer inside his skull, controlled from Washington. The liberals see man as a soul freewheeling to the farthest reaches of the universe—but wearing chains from nose to toes when he crosses the street to buy a loaf of bread.[11]

Yet it is clear enough that controlling either the intellectual (spiritual, moral, religious) activities of man, or his actions concerning physical reality (trade, exchange, production, consumption, ownership), involves the violation of his human rights. Still, in recent years legal decisions pertaining to the liberty to express oneself have too frequently centered around an issue that simply does not relate to human rights at all. In most of the obscenity cases the focal point of attention has concerned whether it is possible to identify or define obscenity at all. In effect the "liberal" approach, exemplified by American Civil Liberties Union spokesmen, to artistic and other forms of human expression rests, in the main, not on any defense of the freedom to give expression to one's artistic, scientific or political ideas, but on the alleged inherent impossibility of identifying obscene or pornographic materials.

No doubt what is and is not obscene is not a *simple* matter to identify. But neither is it a simple matter to identify what constitutes racial, religious, ethnic, or economic discrimination—instances the liberals and the ACLU have never found much trouble with when setting up legal prohibitions against those who engage in them. The legal codes of this country are filled with statutes that address themselves to categories of human action which are delineated only with difficulty.

Now there are several things wrong with basing the argument against censorship on the premise that we cannot know what is obscene. The first is simple: we *can* know what is obscene, and often enough we do. People may not often be able to explain just how they know it, nor what implicit definition of obscenity guides their judgment. But most people have no explanation for their ability to identify tables or chairs or crocodiles either. Still, they know what a chair is and can guide their conduct quite well without the explanation at their fingertips.[12]

True enough, obscenity is a far more complex matter than furniture or wild animals. That it is usually a creation of human beings is one of the tempting grounds for assuming its indefinability. In fact, obscenity is a normative category—it serves to attribute to various forms of human creation an aesthetic quality. Most people, in turn, believe that in art there is no objective standard for judging something good or bad, beautiful or ugly, degrading or dignified. Yet this of course does not demonstrate that artistic standards *do not exist,* could not be identified. In morality, as in art, standards are difficult to identify and, especially, to justify. But none of that shows that standards are impossible.

The second objection to this approach, then, is that those who object to censorship on indefinability grounds can be dismissed by the counter-claim that just in case someone can define obscenity (and they have proven that no one can), we ought to forbid it wherever possible. The liberals have no argument to offer here. They must, logically speaking, allow for the possibility of such standards, especially since there are all too many people who are willing to come forth with some. Another argument is required—one which defends the human right to free expression, not our alleged inability to judge whether that expression is worthwhile or not.

Whether any expression, be it in the context of art, entertainment, politics, science, scholarship, or casual discourse and behavior, is obscene or pornographic or in some other way falls short of valid standards of truth, beauty, taste, and so on ought not be the concern of the legal framework and judgment of a system suited for organizing a human community. It is in this sense, and not because of some indefinability, that "obscenity is your responsibility." Each person and each group of persons in voluntary association ought to be free to choose to say or do whatever they deem proper, and everyone should be protected against any incursion of this freedom.

The only problematic cases here concern slander and libel. Should one be at liberty to make statements about another person that are unjustifiably degrading (obscene) and pass these on to others in trade or exchange? But these cases can be handled in a broader context than obscenity: one does not have the right (ought not have the liberty) to defraud those with whom one is trading. Another area of trouble can be handled with a similar recognition that one ought not trade in information about others which has not been provided voluntarily.

To return to the debated areas of free expression, we need to consider the conservatives' case *for* censorship—the liberals' is only a misguided one against it. As David Brudnoy writes,

A case can be made against allowing anybody, anywhere, at any time (in public) to call Thurgood Marshall a "nigger," or Henry Kissinger a "kike," or, as Bill Buckley drew the example, to produce a *comedy* about the horrors of Buchenwald. So long as we recognize, for instance, that the fabric of society can quite definitely be rent by callousness (such as a rock musical on the fun aspects of the massacre of Hue would do in Saigon or, let's pray, anywhere—or a songfest on TV at Easter time about Jewish "Christ-killings" coupled with a hymn of praise to Adolf Hitler and the memory of the joys of Auschwitz), there *is* a case to be made for censorship.[13]

And, indeed, if we add to this the prospect of advertising a brothel next door to a convent, putting up a billboard advocating abortion across the street from a cathedral, and so forth, the case for censorship appears to be quite plausible.

It is important to notice here Brudnoy's qualifier "in public." A good deal of this kind of thinking rests on the premise that the idea of a "public sphere" is intelligible in a truly free society. The only sense that could be given to it would be in the context of the areas occupied by the government—where, of course, that agency, as any other firm doing business with people, would have jurisdiction. Since this firm would serve all the people in the community who subscribe to it—all of the citizens—its rules could not be directed to exclude some of them. But this follows from the nature of the government's business, from the fact that it serves a clientele with only one relevant set of characteristics, namely that they are human beings. One other sense of "public" that would be possible in the context of a free society is where we would mean areas or buildings that serve the function of transportation—even if that service is provided in the free market it is necessarily public in some respects. Some such "public" places would, conceivably, have rules prohibiting the use of such terms as "nigger" or "kike" (just as most restaurants require wearing a shirt), while others would not, depending on the specification for entry. It is unlikely, of course, that any transportation facility would stay in business long with restrictive conditions favoring whites or blacks or Jews or tall people alone. (The segregation of people on buses in the South was mostly the function of *legally imposed* conditions of use, in municipalities with transportation monopolies protected against competition *by the state!*)

But aside from this general response to Brudnoy's pungent examples (or Buckley's), one must also recall that even without any legal restriction against such forms of free expression, there are a host of other actions that can be taken without violating anyone's rights. Privately initiated boycotts, massive ostracisms, and campaigns of many varieties are available to members of a free society to express dismay with the behavior of others. Vehicles for such expression, such as TV and radio, newspapers, the mail—all of them privately operated, of course—would be available in such a system, even if no *guarantee* exists that there will be sympathy for one's cause.

Moreover, it is a fair bet that in a civilized society, which is what it would take to develop the degree of freedom I am discussing here, such obnoxious cases of free expression would hardly be possible without massive support from industry, the public at large, and so forth. Since these cases serve to illustrate extremes in the first place, they would not be likely, and just in case they would occur, the protesters would have well-developed methods of response—independent of any reliance on bureaucratic exercise of physical force.

Such drastic cases aside, it is obvious that the areas in which censorship now obtains involve nothing of the sort exhibited in these examples. The more common cases are censorship of television commercials, FCC regulations pertaining to the use of "four letter words," publication of books and films with dirty pictures and stories—for purposes of sale to those who are free to avoid them. The founders of the American legal system, while not consistently in agreement with the idea of a free human community developed here, did put forth some of the best principles pertaining to the relationship of government to people's obvious reliance on communication and desire for artistic activity and experience. The founders did not say that people cannot know the truth or cannot know what is beautiful or obscene. Obviously to do so would have rendered their own development of a society which aimed at justice entirely paradoxical—would we have to consider them extraordinary in their ability to tell the truth about the nature of justice?

What the founders recognized was that questions of what is true, false, beautiful, ugly, worthwhile or not, and whether to produce or purchase it, should be left to the discretion of individuals. For this reason they prohibited the government from using its unique competence, the exercise of force, to make determinations about truth, beauty, humor, and so forth. In this the founders of the American republic showed far more respect for human nature than either the conservatives or the liberals do today. For it is conservatives who do not acknowledge the capacity of free individuals to make a correct evaluation of what is presented to them in movies, books, and theaters, and to act accordingly.

Yet the liberal is not far behind in this, for as soon as the material conditions of life are at issue, the liberal generally mistrusts individual judgment and abandons his defense of free expression. It was liberal lawyer John F. Banshaf III who persuaded the Federal Communication Commission to force broadcasters to provide "equal time" against cigarette commercials, leading, eventually, to the prohibition of such commercials on radio and TV. There has not been any sign of protest from the American Civil Liberties Union about such violation of human rights.

Nor have liberals protested zoning ordinances, enactment of laws against the architectural practices and other preferences of private property and home owners.[14] These are all less noticed cases of prohibitions of free expression. It is, of course, in this area that many like to point to the possible harmful consequences—when, for example, the restrictions of private home owners include irrational conditions such as selling only to white people, gentiles, and so forth. But as with all liberties, a person's freedom of action carries with it the possibility that individuals will not exercise correct judgment, will choose wrongly, will even offend and irritate others in what they do. As with those who annoy others by exhibiting pornographic movies or selling filthy books, so there are people who exercise their liberty with the result that proper respect to moral standards has not been shown. Yet while some people with great concern about the moral fiber of our society, about the influence which may be exerted over people who do not even witness obscene art but simply know of its existence, want to prohibit nude dancing in privately owned taverns, so others want to prohibit the exercise of free choice in selecting with whom one shall engage in trade, because they are revolted over the possible influence of the irrational forms of discrimination made possible by this liberty. Yet in both cases the individual ought to be free to do what he will with his own—be it his printing press, movie theater, or night club, as well as his home, firm, or private club. Indeed, the test of principle arises when those acting in terms of such a principle behave most offensively.

Finally, there is yet another important area where censorship goes unrecognized. This is made possible through the practice of establishing governmentally supported artistic, scientific, and scholarly activities. It is of course the money and resources of taxpayers that are used to support such activities.

But the censorship enters in a roundabout fashion. The government generally employs prestigious, reputable members of the academic community to determine how the allocated funds will be distributed among the applicants. Since those on the boards are usually well established in their fields, it is not unreasonable to suppose that they will perpetuate practices and lines of inquiry they consider valid—which means that they will, most often, perpetuate the status quo.[15]

Now it makes no difference whether one considers the method of judgment valid or not. After all, there is probably a tendency for the same process of evaluation to be employed at private foundations. What is crucial is that the funds being spent by the governmental bodies are not given out with the consent of the "contributors." So there is a clear case of censorship of the *(possible)* goals and purposes the forced contributors could have chosen. Obviously, this is not *direct* censorship—governmental *regulation* of artistic, intellectual, educational or scientific activity and the prohibition of the same, but the effective *consequences* of this kind of subsidization amount to no less.

The sample cases which have been discussed thus far should be enough to indicate how pervasive and subtle the practice of censorship is within our often mislabeled "free country." Here, as with state education, every person of the society ought to take the steps within his/her reach to deprive the various levels and branches of government of the legal power to exercise censorship. The seriousness of this issue cannot be overestimated. If even the intellectual activities of individuals relating to various elements of our human community, especially in the thus sensitive area of its political practices, is open to forcible suppression, the prospects for both a good human life and a good human community in which such a life is possible to a person must inevitably diminish for all.

It is at the point when the prospects for free expression become a *legal* impossibility that human beings *owe it to themselves* to turn against their government with overt opposition, including retaliatory force. This constitutes the *right of revolution.* When one considers that shutting down a theater for showing obscene movies can constitute not just the violation of the right of free trade and free artistic expression but an outright depriva- tion of one's means to livelihood, a means that in no way involves the violation of others' rights; and when one learns of concerted governmental efforts to regulate television programming on grounds that some scenes *might possibly* lead to some harm (by influencing some disturbed child in some vaguely damaging fashion[16]); when one considers that these are *precedents* for massive censorship of all radio, newspaper, television or book content (for clearly someone might get the wrong idea from any of these); it is not difficult to imagine that the time is near when revolution could be justified.

Before taking up that topic in detail I will deal with a few additional officially perpetrated and widely supported human rights violations.

Ecology, Conservation, and Human Liberty

Although the philosopher Jeremy Bentham was one of the most severe critics of natural human rights—as mentioned before, he characterized them as "nonsense upon stilts"—he was an advocate of the rights of animals! He argued that since animals have interests of some sort they also have rights; and he wrote:

> The day *may* come when the rest of the animal creation may acquire those rights which never could have been withholden from them but by the hand of tyranny. The French have already discovered that the blackness of the skin is no reason why a human being should be abandoned without redress to the caprice of a tormentor. It may one day come to be recognized that the number of legs, the villosity of the skin, or the termination of *ossacrum*, are reasons equally insufficient for abandoning a sensitive being to the same fate. What else is it that should trace the insuperable line? Is it the faculty of reason, or perhaps the faculty of discourse? But a full-grown horse or dog is beyond comparison a more rational, as well as a more conversable animal, than an infant of a day, or a week, or even a month, old. But suppose they were otherwise, what would it avail? The question is not, Can they *reason?* nor Can they *talk?* but Can they *suffer?*[17]

In our day these thoughts have been taken much further by some philosophers. Peter Singer of Oxford has recently defended the idea that the interests of human beings and other animals ought to be given equal con- sideration, at least, and perhaps more in favor of the latter as against the former. In a book review [18] where Singer comments on the anthology of essays *Animals, Men and Morals* (Taplinger, 1972), we do not merely find a call for more rational treatment of animals. This much could be defended on grounds that human life itself would benefit from such treatment. Nor are we urged to care for animals in behalf of the preservation of our environment, or because we might suffer psychological impairment from wanton aggression upon other living beings. Not that all this is denied. But Singer's point, expressed in approving remarks about the above book, is a different one:

> The book holds out no inducements. It does not tell us that we will become healthier, or enjoy life more, if we cease exploiting animals. Animal Liberation will require greater altruism on the part of mankind than any other liberation movement, since animals are incapable of demanding it for themselves, or of protesting against their exploitation by votes, demonstrations, or bombs.[19]

Leaving aside why liberation movements should be considered altruistic when they involve human beings—is not liberty good for those who will be liberated as well as those no longer tolerated in their oppression of others?—one might ask what the altruism Singer asks for would require. He explains himself quite unambiguously: this book "is a challenge that demands not just a change of attitudes, but a change in our way of life, for it requires us to become vegetarians." And Singer then poses the rhetorical question:

> Is man capable of such genuine altruism? Who knows? If this book does have a significant effect, however, it will be a vindication of all those who have believed that man has within himself the potential for more than cruelty and selfishness.[20]

The argument for animal rights, somewhat different from Singer's equal interest idea, need not be considered here. I will touch on it in connection with my general reply to certain skeptical objections to human rights theory.[21] In the final analysis, however, the argument rests on general skepticism about the possibility of identifying human nature: since we cannot know what is or is not a human being, we cannot deny to things rather like human beings what we want to secure for ourselves. But more on this later.

Singer's is obviously a case of genuine altruism. There is no evidence of ill-intent, of deliberate work for the worsening of the human condition. From the rest of the paper we cannot conclude but that the issues are raised in the spirit of honest philosophical inquiry. Yet it seems to me that if ever a theoretician is guilty of harmful negligence—and many clearly are now and then—Singer in his uncritical review exemplifies such an instance. The simple fact is that the adoption of such full-blown altruism could not but lead to mankind's destruction—especially when one realizes that to move from animal rights to plant rights is not at all less plausible than slipping from human to animal rights. (What with "hearing plants" and such, Singer certainly should renounce even vegetarianism.)

Here are some points against Singer. There is no justification for the claim that feeding oneself on animal flesh requires being cruel to animals. A genuinely selfish life does involve the use of rocks, trees, plants, animals, and other items of nature for human purposes. None of that entails being cruel to anything or anyone. Just as it would be absurd to consider one's dentist cruel for causing pain in one's mouth, so it is illogical to consider whatever pain and suffering may be involved for animals when they are prepared for human use instances of cruelty.

All this is not to say that people are never cruel and wanton in their dealings with animals—or with each other, for that matter. But that is another story entirely. When Bentham asks if we *must* abandon animals to "tormentors," the answer is clear. The appropriate moral advice is that human beings ought to treat all living entities with some consideration for what it means to be a living entity. (Any person who has no sense of the significance of life and absence of pain to those animals unable to protect themselves, is likely unable to appreciate the same for other human beings, even for himself. For a thinking animal, such failure to generalize over relevantly similar cases can only lead a *person* to disaster.)

But this moral advice is far from equivalent to the view that human beings ought to abandon their own welfare for the sake of flies, pelicans, the white whale, or even the Bengali tiger. The question "Why should we do *this?*" simply cannot be answered with even a whiff of good sense behind it. The view usually relies on a sense of sympathy which, in its place and based on empathy with other life forms, is appropriate. But such sympathy and empathy loses its *rational* footing, its very place in reality, if in the process the enormous value of a human life lived well is forgotten. When Socrates observed that a person must love himself to come to love others, he might have added that mankind must appreciate the significance of its own existence before it can learn to appreciate what life can be to other living beings.

Now the above considerations are directed at perhaps the most extreme form of ecologism, a form that defeats the very point of our concern with ecology as a field of science.[22] It is, also, a version of the conservationist creed that few conservationists would embrace—even if their slogans and proposals might logically lead them into the position Singer advocates. What about these other, less drastic forms of ecologism? What about the hundreds of legal measures urged in behalf of birds, trees, fish, and the like, most at the expense of human freedom?

For centuries human liberty has been attacked from all sides in behalf of noble aims. And here again, only rarely have the violations of man's rights to life, liberty, and property emanated from malice. Instead, the source has usually been people's willingness to encroach on the lives of others for such altruistic purposes as to please gods, to erect monuments to the Pharaohs, to do homage to the holy order, and on and on.

This most recent call for depriving human beings of their liberty of choice and action has by now approached monumental dimensions. Of course the call for conservation, generally meaning preserving so-called natural resources for future use, is not quite as drastic as for "animal liberation." In the United States various private and governmental bodies are deeply concerned with conservation—not for its own sake (i.e., that pelicans or redwood trees should simply exist as "inherent goods," independent of the interests of human beings), but for the sake of members of future generations.

The arguments behind this call for conservation usually rely on certain data from the present and past involving land, wild life, water and plant use, and so forth. Those who urge political action for purposes of conservation contend that without restrictions on such use, mankind will soon run out of what is necessary for a decent quality of life. To avoid this allegedly impending disaster, restrictions on hunting, fishing, coal and gas use, logging, irrigation, the use of pesticides, building, research, and various other activities are now in effect and continue to be instituted each day. Many advocate family planning, sterilization, even abortion, with the goal of reducing the size of producing and consuming populations. While in the United States these latter measures have not yet been imposed upon the population by government decree, it is not unreasonable to anticipate that they will, depending of course on how panic-stricken the community and its leadership become.[23]

Presumably without these measures the possibility of life on earth will diminish drastically. Then, since freedom is worthless where life is impossible, it is concluded (usually only implicitly) that there need be no concern with human liberty in the process of attaining conservationist and ecological goals. Implicit in these arguments is a crucial view of human nature: free human beings, unguided (or unhampered) by the strictures of politicians, do not have the capacity to cope with the problems they may face. There is no need at this juncture to list the case histories of free people coping with problems of even greater dimensions than anything that ecologists or conservationists could imagine. This is not a research project but a general discussion of human rights and liberties, so it would be pretentious to offer data [24] that could not be extensive enough to make forceful objections against this new form of hysteria and excuse for violating human rights. Moreover, the arguments of conservationists and ecologists are not in their important respects based on statistics and cases. For from all of that *nothing* follows concerning whether political means are the correct ones to be used to solve whatever problems there are. From the fact that something is generally valuable to us, nothing follows about *who* ought to do what, by what *means*. In particular nothing follows about whether anyone ought to use force against people so as to attain what are perhaps desirable goals.

Yet some might argue that the sins against conservation involve the violation of human rights. And no doubt some do—when, for instance, a firm dumps smoke into the atmosphere, it may well be that the property rights of neighboring owners are violated. When pesticides are used in such a way that their effect reaches beyond the land of the user, this too can involve the violation of someone's rights. *Yet those arguing for conservation measures rarely if ever focus on this element of the cases.* Of course if they did they would notice that the greatest perpetrators of the sins of waste, pollution, and other harmful activities are governments themselves. The institution of public property—with unlimited (democratic, indiscriminate) access—is the most obvious instance of the proliferation of waste and pollution. Beaches, parks, forests, lakes, oceans, roads, schools, recreation centers, monuments, museums, highways, and so on—all of them "owned by everyone" and governed by politicians and their appointees, are all notorious seedbeds of overuse, recklessness, thoughtlessness, waste, pollution, and other activities that can be encouraged by allowing people to act without having to consider the costs and consequences for their actions.[25] Littering, for instance, is not a problem in private clubs, homes, businesses because the cost of cleaning up is taken into consideration by the owners, and it is not "the public" but the private occupants of these areas who must bear the burden of mismanagement[26]

The reader may wonder why roads, highways, and even schools have been included in the list above. The fact is that by opening highways to anyone by some "natural right of access," as well as schools, and other government-run enterprises, immeasurable degrees of inefficiency, waste, and overburdening are encouraged. It takes care and foresight even for a small commune to avoid the irresponsible use of common property. Garrett Hardin's recent essay[27] simply echoes Aristotle's observations on this matter, made 2,500 years ago in his criticism of Plato's ideal communal political system. As Aristotle put it,

> there is another objection to the proposal [to abolish parental jurisdiction and private property]. For that which is common to the greatest number has the least care bestowed upon it. Every one thinks chiefly of his own, hardly at all of the common interest; and only when he is himself concerned as an individual. For, besides other considerations, everybody is more inclined to neglect the duty which he expects another to fulfill; as in

families many attendants are often less useful than a few. Each citizen will have a thousand sons [in Plato's ideal system] who will not be his sons individually, but anybody will be equally the son of anybody, and will therefore be neglected by all alike. Further, upon this principle, every one will use the word 'mine' of one who is prospering or the reverse.[28]

The fact is that the problems which now seem to justify restrictions are not generally attributable to the free actions of individuals, in a legal system where the human rights of each and every person are protected and preserved. Although instances of wanton breach of the private spheres of others are detectable, in fact even those have had the force of bad laws behind them—for example, during the early days of the railroads the government declared the fires set off by sparks from locomotives justified, albeit lamentable, interference with the property rights of owners adjacent to the tracks, thereby setting a precedent for subsequent legal rulings. All, of course, in the "public interest." In general the mixture of private and public property systems has resulted in overuse of those materials that are found primarily in "public" areas. Water, air, minerals, coal, oil, and the like had all been under governmental regulation for decades before the conservation issue emerged in full force.

It is ironic that with the evidence of governmental responsibility for mismanagement of land, water, air and other vital resources, conservationists would call upon the state to rescue us from impending disasters. These as well as other friends of the state fail to recognize, or evade, the unique nature of governments as *experts* at only one activity, namely the use of force.[29] Since force ought to be used only in retaliation against the violation of human rights, calling upon government to do anything else is not unlike calling upon doctors to fix one's automobile, bowlers to teach one how to dance, or sociology professors to teach philosophy. The state's entry into every kind of enterprise must result in constant pressure to use its expertise to suit some groups' purposes. Business, labor, conservation groups, women, men, blacks, Indians, Jews, Arabs, teachers, students, and hundreds of others call upon the government to make use of its power for their *special* purposes. By departing from the *central goal of protecting and preserving the rights of human beings as such,* regardless of special group membership and interest, this consequence is quite logical.

There are, of course, other criticisms one could advance against conservationists, or at least those who overstate the case. Obviously many simply refuse to recognize the capacity for human creativity. Moreover, most are presumptuous enough to be willing to impose their own, rather restricted set of private preferences on the rest of the society—even upon the lives of those not yet born. Many ecologically minded people simply cannot fathom that others, as well as those in the future, might not be thrilled by (or depend on) the same aspects of nature as some of us. Although the reader might believe that all this writer likes in life is a typewriter and some paper to write on, I happen to be very fond of the outdoors. Yet I consider it rather unjust that because I have an automobile, and my life has room for many diverse purposes, I can indulge in occasional trips to the mountains, lakes, and so on, while others who like to dance, play symphonic music in concert halls, read books, sculpt, and the like, are not able to determine what their efforts and income will support but must, lest they be forced to go to jail, contribute to my enjoyment of parks and wildlife. Even if I considered it unusual that someone didn't delight in the songs and sounds of the wild, that others did not consider the colors of the Pennsylvania woods in the fall breathtaking, or did not believe that leopards are stunning crea-tures—even then, it would be immoral to undertake to force these people to "choose" these values.

The advocates of wildlife preserves, conservationists who do not make *efforts of their own* to purchase lands and zoos and pursue other means by which to achieve their presumably highly valued goals, these individuals who lament the lack of altruism in the world but rarely if ever regard it as their own duty to carry out the conservation they advocate, consider it per-fectly just to enlist government to force us all to accept their values, to aban-don our own goals in behalf of what they have chosen for everyone.

Yet their methods can only do harm to their goals. For if they believe that what is right cannot be achieved by voluntary means, if they think that the proper care and caution that is required in dealing with nature *will not* be undertaken by human beings as a result of their own free choices and judgments, one wonders what they anticipate in the long run. Surely if they are in such a minority their battles are of no use. While now and then they may win a few victories, after the fling with this fad is over people will simply turn to others and use the state to further new interests—quite likely at the expense of those that ecologists have identified as proper and worthy of support. The best measure for ensuring greater care and caution in the use of the materials we find around us in nature is to protect each person's human rights, *to identify clearly who has a right to what* (it is rarely considered that *this* might solve the pollution problem), and to keep the system of such protection and preservation as close to its justified task as possible, leaving all other human values in the hands of free men and women to pursue as best they can. That kind of division of labor has the best chance for securing the justifiable interests of all human beings.

A Climate of Power Grabbing

It need not be argued at length that many other projects besides education, maintaining the moral fiber of society, ecological reform, and the arts are supported by government. The objection should be quite clear:

supporting the aims, goals, welfare, wishes, or hopes of some people with grants, special waivers, subsidies, tax exemptions, and so on, involves the violation of human rights. Two types of cases come to mind. We find that religious and educational endeavors in America are exempted from paying taxes. While it cannot be argued that those who take advantage of this situation are wrong, the exemptions are wrong in that others are forced to carry the burdens created by individuals and organizations categorized as religious and educational.

Religion is, after all, just one of the many aspects of human life people may select to support. While this may seem blasphemous to many, there is no reason to believe that one person's religious endeavors are necessarily more worthwhile than another's following sports or astrology. But some people's beliefs and interests, regardless of how noble they are thought to be, never ought to constitute a claim upon others' works, labors, liberty, or life. Yet even in America, with church and state well-separated, the outcome is—because state and virtually everything else have become intermingled—that the tax advantages have become a form of subsidization at the expense of other people's goals and concerns.

Yet the theory of human rights does not imply that when some people are enslaved, all must be. In other words, the solution is not to extend taxation—the coerced support of others' projects—to religious institutions. Priests, ministers, and the many religious organizations and their members ought to be left at liberty to "do their thing," of course. But so ought everyone else.

The same points are applicable to educational endeavors. The elitism that lies behind exempting educational enterprises from the laws that compel the rest of us to "do our duty" is unjustifiable in a society where *all* human beings are said to be subject to the law. Unfortunately the religious and the intellectuals—groups that in fact simply occupy two spheres of mankind's manifold interests and activities, good or bad—carry enough weight to sell many of us the idea that our slavery is more tolerable or justifiable than theirs.

But then there are the cases which do not involve exemptions but outright subsidies. Lockheed Corporation is the most widely known case. The government lent it $500 million so as to save its enterprise—a loan that came out of the taxpayers' pockets, ultimately, and will have to be covered by them as well as by yet unborn taxpayers. This incredible practice of Keynesian economics, deficit spending, whereby present generations of people are encouraged to live off the lifeblood of those who are not yet born (or if born, have no say whatever about what they would have wanted to do with that portion of their lives that will go toward paying the bill) is so unjust that one wonders why no minority movement has arisen in their behalf.

Many people consider it anti-intellectual to engage in protest, to express moral outrage at the choices and actions of one's fellow men. Such outcries are often dismissed as dogmatism and self-righteousness, or as empty emotionalism. (Of course concerning the conduct of businessmen or the activities of politicians, intellectuals do not hesitate to make evaluations, condemnations, and proclamations of moral principle.) While the guilt of *individuals* for contributing to the violation of human rights would be a complex matter to ascertain, it is not so difficult to render judgment about actions, institutions, and policies that systematically involve such violations. Some fingers can be pointed, of course. I have little doubt that John K. Galbraith has, with all his books and articles, contributed to such violations aplenty. He is, to the best of my knowledge, immoral to the extent that he has failed to take heed of the human rights that would be violated by the implementation of his political/economic advice. Many others could be named, most of them in the "public eye." But, in the main, to assess the moral culpability of human beings is a difficult matter and should not be undertaken lightly. That is why my discussion has been kept at a relatively abstract level.

Still, all this does not answer the charge of unjustified moralism. Many professional philosophers believe that people in my field of endeavor ought to refrain from moral judgments. Our business, so the case goes, is to entertain perpetual doubt—metaphysical, epistemological, religious, ethical, political or whatever, just so long as one keeps away from conclusions and from confidence in them.

The fact is that all human beings ought to protest injustice, all ought to resist in a way that is appropriate wrongs done to them and others. For those who fare in philosophical matters the story is no different. Thus I have embarked upon moral judgments within the context of a moral theory that seems to me to be valid, one about which I have no reasonable doubt—and unreasonable doubts do not count. So I shall not recline on grounds of some empty charge of dogmatic or idealistic moralism.

There are so many instances of the violation of human rights around us that we could go on and on listing them even in terms of these broad categories. Since this presentation is based on a system of thought, not on piecemeal opinings, most thoughtful people will be able to draw the proper inferences from what has been said thus far for cases not discussed in detail.

Problems of Justified Killing

Thus far I have not touched on some of the more sensational areas that have a direct connection with the issue of human rights. I have in mind here the problems that are usually discussed under the labels "abortion," "euthanasia," and "mercy killing."[30] By the title of this section, I could include here the many varieties of justified homicide—e.g., self-defense and unavoidable killing of bystanders in protective or defense action either in war or in criminally provoked violent engagements, but these are generally treated properly within our legal system, so I will not deal with them explicitly.

The first point to make here is that the ideal place to settle questions about euthanasia and abortion is in the courts of a free society. Once the principles of the legal system rest firmly on the moral foundations provided by the theory of human rights, their detailed application would have to emerge in the context of a working human community where the problems involved arise. (That, incidentally, is the rationale for invoking precedents in the law. Unfortunately, without that firm foundation reliance on precedents can lead to a morass of contradictions.) It is especially crucial that cases involving new developments in technology, e.g., medicine, pharmacology, and so forth, be subjected to the patient scrutiny that should characterize the legal process. And knowledge of the culture where the principles are to be implemented is required for identifying the numerous criteria of lawfulness, i.e., legal justice, at each stage of a community's history, even when normal, widely anticipated problems arise.

Second, concerning euthanasia we are not dealing with a matter of private conduct. Since the killing of a person by another is involved the problem is open to legal jurisdiction. Since the role of the legal administrators (legislators, courts, committees, and so on) is to identify in detail the proper sphere of authority of each person in a dynamic society, aspects of the relationships between parents and children and the terminally ill and the next of kin fall within the jurisdiction of the law.

In the case of abortion the role of the law is just what is at issue. If the claim is true that from conception the embryo is fully human—i.e., that embryos are human beings at least to the degree infants are—then the relationship between a pregnant woman and the entity within her can be a province of the law. On the other hand, if the embryo, unlike an infant (or even a fetus of six months), is not a human being, then the law must abstain from interfering with that relationship. In terms of the present approach to such matters it would be a crucially important function of the legal administration to consider these issues objectively, independently of myth, religion, or popular desire. It ought to be the function of such legal experts to engage in detailed inquiries about the nature of embryos, fetuses and infants, to make whatever distinctions are biologically, psychologically and morally warranted, and to incorporate the most advanced results of their findings into the legal system. (Instead what such bodies of "experts" now do is debate whether vitamin C should be sold in greater or lesser strength, whether trucks may make pick-ups midway between delivery stops, whether barbers may shave women's legs, what new movies on brushing teeth should be produced by the government and similar issues of "vital significance" to people's rights.)

I do think that present knowledge supports a valid position on abortion—to wit, embryos are parasitic upon pregnant women, who are thus within their rights to elect either to support or to reject this relationship, and fetuses have a similar status up to the point in pregnancy where biological independence is possible without extensive artificial aid. Nevertheless it is not the function of political theory to defend this view, any more than it is its business to defend love and marriage or other human institutions and practices that can have legal significance.

Concerning justifiable infanticide two main points have to be stressed. In cases of so-called catastrophic birth defects, for example, the basic question to be asked is whether it is possible to provide for this entity in line with the obligations parents normally have to their offspring—*can* they prepare it for living the life of a mature human being? If the answer is in the negative without any reasonable doubts, parents would have the right to destroy this entity. The legal resolution of these and similar cases would rest on various details of a valid account of the relationship between parents (or guardians) and children. This, in turn, could change from time to time, depending on the changing opportunities for maintaining or breaking that relationship in accordance with the appropriate moral code. Here again an abstract political theory (that can take account only of the most fundamental matters in human affairs so as to avoid unjustified rigidity) would not be the place to seek answers.

What should be noted in connection with these and related difficult decisions is that in a free society they could not be made by the state. Conclusions on those matters that come to court—because reasonable grounds for charges of violating human rights exist—would be reached by way of the due process appropriate for a legal system in a free society. What is crucial is that doctors in various hospitals could not act as agents of the government. Nor could parents regard them as such. When decisions about malformed children must be made, parents must make them. They may consult doctors and lawyers, read briefs, newspaper articles, and so forth for the best knowledge available on the matter. Most expectant parents, knowing that this is their responsibility, would be prepared for various eventualities. (I would assume that populations would be reduced somewhat with the realization that the responsibility may not be imposed upon others with legal sanction, as now encouraged. The same would likely be the consequence of having to educate a child without coercing others' help for that purpose.) Gradually the legal system would establish precedents for the more unusual cases.

What we now have in all countries of the world, even in the relatively advanced and literate United States, is quite different from the idea advanced above. People involved are usually in the dark, especially about the proper legal approach to their relationship to children at various levels of mental and physical disability. As with the issues surrounding organ transplants, there is a pressing need for identifying the principles by which decisions must be made. Unfortunately few people concern themselves with such basics.

But my point has not been to predict what will be the case within the near future. The focus has been on outlining what could and should be done concerning problems that emerge in a human community. The above are certainly not the only important areas, but they are often dramatic and they have claimed recent attention. Thus they might serve to illustrate how the present moral and political approach would help in coping with difficult, in these cases life-and-death, problems.

Emergency Cases

Since the time Socrates asked if one should return to a madman an axe borrowed prior to his mental aberration,[31] ethics has been flooded with emergency cases as tests for adequacy. If you found yourself in the middle of the Pacific Ocean with a gun but no raft, and met an unarmed person with a raft suited for one, would it be morally right to kill? But few ever ask how you ended up in the Pacific with a gun! Or that person in the middle of a desert with just enough water to keep him alive, and someone dying of thirst right beside him—how did they all get there, and who are they anyway to have made such a mess of things?[32]

Sometimes it is important to dismiss these examples without apologies, because moral dilemmas, which these cases are supposed to illustrate, do not come just this way. When they do occur they are full of details, with people who have a history, character (or the lack of it), and usually enough awareness and thoughtfulness that if a solution is possible they could find it. Part of the attraction of these examples lies in their sketchiness; to pose them as challenges has its obvious appeal—no one in the discussion is prepared for them. But the lack of detail is their weakness as well. For the best answer in those cases is usually that people would have to think fast but carefully and act intelligently, in short, resolve the problem in the best possible way.

Yet that answer is not satisfactory unless we have some general idea of what constitutes "best." What should the general aim be in trying to work out solutions to these problems? Usually the character of the dilemma makes it clear enough: the persons involved need to do as well for themselves as possible while keeping in mind that this is the correct view of their fellow human beings also.

Now if everyone believed in altruism there would be no problem. On desert islands, the person with water would give it to the other chap, and in the ocean the one with the raft would have to jump off to let the wet fellow save himself. Of course, the wet fellow would promptly decline to the raft owner, while in the desert the newly acquired glass of water would just be given back—*ad infinitum*. That is, if we are *conscientious altruists*, in which case the solution to such difficulties is to relinquish one's life as soon as possible. But the present discussion does not provide an argument to show how human beings ought to act for purposes of relinquishing their lives. Instead, we have all along been after a code of conduct that makes life better and better for individuals if they choose to live by it.

In the present section I will not retrace the case for ethical egoism, nor for human rights theory. What I will attempt to do is offer an answer to those who would like to know what is implied by such a moral and political point of view for so-called emergency cases. For despite the occasional misuse of emergency-type examples, there are many actual instances where people face extraordinary situations, ones which require a special interpretation of a legal system and code that is appropriate for generally calm, civilized ways of human life. Although I have previously dealt with the moral implications for the persons dealing with such situations, what will be treated here are the political/legal implications.

First let us consider some aspects of such situations by reference to realistic examples. These are often provided for us in appropriate detail in good novels as well as in records of cases. For example, in the novel *An Operational Necessity* (New American Library, 1969) Gwyn Griffin tells the story of a German U-boat headed for operations crucial to Germany's goals in World War II. In the story the fact that Germany was the aggressor is entirely beside the point. (Some historians even dispute this now.) At a juncture of the journey the U-boat sinks a merchant ship, all in the line of carrying out required war-time operations. Learning of survivors, the U-boat captain decides to destroy the remains of the ship, including equipment that might have helped the survivors to sustain themselves at sea. This operation results in the injury of several of the survivors. Although no gross evidence is left of the sinking, one survivor manages to reach shore and tell of the events. The captain is brought to trial.

The question in court is whether destruction of the debris, with the virtual certainty of both injuries to survivors and the elimination of their chances for reaching safety, was justified. The court acknowledges that leaving debris on the scene could have led enemy search planes to seek out the U-boat, yet this prospect was only that, a likely but not conclusively evident prospect. Did the captain do right to harm the others so as to ensure the safety of his men and the progress of his mission? The captain's defense lawyer then faces him with the following: "I think that the members of the Court will find it very hard to do anything but accept that you took the only rational course. But whether or not it was the right one—" [The captain:] "I can find no difference . . . I only want to say that I see my position like this; I did what I believed to be correct at the time and I am more than ever certain that it was correct now. I was trying to save the lives of my crew—more than fifty men, monsieur, as against some twelve or so of the others. If men have souls—and *I* think they do—then I have saved, in the end, some fifty of these at the expense of a dozen. Is that an outrage against humanity? I was *right*. And whatever the Court may decide I shall still be right. And if they say that I was wrong, that will not change anything. If they find me guilty, I am still right. If they shoot me, I am still right. Nothing—while men can think and have the power to reason—will ever alter that fact!"[33]

Author Griffin provides us with a brilliantly sketched story, with all the relevant facts made evident, with everyone's point of view given fair hearing. Indeed, the reader's moral position is put to a clear test. The following discussion of Mack's will shed some light on the emergency case from the point of view of the ethical egoist, and will also show the direction which legal issues must take.

Consider the case of two men adrift with a plank which can only support one man. Let us stipulate that in this case, all the factors, such as the psychology of each man, are such that it is in the interest of each to survive, and this is at the cost of the other's life. In this case, there is only one possible action for each man that is sufficient (in itself or in conjunction with other actions) for achieving his egoistic interest. These actions are necessary for each of the men. In such an emergency case, rights are significantly absent. Each man ought, given ethical egoism and the stipulations in the case, to seek his own survival at the expense of the other. But neither can be said to have a right to survival. For to ascribe this right to either party would be to ascribe to the other party the obligation to allow the first party's survival at the expense of his own life. But the second party cannot be obligated to allow this, since we know that, given egoism, he ought not to allow it.

Undoubtedly there are actions for each person which are necessary to that person's self-interest. Each person must, for instance, breathe. What is significant, however, is that actions which we tend to classify as actions from which a person is obligated to abstain are actions which, in the normal course of events in a somewhat civilized sociey, are not necessary to the self-interest of the persons who might perform them. . . .

As the plank example illustrates, in abnormal, crisis situations, there is an increase in actions that are necessary to the self-interest of the persons subject to the crisis. In the present view about the possibility of obligations and rights, in such circumstances, persons are less capable of being the subject of obligations and less capable of being the bearers of rights. . . . The reason that rights appear only when reasonably sane societal conditions prevail, and not in emergency and purely chaotic situations, is that one person, say Jones, can only have rights against another, say Smith, to the extent that condemnable actions (the actions from which he would be obligated to abstain, if he could be obligated to abstain from them) against Jones by Smith are not necessary to Smith's well-being. The key feature of reasonably sane societal conditions is that they provide each person with multiple and noncondemnable means of seeking his own well-being.[34]

In the novel referred to it is clear that the captain could not carry out his responsibility to preserve the life and mission of the U-boat without harming obviously innocent people. From the point of view of the present theory it cannot be doubted that he did the *right* thing when he took "the only rational course" available to him.

What usually renders these cases so complicated is that we are accustomed to societies wherein *mutual* interests are desired and pursued and those unwilling to uncover the means to do so are rightfully condemned. Although the refusal to explore harmonious ways is often called "selfish," a rational query would show that it would have been to the guilty party's genuine, rational self-interest to seek and achieve harmony. The important point about emergency cases is that although *mutual* interests can not be pursued, the final arbiter of conduct is still human reason and the central goal of moral conduct is still a person's happiness in life. The rest must be a matter of discovery, although sufficiently well-developed hypothetical cases can be handled even theoretically. The point now is to discuss some of these in connection with the organized protection and preservation of human rights, that is, in connection with the government of a free society. Before that, however, let me explain my approach to emergency cases that arise in less than free societies. After all, we are mostly faced with these in our lives!

Consider the following situation. You are a marriage counselor and a couple with severe problems arrives. They have neglected their marriage, rarely talking honestly to each other. After many years of preoccupation with other matters (though with ample opportunity to make reparations), some trauma, e.g., the suicide of one of their four children, prompted them to come to you. Now what they ask of you is to give them advice as to how they might become a happy couple.

It seems to me that you would have to advise that no miracles should be expected. Indeed, unless virtual superhuman effort is invested, and a complete reformation of character is brought about by both people, there is little hope for the union. It may well be the best choice to get a divorce.

And the same general principle applies to many societies. Abandoning the union is clearly what many political societies ought to do, perhaps ours included. On the other hand, as the Founding Fathers learned from John Locke and made mention of in the Declaration of Independence,

Prudence, indeed, will dictate that Governments long established should not be changed for light and transient causes; and accordingly all experience hath shewn, that mankind are more disposed to suffer, while evils are sufferable, than to right themselves by abolishing the forms to which they are accustomed.

Here again the marriage analogy fits quite well, but it is also clear from what these politically and morally most acute men saw, that "when a long train of abuses and usurpations, pursuing invariably the same Object, evinces a design to reduce them under absolute Despotism, it is their right, it is their duty, to throw off such Government, and to provide new Guards for their future security."

In the United States the idea of abandoning the "union" is considered to be treasonous by most people. Outside of the small camp of revolutionary Marxists and some anarchists, the idea of a violent attack on the government is generally thought of as perverse, if not immoral. I shall come to a discussion of revolution in the next section. For now I simply want to emphasize that there can certainly be occasions in the development of human communities when considerations of reparations, righting wrongs, and so forth simply make no sense. What with the government having been not just permitted but encouraged to violate the rights of people systematically for several generations, the resulting "crisis" situations, which America is experiencing on virtually all fronts, have come to serve as additional excuses (if not having been so designed) to provide greater and greater measures of governmental usurpation of power. They are not crises of a free society but those of a centralized bureaucracy.

As in marriage, there are crises that the *best can* suffer, as when sickness or other traumas occur, and there are bad marriages which engender daily "crises." When the people involved in either personal or political union refuse to (or neglect to) learn from disasters, and multiply errors in the process of feigning reparations, then considerations of the morally and politically appropriate remedies have only academic and, perhaps, limited personal relevance. Aside from my lacking expertise on such topics as oil production, beef consumption, the development of nuclear power, coal mining, and so on, it would be entirely beside the point to deal with them here. For it never is the moral prerogative of the government of a free society to attend to these types of problems. (However "out of touch" that disclaimer may appear to some who are completely convinced that the government ought to handle these matters, there is every reason to decline the invitation to provide political guidelines for what is rightly a matter for people to plan for and choose about in the context of complete economic freedom. Anyone who at this point still believes that governments can do anything ultimately useful in these matters—other than relinquish the usurped power to get involved—simply has not understood the theory being put before him in these pages.)

None of this is to say that genuine, unmanufactured crises cannot face a society of free human beings. Nor that governments cannot themselves face political and legal crises. What it does mean is that the failure of some business, drug addiction, the need of many people for medical attention, the absence of appreciation and financial support for the fine arts, the disappearance of wildlife loved by many among the citizenry, the lack of highly desired educational and scientific services, a beef shortage, and so forth—*none of these matters have anything to do with politics as such.* To treat them as political is to confuse areas of human life, no less than it would be to take a man with a ruptured appendix to the local flowershop. The devastating fact is that in this last case the mistake that would be made need not become the law of the land, whereas piling more and more impossible tasks upon the dockets of government leaves an almost irreparable legal system in the community's lap. With this of course the actual functions, the proper business, of government is of sheer necessity shoved into the background. (So we find the state conscientiously pursuing black marketeers, massage-parlor operators, street peddlers, wage-price freeze transgressors, anti-trust violators, dope peddlers, and dirty-movie makers, while murder, theft, fraud, and assault as well as official, legally sanctioned government improprieties of similar magnitude are widely neglected.)

What then would be crises in the political affairs of a free society? To answer this question I propose to invoke some of the considerations offered by John Locke in his *Second Treatise.* But in offering these answers it is important to warn that no one is warranted in believing that people in a free society would be guaranteed a utopian existence apart from the crisis situations to be considered here. We are dealing here with political matters, and an answer to questions that arise here is not an answer with respect to other problems people in a human community can experience. This was the point of the previous paragraph. Only utopian political theorists take on the impossible task of providing answers to every type of human problem—by politicalizing human life.

In an earlier segment of this work John Locke was mentioned as the first philosopher to offer a political theory centered on the issue of the protection and preservation of human rights. But Locke was not fully consistent, nor did he provide the needed ethical underpinnings for his political theory. This point is worth making in order to preempt the suggestion that reliance on Locke is necessarily infected with his internally inconsistent ethics. The crucial point to note is that Locke's natural rights doctrine is to a large extent paralleled by the human rights theory presented in this work. On the other hand we must remember that the theory itself is insupportable from the point of view of psychological egoism—a doctrine accepted by Locke in places but firmly rejected elsewhere. The present theory rests on a full blown ethical egoism, based on the idea of human nature in terms of which human beings are distinct among living entities in their capacity to choose to direct their faculty of (conceptual) awareness or consciousness. Yet it is important to realize that something closely akin to this notion is integral to Locke's own natural rights theory, so that borrowing from him is warranted.

Locke anticipated emergency problems in political affairs in his *Second Treatise.* In the chapter entitled "Of Prerogative" Locke explained—in language that might mislead some to interpret him as supporting the welfare state but which in fact leaves no room for that interpretation:

> nay, many things there are which the law can by no means provide for, and those must necessarily be left to the discretion of him that has the executive power in his hands, to be ordered by him as the public good and advantage shall require; nay, it is fit that the laws themselves should in some cases give way to the executive power, or rather to this fundamental law of Nature and government—viz., that as much as may be all the members of the society are to be preserved. For since many accidents may happen wherein a strict and rigid observation of the laws may do harm, as not to pull down an innocent man's house to stop the fire when the next to it is burning; and a man may come sometimes within the reach of the law, which makes no distinction of persons, by an action that may deserve reward and pardon; it is fit the ruler should have a power in many cases to mitigate the severity of the law, and pardon some offenders, since the end of government being the preservation of all as much as may be, even the guilty are to be spared where it can prove no prejudice to the innocent.[35]

In other words, as circumstances evolve and there is need to determine quickly what is right and wrong in these new situations, those charged with the administration of justice, with the preservation of a good human community, will find it necessary to make decisions in accordance with the intelligence, character, and imagination that they can muster up at the time, and always in line with the basic principles by which they are empowered in the first place.

If we recall that emergency matters arise not as the rule in the affairs of a community, as illness and sorrow do not arise as constancies of human life (except when completely mismanaged or extraordinarily unfortunate), we must realize that provisions for them must be considered in the light of what we conclude about the normal state of affairs. Human society, as human life, can and ought to proceed along creative, productive, enjoyable, fruitful, and peaceful lines. From this we have seen that political institutions ought to aim at providing for the needed conditions, namely liberty and justice—the protection and preservation of human rights.

Without knowledge of the basic system, the central principles by which human community life is best organized, nothing at all could be discerned about how emergency situations ought to be approached.

Yet mankind does not know all of nature, so it is unrealistic to ask for some static system of laws that will provide for any contingency whatsoever. All the "what if this will happen" questions cannot be answered fully beforehand, simply because the happenings themselves contain the clues to their proper solution. While the temptation today is to provide government measures so as to *preempt* all *unforeseen* situations—thereby making a total fetish out of security at the expense of both security and liberty—rejecting that approach should not lead one to ignore the real question of what is proper for political agents, especially executives, when precedents do not exist. It is this realization that led Locke to discuss the topic of prerogative.

Yet he is clear about the context within which he must be understood. To those who would argue that prerogative should be the rule, not the exception, Locke wrote that "they have a very wrong notion of governments who say that the people have encroached upon the prerogative when they have got any part of it to be defined by positive laws. For in so doing they have not pulled from the prince anything that of right belonged to him, but only declared that that power which they indefinitely left in his or his ancestors' hands, to be exercised for their good, was not a thing they intended him, when he used it otherwise."[36] To this he added a further point:

[S]ince a rational creature cannot be supposed, when free, to put himself into subjection to another for his own harm (though where he finds a good and a wise ruler he may not, perhaps, think it either necessary or useful to set precise bounds to his power in all things), prerogative can be nothing but the people's permitting their rulers to do several things of their own free choice where the law was silent, and sometimes too against the direct letter of the law, for the public good and their acquiescing in it when so done.[37]

Since Locke was no utopian, and did not envision a political system that would solve all problems (especially where *people* are unwilling to act responsibly, to think through their ends and means in political matters), he admitted that sometimes the question would arise, "But who shall be judge when this power is made a right use of?" His answer was that there may be times when no one on earth can judge. As a man with religious commitments, Locke referred to heaven as the place where such issues would be resolved. We can only interpret this as an admission that political matters cannot be *guaranteed* to run smoothly, even when the ground is prepared as well as humanly possible. If one concurs with Locke's *attitude*, the only response one can give to a request for absolute guarantees—that human political problems *will* be solved—is that one ought to do his best, and even without the success that should render the endeavor worthwhile.

After all this it is important to reiterate that the issue of emergency cases cannot ever be a primary in the discussion of ethics and politics. The concept of an emergency means just that. Ayn Rand has given a clear analysis of this in her article "The Ethics of Emergencies":

> An emergency is an unchosen, unexpected event, limited in time, that creates conditions under which human survival is impossible—such as a flood, an earthquake, a fire, a shipwreck. In an emergency situation, men's primary goal is to combat the disaster, escape the danger and restore normal conditions (to reach dry land, to put out the fire, etc.), . . . to return to those conditions under which their lives can continue. By its nature, an emergency situation is temporary; if it were to last, men would perish.
>
> It is only in emergency situations that one should volunteer to help strangers [out of good will, not moral duty], if it is in one's power. For instance, a man who values human life and is caught in a shipwreck, should help to save his fellow passengers (though not at the expense of his own life). But this does not mean that after they all reach shore, he should devote his efforts to saving his fellow passengers from poverty, ignorance, neurosis or whatever other troubles they might have. Nor does it mean that he should spend his life sailing the seven seas in search of shipwreck victims to save.[38]

The same principle that guides a rational person in his personal relationships to others in emergency cases will guide a rational political administrator in his performance of his job in political emergencies. When people refuse to live by rational, moral laws, when legislators are confused, when pressure is exerted by powerful groups for government to violate the rights of others—in short, when he faces unusual degrees of irrationality from either his constituency or his fellow political agents—a rational political administrator will undertake the task "to return [matters] to those conditions under which [politics] can continue." At every turn such an individual—a person for whom the term "statesman" ought to be reserved—would strive to maintain the liberty of the citizens. That is the meaning of "law and order," namely that under the greatest trials a government ought to preserve the human rights of everyone and protect anyone from threats against these rights. Especially so where the threats come from the government of a community, the only agency whose expertise legitimately consists in the exercise of force.

Today, of course, we have government that thrives on crises, that "sails the seven seas in search of victims to save." The government of the United States has lived by "edict in the face of crisis" for as many as fifty years. The Great Depression, brought on by the federal government's intervention as early as 1914 in the relatively free monetary system of the United States and by greater and greater reduction of free market conditions throughout the economy[39]—this event provided those who support total statism with the excuse to make of the government a pseudoemergency unit. But the results leave no doubt about the wrongheadedness of such a course. Moreover, it is self-perpetuating, destructive to the very institution of government, and contributory to the disabling of members of the citizenry to cope with crises with intelligence and responsibility. Clearly, as Spencer put it, "The ultimate result of shielding men from the effects of folly is to fill the world with fools."

In a free society government, as any legitimate business performing some desired function for people, could face occasional emergencies. But unless it has conducted itself with integrity, with its just purpose in mind, those employed in it will be mediocre, morally inferior, professionally incompetent. And its administrators will lose their authority to govern, as would an attorney who misrepresents his client's interest, or a surgeon whose hands begin to shake during operations. The enterprise may eventually have to be disowned, perhaps even cast off.

It is to this last matter that we turn next—the responsibility of members of a human community to depose their government when it loses its just authority to govern. The point of the present section was to demythologize emergencies, to show that they are part of human life and that they no more justify force and the violation of human rights as a systematic feature of a legal system than they justify theft, robbery, burglary, deceit, or murder, for a human being's personal code of conduct. We all realize that sometimes burglaries are necessary—when there is no other way to serve justice; we know that lying to a Nazi SS about the whereabouts of your Jewish friends is not just excusable but your moral responsibility. We know that spies and police undercover agents make an occupation out of what would under normal circumstances be crimes. But none of that justifies making those activities part of an ethical code.

Nor is the emergency prerogative of governments ever properly invoked unless it *serves* justice. Even then it needs to be justified explicitly, at the first challenge. But when all of this has been ignored, when tyranny has set in, what then is the right course of action?

Revolution—But Not for the Hell of It

There are those who, following Emerson, consider consistency a folly of small minds. Indeed, some even contend that irrationality is perhaps a unique *virtue*. It is argued(?) that when one reaches "higher levels of consciousness," there is no need to check one's beliefs or insights by reference to logic and reason. And the claims of the irrationalists have appeal for some people, for they often allow one to be classed among "superior," creative human beings—ones who do not require mundane tools by which to reach knowledge.

Demeaning consistency, however, is itself folly. Without it nothing like understanding is possible in coping with the world. Some of this has already been dealt with in greater detail. The point to be made now is that revolutions, like emergencies, do not warrant going off the deep end—even if when faced with them in any area some people do so. We can understand and even excuse it when fear, panic, or anxiety overcomes us at such times. The crucial issue concerning the nature of emergencies and revolutions is that they do not demonstrate any inherent confusion of nature, some objective condition of contradictoriness in reality—as Marxists, drawing from Hegel, would have us believe.

In the last few decades doctrines of such objective contradictoriness have subtly permeated many fields. With Hegel the inherent contradictions in nature explained the regular recurrence of revolution throughout reality. Marx took over this general metaphysics and argued that society too is subject to violent revolutionary upheavals from time to time. Today some, like Thomas S. Kuhn in *The Structure of Scientific Revolutions*,[40] argue that even the development of scientific knowledge exhibits these periodic upheavals. From Kuhn's admittedly ambiguous theory one might infer that nature itself contains dialectical turnovers, although this is only implicit in what he himself has argued. It is explicit in Kuhn that standards of truth, and therefore rational decisions, are *impossible* at such points within any of the sciences except as a sort of social convention and by hindsight.

Now as sociology—as a report about how those involved in revolutions do in fact behave or what they believe can be done—Kuhn's idea could be correct. Most will have lost their footing when radical turnovers occur in any realm of human life—scientific, ethical, political, artistic, technological, or the rest. And it is likely that many scientists who work on so-called mainstream projects (what Kuhn calls "normal science") will not know where to turn when the rug is pulled from under them by some major breakthrough, by some genius who recasts an entire field of science with some brilliant insight or reorganization of the material of the field. Not even this genius—and we have Einstein's reports to this effect—may be able to *articulate* the full rationale for his contributions, not even he may be able to give a full justification for his confidence in what he puts forth.

But none of this proves the impossibility of judging and acting correctly during revolutions—in science or in politics. The fact that many people get lost, especially in bizarre, rapid-moving times, does not mean that no one *could* discern the correct approach to be taken. Under the strain of turmoil it isn't *likely* that many will keep an open mind and inform themselves of all that bears on the situation. But it could happen. Indeed one might argue that it ought to.

Of course, if people neglect paying attention to fundamentals as they proceed in peaceful times one cannot really hope that in crises they will be able to recover their losses. The goal to keep in mind at *all* times is the same—that is, the purpose of the activity in terms of which the principles are identified—although the peripheral rules will often change. In science the central goal of understanding the different realms of reality should guide those involved and provide them with the anchoring point for identifying the principles of their inquiry at the fundamental level. This is true whatever turmoils are experienced—and when philosophers of science deny there being such an anchoring point, they usually do so based on a philosophical position that advocates the very impossibility of knowing reality.[41]

In political matters the basic goal is social justice or, in somewhat old-fashioned terms, rectitude in social actions. Whether one advocates a policy, organizes a campaign, or forges a revolution, in each case that basic goal must be the motive if one is to preserve morality within the social context. Human rights are the principles of social justice, the standards by which to ascertain whether the basic goal is being pursued effectively—this because of the reliance of such rights on the moral point of view appropriate for human beings in all circumstances.

The question for political action is thus whether human rights can be respected, and how one can do so without endangering the basic political goal. Sometimes, *very rarely*, human rights *cannot* be respected—preserving the principles of a good political community becomes clearly impossible. Then one can no longer invoke them to assist in deciding on the proper course of conduct. Just what the guidelines will then be must be decided in the circumstances, based on the more general ethical code appropriate to human life. The responsibility for that decision lies, of course, with the individual who faces such circumstances.

These points have already been made with respect to emergency cases, and they apply also to political revolutions. Just as in emergencies the goal of action is to restore normal (i.e., proper) human conditions, so also in revolutions. Thus, even if it is the case that human rights cannot be respected in the process of revolutionary action, since the *purpose* of such activities is to establish the right political conditions for people, it is nevertheless to the political principles implicit in the appropriate ethical point of view that one must look in order to do the best that is possible. Anything less than what the above requires of an individual (in line with his particular situation) fails to qualify as responsible revolutionary conduct. This despite the willingness of so many, from Madison Avenue to social science journals, to employ the idea "revolution" stripped of its meaning and its moral import. Political revolutions are not for the hell of it, so they cannot be successfully conducted by satisfying the conditions of a common riot, a massacre, a putsch, or even a rebellion.

I do not want to give the impression that the ethics and politics of revolution are less than difficult problems in both a theory of political affairs and in carrying on with political life. The main concern here is not with formulating policy and strategy for revolutionary conduct. Instead the issue is how any citizen with the goal of justice in his community can best consider the subject of revolution—even when such considerations may not be of direct relevance to his present situation.

What is a political revolution? It is any massive movement within a human community, using whatever tools are available and thought to be justified, for purposes of changing the political system in line with which that community has been governed. On most occasions such revolutions are violent, although this is not a necessary characteristic. The distinguishing feature of a revolution is that the system by which community affairs have been organized, conducted, even thought about officially, is *fundamentally* revised, with some basic principles eliminated, others considerably altered, and yet others newly introduced.

What revolutions accomplish need not happen either with widescale violence or suddenly. There *can* be gradual revolutions, what may be considered the slow revision of one system's principles and the introduction of others that are radically distinct. In fact it is more accurate to consider such gradual turnovers as revolutions than to think of the putschs of Latin America as such—there nothing but the personnel changes while the form of political society remains unaltered. One is impressed then with the relative rarity of revolutions in the history of mankind, considering how many generations of human beings have inhabited this planet: there is evidence of fewer than a hundred different political systems. Moreover, there really have been only a few major *forms* of political organization.

But knowing what a political revolution is does not tell us when one is justified, when people ought to embark upon one. In short, it does not tell us what constitutes a *good* political revolution.

In a substantially statist society—where the majority of human activities are under some measure of governmental jurisdiction even though such activities do not involve the violation of the rights of human beings—there can be many occasions when individuals should resist governmental coercion as if it were coercion perpetrated by common criminals. In both cases the primary focus of attention must be whether resisting is likely to produce greater overall damage than acquiescense. For example, if someone steals your wallet it would be irresponsible to pursue the thief for the rest of your life. If one is the victim of petty thievery it would be unwise to risk death in resisting the holdup.

Nonetheless it is rationally undeniable that certain forms of governmental coercion justify drastic opposition from those who are affected by it. Thus a prospective conscript may find—after careful consideration, not mere arbitrary yield to anger or whim—that he ought to resist being drafted even to the extent of killing those who have come to take him into the military. A composer can conclude that a government's prohibition of the publication of his music is such a severe action against him that he is justified in either withstanding it with force or undertaking a personal vendetta against those who participated in the attack upon him. Such cases can multiply in proportion to the degree of coercion that is found within a community.

While a criminal can be resisted systematically by calling upon the police and the courts to perform the function for which they exist, when the very agents whose function it is to protect and preserve one's human rights violate them, there is nowhere to turn for systematic, organized retaliation. In that situation, then, the just treatment generally expected of the legal system in the apprehension and prosecution of suspected criminals depends upon one's own integrity. That is, in opposing the coercion and aggression of governments people are left to be guided by their own moral values.

It is thus easy to see why people, realizing the responsibility for and difficulty of identifying correct procedures, would be relatively reluctant to embark upon the deposition of their government by force, even when they are convinced that it is justifiable in the most general, abstract sense of that term. Now while the issue of whether to resist the violation of one's rights by government is tied to the context of a person's own situation as long as governmental abuse of power extends only to a certain level of magnitude, at some point human beings owe it to themselves to depose the state. In short, beyond a certain point tolerating a given political system belies a human being's dignity, and to refrain from doing what must be done to oppose the tyranny is plain cowardice. The question is, at what point should people resist *en masse?*

As Locke so eloquently put it,

But if a long train of abuses, prevarications, and artifices, all tending the same way, make the design visible to the people, and they cannot but feel what they lie under, and see whither they are going, it is not to be wondered that they should then rouse themselves, and endeavor to put the rule into such hands which may secure to them the ends for which government was at first erected, and without which, ancient names and specious forms are so far from being better, that they are much worse than the state of Nature or pure anarchy; the inconveniences being all as great and as near, but the remedy farther off and more difficult.[42]

I would argue more specifically that the time for mass revolution comes when total censorship—government ownership or legal regulation of publishing, broadcasting, printing firms—has been imposed. This is because such a move precludes any persuasive, noncoercive, nonviolent means of change.

But to say that people ought to resist their aggressors is not to say that they must make this known to anyone. So that although in fact many of their actions are designed to overturn the state, who plans them and what their exact aim is are another matter. In these matters too the appropriate virtues are called for—discretion, caution, prudence, and so forth.

I have already said that revolution does not necessarily entail violence. That can be its undoing in some circumstances. It does entail whatever actions would, if successful, depose those in power and regain the authority of members of a community to carry out the business that others have no right to interfere in. The only restriction upon any such action is that injustice be avoided wherever possible. Yet this does not provide an explicit principle for identifying the kind of actions open to people in such cases. How would a person act on the principle of resisting a government that violates the good of mankind—i.e., the protection and preservation of each person's human rights—without at once engaging in the "boundless will of tyranny" that is to be opposed by revolutionary action?

Although there can be many kinds of actions and no simple characterization beyond specifying their purpose, some examples will do. If, for instance, some people have identified a system and its adminis-trators as leading (even if not explicitly intended to lead) toward the destruction of the interests of mankind in human communities, they would, if resolved to act responsibly, engage in educating others to recog-nize theirs as a tyrannical system and in the proper actions to be taken. Education, then, is perhaps the first and foremost vehicle by which the purpose of a political revolution should be achieved. On the other hand, if even education would fail to secure this very purpose—leaving those who understand their responsibility powerless because their efforts reach hostile ears and elicit even further tyrannical measures—it may be right for the revolutionaries to embark on carefully designed but secretive and subtle measures by which to undermine the power of the tyrant(s). Also, when large enough numbers in a community have acknowledged their respon-sibility to resist and enough force can be assembled to carry out a successful violent challenge, then careful planning and action might be undertaken, but only with the clear understanding that the power gained will not be used in the manner that made for tyranny in the first place. In short, the design of a free society and the support for it must be at hand before any revolutionary plans are carried out, violent or not.

In a recently made film—*State of Siege*—there is a crucial scene where the revolutionaries are confronted by their hostage. The question he asks is, "What is your alternative?" And the leader of the revolutionaries replies with a confession of ignorance, adding only that those like his adversaries would be excluded. But no one has a right to advocate revolution unless an alternative to tyranny has been designed and acknowledged by him. He may have a moral justification for resisting tyranny, but the call for revolution—or engaging in revolutionary programs—requires more. That involves a promise to bring about a fundamental change in the direction of justice, and a plan for doing so.

For those who pay no attention to political issues the question of what is morally justified vis-à-vis political conditions such as tyranny can have little if any meaning. First they would need to gain political understanding, which by the nature of the problem is exactly what they lack.

Of course the immediate question most people will ask is whether the present political conditions in the United States justify revolution. There are some problems with answering this question.

First of all, I am personally sensitive enough to the degree to which there already exists a systematic abuse of governmental power, one aspect of which is the wielding of political influence with respect to almost every area of life. So I am reluctant to go on record about whether I would now call for revolution or which variety of it I might support, if any.

Second, it is clear that for some people there is still the opportunity to resist state intervention within the limitations of existing law. Also the majority in the United States still consider the basic political conditions here virtually flawless and explain any failures by reference to single events, mistakes in judgment, people with inexplicable flaws, unloving parents, alienation, et cetera. Moreover, those who do propose more searching explanations rarely advocate the adoption of a political/legal system that is, indeed, appropriate for human beings.

Finally, unless one can offer the required conditions for the success of revolution, other means to achieving a better moral/political system ought . to be advocated. Ought implies can, and anything like an overt attack upon the government of the United States by the people in general could not be successful when it is the majority of the people who keep that government acting as it does.

But something like a revolution is supported by the theory advanced in this book: a revolution of attention! By what has been said thus far it is clear that every individual capable of making the effort ought to, as a matter of his moral responsibility, his rational self-interest, pay attention to political affairs. Politics ought to be a personal concern for everyone.

It is obvious that some degree of attention is warranted in matters of health, nutrition, education, environment, friendship, love, and so on, even when there is no imminent problem. One must at least know where to go for help when sickness strikes; one needs to know of the available automobile mechanic, TV repairman, plumber—or at least the Yellow Pages—so as to be prepared when troubles arise in these areas. Politics too would be just one of the many issues to keep in mind, perhaps only in the back of one's mind, in a free society. Without politics engulfing one's life from virtually all sides there would be little reason why those not employed to serve as governmental agents ought to do more than keep the general requirements of a good society in mind and pay only sporadic attention to the details.

But this is hardly what has been mankind's condition. Nor is it now, although it was within the history of the United States that people could for a while enjoy the comfort of going about their own business and keeping politics at a distance. This ought to be the norm, and for a while it was, at least for some segments of the population. (There have always been minorities against whom the existing tyrannical aspects of our mixed legal system functioned severely; blacks and Indians, and at times Orientals, at others Germans, and then also women, and homosexuals, have found themselves attacked by governments *en masse*. Unfortunately, instead of demanding general adherence to human rights, members of these frequently oppressed groups too often demand extra privileges for their group as a group, most recently by way of governmentally supported employment quota systems.) The current worldwide violation of human rights by states and their friends (intellectuals, artists, and the whole host of advocates of statism) no longer enjoys the small outpost of opposition that was provided in at least some measure in the original political tradition and institutions of the United States. As such, every person ought to concern himself with the general political conditions which are increasingly productive of the violation of human rights.

Without the proper attention from people, bombarded as they are by misguided cries about crisis, self-sacrifice, the welfare of the nation or some group, and other rhetoric that is overtly or inadvertently calling for support of statism, no type of revolution can succeed, be it violent or peaceful. It may indeed be true that in our time the various countries of the world will have to experience general devastation, political as well as other forms of disaster; as in the lives of many individuals, so in the lives of human communities, often only such drastic traumas elicit awareness of the need to think through matters and act accordingly, although there is no guarantee that it will not be too late.

Again Locke makes the point well:

Where there is no longer the administration of justice for the security of men's rights, nor any remaining power within the community to direct the force, or provide for the necessities of the public, there certainly is no government left. Where the laws cannot be executed it is all one as if there were no laws, and a government without laws is, I suppose, a mystery in politics inconceivable to human capacity, and inconsistent with human society.[43]

Yet for those who will make the effort to foster the integrity if not of their political system—for that may be impossible—at least of their political ideals, the problem of revolution must in the end emerge in the following light, provided by Locke again:

> If the innocent honest man must quietly quit all he has for peace sake to him who will lay violent hands upon it, I desire it may be considered what a kind of peace there will be in the world which consists only in violence and rapine, and which is to be maintained only for the benefit of robbers and oppressors. Who would not think it an admirable peace betwixt the mighty and the mean, when the lamb, without resistance, yielded his throat to be torn by the imperious wolf?[44]

In recent years we have witnessed a remarkable development in the world—the protest of several Russian intellectuals against their government's violation of human rights. While in the United States the concept and the protection of human rights have been increasingly subverted by intellectuals and political administrators in their respective realms, in the Soviet Union human rights have emerged as an issue, even if distorted by officials who now pay lip service to the concept. When Andrei Sakharov was recently asked why he engages in activities that can have no noticeable impact, he replied in a vein in which I would like to be understood in the face the minuscule impact in this country also of the political theory of a free society:

> You always need to make ideals clear to yourself. . . . You always have to be aware of them, even if there is no direct path to their realization. Were there no ideals, there would be no hope whatsoever. Then everything would be hopelessness, darkness—a blind alley.[45]

CHAPTER 7

This, of course, does not suggest that skepticism is trivial; on the contrary it shows how profound a position of the mind it is. Nothing is more human than the wish to deny one's humanity.

Stanley Cavell

Facing some Critical Considerations

On Criticism

To criticize is to evaluate according to a standard, to judge by invoking some criterion of good. The present theory is itself an attempt to establish standards of political judgment and action. One of its purposes is therefore to guide one in the evaluation and criticism of political decisions and policies, including those one might consider undertaking. To criticize the theory itself must also involve some standard. Since the theory ranges over problems and issues in general philosophy and over several of its branches in particular, to criticize it involves reference to standards on a variety of philosophical fronts.

Perhaps the most persistent criticism emerges from philosophical skepticism. Philosophical criticism at a very basic level does indeed center on whatever conception of knowledge is used in the course of the development of a theory. This means that one can turn to a theorist and ask what he takes as knowledge. So although what he claims to know may fit his conception, his idea of knowledge may still not be adequate. When criticism rests on thoroughgoing skepticism it involves the claim that human beings cannot know reality, that there is no valid idea of knowledge, and thus it must be false to believe that one knows anything about anything whatever.

In the next section of this chapter I will provide an outline of a view of knowledge in terms of which skeptical challenges aimed at the attempt to develop some theory, especially within political philosophy, may be met. But first let me indicate why all this is important, despite its apparent departure from the main task of this work.

It is probably not widely realized outside of academic circles—ones that nevertheless have an obvious impact on the intellectual atmosphere of a culture—but to advance and be in agreement with a political theory is widely frowned upon today. Even when academicians engage in political action they tend, in the main, to divorce this from their professional intellectual activities. (Bertrand Russell was almost a caricature of this sort of academician and philosopher.[1])

To all this there exists a background: for many decades, even centuries, philosophers and other intellectuals in the West have been doubtful about the capacity of human beings to know reality. Radical skepticism is widely embraced even today; that is, many accept the idea or hold a deeply felt attitude that we are caught in individualized (or, at times, socially imposed) illusions about reality and our place in it. When people disagree on some issue, even in what is often thought to be a safe territory, namely the natural sciences, the discussion often bogs down in questions about whether we can after all know reality, whether people can ever find a common ground independent of their biases, prejudices, even independent of allegedly inherent or innate mental limitations, from which to develop some mutual understanding of what there is. The common answer is in the negative—and the efforts of thinkers are spent on the question of what we can substitute for such independent, objective common grounds. (Social success, loving tolerance of any and all views, living by the guidance of our instincts, mystical inspiration, drug-induced "higher" consciousness and the like are often suggested.)

Although such basic skepticism is pervasive enough, skepticism concerning values—ethical, political, and artistic judgments—is even more widely touted. Because of such a cultural fact, presenting fundamental obstacles to anyone who sets out to establish the existence of certain values, some discussion is owed to the point in a work such as the present, especially since the more general skepticism and that with which knowledge of values is attacked have much in common.

In addition, the skeptical attitude is not showing any signs of giving way to anything like confidence in man's capacity to know, even though there has been much dissatisfaction with the *results* of skepticism in the last few decades. People are concerned about wars being fought that lack any moral justification, with laws passed without a political framework to give them credibility, with ideologies that have no intellectual backbone and yet are used to rationalize oppression, terror, and other horrors. So while understanding and explanation are lacking, discontent is widespread.

In the wake of this the substitutes are gaining intellectual footing. Even in the sciences the idea that knowledge and understanding of reality are possible is being challenged by the view that theories which have gained widescale support are really unfounded and rely more on social acceptance than argument. Kuhn, as mentioned before, has put forth a doctrine such as this. The substance of such ideas can be harmful to the integrity of science, of course. But it is even more damaging to the search for understanding in personal and political affairs. For in science reality does not itself behave differently simply because scientists have curious ideas about their own activities. For us, however, these theories can become the quicksand of human action where solid foundations are needed.

Yet however important it may be to offer a well thought out defense of man's capacity to know the world, as well as of some of the beliefs that have earned the status of knowledge, the task is made virtually impossible by one feature of the skeptic's position. The skeptic denies that people can know the world. By this he has also deprived himself of any standards that another who wants to establish the validity of human knowledge will have to invoke to carry out his own task. If I believe that no one *can* know anything, not just that few or even none do know much, I have also admitted that I know of nothing that would serve as standards or criteria for contradicting my position. In a way, by an act of choice the skeptic has thus made discussion of the problem of knowledge impossible, at least when taken quite strictly and seriously about his own views.

Yet this is also the skeptic's downfall. He has failed to admit that his own pronouncement requires a great deal of prior knowledge even to make sense, let alone to qualify as true. By opening his mouth to discuss, the skeptic has provided evidence of his own confusion. For how does he know that what he is doing is denying something? Does he *know* what a denial is so that he can deny that people can know? And what does he know of human beings if he, as a human being, cannot know anything? Surely the alleged discovery that people cannot know reality is loaded with information about people, reality, and what sort of relationship can and cannot occur between these.

Some skeptics have tried to escape this bind. They have tried to maintain that while knowledge of reality is impossible, knowledge of ideas is not—so they could know that the idea "knowledge" is meaningless, incapable of ever being used to pick out something in reality. Thus they can know that whenever one thinks he knows something, he cannot be saying what is true. Except, of course, when this truth pertains to ideas. So in the end these skeptics will maintain that we can never *know that we have knowledge* of reality. This is a sophisticated variety of skepticism in that the skeptic does not actually claim to know that no one does know or even can know reality, only that no one can know *whether* he has any knowledge of reality. Maybe you and I know quite a lot, but we are barred from finding this out.

This view owes its formulation to those philosophers who have argued that the world consists of two separate, although perhaps at times connected, realms, the mental and the physical. From the time of Descartes this idea has carried considerable weight in the modern world, although Plato held to a version of it also. As pointed out earlier in this work, we owe to this view many popular distinctions—e.g., theory versus practice, mind versus body, a priori versus a posteriori sciences, empirical versus conceptual, and so forth. In short, the skeptic who claims to know the mental realm, including that mind cannot know of its own capacities and achievements in the realm of knowledge, relies on a definite philosophical position about mind's relationship to matter. As such he is really not entitled to call himself a skeptic, for knowledge of that relationship must come before he can invoke it to save himself against the charge that he is caught in an inconsistency. As D. W. Hamlyn points out, "Skepticism without grounds is empty, and empty suggestions need not be regarded seriously."[2] Yet how could the skeptic offer grounds for his views if, by their very meaning (if he is right), he could never know whether these grounds are real or illusionary?

All these points against radical and mitigated skepticism omit an important consideration. When one is skeptical about something in the ordinary sense of the term, one simply has reasonable doubts about the nature of what is at issue. A religious skeptic doubts the existence of God because he has reasons indicating that claims that God exists are insufficiently supported. In this sense skepticism is an extremely healthy approach to many issues, especially when raised in the context of politics.

And one simply cannot reject out of hand this sort of skeptical attitude toward efforts to provide a theory of human knowledge. Quite frankly many of them have been inadequate by ordinary standards—they have not demonstrated that the kind of thing they believe knowledge is exists. Skeptics have shown us that those who believe that knowledge consists of proving one's beliefs exclusively on the basis of infallible sense impressions are wrong; such proofs do not exist. Nor have those who account for human knowledge on the basis of innate ideas, fixed eternal forms, conventional beliefs, intuitions, and so on, fared better.

To perform the task of developing an adequate theory of knowledge here would be impossible. What I aim to do is to sketch an idea of knowledge that, fully developed, would identify, as best as possible for now, a distinct aspect of reality: man's correct identification of some fact.

Knowledge in Brief Focus[3]

To know something a person must be prepared to prove or show that what he believes is true, and his support in behalf of what he believes must constitute the best possible in the circumstances pertaining to the sort of thing he knows. To indicate what all this involves we need to spell out what it is for beliefs to be proven and what it is for a support to be the best in some area of concern. (Beliefs are usually made evident in statements, and when we speak about proving or showing that they are true, we are safe to refer to statements, the more tangible items in these areas of concern.) A preliminary point is that when we ask about truth, we (ought to) consider the *character* of some belief or statement. Although people commonly refer to "truths," there are no such things hanging about in reality for us to grab at and occasionally catch. Instead it is those entities capable of entertaining thoughts, forming judgments, believing this or that, or saying such and such that *produce* what is true. As with most important enterprises, this requires invoking standards. Of course, just as once in a while a good thing comes about by accident or without much care and attention, people can say and believe what is in fact true even though they did little to make sure that it would be. What we are after is the standards to be invoked when attempting a careful, deliberate and successful production of a true statement, theory, and so forth.

There is of course a difference between what someone must be able to produce when he claims to know something and when he offers a statement as a hunch, a first impression, something he believes but does not know, something he thinks may well be true, is very likely true, and so forth. It should be clear that to believe that something is the case needs far less to make it reasonable than to know it to be the case. If I say "The president has ulterior motives for signing this bill," I would need little to demonstrate that my belief is at least reasonable. I must come up with a good deal more if I offer this as something I know: I need proof.

To establish the truth of what we think or say, we need to discover whether the appropriate standards for doing this can be met. Not that these steps need always be followed at the time we formulate a belief, but they must be met to establish that we do have a true statement or theory at hand. What this will involve in the various realms we are concerned with is calling on facts we already know to support what we believe to an extent that reasonable contradictory claims (i.e., those consonant with the purposes we have for making our statement or holding our belief) would be excluded. In some cases, when many conflicting pieces of information emerge from initial investigation, we will have to dig far indeed. Some are unwilling to do this; others argue that it cannot be done because we will always meet a point where we must stop, yet disagreement is rationally possible. But this latter view is indefensible—its own tenets make it incapable of justification, of support. So we can explore how we would have to proceed to satisfy the requirements outlined above.

For example, suppose that as I sit typing I am called to the phone and asked whether my basement is flooded. I would, at this time, flatly report that it is not. I believe this to be true, and would even defend the claim that I *know* my basement is not flooded. In order to have the justification needed for this I would first of all have to *understand* what is meant by the claim "My basement is not flooded." The concepts used in this statement must themselves be meaningful, i.e., must be capable of being used to mean something, to be employed to pick out, refer to, mention or designate. This requires that the words (linguistic tools) used to express the concepts be clearly definable. And that in turn requires that the idea of defining something could itself be made clear, at least in crucial and searching circumstances—an issue to be taken up in the next section.

When I say that my basement is not flooded I am letting another rely on what I have recognized about a part of reality. Yet I can learn a good deal more about that part. How could it be possible for me to say something *true* when I may soon learn something new about the matter? What if new facts prove to be in conflict with what I now believe to the point where I conclude that I know? Would that indicate that I really did not know? And if this is possible in one case, is it in all cases—are we obligated to admit that we cannot know anything?

These questions arise when one conceives a true belief or knowledge as a final belief. No doubt people do make mistakes—what they concluded they knew they did not in fact know. From this it follows that people are not infallible. It does not follow that they must in each case be in error or be unable to tell whether or not they are in error. The *possibility* of being wrong—a rather widespread situation for human beings—has nothing at all to do with whether on any occasion one is right or wrong. It is simply the condition of knowledge; people can be wrong *and* they can be right, they can believe what is true or what is false. Whether here and now it is one or the other must be determined on the basis of what counts as the highest standards of knowledge in the area of present concern.

To return to my basement for a moment, I had been there before typing. And it had not rained since then, nor had there been any evidence of a break in the water pipes. It is, in addition, a solid building we live in, and the basement has not had any flooding during our occupancy. I know these facts. As indicated above, to establish the truth of my belief about my basement I need to understand what a basement is, what flooding is, what it is for something to be mine in the relevant sense, and how a question may be answered in the negative. But I also must know the situation with my basement, something that is possible only if I have the above understanding and have experienced what is recounted above. It is in this sense that I can achieve the highest standards of knowledge relevant to what was at issue in the present case, and thus be sure that what I believed is true, that I know that my basement is not flooded.

Of course concepts can change their meaning from one context and one time to the next. "Flooding" might come to mean "filled with X," and depending on what I then know of X in my basement I may have to answer that my basement is flooded. Moreover, at that time someone might recall my answer given today and maintain that I was wrong to say, back then, "My basement is not flooded" if X then filled it. But he would be wrong to hold this view. Being filled with X is not today understood as flooded—i.e., the idea is not now used to identify such a state of affairs. Which is not to say that it could not, but that possibility, even should it come about, does not count against using concepts as best developed at some stage, and having been correct in doing so.

Now the question arises, if truth is not fixed, if concepts that are involved in true beliefs can change, and new items can be discovered, how could there be an independent, objective reality at all? The answer to this was hinted at before. Briefly, there is a difference between facts and truth. Facts are what they are; reality is what it is. Even when we have more to learn about it or when it changes, it is and it changes independently of what we believe or say (although our saying things can itself bring about changes at times, but this is another matter). Our awareness of facts and our best rendition of them in thought and speech can change, improve, or deteriorate as well as remain constant through time. There are some things about the world that are quite evident at first inspection, even if many deny them (that too is a different matter), and other things that require continuous or renewed investigation. Both reality and the prospects of conscious life appear to be infinite, so it is not surprising that knowledge grows. Yet the very fact that we know of this much indicates that there is something we have understood quite well by now.

These admittedly obvious points need to be made because some try to deny that we can say things that are true, that we can have knowledge of reality, on grounds that the Truth can never be known. And by this they usually mean a final, unchangeable, noncontextually rendered, and "completely precise" statement such that under no circumstances would we have to change it. "Precision" then becomes an impossible goal, as does "completeness." The conclusion usually drawn is that we can never know—have conclusively justified true beliefs—about anything. What should actually be concluded, however, is that there are many cases when in one context a belief or statement will be true and in another context—the concepts have changed their meaning somewhat, new facts have been brought to light or more precision is required—it could well not be true. Both time and circumstance can warrant change in the rendition of some statement or belief, without depriving what was stated or believed earlier of its status.

The dropping of such context has led some to assert, e.g., that tables are not really solid at all, for at the atomic level there are obviously holes and anything with holes in it cannot be solid. (And this was said by the famous physicist Arthur Eddington.) Squarely put, to ask for the kind of precision needed in subatomic physics when building a landing strip for airlines would lead to the failure to build any landing strips! Such confusion of contexts has also led people to deny the existence of certain things because they could not be measured in ways we measure others. Thus some psychologists say that thoughts cannot be measured in ways bodily movements can, so there must not exist any such thing as thoughts, or, at least, we could never know of their existence. This assumes that we have already developed all the measuring standards appropriate to dealing with reality and that, among these, only those used in physics are valid procedures. The entire approach is question-begging. It assumes that there is only one kind of thing in reality, namely sensible matter. What is being crucially left out of such specifications of what will count as knowledge is that the standards to be met in order to justifiably claim knowledge, accuracy, measurement, and so on are in important respects specific to the subject matter and to the purpose at hand.

When we look at statements made some years ago about some area of reality we can fall into similar problems. We can impose requirements on people then that can only be met today. Thereby we also imply that they must have been wrong about what they believed. Yet usually this is not so. The meaning of what they said might have been extended beyond justification, as it often is today when people are too eager to extend ideas found sound in one area to explain everything under the sun. But quite often those in the past had it right, and this only means that they met the highest (then) possible standards of accuracy and truth within some field, given the definitions and meaning of what they believed. And that these latter were fully justified as well, in the context of their knowledge.

What does all this tell us about knowing right and wrong, about moral and political knowledge? That the standards of truth in a moral context could well be different from others, just as they are different in physics and psychology. I have already discussed those standards in my chapter dealing with human virtues and human excellence. It is by an understanding of human nature that their identification was rendered possible. The realm of morality and the standards of what counts as a true statement (judgment, belief, or theory) pertaining to that realm can be identified in the course of the general attempt to come to understand the world that we experience and must cope with for purposes of our successful existence.

In morality as well as in politics we deal with what concerns human beings alone, and here, as in other areas of interest to us, we must be able to provide ourselves with standards of truth. Yet even more importantly, we need to identify these standards so as to be able to guide our own conduct successfully, to distinguish not just truth from falsehood but right from wrong. We need to know what is right, to spot where we have been unsuccessful in that attempt, even if only by hindsight, so that our conduct, policies, institutions, and the like accord with the requirements of our nature, so that we can live well as the kind of entities we are.

To learn more about what the knowledge we need for that purpose involves, we need to examine another feature of the theory of knowledge that underlies the present investigation. This feature is generally called the theory of definitions. It is a crucial and perhaps the most controversial aspect of the present work from the point of view of what is most basic to the present theory; human rights theorists have had enormous difficulties with it.

Even among philosophers who have arrived at conclusions that back up the present theory of knowledge, the idea that we can identify the nature of what exists, that we are capable of formulating sound definitions of concepts, has little support. Theories of definition—or more appropriately discussions of the idea—usually culminate in the view that we cannot formulate *correct* definitions. All we might be able to do is agree on some convention, maybe get used to restricting our employment of concepts in certain ways, or stipulate that we will use words in some specific sense only. These are called nominalist, conventionalist, or pragmatic accounts of definitions, all of which deny that there can be a rational, binding *justification* for a definition of some concept or idea. Some even argue that all attempts to provide a theory that would support the possibility of such justification are no more than attempts at persuasion or, more likely, attempts to give credence to some people's efforts to persuade as against others'. (This is known as the "persuasive definition" theory.) Here the point that to persuade one might in fact need conclusive arguments is forgotten. So it may be true that one is aiming to persuade people to employ a certain definition; but it does not follow that one has no conclusive ground for expecting that they do so.

The overall purpose of the present theory of human rights has been to understand what human rights are, what those conditions are that are right for human beings in society because they *are* human beings. Thus our concern is linked intimately with the problem of definitions. Human rights are what people have because they are human, not because they belong to a club, race, union, gender, or some other special classification of human beings. Nor does a person possess these rights by virtue of being a living entity—an animal or plant. We have these rights, if indeed we have them, because of our humanity. So we need to deal with the issue of whether we can know the nature of something, so that we can establish our capacity to know what is human as distinct from other sorts of being.

If a definition of man cannot be known, then the case for human rights could never get off the ground. The kind of beings we are is stated, if it ever is, or would be, in the definition of the concept "human being." It is only if human beings can provide that, that anyone has the logical as well as moral justification for claiming his human rights or the human rights of anyone, and acting to establish a human community in which such rights are protected and preserved. First, then, it will be necessary to give definitions some heed.

On Defining Concepts

In this discussion of definitions I will focus mainly on the philosophical problems that theories of definitions have encountered. I will try to discuss the matter in fairly straightforward terms, using as little of the jargon as possible. As such I will not be developing a full-blown theory. Instead I will try to update something that has been part of the fabric of human thought and communication throughout its existence, and was identified well by Aristotle, who made clear the function of definitions in human affairs.

In thinking about definitions most people have in mind a statement such as "By 'government' I mean 'a group of people who administer the rules of human interaction within a given society.'" Yet this is misleading in that the concept "meaning" does not quite capture what a definition is. In the above case, for example, the concept "government" actually means whatever one can successfully refer to, mention, designate, indicate, or signify by using it in thought and language. So to mean something by the use of a concept already requires that it be defined clearly enough. A definition will provide that concept with its borders, the limitations on the range of the concept's applicability. It does not state all of what can be meant by a concept, only what at minimum *must* be meant by it. Put more rigorously in a way common to philosophy, a definition states the necessary and sufficient conditions for employing some concept; it provides us with the criterion or standard by which we can tell whether a concept is appropriate in some context of use.

A problem that has plagued those who have held that we can provide concepts (terms, words, ideas) with the correct definition goes hand in hand with the problem raised earlier concerning human knowledge. Since what we know is known via our employment of concepts, and each statement of what we know uses words that express these concepts in a person's language, can our knowledge ever grow when the definitions provided at any given time serve as the standards of our employment of these concepts? In short, the idea that concepts can be defined correctly would seem to fly in the face of something obvious, namely that we do change the way our concepts are used, we expand on the areas covered by them, or sometimes we restrict them and introduce new concepts to cover some of what had previously been taken care of by the old.

The problem here stems from a fact that has been noted in connection with various issues throughout the discussion in this work. In some areas of knowledge a given definition will suffice for a very long time. Thus in mathematics we can define "square" in a way that has not changed in centuries. The concept "human being" was defined by Aristotle as "rational animal." Some philosophers who have defended the view that there can be correct or good and incorrect or bad definitions for all terms in the language—although perhaps different types of definitions will be needed for different types of terms (ostensive, operational, conventional, real, and so on)—have argued that once a *correct* definition is found, that definition must forever stay as it is when identified. In other words, adequate definitions were conceived as timelessly fixed, unchanging.

This view does run contrary to the fact of growth and change in our ideas, in line with the growth in human knowledge. Clearly anyone seeking a final definition of all concepts will be disappointed—we will never be able to stop either reality's own evolution or the continued increase in understanding of reality either by human beings or some other entities capable of conceptual knowledge. The question then is, can there be some other idea of definitions that will account for the purpose definitions are thought to serve (and seem certainly to be needed for in science, law, or business) without setting for itself an impossible goal such as the above? I think that the alternative of contextually valid definitions can succeed as an answer to this query.

The idea here is not very difficult, although to show that it is sound would take a good deal of space and effort. Fortunately several philosophers have worked on the problem.[4] Some have discussed it explicitly in terms of the theory of definitions, others have handled it as the issue of the natures of things, or universals. For when we talk about definitions, we are also considering whether the idea of the nature of something—e.g., the nature of man, the nature of government—is sound. At any rate, the basic idea here is that although human knowledge may grow—or decline, for that matter—at each of its stages within various fields of interest, the best definitions of concepts can be provided. Within the context of knowledge one can then formulate the correct definition of such notions as "science," "government," "justice," "wife," "atom," "electron," "triangle," "physics," "vehicle," "freeway," and so forth.

Obviously some concepts change rapidly, and most have quite legitimate uses in a variety of circumstances; consider, for instance, that the concept "universal" is used to mean one sort of thing in philosophy and quite another sort in an automotive shop. There are also identical words that serve to express totally unrelated concepts, e.g., "kind" or "import." These last are understandably rare. Some ideas may never stay put long enough to be defined on any widescale basis, e.g., such slang terms as "groovy," "hip," and the like. Yet others need never be redefined once they have been understood by human beings, e.g., "existence" or "reality."

Of course, whether what I have said is viable is certainly open to discussion. Many philosophers would reject it, on various grounds. For example, and this is an objection to most theories of definitions, if definitions always require a statement that contains certain concepts, do we not reach the dilemma of an infinite regress in our attempt to define all concepts? However open-ended definitions can be with the contextual approach, this problem will not be solved by that feature. One solution would be to argue that all definitions need not be *stated*—e.g., ostensive definitions might not require any statement whatever. Certain features of reality might simply be evident to any attentive person, they may be on view, directly displayed. Reflection would then lead one to realize that any concept by which we would think of these aspects of reality is implicit in all else that we know. (The concept "existence," for instance, is implicit in all thinking, and its range of application can be clear to anyone concerned: everything that is is meant by it.) Yet even these concepts may be clarified by some discussion, however integral they could be to all our thinking, however unusually would have to approach and understand what they mean.

One advantage of this approach to definitions is that it allows for enormous diversity without, however, sanctioning arbitrariness. It also relies on a theory about the way human beings must formulate definitions: by using their minds to engage in differentiation and integration of the material that they obtain through perception. There is a responsibility involved here that is well captured in the following passage by Barry Stroud:

> Logical necessity . . . is not like rails that stretch into infinity and compel us always to go in one and only one way; but neither is it the case that we are not compelled at all. Rather, there are the rails we have already travelled, and we can extend them beyond the present point only by depending on those that already exist. In order for the rails to be navigable they must be extended in smooth and natural ways; how they are to be continued is to that extent determined by the route of those rails which are already there. I have been primarily concerned to explain the sense in which we are "responsible" for the ways in which the rails are extended, without destroying anything that could properly be called their objectivity.[5]

By "logical necessity" philosophers often mean the necessary and sufficient conditions for something being the case, for our use of a concept to mean something *definite*. (It pertains to the *logical* implications of the meaning of some idea.) Stroud indicates the sense in which the idea of definition being considered here makes room for that element of growth, even inventiveness or creativeness that many people talk about when they show dissatisfaction with the traditional conception of "fixed natures." Yet this idea is not conducive to the advocacy of arbitrariness.

In the present discussion I have attempted to outline some of the distinctive features of a theory of definitions that has underpinned the entire discussion of the present book. This theory has been developed by various philosophers throughout history. Today it is well expressed in the following passages by Ayn Rand:

To know the exact meaning of the concepts one is using, one must know their correct definitions, one must be able to retrace the specific (logical, not chronological) steps by which they were formed, and one must be able to demonstrate their connection to their base in perceptual reality.

When in doubt about the meaning or the definition of a concept, the best method of clarification is to look for its referents—i.e., to ask oneself: What fact or facts of reality gave rise to this concept? What distinguishes it from all other concepts. . . .

The essence of a concept is that fundamental characteristic(s) of its units on which the greatest number of other characteristics depend, and which distinguishes these units from all other existents within the field of man's knowledge. Thus the essence of a concept is determined *contextually* and may be altered with the growth of man's knowledge.

(Who decides, in case of disagreements? As in all issues pertaining to objectivity, there is no ultimate authority, except reality and the mind of every individual who judges the evidence by the objective method of judgment: logic.)[6]

It is not to be expected that this short exposition of the view of definitions that I consider most appropriate will be fully convincing. I have already said why it cannot be expected that radical skeptics will agree. Even those who would like to see a detailed justification of one's case will be unsatisfied, I am sure. But to defend the view in full would require matching it against numerous alternatives, as well as confronting it with all the questions a theory of this sort must answer.

Yet there is even an initial plausibility to this view beyond what most enjoy. It seems to take care of the central objections raised against traditional theories of definitions while preserving their widely admitted usefulness in human affairs. Most importantly, it explains disagreements not by reference to some inherent limitation of the human mind, or some intrinsic confusion of nature itself, but by reference to man's capacity for error as well as negligence and carelessness—the willingness of many people to quite often abandon their responsibility to use their minds in the task of coping with reality. The present view of definitions and knowledge ties in with the moral theory advanced earlier. In *human* affairs, knowledge is a life-and-death issue. And morality, too, concerns itself with the successful life of human beings, something that has a great deal to do with how well they use their minds.

From this point on I shall let the topic of human knowledge rest. I have already argued for the idea of human nature that underlies the human rights theory advocated here. While brief, that discussion can now be more fully appreciated. We can arrive at a definition of man, while not denying that man could change, human nature could evolve into something other than what it now is. But until evidence is provided that that is happening and not just possible, we are entitled to work for the realization of those goals that are appropriate for people given what they *are*.

Some Heed to Critics Galore

My plan is here to state the views of some major critics of human rights theory in summary form and to respond to them fully enough to indicate the direction that the counterargument would take. Given what has already gone before in this work, this is all that seems necessary here.

In her paper "Natural Rights"[7] Margaret Macdonald argues that man has no fixed nature, and therefore no natural rights. When men claim to have rights what are really being referred to are common human preferences, goals, aspirations, or values, which can be defended only as one defends one's aesthetic tastes, by reference to subjective factors. The rights to life, liberty, equality or whatever, she believes, are widely expressed preferences that, although people have fought for them valiantly, are nothing like the truths of science, which can be firmly established.

In response to Macdonald, she is wrong on two important counts. First, a theory of human (natural) rights does not require belief in "fixed natures." The theory of definitions presented earlier will suffice to make this point clear. Second, Macdonald is wrong, although far from alone, to think that there is such a crucial division between the facts of science and the facts of ethics and politics—what is good and right for human beings generally and in their social circumstances. True, the kind of precision necessary to physics or mathematics is not to be found in ethics and politics, but the *kind* of precision found in biology is also different from that in chemistry. As Aristotle said many centuries ago of the subject matter of ethics, "Our discussion will be adequate if it has as much clearness as the subject-matter admits of, for precision is not to be sought for alike in all discussions, any more than in all products of the crafts." Indeed, Macdonald's denial of the capacity for truth to statements about what is good and right on grounds that one can not accommodate the standards used in the physical sciences amounts to asking a student of botany to use the tools of nuclear physics.

Another criticism of human rights theory comes from Kai Nielsen.[8] He argues that since we can imagine—and very brilliant philosophers have indeed imagined in great detail—moral and political systems variously suited to several conceptions of the nature of man, this must mean that human nature is not fixed, that man might be different from how human rights theorists have conceived of him. If that is so, we cannot identify any human rights. So Nielsen reluctantly concludes that "As much as I value a respect for human beings, all human beings . . . it seems to me quite evident that we do not know that there are any universal human rights."[9]

To Nielsen the response would have to go along the following lines: First, he also has the idea that to know that there are human rights must either amount to knowing some scientifically established fact about people—e.g., that they all and invariably benefit from something in the way they can benefit from a nutritious diet—or to knowing some logical truth, some unchangeably fixed nature of man which would not be deniable without obvious self-contradiction. Second, that very important people have imagined man to be other than what he is simply cannot be used to prove anything about human nature, nor about what we may or may not know of people's human rights. All it proves is that the human imagination is indeed powerful. Nielsen focuses on Friedrich Nietzsche's idea of a "master morality" suited for his "overman," the superior human being with the rare and exclusive capacity to overcome the obstacles to man's growth. Yet Nietzsche was one of the least systematic philosophers. Even if he had inquired into it with as much care as is needed for formulating a general account of human nature, even if he had developed a rigorously argued moral theory, it does not follow that we must accept his conclusions, or that we need to incorporate his conjectures into a theory of human nature and morality. His value is in offering us certain insights, but his faults are there also in his refusal to acknowledge all persons as equal in moral capacities, never mind that each one can do with this moral capacity more or less well in life.

Ultimately Nielsen's objections come down to saying that since others disagree with the idea of human nature in human rights theory, we cannot know that people have such rights. Yet, of course, people disagree on virtually anything under the sun—in England the Flat Earth Society goes to great lengths trying to show that spaceship pictures of a round earth are frauds. Do we concede that we cannot know that there are principles of geophysics, or cannot know facts about the nature of our planet? Nietzsche or no Nietzsche, his imagination and Nielsen's as well cannot be considered relevant to the case for human rights.

William T. Blackstone[10] has been a defender of human rights, but his theory allows for a certain characterization of them that conflicts with what I have advanced. Basically Blackstone believes that there are human rights but their existence (not their acknowledgment) depends on society's having a certain "desired ideal" about what a human community should be. As one might gather, the difference between Blackstone's theory and what has been offered in this book is at a level not simple to discern. Nevertheless it is crucial, because on it hinges whether human rights are rationally defensible or conventional.

Blackstone's reference to some "desired ideal" rests the case for human rights on grounds similar to Macdonald's. A feeling or desire is the court of last resort in our search for a foundation, and although an ideal may well be *desired*—many have been, some of them disastrous—it could be indefensible by rational argument. For a desire or feeling is not a judgment, and as such there are no standards that must be satisfied in justifying a desire as there are when one tries to defend judgments. If human rights cannot find themselves a firmer foundation than what people happen to desire in the way of a human community, then human rights are indefensible. As such, Blackstone's case for human rights, in some ways related to the one offered here, is built on quicksand—the extremely varied and variable desires of mankind.

One of the most challenging arguments related to human rights was propounded some years ago by a number of philosophers who defended what they called *prima facie* rights. Gregory Vlastos,[11] a recent defender of this revision of human rights, says that human rights are *prima facie* in "that the claims of any of them may be over-ruled in special circumstances."[12] Although according to Vlastos all rights are prima facie, he also contends that they have "a fundamental place . . . in our scheme of justice,"[13] meaning that any just system of law would be based on them. The point is that human rights are really prima facie and not absolute (as argued in this work) because there are cases when people ought to disregard the rights of others, as when the property rights of some landowner ought to be disregarded to save someone from a burning house, or when public authority may or even should requisition hoarded food during a famine. Vlastos also cites punishment as an instance of overruling human rights, so that he claims not even John Locke could have believed human rights to be absolute.

There are important points here, and I want to discuss them quickly. Vlastos is right to say that human rights ought to be disregarded sometimes. But he is wrong to think that they are disregarded when someone is punished for having violated another's human rights—such punishment is like the payment of a debt or the delivery on a promise: it is the logical, moral consequence of a freely chosen act.

Vlastos is also wrong to think that human rights could be disregarded *as* fundamental features of a scheme of justice, a system of just laws. For nothing can be both fundamental and capable of being overruled in the context of the same system. What he could have argued is that *within the context of morality* the moral point of view from which human rights are derived is more basic than human rights and a scheme of justice. Indeed, the egoistic morality in terms of which human rights are justified is more basic, and, as discussed before, when no choice other than one's life or another's is open to a person, one simply cannot pay heed to the issue of human rights. This is an emergency case, not one suited for the normal conduct of a human community, i.e., a just legal system. All this, however, does not render human rights less than absolute *within the context of a scheme of justice,* i.e., politically. There, indeed, each person's human rights must be fully protected, and the right to life is most basic, thus absolute, in any system that adopts the principles of justice.

The reason that Vlastos opts for a theory of *prima facie* rights is that he believes every person has two great moral values which the state ought to protect and preserve: freedom and happiness (or well-being). Unlike the founders of our system, Vlastos thinks one has a natural right to happiness, not to its pursuit. He therefore argues for a legal system in which both something called welfare rights and freedom rights are protected and preserved. Yet, as we have seen, there is a difference between the values of human happiness and human (political) freedom. Happiness is each individual's most general moral goal, to be pursued and achieved by choice and effort, respectively, not produced for him by others. Political freedom is the common good of a human community by which people are enabled to achieve their personal moral goal—happiness. The latter is a matter of personal achievement—that is why it is a moral goal—the former an achievement of a community—that is why it is a political goal. Vlastos mixes these two values because he is interested in guaranteeing everyone some degree of happiness (even if he is either unfortunate enough or unwilling enough to fail to achieve it), yet is keenly aware of the dangers of a benevolent dictatorship where all human liberty is sacrificed for well-being and security (the absence of the risk of failure in striving for happiness without guarantees). What happens is that neither can be fully achieved; each must be compromised.

More importantly, however, Vlastos deprives political liberty of its moral foundation by putting human happiness and political liberty within the same category of values. It is only because it is man's moral purpose to achieve happiness that he can justify political liberty. Liberty by itself is not a value, whereas human happiness is. Freedom, if it were not necessary to the achievement of goals on the part of those who have it, would not have any value. But by abolishing this distinction between the two values, Vlastos renders liberty indefensible and happiness a matter of politics, not morality. *Prima facie* rights is an invalid concept, although Vlastos is at least correct to indicate that human rights are not the most basic values of human life, only the most important political values, the basic values of a human community.[14]

Another but far more remote criticism of human rights originates in Marxism. There are today so many Marxists that it is difficult to know whom to select as the standard-bearer of that doctrine, so it will be best to discuss Marx's own position relative to human rights as advocated in this book. The crucial feature of his philosophy in this connection is his idea of man. Marx believed that the universe advances in a definite direction along precise and systematic lines. He regarded socialism as the science that studies the advancement of human history, and interpreted the history of humanity (as everything else) as following the laws of dialectical materialism.

The central feature of all of these laws consisted of a process whereby everything that exists contains within it its own negation or, as we might say more simply, each entity that exists is in conflict with itself. So each entity surges on to become another entity that is not just a combination of the opposites but a *qualitatively* different and better entity than the previous combination. This process continues, with each new entity developing internal conflicts or contradictions until it achieves a final resolution that abolishes conflict altogether. In fact communism, although not discussed by Marx in sufficient detail to know what it would amount to, was to be the culmination of the process of development involving what we know as human beings.

In line with Marx's thought, man is today alienated from himself, still embodying self-contradictions, and therefore reaching toward a higher stage of development in accordance with the laws of dialectics. Today we have only the human consciousness of class members, not some unified, consistent, fully developed human nature. That would come only through the realization of socialism and after that communism. The conclusion was that there could be no such thing as human rights until human nature is fully realized.

In fact Marx argued that the mention of human nature at this time is actually an ideological product of class consciousness, specifically of the class consciousness of the bourgeoisie, i.e., the propertied class. Since human rights theory had gained its fullest articulation in John Locke, and Locke had indeed argued for the claim that each person has the natural right to life, liberty and property, Marx's charge, made by both him and Engels and more recently by C. B. MacPherson,[15] had some plausibility. Locke as a member of the bourgeoisie had simply put forth the ideology of his class, the prime object being to protect the interest of that class. Locke gave this argument some fuel by frequently providing his critics with more talk of property rights than any other rights, as well as by downgrading at times those who did not possess wealth.

Marx argued further that this emphasis on property was a perfectly natural aspect of the development of history in accordance with dialectical laws. Although at times he used very moralistic language against capitalists, as do his current followers, Marx never doubted the essential role of capitalism in the development of humanity. He said that capitalism would develop the tools of production so that the state could appropriate them in socialism, and they could be usefully employed to abolish scarcity in communism.

The way in which the different stages of development were to come about was via revolution. Because the classes possess conflicting ideologies and cannot understand each other's language, their conflicting interests will not be settled by discussion, commerce or compromise. Only revolution can resolve the self-contradiction within humanity. (This Marx later revised. But it formed the basis of the Marxist ideology and was only abandoned here and there, when useful to the party and subsequent intellectuals.) Human rights theory as articulated in the American political tradition is just one of the ideologies to emerge in the ongoing class conflicts throughout history, but the ideology certainly has no claim to truth according to Marx's system, since human nature, from which human rights derive, has not yet been realized.

To argue with Marx would require careful examination of his entire system. There are so many divergent elements that come together in Marx's thought, from Hegel, Kant, Hobbes, Hume, Feuerbach, Stirner, Saint Simon *et al.*, that it is impossible to simply outline or briefly criticize his thought. What *can* be said is that logic does not find a central place in it. Unfortunately Marx had many conflicting claims within his system, but even more unfortunately, it is unclear to what extent he managed to explain these away by his endorsement of the presence of contradictions in *everything*. Nor is it clear that he can even make plausible his adoption of Hegel's dialectic within a purely materialistic system. (Sartre criticizes Marx on this very severely.)

Even more importantly, there is no clear clue in Marx where ideology ends and science begins—why, for instance, must Locke be giving voice to ideology (class-bound), while Marx voices scientific truth, which is not conditioned by class membership? And Marx did believe that his views were not so conditioned, yet he did not explain why *others* could not resolve their class disputes by becoming scientific about them. The Marxist argument thus contains something disingenuous by elevating Marx himself out of the ordinary human situation to a perspective with what is called a "God's-eye view." No doubt Marx made some important observations about the social conditions of man, at least at his time, and no doubt he was impressed by some of the turmoil of his times to the point that he selected turmoil itself as the paradigmatic law of existence. We need not, however, accept his generalizations—the "blow-up" principle I have described elsewhere seems to have operated in Marx's case.

Marx's argument against human rights rests on a dubious conception of human life and history. His idea of man and what is right for man involves some new entity in a hardly recognizable human society, while human rights theory deals with man today, as a part of nature. If a new species does emerge, that must be dealt with in its time.

There are other objections to human rights that could be cited, but throughout this book I have touched on virtually all of them directly or indirectly. What seems so difficult for most people to acknowledge is that compromising principles is fatal to the good principles, the sound ones. The Watergate scandal was an excellent, although not the most drastic, illustration of this fact, although few have drawn the proper lessons from it. But many people seem to believe that we must compromise our ethics, as well as our politics, in order to make peace with those who have little or no regard for them.

So much for considering criticism. To go beyond this would require entering the technicalities of academic philosophy, and my purpose has not been to do that kind of battle here. Contrary to Kai Nielsen, then, I must conclude from all the above that human rights exist; we can know that well enough. Unfortunately they are evaded, violated, and intellectually attacked too widely for us to have justified expectations for their better prospects in our lives and institutions.

CHAPTER 8

It has frequently been noticed that the surest result of brainwashing in the long run is a peculiar kind of cynicism, the absolute refusal to believe in the truth of anything, no matter how well it may be established. In other words, the result of a consistent and total substitution of lies for factual truth is not that the lie now will be accepted as truth, and truth be defamed as lie, but that the sense by which we take our bearings in the real world—and the category of truth versus falsehood is among the mental means to this end—is being destroyed.

Hannah Arendt

On the Prospects of Human Rights

Human Life, Human Good, and Human Rights

AT the outset we need to talk about the applicability of the idea of prospects to human rights. What may seem strange about considering this is that if human rights exist, then surely it makes no sense to question their prospects—no more than to ask about the prospects of the sun or moon or the law of gravity. But the comparison cannot be made if one understands what it is for there to be human rights.

Obviously human rights do not exist in the fashion of the sun, the moon, or even the law of gravity. Rather they exist in the way an obligation, a responsibility or a duty might exist. That is to say, if I ought to further my career, or if you ought to help your son to understand his relationship to the family, then my responsibility to excel at my work *exists*, and your responsibility as a parent *exists*. In the same way, if everyone in a human community ought to refrain from obstructing other people's choices and actions when these pertain to their own lives, then the human right to political liberty *exists*. Of course the existence of such facts is not ascertained by looking through microscopes, or by elaborate mathematical calculations, or by psychological experimentation—all of that is not suited to discovering and identifying human rights. It is unjustified and indefensible to ask that we go about learning of human rights as we do about sunken treasures, quasars, or the best price of chicken this week.

On the other hand, it is true that most of the facts people may run across will not be very controversial (although at certain levels of complexity the facts in almost any area of concern will be questioned), while the facts of ethics and politics, not to mention aesthetics, are steeped in perennial debate. (Many take this as evidence that no defensible conclusions *could* be reached on these matters.) Perhaps it is just because values are at least implicitly so integral to our every choice and action that we are so concerned to have our own views about them flourish—or to deny that there are any facts about such issues, any demands that we support what we have concluded.

As such, it does make sense to ask about the prospects of something that exists, something that constitutes a fact in the universe. If people come to acknowledge the existence of human rights and the truth of the moral and political principles underlying the theory, then the prospects of human rights will be good, but if this does not happen they will be bad. So this final chapter is devoted to a brief discussion of whether it is more or less likely that human rights will be acknowledged, and of some initial obstacles and doubts which might stand in the way of their instantiation.

It may help to retrace the positive thesis developed here. We began with the stipulation that to justify claims about what people ought to do we had to appeal to a standard. This itself had to be established as the standard applicable for our purpose. And our purpose has been to identify how human beings might best live their lives in a human community.

It would not have been sufficient to start from what some people would much like others to do, what I or my philosophical allies prefer or would prescribe on grounds that we find these modes of conduct appealing. Nor would it have been enough to invoke some ineffable grounds such as "the will of God," "our intuitions of what is right," "things known to the heart," or "what the experts in their wisdom have decided." It was necessary to appeal to what anyone who would care to investigate the matter *could* learn—unless his normal functions are unusually impaired—even though there is no way to ensure that this investigation *will* be undertaken or done well, or concluded with self-confidence in the face of opposition.

What seems to be the standard clearly accessible in the effort to learn what is good for human beings is human nature, what each person is *essentially*. Although some careful thinking is required to trace down this approach, especially since the fact of man's freedom of choice may seem to class our species within some strange, unnatural, even mysterious or divine group of unexplainable entities, the idea is not really that complicated. Thus ethical and political principles are justifiable—in that they pertain to the conduct of men and women—by reference to human nature. Anything else presupposes some standard that applies not to people but, for example, to gods, angels, society, State, culture, tradition, heritage, future generations, or ecology.

The claim that people should strive to protect and preserve human rights must also be justified by reference to human nature. Such a justification would succeed only if this protection and preservation are good for people in some circumstances, namely when they live in human communities. In this broad sense, human rights are justified by reference to each individual human being's self-interest—not what he thinks is his self-interest, not what he feels he would like, not his wishes, wants or deepest convictions, but his actual, rational self-interest as a human being. This indeed is the egoism that has given the moral support for the human rights theory presented above, and it has been advanced by philosophers from Socrates, Plato, Aristotle, Locke, and Spencer, to Rand, Mack and myself in one form or another. In short, the present human rights theory has focused on the rational self-interest of people with respect to their most basic principles of community action, organization, leadership, crises, emergencies, and whatever else requires the most general guidelines of political conduct.

Obstructions in the Current Moral Climate

An important consideration for purposes of discerning the likelihood of better prospects for human rights is the popularity of the moral theory of altruism. It is implicitly and explicitly advocated by virtually all intellectual forces, from the most to the least sophisticated (e.g., from complex defenses of altruism and equally complex attacks on egoism in philosophical journals, to very commonplace advocacies by way of television programs, the pulpit, and children's fables, as well as throughout the volumes of literature wherein the moral nature of human beings is exemplified, discussed, and projected). Undoubtedly many respond to the examples set by those whom they admire or simply accept as authorities about human affairs. Although people ought to exercise a critical approach to these individuals and institutions of leadership, they do not often do this. They as well as the leaders carry the responsibility for perpetuating a moral point of view and the corresponding actions, institutions and laws.

Altruism is simply incompatible with the advocacy of human rights, although it is not at odds with their legal recognition and protection and preservation: an altruist is free to advocate his doctrine that all men ought to choose to live for others' sake, to pursue the happiness of other people; he is also free to act on this doctrine when that does not violate people's human rights—even though some altruists believe that violating others' rights is part and parcel of being an altruist. Strictly speaking, however, altruism does not entail or imply forcing others to act as they would not act freely, although forcing "goodness" on others is widely practiced in its name. Altruism merely implies that each person ought to choose to perform actions with the goal of benefiting others. It is another matter to force people to act in accord with the altruists' beliefs, or to force them to accept benefits.

The pervasiveness of this morality is incalculable, partly because the so-called "value-free" social sciences usually give it support via their resultant conventionalism. Unless the altruistic morality is countered on the philosophical educational level, the ethical code that underlies human rights theory will not gain an intellectual foothold in the culture. This will also prevent its development as a respectable, defensible political philosophy. As matters stand today, with the intellectual presentation egoism is given and the institutionalization of altruism in public policy, there is no moral support for the political system which incorporates human rights theory.

The "Value-Free" Defense of Political Liberty

While the justification for any course of conduct must ultimately *square* with morality, the defense of a system of laws as against other systems must *be* a moral one. Prudence, efficiency, or aesthetic appeal—which bolster the "pragmatic" and "utilitarian" arguments—will not by themselves render a society good and just.

Many people forget this when they argue for freedom. Today when the free society is defended it is usually on such nonmoral grounds. To name just a few who are now engaged in research and analysis pointing to a free market approach to the problems facing us, the ranks include Milton Friedman, Yale Brozen, Harold Demsetz, Armen Alchian, Sam Peltzman, James Buchanan, Henry Manne, Gordon Tullock, David Friedman, and Roger LeRoy Miller.[1] All of these are economists, and most maintain that the defense of freedom must come from economists. Some argue that scientists simply do not deal with moral values. Others contend that values cannot be justified anyway, so efficiency is what we must look to in the defense of our economic and political systems.

Of course a good deal of what people do in a social context is economic. Even love, family life, church, and art include economic aspects. The human rights to life, liberty, and property all involve some economic matters, and a country with a legal system based on the principle of human rights and political freedom must enjoy a free economy. As the Soviets have so keenly observed, if the economy of a country is free its politics will soon follow suit.[2] Defending the free economy is, then, almost the same as defending political liberty.

The appeal of the economic argument usually comes from a certain conception of science. In line with the idea of knowledge prominent in intellectual circles, science is viewed by many as the most reliable source of knowledge because it is carefully tied to sensory impressions—observations, measurements, statistics, and other sorts of empirical data. Social scientists from the inception of their disciplines have, in their desire to gain the status of physical sciences, turned increasingly to producing such empirical findings. And, having done so, they often consider themselves to be in possession of the best arguments in matters touched upon in their field. Actually there is no reason to concede that science must be exclusively empirical, or that good arguments and sound theories are not to be found outside the framework of science. But many people believe this. So the appeal of an exclusively economic defense of freedom is understandable. Yet, we shall see, there is something lacking in it.

Briefly, those economists who support the free society argue that the aims of various governmental programs and regulations, all of which constitute market interventions, can be achieved more efficiently within a free market. Their evidence for this consists of empirical studies, usually comparative investigations of historical periods and present enterprises where economic activity was or is carried on with and without state intervention. In addition there are studies which simply point out or predict the effects of past or planned government schemes.

For example, a recent study examined the common notion that advertising leads to higher prices for the advertised products. Prices in the optometry industry in two different states were looked at and it was found that the prices of eyeglasses are lower where optometrists can (are allowed by the state to) advertise their products. Now this study not only goes against a thesis about advertising widely accepted in economic and popular circles, but it also gives some evidence for the claim that governmental interference in the activities of at least one industry has a generally undesirable and unplanned effect. Many such studies have been published in *The Journal of Law and Economics* and other academic journals.

A number of people, most notably Milton Friedman, have gone on from this sort of evidence to argue vigorously for a reduction of government activities in the economic realm. The general case is that government intervention is ineffective for purposes of achieving the stated goals for which it is instituted and carried out. Monopolies are not eliminated, prices are not cut, wages are not improved for those who are considered poor, the environment is no cleaner, competition is not increased, education is not delivered, housing is not provided for those who are said to need it, and so forth. In addition to the failure to attain the purposes which are used to justify the need for regulation, the cost of the regulatory activities has merely been a burden on the economy—people's buying power has been reduced and their funds taxed away without significant results in the areas used to justify the increase in appropriations.

It would appear that with the studies produced by these economists, the conclusion from them should lead rational people to change their minds about the value of governmental intervention. In short, there should be less popular support for it and more for the free economy. While there is some evidence of government's increased concern with efficiency and cost considerations, there has not been a great surge of support for the free market, even though many have read Friedman's columns in *Newsweek* and have been made aware of the case for the free market from various sources. I want to suggest a reason why this is so: the case for the free market cannot be made conclusive with arguments based on economic considerations alone. While opposition can be expected from many sources even if there is a better case, one that offers a conclusive argument, I suggest that it would be considerably weaker if some additional matters were introduced.

One important feature of the kind of argument drawn from empirical research is that it is, by admission of the scholars themselves, a value-free approach to social problems. That is to say, as economists and (social) scientists they do not take a position on whether the free market is morally superior to a socialist or welfare-statist economy. At best they may admit to taking a utilitarian approach. By this they must mean that given the values accepted and announced by those interested in governmental activism on the economic front, they can show in an overwhelming number of cases that without government's "coming to the rescue" the desired goals are more likely achieved and with less overall cost to the economy than is (or would be and has been) done with governmental intervention.

In turn, those who argue for intervention often admit that what government is (has been or might be) doing does not always reap satisfactory results. Ralph Nader is a prime example: he has been one of the most persistent critics of the federal regulatory agencies, showing their incompetence, inefficiency, and even bias (e.g., in their judgments concerning matters that might benefit or impede the interest of regulated industries). Yet Nader does not call for the abolition of these governmental bodies. He advocates making them more efficient, installing better people, and increasing their power. We are entitled to ask, then, how it is that two groups of people, equally convinced (at least in many cases) of the inefficiency and high cost of governmental intervention, conclude with such diametrically opposed views from the same evidence![3]

The source of the discrepancy in the face of such clear agreement should interest the value-free economists: Ralph Nader and the others who advocate governmental intervention in the economy explicitly commit themselves to values. While they may not be able to demonstrate their validity, we might say that "these values are widely held by people." They include a safe toy, protection from "nasty businessmen," low prices, education of the young, a better environment, flourishing fine arts, quality in TV programming, and so on. In general their advocacy of government intervention is based on commitment to the values of "social justice," "equality of opportunity," "protection of the people," and "the general welfare." These are the *ethical* purposes for which Nader and company ask the statist measures we all know well.

Without the benefit of ethics the value-free economists can only respond to Nader by citing the same historical evidence of failure, cost/efficiency data, and the pervasiveness of corruption and political favoritism. To which Nader can reply, "Wait until I get the right folks in the driver's seat" (with *seat belts* of course, i.e., regulatory supervision of the regulators). To this the economists have no argument to show that the values enhanced by eliminating the inefficiency, high cost, corruption and politicking *ought not* be pursued in that way—because the supporters of these governmental activities are sacrificing something of enormous value, namely individual liberty, in their efforts to secure what they want by the means they have chosen.

Of course, in that history speaks against the success of such an approach, the economists have good common sense on their side. But this cannot match the ethical argument. We must all admit that the values we are committed to often involve taking extraordinary risks. We are honest in the face of losing our jobs—and are often commended for just such loyalty to our values. We risk life and limb to save someone's life or health. We fight for justice and peace to the point where even the mention of cost and efficiency becomes laughable if not odious. To suggest that low efficiency should lead us to stop swimming toward a person who is drowning is properly considered not just irrelevant but revolting. One can point to thousands of major and minor cases, both recorded and unrecorded in history books, where cost and efficiency rightfully had no bearing at all in light of the gravity of the purpose at hand. Life, liberty, justice, property, equality, integrity and all the other values for which people have risked everything conceivable they could part with—all these surely have often been worth the risk, or at least warranted it.

If we now look back upon the dispute over whether governmental efforts to secure the goals sought ought to be continued, we will observe that the argument which ends in support of that course relies heavily on the above considerations. Surely, the point is often made, if there is a *chance* to make progress toward the ends desired, we ought to take the risks of even great losses in monies, time, and materials. And the type of goals mentioned earlier are clearly desirable. Who would deny that eliminating poverty is important, worthy of considerable expense? Who wants to claim that equality of opportunity does not deserve sacrifice? Education, the quality of the environment, and so forth—all are widely acknowledged, even if not clearly understood and fully justified, goals to be sought, to be pursued even at the risk of significant losses.

What force does an economic analysis by itself have in the face of such claims? I suggest, not enough. Unless defenders of the free market can justify their support with more than the empirical research our economists produce, their case is doomed to failure. For what they are asking is that people change their views as to what *should be* done, in order to achieve goals that most would not admit can be calculated in purely economic terms.

I am not, of course, suggesting that there is no value in what our economists have given us. By showing that economic activities can be carried out with more efficiency when men are left free in such matters, they have supplied the "can" in "Ought implies can." But the point of all the above is that what we ought to do with the information offered is not derivable from that information alone.

Moreover, from the point of view of empirical economics there is another problem with what we are offered by the researchers. Such studies tell us what happened in the past or what is happening now. Strictly speaking, this does not produce anything conclusive about what can or cannot happen in · the future, particularly when human beings are involved. Many people argue precisely that a shortcoming of empirical economics is that it gives us no laws or principles, only history. And history can be controlled by man.

At this point another, less familiar, school of economics might provide some help. The Austrian School following Ludwig von Mises[4] concludes against the promise of governmental intervention on what are called a priori grounds. Here the argument is that the very nature of economic activity militates against the successful fulfillment of such promises. This would match the situation mentioned above, where someone pursuing a course of action is told that doing it in the way he is simply *cannot* lead to the desired results. There are some difficulties here also, mainly connected with two factors: *(a)* a priori scientific methodology in the social sciences is almost universally eschewed, thus it simply does not provide a persuasive case these days (i.e., arguments that have persuasiveness apart from their logical power), and *(b)* many who support government intervention simply do not consider economic weakness a socially dangerous result, preferring, instead, to provide the society with moral guidance even if it means economic ruin. Although it is not clear that either of these points is fatal to the a priori approach, nonetheless, it too lacks a moral foundation and, therefore, is unable to counter the arguments in behalf of the second point. (Thus while I agree with von Mises that under socialism economic calculation the vital function of market signals is rendered impossible, I am not sure that socialists—at least the more ideological types—are really concerned with that over and above the import they attach to lending moral guidance to society.)

Neither the empiricists nor the a priorists provide a moral justification for keeping the government out of the economy, that is to say, out of the lives of individuals when acting in voluntary cooperation with each other. Both Milton Friedman and von Mises and those like them *prefer* freedom to coercion—in the bulk of social relations. Nor is this preference a weak, casual one for any of them. But it is still just a preference. They believe there is no moral justification to offer for it, and they make their case for the free market independently of such a justification.[5]

Needless to say there are many who do offer a moral defense of the free market—the free society, that is. Three important values are considered to be in great danger if not entirely forgotten and obviated by the introduction of government intervention—at least three that we can identify as universal values. (There are many other values which individuals could choose to pursue if they were not prevented from doing so by government—directly, through regulation of their activities and indirectly, through expropriation of their economic capacity to do so. As Bastiat made so clear,[6] what is not *seen* and *might have been* is difficult to identify, but a little thought can bring these into focus also.)

First, justice. When people are regulated in their economic activities, they are ordered to act in ways they might not have wanted to act. This in effect imposes a fine or penalty on them even though they have not committed a crime—most certainly it has not been proven that they have. Such "preventive" measures are said to be justified by what such people *might possibly* or *could* do without regulation. Thus a toy manufacturer is ordered to discontinue the production of some toy on grounds that it *might* hurt someone. It is true enough that such a product may be manufactured negligently, in which case the producer should be charged and proven guilty of criminal negligence, fraudulent advertising, etc. Yet it is not only such cases that currently come under the preventive efforts of government. Even when through no fault of the producer someone's abuse of a product leads to harm, it is the producer who is now penalized *for this possibility!* Obviously such regulations are already in violation of the "presumption of innocence" provision of due process in a free society. Such cases are so widespread that they boggle the mind—virtually all federal regulatory measures dealt with by such agencies as the FCC, FAA, CAB, FDA, ICC, and FTC gain their legitimacy in law from the argument that industry and business *might* act irresponsibly and, even more, that not the buyers but the producers must protect against the misuse and abuse of the product. The injustice here is staggering. People are treated as they certainly do not deserve to be.

Second, equality. By prohibiting some people from pursuing their goals (by taking their income and spending it on projects others select), while authorizing others to decide for these people what their effort (income, time, life!) will support, a clear case of violation of the principle of "equality under the law" has been perpetrated. And this again is a basic principle, not just a legislated feature of a legal system. It is one that ought to guide any legal system—for it embodies the recognition of each person's equal moral status before the law, i.e., that unless demonstrably inferior in political/legal status (e.g., one who has violated someone's human rights), everyone must be accorded the same protection of his or her rights.

Third, moral responsibility. When some people forcibly assume the responsibility to direct others' lives, when they take it upon themselves to make decisions about what others ought to do, they deprive them of the moral responsibility to choose and act on their own. By robbing individuals of the responsibility for their own moral character, of the liberty to choose and act, their humanity is undermined. What they do or fail to do does not have consequences for them; the cause and effect relationship between judgment/action and consequence is broken—or at least rendered undetectable. This cannot but lead to moral disorientation and frustration—as well as eventual disregard for morality. In addition, people's capacity to judge those who govern will most likely diminish; they would very likely become unable to evaluate their actions, even though these now shoulder the bulk of the responsibility for the lives of the governed.

For each of these cases we can cite numerous empirical consequences. The economists have demonstrated many of them, without explicitly connecting them, however, with the moral (political) issues at hand. But this much is clear: justice, equality and moral self-responsibility, justifiable values for people, are obstructed by the practices advocated by those who want to improve as opposed to abandon the regulatory activities of the government. Clearly, one of the major issues is intervention itself. That activity alone violates each of the above moral values.

Of course we have not yet considered these values comparatively, in contrast to the values sought by way of governmental intervention. It must be made clear that the latter are not themselves in question, necessarily—we can all accept that equality of opportunity, the general welfare, adequate housing, low prices, high wages, and so forth are important goods for people to seek. The issue is that certain ways of trying to achieve them not only do not work (and this is where empirical economics is important), or cannot work (if we take the Austrian analysis seriously), but must lead to the loss of values that are more universal and thus more worthy of pursuit, protection, achievement and support than the ones we have been attempting to achieve by way of governmental intervention.

Unless a moral justification is offered for freedom and the free market, and until the economists are willing to admit its importance, the argument for freedom will be fruitless. Freedom is, to many, a utilitarian value, only—a better means toward the achievement of certain desirable goals. But it is far more than that. It is a political value, the basic principle of a just, equal and morally responsible political community, without which not only efficiency and money, but great moral values are lost.

Business and Liberty

One factor which dims the prospects of human rights is that, although many people believe the contrary, capitalism is not uniformly or consistently desired by businessmen. Every time capitalism is condemned it is assumed that those involved in both large and small businesses want freedom, at least freedom in the economic realm. This belief is partially derived from an essentially Marxist idea of class consciousness which, as discussed earlier in this work, is invalid. Yet the idea is propagated not so much by conspiring Marxists or socialists but by people anywhere discussing the free market. The accepted conclusion is that capitalism benefits only the rich and, therefore, if it is to be instituted in a culture they of course would do so, even if only inadvertently. Even many supporters of capitalism tend to believe this.

A recent widely publicized event gives evidence of the above: the so-called "Powell Memorandum."[7] In the early part of 1972 Jack Anderson reported in his Washington column that before Justice Lewis Powell of the U. S. Supreme Court assumed that position he had been asked to do a report for the Chamber of Commerce on the current status of free enterprise. This report came to be called the "Powell Memorandum," and its conclusion stated that the "American economic system is under broad attack. . . . We are not dealing with sporadic or isolated attacks from a relatively few extremists or even from the minority socialist cadre. Rather, the assault on the enterprise system is broadly based and consistently pursued. It is gaining momentum and converts."[8]

The idea behind the report was to induce or at least instruct the chamber to go to work on revitalizing the free enterprise system by an educational counteroffensive. "As the experience of the socialist and totalitarian states demonstrates, the contradiction and denial of economic freedom is followed inevitably by governmental restrictions on other cherished rights. It is this message, above all others, that must be carried home to the American people."[9] (Ironically, perhaps to prove his own predictions, Justice Powell was among those on the Supreme Court who voted for allowing greater censorship by governments throughout the United States—in the several obscenity cases decided by the court in the early 1970s.)

Although these were important insights, a flaw permeated the Memorandum as well. One was Powell's belief that the attacks started only about ten years ago. But an even more important flaw involved the belief that membership in the Chamber of Commerce would indicate anything like a genuine concern with human liberty.

Throughout the business world people have been supporting the attack on the capitalist system since it was introduced to mankind. Today, as before, it is the intellectuals who provide the philosophical, economic, sociological, psychological and political theories that render the arguments against the free society respectable—but the business community does little to discourage these efforts, and often furthers them through direct action. It is businessmen who have decided to call on the government to help finance their ventures rather than attempting to sell them on the free market with the attendant risks. For instance, when the transcontinental railroads were constructed the taxpayers had to fund them and property owners had to give up their land to provide the right of way. It was businessmen who initiated the antitrust laws—when some of them had gained immoral assistance from government and had consequently grown in power so that others were forced out of competition. After all, when the government "assists the competition," it is like giving some of the competitors guns with which to shoot others, or putting lead into some of the runners' shoes in a marathon race. When laws can be passed to help some at the expense of others, no wonder that the results are unfairly uneven. But the government is then called upon to even things up.

Nevertheless, Justice Powell believes that the attack on the system "has gradually evolved over the *past two decades, barely perceptible in its origins* and benefiting from a gradualism that provoked little awareness much less any real reaction."[10] The sorry fact is that businessmen have been as fully responsible and long-engaged as others in the erosion of the free market and the legal system that gave it at least a partial chance throughout the early history of the United States. They have produced movies condemning it, commercials demeaning it, business deals with politicians at home and abroad that violated it, and suits in court which have clearly demonstrated that they have no interest in it at all.[11]

And all this may be expected. People do not change their basic values because of professional association, a clue also to foreseeing the prospects of anything valuable emerging from the "Powell Memorandum." There is no business class—there are only people who happen to have chosen business as a career. Since businessmen are not usually in the business of putting forth ideas they appear to some to have no beliefs about politics, ethics, economics, and so forth. But just investigate which books they publish, what movies they produce, to what foundations they give their tax-deductible contributions, what sorts of foreign countries they enter for purposes of investment, what kind of contracts they draw up with the business interests (usually governments) of foreign nations—and there you will have clear evidence of how divergent the so-called class consciousness can be.

It is just as mistaken and futile to believe that businessmen will help the cause of human liberty as it is to believe that labor will hurt it. The simple fact is that opposition to human liberty is indeed pervasive, so one may suppose that among the members of any professional, racial, ethnic, national, or other identifiable group, few will advocate or act on the principles of a free society. Whatever the cause of lack of support for human liberty in our time, it is not that there are but few opportunities for the "capitalist class" to support it. Some have argued convincingly that those involved in the management of businesses are very likely as much under the influence of anti-libertarian ideologies, if not more, as are those teaching classes, writing bestsellers, lecturing from the pulpit, and running for political office. It is useless to wait for them to revitalize a system they have opposed throughout with actions if not words.

The prospects of liberty do not lie with "capitalists" (so-called only because of Marx's distortion of what the free market involves—the *rule* of those who have capital, property in wealth and money). A capitalist is not necessarily a businessman, and a businessman is not necessarily a capitalist: to be a capitalist is to *adhere to the principle* of the human right to private ownership of goods and services, not just to be an owner of great wealth. In fact, many members of communes in this country are capitalists without realizing it, in that they act on the principle of voluntary cooperation and would not think of forcing others to get involved in their freely chosen arrangement. So much for class consciousness.

Financing Government in a Free Society

Whenever a comprehensive, systematic theory is proposed concerning any area of scientific or philosophical inquiry, there are problems it must solve or be declared inadequate. This is as true of political theory as it is of physics or biology. But because political theory pertains to human action and the basic organization of a human community—as these *should* be—its success cannot be tested by performing carefully controlled experiments or by carrying out observations (as in high energy physics or astronomy, respectively). When considering theories pertaining to the best social organization of human beings, one must adapt the tests to the subject matter, to the fact that man is a free agent—he can choose to judge and act and is, thereby, an entity that *can cause some of its own behavior*. Thus, for example, it won't do to catch some people and put them into a laboratory space, because from the very beginning such a procedure would have violated some of the conditions that certain theories require, especially the theory of human rights under consideration. Even to obtain volunteers, put them in an experimental setting, and, e.g., assign no authority to any particular person or group, and observe how they manage to work out their problems, would not be very helpful because, being free, they could have done otherwise—they could have come up with a better or worse solution.

How then can we test a theory such as the present? What do we have to do to show that it can provide solutions to the problems that require solution and do so better than other approaches? Throughout this work the answer to these questions has been at least implicit. The method is characteristic of all of what are called "normative" fields of inquiry, areas that involve what ought to be done, what should be adopted and practiced, what is good or right for human beings as such, in general or in social circumstances. We need to construct hypothetical situations, imagine people facing certain problems, and see how these would have to be approached in terms of the different theories proposed to take care of them. (There are some theories in the field of politics that only appear to be of a normative variety. For example, Marx's theory invokes the language of ethics and politics, but in fact his system has no room for what ought to be done because, when cleaned up and made reasonably consistent, it amounts to a mechanistic account of what *will* happen in human history, not of what *should* happen. Although mitigated by inclusion of the dialectical principle so that it changed from simple action/reaction to a triadic or state/negation/resolution mechanism, it still allows no place in the system for genuine human agency.)

One of the most crucial requirements of the present theory is that a human community *could be* constructed, instituted, or established which excluded any systematic use of force where no prior force had been initiated. So the human rights of every person could be respected without any violation of them built into the system itself. (Of course errors and corruption could occur, but these are not systematic violations of human rights. This theory does not *predict* that human beings will not err or that they will always do the right things. That would again be to confuse political with physical theory.) One of the specific features of the theory is that since each person has the unalienable right to acquire and keep items that are not owned by someone else or that are for sale or given away to him, and since taxation is the expropriation of such items from people who have the human right to keep them, the practice of taxation is a violation of human rights.

Now it is often argued that this conclusion would render it impossible for a government of a free society to acquire the means by which it could carry out its justified activities. In short, it is contended that the present theory could not be established consistently. The agency commissioned with protecting and preserving the human rights of those under its jurisdiction would have to violate those rights in the process of doing so! If true, then the theory would require that a good human community be based on contradictory principles—do and do not violate human rights. That in itself renders the system proposed *impossible*. And from the more general principle that one ought to pursue only that which *can* be achieved, one would have to conclude that the system of social organization I have been defending and advocating should in fact be rejected in view of its impossibility.

Before I answer this central objection to the theory under inspection, let me mention that the problem of taxation—of providing funds for a community-shared service, namely government—is similar to situations called externalities by economists. The benefits of some good are said to be obtainable only through collective operations involving coercion. Thus clean air is often thought of as an externality, in that while it is of admitted long-term benefit to everyone, it is not of short-term benefit to enough people in a community so that they would act to protect it. Such other items as parks, education, lighthouses, and so on have been classed among externalities. Usually these sorts of things benefit everyone but they are too expensive to obtain individually. So the idea is that individuals left free to choose would forego this benefit for more immediate and less costly ones, only to come eventually upon disaster.

I have examined a great many discussions of this issue and have found the force of them wanting. Usually they are based on an untenable view of human nature—namely that people are unaware of the fact that some goods can be obtained only by way of cooperation and that the long-range benefits far outweigh the short-term ones, so they simply charge ahead thoughtlessly. While this may be true in some cases, particularly with our present system where individuals have little responsibility for such matters, it does not follow that it must be true in all community circumstances. The assumption of hedonistic (immediate pleasure-seeking) motivation on the part of all people as a matter of innate human nature is false. It is contradicted in many cases. Moreover, the conclusion that individuals would fail to see the gains of cooperating is lent credence by the frequent use of what has become known as the prisoners' dilemma as a model on which to base analysis of the problem of externalities. The prisoners' dilemma involves the alternatives available to two prisoners who could both remain silent about each other, both rat on each other, and so forth, such that depending on their choice they either perish together, stay alive together, or lose and benefit in several different ways. The crucial points for our purposes are that only two persons are involved and they are unable to communicate with each other or anyone else. It is thus a questionable practice to base a problem of some human community on what may or may not happen in such situations. To take that model and impose its difficulties upon communities in general is not a good way to consider problems of free people in a community where their freedom is protected. In the latter situation they can at least employ the social scientists to figure out the best way to secure externalities!

In the main the externalities problem does not concern us here. True enough, many economists have taken it upon themselves to treat what are in fact political and ethical questions as if they were economic ones. What usually happens with this kind of intellectual imperialism is that the issues of the field being conquered are artificially translated into the language of the conquering field. Thus economists make ethics into a theory of cost/benefit calculus, but with no standard of what constitutes benefit and loss except the *arbitrary desires* of those involved, thereby evading the crucial problem of ethics and politics.

I in turn am well aware that I will be talking about an issue that is generally best left to economists, namely the means by which to finance the administration of a legal system in a free society. My own coverage of this issue draws from what I have learned from those who have considered it from the point of view of economics and politics. My purpose will be to demonstrate at least one solution which avoids the charge of theoretical inconsistency raised earlier.

The justification and need of government arises from the fact that in order to live together without constant private militarization and wars, individuals require the protection of an agency that operates according to objective laws, one whose aim is the protection and preservation of the human rights of all. Human life in a community—where the benefits of mutual endeavors, cooperation, and so on can be taken advantage of—involves making and accepting promises pertaining to acts and events in the near or far future.

To insure such promises against violation, it is best to make certain provisions for the imposition of penalties upon those who would abrogate contracts. This is due to the fact that human beings can change their minds without regard to the harm this will do to those with whom they have endeavored to cooperate. While it is true that once a promise is broken, the culprit will not likely gain the confidence of others in such matters, one cannot be protected against promise-breaking by that prospect alone. After all, many people act against their own interest and simply may not care if what they do brings them ultimate harm. So each individual has a personal stake in providing for the protection of his own best interest, even if the consequences of promise-breaking will be harmful enough to the culprit himself. (None of this implies that people ought to look upon each other as tending toward the violation of promises. A promise-breaker may indeed have good reasons for his action and yet have caused harm to his victim, so that he ought to vindicate himself by paying damages. Nor can we know all those with whom we conduct business in a complex society. So protecting against promise-breaking is rational even when a person has a benevolent view of human nature.)

Such provisions can be made in numerous ways, including outright insurance policies paid for by all parties to promises—i.e., all those who have entered into some contractual agreement. Various arbitration agencies could be hired to adjudicate such disputes as may arise from the breaking of contracts or charges to that effect.

However one might insure against losses from contract violation, there is an element of such protection that ties in directly with the legal system itself. The administration of justice in a free society must be ready to provide the ultimate guidance in the determination of guilt or innocence, responsibility or the lack of it, in matters where charges of contract violation have surfaced. For such charges at bottom pertain to whether someone's human rights have been violated. If a movie star is signed up for a five-year contract and is paid a given amount of income for such an exclusive contract, yet he proceeds to make movies for other companies in secret, he has *stolen* some of his income. Once this is suspected, the star may be charged with fraud, a form of violation of property rights. Of course, the matter could be settled out of court via a mutually agreed upon arbitration agency. But should the dispute persist, the matter would have to end up in a court of law where the charges would be examined in full detail, by rules of evidence developed in accordance with a system of objective law.

The point of all this is that since every valid contract imposes a potential burden upon the legal system, every contract could be assessed with what I will call a contract-fee. Anyone who has the faintest appreciation of the number of contracts drawn within the time span of just one day will immediately see the possibilities in such a scheme for financing a government. Since entering into a contractual relationship is itself an entirely free or voluntary matter—one *could* simply stay with friendly promises—and since such relationships are just what a legal system makes so lucrative, it is most reasonable to charge those so entering with a fee for the services coming to them because of the nature of a contract. If one enters into a valid contract, i.e., some agreement that does not violate human rights, one is entitled to expect and receive the enforcement of that contract. Since this is a service, it should be paid for by those who receive it.

When one considers the very limited task of governments of free societies, as well as the anticipated production, trade and exchange that people could engage in without legalized force and management by a legally immune central authority such as government, the prospect of financing the justified activities of government is clear enough. The contract-fee solution is not the only one that could be invoked. Many would benefit from courts, police and military service even though not entering into contractual agreements. It is possible that any service the police might render would be charged to individuals' accounts, payable every month, half year or so on. Thus road owners could either hire their own traffic guards and pass the charges on to travelers, or could request that the police carry out the function directly, much along lines familiar to us today.

There might also be temporary means by which governments could be funded. In national emergencies when heavy armaments are required the government might institute a lottery system or ask for outright donations—surely if it is an emergency, it can be demonstrated that this is so. In which case the people ought to give their support. If they do not, those who still think the system is worth saving would have to take the matter upon themselves. If this fails, then so be it. The fact that many people in a human community are unwilling to defend themselves against dangers from outside or inside does not justify the few to do anything harmful against the many. (I have already discussed this under the topic of emergency cases.)

Financing the administration of a just legal system is really no great problem. Most people think it is only because they have never heard of that prospect. (Just as the idea of a completely private postal service is unheard of and outrageous to some. But in Europe the extent to which such industries as Penn Central, Greyhound, and American Airlines are private would be considered entirely impossible.) In some respects paying those who administer and enforce the laws is then a problem for those who want the service and those who want to perform it. It is not a political problem at all, given that we have seen no merit in the charge that governments must violate human rights in order to obtain payment for their services. The details of such measures are the province of the field of public finance and not political theory. Admittedly, few in public finance are now concerned with how governments can be funded without recourse to coercion and expropriation. (At present those in the field are somewhat like advisers to pickpockets—they are aiding and abetting an immoral practice which is unfortunately sanctioned in some circles.) At any rate a certain question posed to proponents of a political theory has been answered from the point of view of human rights theory. As such it goes some way toward demonstrating that the theory is indeed suited to solving the problems of human communities should people adopt it.

On Securing Liberty

People can choose between right and wrong. So even if it is right for them to choose to put into effect a legal system based on human rights, they can of course fail to do so. Thus the establishment of such a system is not some historically inevitable prospect, something being enacted by historical law. Yet some classical liberals—e.g., Mill—believed that mankind is progressing necessarily toward some greater stage, very much as Marx did, only without the latter's specific theory of the dialectic. There can of course be progress of human community life in a better and better direction, as well as regress. But in either case it is the achievement or failure not of a historical law but of individual human beings.

Books like this one aim to contribute to the achievement of human liberty, and this they try to do by convincing those who will consider the ideas that it is the proper goal to be sought after. But neither books nor airtight arguments can *make* people do what is right—something that frustrates most social reformers and, these days, social engineers. There is no guarantee of freedom in the politically relevant sense. It must be chosen by human beings, of their own free will! That is to say, they must choose to refrain from the initiation of force, from coercion that is not defensive, from aggression—and from establishing legal institutions by which such practices are rendered pervasive and difficult to resist.

Those who have spent some time defending the free society against opponents and skeptics should never underestimate the difficulty of their task. Liberty is not a self-evident value—it must be explained to many, and often wrong ideas connected with it must be cleared up. While one can expect people to make some effort to grasp the worth of the absence of unprovoked coercion, in fact the understanding of political and economic liberty and of the theory of human rights which underlies both takes active minds, an effort that not all people will exert. Some, in fact, will evade these matters, either by refusing to consider them or by coming up with unreasonable challenges (e.g., "Well, but even if you are right, it might not work anyway—then what will we do?").

Yet as many who have fought with both pen and arms have realized, it is not always worth concentrating on gaining converts—persuasion is often not the best means by which to fight for one's principles. Opponents of human liberty are rarely if ever simply ignorant. To fail to realize this would be to tolerate oppression, the violation of people's rights, the enslavement of millions and other evils as if they were accidents of nature or historically inevitable. It would be to refuse to acknowledge that human beings are responsible for most of what is wrong in human life. Just as they are responsible for most of what is right in it.

Often, though not always, those who oppose political liberty do so because they evade their responsibility to think through the implications of what they know very well about human beings, to think seriously and carefully about what they must do, including defend and advocate various principles, so as to live the life appropriate to a person in a social context. It is after all no secret that free men work harder and better than slaves, especially on creative endeavors—I did not discover this yesterday, nor was it noticed only in recent times. Nor is it a secret that the American political climate of more rather than less protection and preservation of liberty has contributed in an essential, crucial way to a better life for people than what others experience throughout the world. And by this I am not talking about such isolated factors as better symphony orchestras, collections of rare china, medical care or air conditioning systems. (The idea that the richer natural resources of the American continent can account for the boom in living standards here was discredited long ago—e.g., by Schumpeter. Capitalism is a necessary condition, though not sufficient, for the *innovativeness* that is essential for a rise in living conditions on the scale experienced in American history.)

What "better" means, the way in which people are better off, is that the United States' legal/political system encourages the greatest degree of personal, moral growth, the greatest individual responsibility for self-improvement on all levels, and the widest degree of justice—treating people as moral agents, not tools for others' uninvited employment—within the social realm. A better life must, first of all, be a morally good one, and the society that is most free provides the greatest opportunity for it. (Those who will protest that this last is but an empty tautology have simply failed to understand the bulk of this work. It may be a tautology of sorts, but it clearly is not empty! Not if it is sound.) Unless one accepts some irrationalist doctrine of the human good, or believes that man is by nature tilted toward greater evil than good, one is not going to be able to deny that the United States, with its more rather than less free institutions, has been better for human life in general than other nations in human history known to us.

That the system of free enterprise, as far as it went, had produced goods not only for Americans but for members of other societies far above even the most optimistic expectations of the level of human welfare possible to mankind—this simply cannot be denied without absurdity. Those who deny it usually hold to some mystical standard of human welfare—witness the obscurantist indictments of Western culture, especially capitalism, one reads in books emulating Eastern mysticism, tribalism, and feudalism. Many have recently charged Americans with consuming 30 percent of the world's energy while constituting only 6 percent of its population. A neglected statistic is that *Americans produce more than 30 percent of the wealth of the world,* some of it going directly and indirectly toward upgrading the well-being of those living in other regions. Who is it that provides foreign aid, technological know-how, entertainment (admittedly with some of its drawbacks) to the rest of the world each year, with little gratitude and much envy and disdain as the usual response, especially from those who "speak for" the people?

While much of the opposition to the free society stems from evasion and blindness, it often takes the form of eloquent and sophisticated argument and oratory. Opponents of liberty are not stupid, or mentally impaired—although some self-impairment will result from rejecting reality in favor of utopian dreams and wishful thinking(?). It is only when one puts an unqualified faith in IQ that brilliance is mistaken for inherent worth. Virtuosity, without a resolve to identify the truth of the matter in some field and often in fact coupled with the very denial of that possibility, must not be allowed to parade as depth of understanding. None of this is profound or original, but it is worth keeping such matters in mind throughout one's investigation of competing efforts to make sense of any area of life. The point is, " the devil" isn't brainless. Nor need evil be what cheap television shows feature as paradigmatic—blatant cruelty, ruthlessness, the attitude of actively desiring that suffering, destruction, pain would permeate the world. Few of the guilty engage in malice. Most manifest their irresponsibility by self-deception, negligence, blind devotion, ordinary compromise of principles. (How worthy it would be if critics of the Watergate affair did not believe that Mr. Nixon is the evil demon incarnate, but recognized him and his cohorts as most probably the usual run-of-the-mill irresponsible bureaucrats—merely caught with their pants down, something most of the others who have inhabited Washington managed to escape.)

With these and similar matters in clear focus we can now state that each human being has the moral responsibility—as a person and not as some obedient servant of God or the State—to take certain steps to secure for himself optimal political and legal conditions, to do the best in his capacity and situation to understand these matters and to work to realize the conclusions within the context of his own individual life. Learning about and discussing politics is not a mere parlor game but a genuine human responsibility. Hard times—when liberty and, therefore, a good deal of what is crucial to human life in society, are in danger—warrant extra doses of attention to politics. The considered and discriminate advocacy of liberty is, under such circumstances, each person's moral responsibility.

Yet, as implied, this should not lead to anything like wasting one's energy and time. While those who are professionally involved in political affairs ought to continue to discuss and debate the issues even when the prospects of clear communication are minuscule, others ought to find more suitable ways by which to secure for themselves the freedom from which each person's life can only benefit. When a culture is mainly hostile to the ideals of a free society, education will bear the burden of fostering and defending those ideals—for surely many people have no idea what consistent regard for human rights would involve, so how could they give it their support? And even those who are hostile to liberty have what would best be called their more rational moments—people are free agents and *can* change their minds.

Some of this will, I am sure, seem rather arrogant to many. Why should others change their minds? Shouldn't advocates of human liberty consider this as an option? What, in short, makes me so sure? Am I justified in my confidence?

In response to these questions I must direct the reader to what has gone before in this book. In a way even to ask these questions demeans any person's ability to cope with reality. The present work outlines what has emerged as a sound analysis of human political affairs. Is it sound, in fact? By the standard of soundness that makes sense, yes. Anything further cannot be requested by a rational person, for soundness is based on the nature of reality, on what is fundamental to all existence, and on what is implied by the careful consideration of reality through an active human consciousness. Those who ask for more would seem to have something out-of-mind in mind, something that is simply not.

On that basis, then, I can only end by admitting that the future can produce new human discoveries—or, better put, human beings can produce discoveries in the future—and it is each person's responsibility to evaluate the relevant discoveries to see if they require addition, modification, revision, and/or expansion of the conclusions he or she has formed about some important aspect of life.

If such a claim to knowledge is arrogance, so be it. For surely a sound conclusion is not an unheard of feat for a human being, given the record of man's achievements in such a creative endeavor. It would be like chiding Bobby Fisher for priding himself on his ability to play chess, or Aristotle for making a claim to philosophical accomplishments. In the end I can only hope that the reader will have enough arrogance to undertake to examine this work critically and pass judgment. No one can do this *for* him.

Yet it is not enough to sit and nod. There are people around who agree with what I have said thus far; indeed, people who write on these topics, who may even integrate some of these ideas with their everyday activities, who are motivated, by and large, to do something here and there concerning their political existence in line with the principles discussed in this book.

Many of these same people, however, tend at times to do little more than spout lofty principles. They recite passages from books, go to meetings to talk to others of their own persuasion, produce vehement rhetoric about much of what we have been considering. Some become so fanatical that they blame rain on government and condemn the state for their own ineptitude. Others make adherence to their ideas a regular profession, as if political advocacy could be the sum total of living a full and productive human life. The point is simply that ideas can be mouthed, given even the most eloquent lip service, and the best of them will suffer when people do nothing more than this. I have been emphasizing the value of sustained attention to living, of choosing unflinching commitment to reason. All this must have practical effect, or the rationality is merely feigned. Moral principles can be made ritualistic rules of conduct in some limited areas of life, allowing one to be self-satisfied with the *image* of being a good person. Having unsound ideals is not the only way to be negligent in one's life—one can *profess* the soundest morality in contention and still be a fraud about it. And this applies to one's politics as well.

It is perhaps the most deceitful of performances to profess good ideas and valid political theories but subvert them in practice by negligence, omission, inattentiveness to the opportunities that exist to implement them, or even just advocate them. Every human being has the right to defend his political well-being. That is a political matter that ought to gain the recognition of a legal system that aims to serve justice. But each person ought to make the effort to take as much advantage of this right as the circumstances of his life will allow. This is a moral matter. And about this nothing much can be done by someone who values human liberty except "talk, talk, and talk some more." And those who espouse the ideals set forth and defended in this book without making the effort I am speaking of are not just negligent, as are the many who have failed to gain an understanding of their own political welfare—they are treasonous, they betray and debase the great value of the ideas they have decided to accept "in theory."

The homage to be paid should go to those who integrate their philosophical framework with life itself, at every turn where the possibility arises. When this is done, most people will come to find the flaws in their views should they contain some. Reality cannot be cheated for long. It is those great heroes of the world, from Aristotle on, who have never required less of their own lives that I wish I could thank personally. Not because they did it for me, but because in doing it right, they managed to make it possible for me to have confidence in doing it for myself. They have been, as one might say, the empirical evidence in support of the point of view I have tried to defend here, both moral and political.

Conclusion

In a quick overview, I offered a sketch of the history of the concept of human (natural) rights. I discussed the nature of human rights as understood within the context of a human community and the history of thought about such communities. Next I provided the moral justification for the political principles that were identified as man's rights, by defending the view that human excellence consists in the sustained choice to be rational to the degree of one's individual capacity. Next I argued that this notion, and the idea of human nature involved, support the conclusion that in a social context each person possesses certain rights by virtue of being a human being. From here I moved on to a consideration of the role and function of government, if any, in a human community the legal system of which is based on human rights; I argued that proper government consists of those institutions designed by members of some human community for purposes of protecting and preserving a system in accord with human rights. Next I considered some of the implications of the overall theory for purposes of evaluating the realpolitik of our present society, indicating that most of the laws and institutions and the policies flowing from these constitute violations of human rights, although exceptions exist in America more than elsewhere known to me. Then I examined some features of the theory that have come under reasonable criticism, trying to answer both relevant and in some cases less compelling but still prevalent objections. Last I considered the prospects for the implementation of the human rights identified in this work, given the present intellectual and political climate in the United States, observing that trends are not favorable.

In this conclusion I want to add an afterthought or two. First, I want to make a point about utopianism. After one has proposed and argued for a theory, it is wise and reasonable to ask, can it be realized at all, or is it, like some others that have gained prominence in history, a mere unattainable (although to some appealing) ideal? Then I also wish to make a point about the persuasive character of theories and books in the field of ethics and politics.

It has not been my task to argue for ideals that are unreachable—frankly, I haven't the time for that. Although there is a respected tradition which holds that political philosophy *should* propose ideal systems of that sort, I consider this approach wrongheaded and dangerous—but mostly unjustifiable when dealing with human affairs. In making plans for one's life or for the institutions in one's society many forget about those for whom the plans are devised, namely human beings. This produces means unsuited for what people can achieve. Guiding oneself in life by impossible goals must involve going against reality—it would be like knowingly increasing the buoyancy of a submarine when trying to have it descend further. As mistakes or close enough approximations high aspirations may not be harmful. Then one is still admitting that further knowledge would make the task a more realistic one. But when one *knows* that some goals are impossible, it is criminal to sell people methods suited to their achievement. Goals such as perfect competition, full employment, guaranteed happiness, perfect ecological balance, free medical care for all, peace forever, and the like have guided both personal and political conduct often enough—with horrible consequences for almost everyone involved. They ought to teach the lesson well: avoid utopianism. It encourages irresponsible hypothesizing of conditions for the future and leads to policies for moving from the present toward what *could* not even exist. Meanwhile real solutions, which may be far more modest, are neglected and, eventually, people grow cynical about all attempts to solve problems.

The present theory does not admit of the value of utopianism. Impossible dreams no, difficult to achieve goals yes! If they are worth it.

But to convince people that some goal is worthy of pursuit is not a process with only one participant. There is no way that even the best argument can *make* someone move out to reach for the best goals in life. There are many personal and cultural factors that enter into the process of persuasion, even if the thesis of which someone is to be persuaded is sound and the arguments are all in order. People sometimes like to just continue with old ideas—it does take a hell of a lot of effort to go through most of one's implicit and explicit beliefs and see if they will hold up against challenge. What if in the end the challenger really had nothing to offer? Why waste time? Who is he to tread on the views one has lived with for years and gotten by with comfortably enough?

An author can only hope that there is some common ground on which trust has been established, however harsh some of his views may be for those he wishes to convince. Obviously if all of the reader's views were alien to the author communication could not even begin. But we are in a world we are capable of understanding quite well, provided we give it our attention. So we are already together on some issues, simply by living and doing whatever we are doing. And surely one of the merits of our case is that it claims no special status for those who can understand it. Moreover, it is supposed to be, if the homework has been done, fully consistent with the facts anyone may know who exerts the effort to look and think, facts that face everyone everywhere. So long as these are kept in view and the present work is understood clearly enough, the theory I have developed will, if correct, integrate well with the rest of one's knowledge.

There is no reasonable doubt that the free society is the soundest and best possible human society. As such it may appear utopian. And for that reason alone many will turn away from it, even leave the arguments unexamined. But every person owes himself the acknowledgment that present society could be better than what it is—even if it could be much worse. And he also owes himself the confidence in man and in the individual person that he/she is to undertake some effort to improve his political circumstances. There are many other matters to be taken care of, and I have not tried to promise solutions for them. Others have done fine work in medicine, building construction, nutrition, plastics, chemistry, movie making, and so on, so that political thinkers need not bother with that. Yet everyone owes himself some attention to political matters, and my last appeal is for such attention. There is evidence to prove that people have made a mess of things in the world politically, but that they can make the reparations as well. And today there is need for even more than reparations. A radical reconsideration of the prominent political attitudes and ideals in our culture is fully in order.

Notes to Chapter 1

1. *Natural Right and History* (Chicago: University of Chicago Press, 1971).

2. Jeremy Bentham, "Anarchical Fallacies," in A. I. Melden (ed.), *Human Rights* (Belmont, Calif.: Wadsworth, 1970), p. 32.

3. I must stress that rationality is not being emphasized in preference to the value and role of man's emotions. The former is man's distinctive means of consciousness—how knowledge is achieved—while the latter are responses man can have to what he values or abhors, and so on. Emotions are not cognitive activites but experiences people have in response to the world, including themselves. There is no conflict between these two features of human life, although conflicting desires have been interpreted as conflicts between desires and judgments, and vice versa, competing judgments have been taken as judgment in conflict with feeling.

4. Aristotle, *Nicomachean Ethics*, 1134b(18)-1135a(14).

5. Margaret Macdonald, "Natural Rights," in Melden, pp. 40-60.

6. Strauss, op. cit., p. 156.

7. Raymond Polin, "The Rights of Man in Hobbes and Locke," in D. D. Raphael (ed.), *Political Theory and the Rights of Man* (Bloomington, Ind.: Indiana University Press, 1967), pp. 16-26.

8. C. B. Macpherson, "Natural Rights in Hobbes and Locke," in Raphael, pp. 4-5.

9. Cf. Wilmore Kendall, *John Locke and the Doctrine of Majority Rule* (Urbana, Ill.: University of Illinois Press, 1941).

10. Strauss, pp. 202-250.

11. Ibid., p. 248.

12. Quoted in Strauss, p. 249.

13. Ibid., p. 250.

14. Ibid.

15. Alan Ryan, "Locke and the Dictatorship of the Bourgeoisie," in David M. Armstrong and C. B. Martin, *Locke and Berkeley* (Garden City, N. Y.: Anchor Books, 1968), pp. 231-254. See also John W. Yolton, "Locke and the Law of Nature," *Philosophical Review* (Oct. 1958), pp. 477-498.

16. Cf. Bernard Bailyn, *The Ideological Origins of the American Revolution* (Cambridge: Harvard University Press, 1973); *The Origins of American Politics* (Cambridge: Harvard University Press, 1967); David L. Jacobson, *The English Libertarian Heritage* (Indianapolis, Ind.: Bobbs-Merrill, 1965). In a short but packed essay Murray N. Rothbard discusses the divisions on these ideas among those in the historical professions. In "The American Revolution Reconsidered," *Books for Libertarians* (July 1974), pp. 6-8, Rothbard points out that both left (Marxist) and right (conservative) oriented historians tend to denigrate the ideological, philosophical aspects of the revolution—the former emphasizing class and economic aspects, the latter stressing that the revolution was really quite tradition bound. Neither allows for the power of ideas. Bailyn's several works, however, clearly demonstrate that such "explanations" of the revolution are wrong.

17. Kai Nielsen, "Skepticism and Human Rights," *The Monist* (October 1968), p. 594.

18. Tibor R. Machan, *The Pseudo-Science of B. F. Skinner* (New Rochelle, N. Y.: Arlington House Publishers, 1974). This work aims to show that Skinner has a questionable

philosophical support, not a scientifically backed demonstration for his political conclusions.

19. David Hume, *A Treatise of Human Nature* (Garden City, N. Y.: Dolphin Books, 1961), p. 423.

20. David Hume, *Enquiries Concerning the Human Understanding* (Oxford: Clarendon Press, 1957).

21. Ibid., p. 164.

22. Ibid.

23. Ibid., p. 364.

24. Among those who have expressed this general approach to the question of the nature of values (morality, politics, aesthetics) are Margaret Macdonald, A. J. Ayer, Bertrand Russell, and most of those who call themselves positivists in both social science and philosophy. It is crucial that the basis of all these views consists of what is essentially a negative or critical thesis about whether judgments or statements as to what ought to or should be the case, be done, and so on can be true or false.

25. R. M. Hare, *The Language of Morals* (Oxford: Clarendon Press, 1952).

26. C. L. Stevenson, *Ethics and Language* (New Haven: Yale University Press, 1944).

27. Kai Nielsen, "On Taking Human Nature as the Basis for Morality," *Social Research* (Summer 1962), pp. 170-176; "The Myth of Natural Law," in Sidney Hook (ed.), *Law and Philosophy* (New York: N. Y. U. Press, 1964), pp. 122-143.

28. Macdonald.

29. Nielsen, "Skepticism. . . ."

30. G. E. Moore, *Principia Ethica* (Cambridge: University Press, 1903).

31. Kai Nielsen, "The Myth of . . ."; Alf Ross, *On Law and Justice* (Berkeley: University of California Press, 1959).

32. R. W. Beardsmore, *Moral Reasoning* (New York: Schocken Books, 1969); Ernest van den Haag, *Political Violence and Civil Disobedience* (New York: Harper and Row, 1972).

33. W. D. Falk, "Goading and Guiding, " in Rosalind Ekman (ed.), *Readings in the Problems of Ethics* (New York: Charles Scribner's Sons, 1965), pp. 204-228; Stanly Cavell, *A Claim to Rationality* (Harvard University: Unpublished Doctoral Dissertation, 1961); Henry B. Veatch, "Good Reasons and Prescriptivism in Ethics: A Metaethical Incompatibility?" *Ethics* (April 1970), pp. 102-111; Edward F. Walter, "Empiricism and Ethical Reasoning," *American Philosophical Quarterly* (October 1970), pp. 264-269; Dorothy Mitchell, "The Truth or Falsity of Value Judgements," *Mind*, pp. 67-74.

34. Ernest van den Haag, "Author Replies," *The Intercollegiate Review* (Winter 1972/73), p. 144. Van den Haag writes: "There is no chance of agreement on what is 'suited to human beings essentially.' Gandhi, Hitler, Prof. Machan, Billy Graham, Mao Tse Tung, Ayn Rand and I would not agree. Nor do we have a method or experiment to settle our disagreement." Yet lack of agreement does not prove its impossibility, nor is the experimental approach the only one by which agreement can be achieved. In his recent work van den Haag is defending the legal positivist line against natural rights theories, following, by his own admission, Bentham, Austin, Hart, and Kelsen. It is interesting to note that this line is used by all types of critics of natural rights: left liberals such as Kai Nielsen, Margaret Macdonald, and conservatives such as van den Haag. There are also pure classical liberals such as H. L. A. Hart who have defended the "autonomy of law" doctrine.

35. Stephen Toulmin, *The Uses of Argument* (Cambridge: University Press, 1969).

36. *Critique of Pure Reason.*

37. "Universal Declaration of Human Rights." Melden, pp. 143-149.

38. Ibid.

39. William T. Blackstone, "Equality and Human Rights, *The Monist* (October 1968), pp. 616-639.

40. I am here thinking of the notion of "right" developed in the German tradition starting with Hegel's critique of classical liberalism. Cf. Leo Strauss. This right-wing tradition started by Hegel was best exemplified by Thomas Hell Green (1836-1882) in his *Prolegomena to Ethics*.

41. Here was a clear illustration of the American conservative's paradox: while conservatism has what is basically a *liberal* tradition to uphold in economics and civil liberties, the emphasis on religion and elitism dilutes this commitment, resulting in the conservative's willingness to sacrifice intellectual freedom. Thus one will find economic laissez-faire advocates such as Professor Gary North writing approvingly of the Supreme Court's decision to refuse to protect individuals against the forces in their community which would prohibit trade between movie house managers and customers who wish to see obscene films. (The liberals, in turn, can defend the individual's right only by denying that obscenity exists!)

42. Nielsen. For additional discussions see M. P. Golding (ed.), *The Nature of Law* (New York: Random House, 1966).

43. See note 35.

44. Ibid.

45. Melden, pp. 61-75.

46. Ibid., pp. 76-95. I have listed only several distinctive approaches to human rights. For varieties along the above lines see *The Philosophical Review* (April 1955); Ervin H. Pollack (ed.), *Human Rights* (Buffalo, N. Y.: Jay Stewart Publications, 1971); *The Monist* (October 1968), and so on. (In this last, especially noteworthy is M. P. Golding's "Towards a Theory of Human Rights," pp. 521-549, where Golding outlines the three stages of argument to be followed for purposes of a successful defense of anything that could rationally be called a human rights theory. In my "A Rationale for Human Rights," *The Personalist* (Spring 1971), pp. 216-235, I follow through on an outline of such a defense, and in the present discussion also I have had Golding's suggestions in mind.)

47. Machan, *The Pseudo-Science of B. F. Skinner* (New Rochelle, N. Y.: Arlington House, 1974).

48. Cf. John Hospers, "Freedom, Psychoanalysis and Moral Responsibility," in William T. Blackstone (ed.), *Meaning and Existence* (New York: Holt, Rinehart and Winston, 1971), pp. 497-507.

49. B. F. Skinner, *Beyond Freedom and Dignity* (New York: Bantam Books, 1972).

50. Thomas S. Szasz, *The Myth of Mental Illness* (New York: Dell Publishing Co., 1961). For a critique see M. L. Zupan, "Is Mental Illness a Myth?" *Reason* (August 1973), pp. 4-11.

51. Peter Breggin, "Is Psychosurgery on the Upswing?" *Human Events* (May 5, 1973).

52. Karl Menninger, *The Crime of Punishment* (New York: Viking Press, 1968). For a criticism of the "crime is illness" thesis see Herbert Morris, "Persons and Punishment," *The Monist* (October 1968), pp. 465-501; Walter Berns, "Justified Anger: Just Retribution," *Imprimis* (June 1974). (For the record, I differ with Berns on the issue of capital punishment. One may deserve to be killed, granted, but it is not the case that someone else *ought to* kill him, especially when being wrong can be of such irrevocable magnitude.)

Notes to Chapter 3

1. Aristotle, *Nicomachean Ethics*. For Aristotle the discussion of ethics forms part of a comprehensive doctrine—although not necessarily one that cannot be revised in line with new knowledge, as in Plato. Contemporary philosophy has, in the main, eschewed this systematic approach in favor of piecemeal criticism, analysis, and so forth, following the post-Cartesian idea that a philosopher has no business being concerned with facts of nature. One can find many philosophers today whose paper published in one journal will be inconsistent with that published in another, whose ideal is an *open* mind, one that can *yield* easily to any new possibilities. Even this ideal reflects the passive-mind doctrines dominant in modern philosophy. Yet there is also a justified fear of grand speculative doctrines in the face of rapid developments within the various branches of science that seem, at least to some philosophers, to threaten all substantive philosophical doctrines.

2. The following provide groundwork for points being made in this discussion: John Yolton, "Action: Metaphysics and Modality," *American Philosophical Quarterly* (April 1973), pp. 71-85; E. H. Madden and Rom Harre, "In Defense of Natural Agents," *The Philosophical Quarterly* (April 1973), pp. 117-132; Roger W. Sperry, "Mind, Brain, and Humanist Values," in John R. Platt (ed.), *New Views of the Nature of Man* (Chicago: University of Chicago Press, 1965), pp. 71-92; Nathaniel Branden, *The Psychology of Self-Esteem* (Los Angeles, Calif.: Nash Publishing Co., 1969); Milton Fisk, *Nature and Necessity* (Bloomington, Ind.: Indiana University Press, 1974).

3. For more detailed discussion of these issues see J. M. Boyle, *et al.*, "Determinism, Freedom, and Self-Referential Arguments," *The Review of Metaphysics* (September 1972), pp. 3-37; James Jordan, "Determinism's Dilemma," *The Review of Metaphysics* (September 1969), pp. 48-66.

4. There are too many existentialists now to be confident about the claim that all are subjectivists. Even Kierkegaard's subjectivism may have to be reevaluated when we consider that he was responding to an objectivism advanced in conjunction with mechanism and full-blown determinism. Sartre's subjectivism is, in turn, mitigated by his quite objectivist doctrine of "authenticity versus bad faith." Most of these disputes must be understood in light of the false dichotomy between mechanistic determinism and the freedom of the immaterial soul (will). For a view of Aristotle's notion of the soul see Henry B. Veatch, *Aristotle* (Bloomington, Ind.: Indiana University Press, 1974). Veatch advances the thesis that Aristotle holds an aspectival view of the relationship between mind and body. For the way in which this can contribute to the resolution of subjectivism versus objectivism in ethics see Book II, Chapter 2 in Machan, *The Pseudo-Science of B. F. Skinner* (New Rochelle, N. Y.: Arlington House, 1974).

5. Eric Mack, "How to Derive Ethical Egoism," *The Personalist* (Autumn 1971), pp. 736-743.

6. Ibid., p. 735.

7. Ibid., pp. 736-737.

8. Ibid.

9. Ayn Rand, *For the New Intellectual* (New York: New American Library, 1963), p. 132. Rand holds that "Happiness is a state of non-contradictory joy—a joy without penalty or

guilt, a joy that does not clash with any of [one's] values and does not work for [one's] own destruction. . . . Happiness is possible only to a rational man, the man who desires nothing but rational goals, seeks nothing but rational values and finds his joy in nothing but rational actions."

10. Laszlo Versenyi, "Virtue as a Self-Directed Art," *The Personalist* (Summer 1972), p. 282.

11. Veatch, *Aristotle*. A pervasive objection to Aristotle has always been that he believed all things to be pursuing goals, all motion in nature to be purposive. Veatch argues that "Aristotelian final causes are no more than this: the regular and characteristic consequences or results that are correlated with the characteristic actions of the various agents and efficient causes that operate in the natural world. Of course, if the agent or efficient cause from which a certain action proceeds should happen to be a human being, or, more precisely, an intelligent being, then clearly the final cause might well be the purpose, goal and, in this sense, the end of that intelligent being who initiated the action." (P. 48.)

12. Mack, p. 737.

13. Friedrich Nietzsche, *The Will to Power*, Book I, No. 1.

14. Cf. Richard B. Hall, *Morality and Reason for Action* (University of California at Los Angeles, Unpublished Doctoral Dissertation, 1973). This work shows that altruistic moralities cannot provide a rational motive for human action. This supplements my point that unless we find that egoism can be a moral point of view, no chance of a rational justification for moral conduct exists for the actor himself.

15. Cf., K. Baier, *The Moral Point of View* (Ithaca, N.Y.: Cornell University Press, 1958(?); "Ethical Egoism and Interpersonal Compatibility," *Philosophical Studies*, December 1973, pp. 357-68; D. Gauthier, "The Impossibility of Rational Egoism" and W. Quinn "Egoism as an Ethical System," *The Journal of Philosophy*, August 15, 1974, pp. 439-55 and 456-72; K. Nielsen, "Egoism in Ethics," *Philosophy and Phenomenologic Research*, June 1959; "On the Rationality of 'Rational Egoism'," *The Personalist*, Autumn 1974, pp. 398-400; S. A. Smith, "Ethical Egoism and Value," *Southern Journal of Philosophy*, Spring 1974, pp. 95-102; J. Rachels, "Two Arguments Against Ethical Egoism," *Philosophia*, April-July 1974, pp. 297-315. Most of the above hold, with Nielsen, "that ethical egoism is not a possible ethical view." Some hold, with Rachel, that egoism is wicked. None of these examine defenses of egoism by Mack, Rand, Hospers, *et al.*

16. Disputes about Kant's ethics are a regular profession by now. The basic idea is that so-called prudential conduct—aiming for the achievement of what will benefit the agent—could not be morally significant because one could never be sure if one acted on principle ("out of duty") instead of from habit, desire, impulse, and so on. The idea, proposed by Aristotle, that morality can be cultivated—one can develop character—is foreign to most post-Kantian ethicists. And they seem to accept the idea that actions can spring exclusively from desires, i.e., emotions; the intentional character of actions, however, makes it impossible to account for them in terms of such passive features as emotions or impulses.

17. Friedrich Nietzsche, *The Anti-Christ* (Baltimore: Penguin Books, 1968), pp. 121-123.

18. Kant is simply wrong to think that people are inherently inclined toward selfish conduct—one need but listen to reports from psychotherapists to find out how wrong this view is. (The idea, however, did gain respectability in light of the dominance of psychological egoism, a doctrine that emerged powerfully in the philosophy of Thomas Hobbes.) In fact, however, selfish intentions must often overcome unselfish inclination.

19. I am indebted to Ayn Rand in the precise identification of the appropriate virtues. See her *For the New Intellectual*, pp. 128-131, for the details. It should be noted that the nature of virtues as advocated by Rand must be understood in terms of her epistemology. The sort of objections levelled at moral absolutists, whose doctrines are closer to Plato than to Aristotle, simply do not have force against epistemological objectivists.

20. For a full illustration of some of these points one would benefit from reading Ayn Rand's *Atlas Shrugged* (N.Y.: Random House, 1957). Also see my brief discussion of the film *Casablanca* (below). To appreciate the contrasting versions of egoism alluded to here, see John Beverley Robinson, "Egoism," *Reedy's Mirror*, Fall 1915 and W. F. R. Hardie, "The Final Good in Aristotle's Ethics," *Philosophy*, Vol. XL (1965), pp. 277-95. Critics of egoism accept without question or explicit mention Robinson's view that "Modern egoism . . . is the realization by the individual that he *is* an individual; that, as far as he is concerned, he is the *only* individual."

21. Richard Taylor, *Freedom, Anarchy, and the Law* (Englewood Cliffs, N. J.: Prentice-Hall, 1973), p. 22. In this connection Rand writes: "it is on a desert island that [man] would need [morality] most. Let him try to claim when there are no victims to pay for it, that a rock is a house, that sand is clothing, that food will drop into his mouth without cause or effect, that he will collect a harvest tomorrow by devouring his stock seed today—and reality will wipe him out, as he deserves; reality will show him that life is a value to be bought and that thinking is the only coin noble enough to buy it." *(For the New Intellectual*, pp. 127-128.)

22. Ibid., p. 23. Theft is not a primary vice because one must first be dishonest (or evasive or lack integrity) so as to convince himself that taking what is another's is what he ought to do. Theft amounts to the translation of a broader category of vice into the social realm. Taylor never deals with virtues such as courage, honor, integrity. Yet these are character traits that may have no social consequences whatsoever.

23. Kurt Baier, "Ethical Egoism and Interpersonal Compatibility," *Philosophical Studies* (December 1973) pp. 357-368.

24. Tibor R. Machan, "Some Considerations of the Common Good," *The Journal of Human Relations* Fall 1970) pp. 979-994. (This paper appears in slightly revised form in Machan, *The Pseudo-Science of B. F. Skinner.)* See also Robert F. Sasseen, "Freedom as an End of Politics," *Interpretation* (Winter 1971) pp. 105-125.

25. Kurt Baier, *The Moral Point of View* (Ithaca, N. Y.: Cornell University Press, 1958), pp. 180-190.

26. Ibid., p. 190.

27. Hannah Arendt, *Eichman in Jerusalem: A Report on the Banality of Evil* (New York: Viking Press, 1964). Arendt's specific ethics is not of interest here. I want merely to call attention to her recognition of the important fact that evil need not be premeditated, malicious, deliberate.

28. Rand, p. 178. The full quote will help to reemphasize the sense in which the concept "rationality" is used throughout this work: "Moral perfection is an unbreached rationality—not the degree of your intelligence, but the full and relentless use of your mind, not the extent of your knowledge, but the acceptance of reason as an absolute." For a discussion of the prevalent, instrumentalist uses of the concept "rationality" see John O. Nelson, "A Critical Review of *Reason and Teaching*" (Scheffler), *Reason Papers* No. 1, pp. 111-116.

29. For a more detailed discussion of the relationship between volition and rationality—including the nature of the choice involved in initiating thinking—see Branden, Chapter IV, "Man: A Being of Volitional Consciousness." Aside from the discussions cited in note 2, see also Isidor Chein, *The Science of Behavior and the Image of Man* (New York: Basic Books, 1972), and A. R. Louch, *Explanation and Human Action* (Berkeley, Calif.: University of California Press, 1969).

30. R. W. Beardsmore, *Moral Reasoning* (New York: Schocken Books, 1969), p. 137.

31. Ibid., p. x.

32. Jon Wheatley, "Reasons for Acting," *Dialogue*, vol. 7, no. 4, p. 564.

33. Beardsmore, p. x.

Notes to Chapter 4

1. For a discussion of the kind of justification one would need for moral and political principles see Robin Attfield, "The Logical Status of Moral Utterances," *The Journal of Critical Analysis* (July 1972) pp. 70-84.

2. Cf. T. R. Machan, *The Pseudo-Science of B. F. Skinner* (New Rochelle, N. Y.: Arlington House Publishers 1974), Chap. 5.

3. Ayn Rand, "Value and Rights," in John Hospers (ed.), *Readings in Introductory Philosophical Analysis* (Englewood Cliffs, N. J.: Prentice-Hall, 1968), p. 382.

4. Henry Aiken, "Rights, Human and Otherwise," *The Monist* (October 1968) p. 519.

5. This is not the same as the claim that people ought to exercise their liberty in any way they wish or feel or desire or even want. It is perfectly sensible to hold that someone ought to be free from interference from others in his conduct *and* ought, also, to conduct himself in certain specific ways. For the connection between morality and political liberty see Alan Gewirth,. "The 'Is-Ought' Problem Resolved," Presidential Address, 72nd Annual Western Meeting of the American Philosophical Association, April 26, 1974. Consider also the contrast: Ayn Rand: "Force and mind are opposites: morality ends where a gun begins," versus Andrew Kopkind: "morality . . . starts at the barrel of a gun."

6. Robert Nozick, "Distributive Justice," *Philosophy and Public Affairs* (Fall 1973) pp. 45-126; see especially Part II, Section 3, "The Original-Position and End-Result Principles," pp. 94-100. (This paper is now a chapter in Nozick's *Anarchy, State, and Utopia* [New York: Basic Books, 1974].)

7. Ludwig Wittgenstein, *Philosophical Investigations* (New York: Macmillan, 1968), No. 66.

8. The present theory, unlike justifications of the free society provided by, e.g., Milton Friedman, F. A. Hayek, Karl Popper *et al.*, does not require the paradoxical doctrine that human beings *cannot* know what is right or wrong, that they *cannot* tell when another does wrong, when people are guilty of moral irresponsibility. This view is a paradox for defenders of any political system, since the defense of such a system necessarily involves statements concerning what is right or wrong and, thus, an implicit claim that the advocates have themselves managed to identify something they maintain no human being can identify.

9. F. A. Hayek, "The Results of Human Action but not of Human Design," in *Studies in Philosophy, Politics, and Economics* (New York: Simon and Schuster, 1969), pp. 96-105. My point here differs from Hayek's somewhat in that Hayek seems to think that whereas designing or planning social order is a feature of a rationalistic viewpoint, allowing for *spontaneous forces* to operate is more in line with the Humean outlook. On the other hand Hayek admits that by "rationalism" he is not talking about Aristotelian ideas of reason but post-Cartesian ones.

10. F. A. Hayek, *Law, Legislation and Liberty* (Chicago: University of Chicago Press, 1973). Indeed, many today think that central planning is rational while laissez faire is letting irrational forces operate in society. As if having some utopian plan that happens to *envision* orderliness constituted rationality in political affairs! It is unfortunate, however, that defenders of liberty have allowed the idea of rationality, even if so debased as it is in the above context, to become the property of totalitarians.

11. Tibor R. Machan, "A Note on Conceivability and Logical Possibility," *Kinesis* (Fall 1969) pp. 39-42; Jose A. Benardete, "Is There a Problem about Logical Possibility?" *Mind* (January 1967) pp. 342-352; Arthur W. Collins, "Philosophical Imagination," *American Philosophical Quarterly* (January 1967) pp. 49-56. Since the idea "logical possibility" is often linked with the idea "necessary truth," it is helpful to point out that one need not give up the latter to abandon the former; see Charles Evans, "Salvaging Necessary Truth," *The Journal of Critical Analysis* (April 1972) pp. 24-33.

12. Herbert Morris, "Persons and Punishment," *The Monist*, pp. 465-501. See also J. Roger Lee, "Reflections on Punishment," in T. R. Machan (ed.), *The Libertarian Alternative: Essays in Social and Political Philosophy* (Chicago: Nelson-Hall, 1974), pp. 56-68. The view of punishment consistent with the present theory combines retributivist and utilitarian notions: there cannot be a separation of morality into deontological versus teleological (or consequentialist) positions; that would be to attempt to drive a wedge between intentions and behavior, to break up action into two *separate* parts and regard only one as morally significant. In punishment also, it is actions that are punished, neither only intentions nor only their consequences, i.e., behavior. Yet it must also be noted that punishment is often a device for self-protection, and current worries about its effects upon criminals are simply misguided in omitting from consideration that some people ought to be put away *for our sake*, not for theirs.

13. Ayn Rand, *Introduction to Objectivist Epistemology* (New York: The Objectivist, 1970). See Chapter 7, note 6.

14. See Chapter 7, note 5. See also Hanna Fenichel Pitkin, *Wittgenstein and Justice* (Berkeley, Calif.: University of California Press, 1972), especially Chapter IV, "Context, Sense, and Concepts."

15. See Chapter 3, notes 2 and 29.

16. See note 1.

17. Ayn Rand, *For the New Intellectual* (New York: New American Library, 1963), pp. 182-183.

18. Rand, "Values and Rights," p. 382.

19. John Locke, *Second Treatise on Government*, Chapter 5 ("On Property").

20. John Hospers, "Property," *The Personalist* (Summer 1972) p. 263. For a criticism of some aspects of the present theory see George Mavrodes, "Property," pp. 245-262. For an ordinary language analysis of the concept see Frank Snare, "The Concept of Property," *American Philosophical Quarterly* (April 1972) pp. 200-206. Also see note 26.

21. Mechanistic determinism and the accompanying psychological egoism—"everyone is always selfish" or "all people pursue their self-interest" or "everyone does only what he really wants to do"—are often invoked to defend capitalism on "scientific" grounds. See John Brill, *Anti-Utopia* (Columbia, Mo.: Lucas Brothers, 1940), a little known work, for a clear example of this view, one held in more sophisticated forms by many economists.

22. Norman Malcolm, *Ludwig Wittgenstein, A Memoir* (London: Oxford Paperbacks, 1958), pp. 31-32.

23. Herbert Spencer, *The Man versus the State* (Caldwell, Idaho: Caxton Printers, 1940), p. 22.

24. Cf. Thomas McPherson, *Social Philosophy* (London: Van Nostrand Rinehold Co., 1970), pp. 130-139.

25. *The Watergate Hearings* (New York: Bantam Books, 1973), p. 521.

26. James Sadowsky, "Private Property and Collective Ownership," in Machan, p. 123. See also Israel M. Kirzner, *Competition and Entrepreneurship* (Chicago: University of Chicago Press, 1973), and "Producer, Entrepreneur, and the Right to Property," *Reason Papers*, no. 1, pp. 1-17.

27. Roger Donway, "Markets and Morals," *The Freeman* (April 1974) p. 197.

28. Leo Strauss, *Natural Right and History* (Chicago: University of Chicago Press, 1971), p. 127.

29. Ibid., p. 131.

30. Ibid.

31. Ibid., Chapters I, II, and VI. See also Rosco Hill, "Legal Validity and Legal Obligation," *The Yale Law Journal* (November 1970) pp. 47-75; Bruce Goldberg, "Natural Law: Some Considerations," *Modern Age* (Summer 1966) pp. 269-277. Many who reject the case for defining a valid legal system in terms of its moral, i.e., natural law, contents focus on the problem that some laws that are obviously morally objectionable are nevertheless laws. Yet a natural law approach need not deny this, as long as the systematic *aim* of the legal framework remains fundamentally wedded to justice. (I will have more to say about this when discussing the right to revolution.)

Notes to Chapter 5

1. Murray N. Rothbard, *For A New Liberty* (New York: Macmillan, 1973); *Power and Market* (Menlo Park, Calif.: Institute for Humane Studies, 1970); *Egalitarianism as a Revolt Against Nature* (Washington, D. C.: Libertarian Review Press, 1974). These are Rothbard's major works in social and political philosophy. He has also authored several volumes in economic theory and history and the first volume of his multivolume history of America will be published in 1975 by Arlington House.

2. For a detailed discussion of the views of these individualist anarchists see James J. Martin, *Men Against the State* (Colorado Springs, Colo.: Ralph Myles Publishers, 1970).

3. Murray N. Rothbard, "Will Free Market Justice Suffice—Yes," *Reason* (March 1972) p. 19.

4. Jarret B. Wollstein, "Public Services under Laissez-Faire," *SIL Pamphlet* (Philadelphia, Pa.: The Society for Individual Liberty, 1969). This is a neglected little work showing how the prospects for supplying services and goods ordinarily thought to be inherently tied to governments are very excellent in a free economy. See also Chapter 8 in this book, pp. 253-279.

5. Mr. Childs, a personal friend, has made his views clear to me, although these observations are not in writing.

6. This translation was provided by Fred D. Miller, Jr. For his discussion of the 'polis' see "The State and the Community in Aristotle's POLITICS," *Reason Papers*, no. 1, pp. 61-69.

7. David Kelley, "The Necessity of Government," *The Freeman* (April 1974) pp. 244-245.

8. Ibid., p. 245.

9. David Friedman, *The Machinery of Freedom* (New York: Harper and Row, 1972).

10. Ayn Rand, "Censorship: Local and Express," *Ayn Rand Letter*, vol. II, no. 25. For a detailed critique of recent Supreme Court arguments involving governmental control of intellectual activities, see "Thought Control," *Ayn Rand Letter*, vol II, no. 26, and vol. III, nos. 1 and 2.

11. Andrew McLaughlin, "Freedom versus Capitalism," in Dorothy James (ed.), *Outside Looking In* (New York: Harper and Row, 1972), p. 135.

12. Michael P. Lerner, *The New Socialist Revolution* (New York: Dell Publishers, 1972), p. 298.

13. R. M. Hare, "Rawls' Theory of Justice," *The Philosophical Quarterly* (July 1973) p. 251. See also Charles Frankel, "The New Egalitarianism and the Old," *Commentary* (September 1973) pp. 54-61.

14. John Rawls, *A Theory of Justice* (Cambridge: Harvard University Press, 1971), pp. 101-102.

15. Robert Nozick, "Distributive Justice," *Philosophy and Public Affairs* (Fall 1973) pp. 121-122.

16. Ibid., pp. 117-118.

17. Rawls, p. 104.

18. Nozick, pp. 108-109.

19. I have unfortunately lost my source for this quotation but transcripts of the *"Firing Line" program* will easily document it.

20. Agnes Heller, "Towards a Marxist Theory of Value," *Kinesis* (Fall 1972) p. 76.

Notes to Chapter 6

1. For example, David Hume's skepticism developed in answer to the rationalist attempt to model knowledge on the deductive sciences. Ludwig Wittgenstein's criticism of definitions—and his subsequent suggestions that concepts cannot be defined by citing necessary and sufficient conditions for their employment—developed in opposition to the rigid formalism of logical atomists and positivists. Just how ancient this problem is in philosophy may be best appreciated from reading Charlotte L. Stough's *Greek Skepticism* (Berkeley, Calif.: University of California Press, 1969).

2. Many students of Ludwig Wittgenstein held that their teacher proposed no theories in philosophy and thus had no theory of knowledge, theory of language, theory of mind, and so forth. However, an appropriate revision on the concept of theory itself, allowing that there can be open-ended theories, would avoid the paradoxes generated by such claims.

3. Aristotle (Philip Wheelwright, translator), *Selections* (New York: Odyssey Press, 1951), p. 167.

4. Murder is, of course, a horrible and tragic event. Some will claim that characterizing it as the violation of someone's human right to life is just too systematic, lacks the impact of the actual experience. True enough, words do not generally serve to transmit the full impact of what they are used to communicate about. But it is equally true that such a complaint misses the point of just how grave it is to violate another's human rights.

5. For additional discussions of compulsory education see William F. Rickenbacker (ed.), *The Twelve Year Sentence* (LaSalle, Ill.: Open Court, 1974). See also my " 'The Schools Ain't What They Used to Be . . . and Never Was,' " in Machan (ed.), *The Libertarian Alternative* (Chicago: Nelson-Hall, 1974), pp. 245-261.

6. Personal communication from Senator Javits on United States Senate letterhead, November 1, 1973.

7. For how some scientists have abused the idea of possibility—by employing the philosophical idea "logical possibility" in justifying research ventures—see Mortimer Taube, *Computers and Common Sense* (New York: McGraw-Hill, 1961). See Chapter 4, note 11.

8. Rickenbacker, pp. 164-191. Also see the numerous papers by E. G. West—listed in Rickenbacker's book—on political, economic, and historical factors of compulsory education.

9. Ibid.

10. Ivan Illich, *Deschooling Society* (New York: Harper and Row, 1972), p. 16.

11. Ayn Rand, "Censorship: Local and Express," *Ayn Rand Letter*, vol II, no. 25, pp. 2-3.

12. It is one thing to have knowledge of what something is—of the nature of something or how to define the concepts of it—and another to articulate competently what one knows. Not everyone is prepared for verbalizing what he knows, nor would most bother with trying.

13. David Brudnoy, "Decriminalizing Crimes Without Victims," *New Guard*, April 1973, p. 7.

14. See Bernard Siegan's *Land Use Without Zoning* (Lexington, Mass.: D. C. Heath and Co., 1972) for a discussion of how zoning does not achieve its announced aims.

15. This is another harmful consequence of governmentally financed education and scholarship. With tax exemptions for institutions whose research is approved of by the state

academic boards it is not likely that research that challenges established doctrines, especially in the social sciences and the humanities, will gain the support enjoyed by studies well within the state sanctioned lines of thought. Those intellectuals who support socialism rarely focus on this, fearing, instead, that if they depended solely on private contributions and tuitions their work may be subjected to such crass checks as market forces. I have not conducted a study in motivation concerning these matters, but in the academic profession this resentment against submitting what one does to the forces of the market, instead of the select boards in educational bureaucracies, is plainly evident.

16. Edith Efron, "A Million-Dollar Misunderstanding," *TV Guide* (November 11, 1972) pp. 8-13. See also Norval Morris and Gordon Hawkins, *The Honest Politicians's Guide to Crime Control* (Chicago: University of Chicago Press, 1970), Chapter 3; the authors adequately dispose of the case for censorship of television programming based on alleged harm to children.

17. Jeremy Bentham, *The Principles of Morals and Legislation*, Chapter XVII, Section 1, footnote to paragraph 4; quoted in Peter Singer, "Animal Liberation," *The New York Review of Books* (April 5, 1973) p. 17.

18. Ibid.

19. Ibid., p. 20.

20. Ibid.

21. Cf. Joel Feinberg, "The Rights of Animals and Future Generations" in William T. Blackstone (ed.), *Philosophy and Environmental Crisis* (Athens, Ga.: University of Georgia Press, 1974). In this discussion Feinberg attempts to show, among other things, that animals have rights. He argues first that we cannot define "human being" in such a way that the definition will not also cover many animals. So he accepts the consequences, namely that living beings capable of suffering have rights against those capable of avoiding inflicting such suffering, thus arguing that human beings violate animals' rights when they inflict suffering on them. He also argues, more tentatively, that human beings owe it to all species of animal to preserve them for posterity, to keep the species alive. Both of these points are in conflict with the present theory—animals have no rights since they cannot choose to be rational and pursue moral goals, and human beings have no natural duty to preserve any animal species since their only justifiable responsibility is to pursue their rational self-interest. Of course, within the latter would fall various efforts to deal with animals without cruelty, and so on.

22. Less drastic proposals than these have, of course, been offered. Advocates of human rights, for example, have argued that most environmental problems stem from governmental (forcible) creation of demand for goods and services (often in response to demands by pressure groups) that would otherwise be too costly; the failure of the legal system to identify the proper sphere of authority/responsibility concerning the use of items (e.g., land, water, air)—that is, the "free goods" problem. But some problems must be accounted for in terms of natural events—e.g., earthquakes, volcanos, draughts, fires, floods, and so on. In dealing with these cases human beings often contribute to ecological balance by preventing natural disaster.

23. Some such as William Schockley advocate forced sterilization on grounds of the "public interest." Without so many "free goods" the likelihood of population disbalance would be reduced severely—people could not count on feeding, educating, keeping their children healthy beyond *their* means.

24. Excellent arguments against the space-ship earth concept and anti-technology in general may be found in Peter Beckmann, *Eco-Hysterics and the Technophobes* (Boulder, Colo.: Golem Press, 1973).

25. Cf. Edwin G. Dolan, *TANSTAAFL, The Economic Strategy for Environmental Crisis* (New York: Holt, Rinehart and Winston, 1971); Douglas C. North and Roger LeRoy Miller, *The Economics of Public Issues* (New York: Harper and Row, 1971); Angus Black, *A Radical's Guide to Self-Destruction* (New York: Holt, Rinehart and Winston, 1971).

26. A pioneer in environmental studies, Garret Hardin explained the problem of "free goods" with special focus on ecological matters in his "The Tragedy of the Commons," in Hardin, *Exploring New Ethics of Survival* (Baltimore: Pelican Book, 1973), pp. 250-264.

27. Ibid.

28. Aristotle, *Politics*, Book I, Chapter 13.

29. David Kelley, "The Necessity of Government," *The Freeman* (April 1974) pp. 243-248.

30. Cf. Marvin Kohl, *The Morality of Killing* (London: Peter Owen, 1973).

31. Plato, *Republic*, Book I, 331e-332b.

32. In theories of ethics extreme cases do serve the purpose of providing difficult testing grounds (no less than rough roads are used to test tires, and so on). But in most instances these extreme cases are not spelled out clearly. Often their statement presupposes an understanding of right and wrong, as it is often labeled, intuitively.

33. Gwyn Griffin, *An Operational Necessity* (New York: New American Library, 1969), pp. 338-341.

34. Eric Mack, "Egoism and Rights," *The Personalist* (Winter 1973) pp. 19-20.

35. John Locke, *Second Treatise on Government*, Chapter V, "Of Prerogative," No. 159.

36. Ibid., No. 163.

37. Ibid., No. 164.

38. Ayn Rand, *The Virtue of Selfishness* (New York: New American Library, 1966), pp. 47-48.

39. Cf. Murray N. Rothbard, *America's Great Depression* (Princeton, N. J.: Van Nostrand, 1963). The irony is that when by the late 1920s the economy began experiencing the consequences of this kind of subtle meddling, the socialists promptly blamed the resultant troubles on capitalism. Thus government activism picked up. All this is not to say that many businessmen did not contribute to the rise of statism. Cf. R. A. Childs, Jr., "Big Business and the Rise of American Statism," in Machan, *The Libertarian*, pp. 208-234. For a quick but incisive overview of recent political affairs see Jerome Tuccille, *Who's Afraid of 1984?* (New Rochelle, N. Y.: Arlington House, 1975), Section II.

40. (Chicago: University of Chicago Press, 1970). For a discussion of Kuhn's ideas see Imre Lakatos and Alan Musgrave, *Criticism and the Growth of Knowledge* (Cambridge: University Press, 1970). See also Roger Trigg, *Reason and Commitment* (Cambridge: University Press, 1973) and Carl R. Kordig, *The Justification of Scientific Change* (Dordrecht, Holland: D. Reidel Co., 1971).

41. Kant held that because human knowledge is produced by man's consciousness and is, thus, processed knowledge, we could never know the nature of something beyond how it appears to us. For Kant, however, strict knowledge of the nature of something would have had to be unconditioned, pure knowledge, literal merging or communing with the thing itself, without the mind interfering by way of its means or categories of understanding. But this is not knowledge, except in the Biblical sense perhaps. Nor is knowledge itself processed, only the result of certain processes, perhaps.

42. Locke, "Of the Dissolution of Government," No. 225.

43. Ibid., No. 219.

44. Ibid., No. 228.

45. Quoted in Hedrick Smith, "The Intolerable Andrei Sakharov," *The New York Times Magazine* (November 4, 1973) p. 71.

Notes to Chapter 7

1. Russell is known for his fervent political activism regarding twentieth-century political events. Both he and Jean-Paul Sartre participated in the unofficial war tribunal against the United States' involvement in Vietnam. Yet Russell's philosophy has no room for objectivity in ethics or politics, just as Sartre proclaimed himself an avowed subjectivist in ethics.

2. D. W. Hamlyn, *The Theory of Knowledge* (Garden City, N. Y.: Anchor Books, 1969), p. 49.

3. Throughout this discussion I am drawing on what I have learned from such philosophers as Rand, Cavell, Austin, Wittgenstein, Veatch, Toulmin, Madden, Harre *et al*. I would not guarantee that any of these can fully agree to my position.

4. In the theory of definition I am indicating a modified Aristotelianism advanced by Rand, Veatch, Madden and Harre, cited elsewhere in this work.

5. Barry Stroud, "Wittgenstein and Logical Necessity," in George Pitcher, *Wittgenstein* (Garden City, N. Y.: Anchor Books, 1969), p. 496.

6. Ayn Rand, *Introduction to Objectivist Epistemology* (New York: Objectivist, 1970), pp. 45, 48-49. Unfortunately Rand's views are rarely discussed by contemporary philosophers. Those who consider her worthy of serious consideration generally meet with disdain, mainly, one may suppose, in view of her unabashed support of laissez-faire capitalism and the American political tradition. Neither conservatives, who find her rationalism and atheism bothersome, nor liberals, who despise her political philosophy almost in toto, have elected to discuss her ideas in a way they would never hesitate to discuss Marcuse, on the one hand, and John Stuart Mill, on the other.

7. Margaret Macdonald, "Natural Rights," in A. I. Melden (ed.), *Human Rights* (Belmont, Calif.: Wadsworth Publishing Co., 1970), pp. 40-60.

8. Kai Nielsen, "Skepticism and Human Rights," *The Monist* (October 1968) pp. 573-594.

9. Ibid., p. 594.

10. William T. Blackstone, "Equality and Human Rights," *The Monist* (October 1968) pp. 616-639. (Blackstone is still writing on human rights and his views have changed somewhat from what they are in the above paper. Nevertheless his mode of securing a justification for human rights in this paper is one crucial alternative put forth in recent times.)

11. Gregory Vlastos, "Justice and Equality," in Melden, pp. 76-95.

12. Ibid., p. 82.

13. Ibid., p. 84.

14. For a more detailed criticism of Vlastos' paper see my "Prima Facie versus Natural (Human) Rights," *The Journal of Value Inquiry* (forthcoming).

15. C. B. Macpherson, *The Political Theory of Possessive Individualism: Hobbes and Locke* (Oxford: Clarendon Press, 1962).

Notes to Chapter 8

1. Those listed are educators at such institutions as the University of Chicago, University of Virginia, University of California at Los Angeles, and so forth,'usually associated with the "Chicago School" of economics and its offshoots throughout the academic community. Many of them are classical liberals in their political preferences but deny that this preference has objective justification beyond the empirical work they provide.

2. Many Eastern European (Soviet Bloc) countries have seen the emergence of economic thinking that is closer to neo-classical economics than even some Western economists accept. Since the famous Lieberman program in the Soviet Union, so-called liberalization in the direction of a less centralized economy has been a repeated political issue.

3. For more concentrated discussions of these matters see my "The Moral Imperative of the Free Market," *New Guard* (April 1974) pp. 17-20, and "Liberty: Economic versus Moral Defense," *The Occasional Review*, Fall 1974, pp. 63-82.

4. Ludwig von Mises, *Human Action* (New Haven, Conn.: Yale University Press, 1949); Murray N. Rothbard, *Man, Economy and State* (Los Angeles, Calif.: Nash Publishing Co., 1971). Rothbard defends Mises' method without, however, accepting the latter's implied subjectivism in ethics.

5. For a detailed analysis along these lines see David Friedman, *The Machinery of Freedom* (New York: Harper and Row, 1973). A criticism of Friedman's value-free defense of the free market can be found in Eric Mack's review of this work in *Reason* (March 1974) pp. 12-19.

6. Frederic Bastiat, *Selected Essays on Political Economy* (Princeton, N. J.: Van Nostrand, 1964), p. 2.

7. Lewis F. Powell, Jr., "Confidential Memorandum; Attack on American Free Enterprise System," U. S. Chamber of Commerce, Education Committee.

8. Ibid.

9. Ibid.

10. Ibid.

11. In this connection see Joseph Schumpeter, *Capitalism, Socialism and Democracy* (New York: Harper and Row, 1942). Schumpeter defended capitalism's merits as an economic system, *especially* on grounds of its aid to "the masses." He also predicted its fall on grounds that businessmen would undermine it by their shortsightedness and because intellectuals would attack it constantly. I can only concur with Benjamin A. Rogge when he answers this prediction by the modest commitment: "I know only what I try to do about it, and that is to talk, and talk, and talk—and that isn't much." Well, perhaps it is. (See Rogge, "Will Capitalism Survive?" *Imprimis* [May 1974] p. 6)

In support of Schumpeter's defense of the record of capitalism see F. A. Hayek (ed.), *Capitalism and the Historians* (Chicago: University of Chicago Press, 1954). For additional discussions of the overall benefits wrought from the existence of a relatively free economy in America's early history, see John Hospers, *Libertarianism* (Santa Barbara, Calif.: Reason Press, 1971). For essays touching on various ethical and political issues connected with the free economic system see Ayn Rand, *Capitalism: The Unknown Ideal* (New York: New American Library, 1966).

Index

About the Author

Tibor R. Machan is a professor of philosophy at State University College at Fredonia, New York.

Born in Budapest, Hungary, Machan immigrated to the United States from Munich, Germany in 1956, and later served in the U.S. Air Force.

He earned his undergraduate degree at Claremont Men's College in 1965; an M.A. degree from New York University in 1966, and a Ph.D. from the University of California at Santa Barbara in 1971.

Dr. Machan is editor of *Reason*. His articles have appeared in *Educational Theory, The Personalist, Journal of Aesthetics and Art Criticism, Journal of Human Relations, Barron's, Freeman, Individualist, New Guard,* and *Indian Libertarian,* as well as *Reason*.

Dr. Machan is editor of *The Libertarian Alternative: Essays in Social and Political Philosophy* (Nelson-Hall, 1974) a collection of thirty-seven essays by thirty prominent exponents of libertarianism.